Darren J. O'Byrne

Human Rights

An Introduction

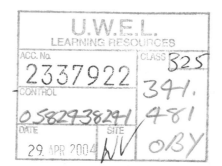

Longman

An imprint of **Pearson Education**

Harlow, England · London · New York · Reading, Massachusetts · San Francisco
Toronto · Don Mills, Ontario · Sydney · Tokyo · Singapore · Hong Kong · Seoul
Taipei · Cape Town · Madrid · Mexico City · Amsterdam · Munich · Paris · Milan

Pearson Education Limited
Edinburgh Gate
Harlow
Essex CM20 2JE

and Associated Companies throughout the world

Visit us on the World Wide Web at:
www.pearsoneduc.com

ISBN 0 582 43824 1

British Library Cataloguing-in-Publication Data
A catalogue record for this book is available from the British Library

Library of Congress Cataloging-in-Publication Data
O'Byrne, Darren J.
    Human rights : an introduction / Darren J. O'Byrne.
        p. cm.
    Includes bibliographical references and index.
    ISBN 0-582-43824-1 (pbk.)
    1. Human rights.   I. Title.

JC571 .O29 2003
323—dc21

                                      2002023047

10 9 8 7 6 5 4 3 2 1
06 05 04 03 02

Typeset in 10/12.5pt Book Antiqua by 35
Produced by Pearson Education Malaysia Sdn Bhd,
Printed in Malaysia

CONTENTS

Foreword   x

Acknowledgements   xiii

Introduction   1

Thinking about human rights   1
Human rights abuses in the world today   5
The scope of human rights research   10
Human rights and theoretical traditions   17

CHAPTER ONE

Theorising human rights   26

What are human rights?   26
A brief history of human rights theory   28
Are human rights universal?   37
Are human rights incontrovertible?   44
Are human rights subjective?   49
Ethics and social practice   55
Modernity and democratisation   59
The state and human rights theory   62
Essay questions   66
Notes   66
Further information   71

CHAPTER TWO

Regulating human rights   72

Who protects human rights?	72
A brief history of human rights regulation	74
Human rights and world politics	76
The United Nations	79
Human rights and the law	87
Human rights and social movements	93
The state and human rights regulation	100
Essay questions	102
Notes	102
Further information	104

CHAPTER THREE

Censorship   106

What is censorship?	106
A brief history of censorship	109
Censorship and democracy	115
The theoretical discourse on censorship	125
Pornography and obscenity	126
The state, censorship and human rights	129
Essay questions	134
Notes	134
Further information	137

CHAPTER FOUR

Political prisoners   139

What is a political prisoner?	139
A brief history of political prisoners	142
Political policing	145
Political prisoners and just punishment	147
Exile and house arrest	154
'Disappearances' and extra-judicial executions	155
The state, political prisoners and human rights	158
Essay questions	160
Notes	160

CHAPTER FIVE

Torture 164

What is torture? 164

A brief history of torture 168

Torture methods 171

The theoretical discourse on torture 179

Understanding torturers 181

Medical involvement in torture 184

The trade in torture equipment 189

The state, torture and human rights 191

Essay questions 192

Notes 192

Further information 196

CHAPTER SIX

The death penalty 198

What is the death penalty? 198

A brief history of the death penalty 201

Execution methods 208

Understanding the death penalty 212

The theoretical discourse on the death penalty 217

'Race', class and the death penalty 222

The experience of Death Row 226

Medical involvement in the death penalty 228

The state, the death penalty and human rights 230

Essay questions 233

Notes 234

Further information 239

CHAPTER SEVEN

Apartheid 241

What is apartheid? 241

A brief history of apartheid 242

Understanding apartheid 247

Apartheid, caste and social stratification 252

Gender and apartheid   255
The state, apartheid and human rights   258
Essay questions   259
Notes   259
Further information   262

CHAPTER EIGHT

Slavery   263

What is slavery?   263
A brief history of slavery   266
'Race', citizenship and slavery   274
Understanding slavery   276
The experience of enslavement   282
The state, slavery and human rights   289
Essay questions   291
Notes   291
Further information   297

CHAPTER NINE

Genocide   299

What is genocide?   299
A brief history of genocide   303
Understanding genocide   311
Political genocide   321
The experience of the concentration camp   323
The state, genocide and human rights   324
Essay questions   328
Notes   328
Further information   335

CHAPTER TEN

Refugees   337

What is a refugee?   337
A brief history of refugees   342

'Race', citizenship and refugees   348
Refugees and border controls   353
Refugees and the media   355
The experience of displacement   358
The state, refugees and human rights   362
Essay questions   363
Notes   364
Further information   367

Conclusion

368

New directions in human rights research   368
Women and human rights   369
Children and human rights   374
Business and human rights   381
Poverty and human rights   384
The environment and human rights   387
Human rights in a globalised world   389
Essay questions   393
Notes   393
Further information   396

Appendix

Universal Declaration of Human Rights   398
International Covenant on Civil and Political Rights   405

Name index

426

Acts and Conventions index

429

Subject index

432

Foreword

It is late at night. The air is hot and heavy in the expectation of a thunderstorm. I am sitting at the computer writing this foreword, with half an ear on my crackling radio tuned to the World Service. News from around the world is grim. Political violence has intensified in Zimbabwe. Hundreds have died in confrontations between armed opposition groups and the paramilitaries. In Barcelona the XIV International Aids Conference, in seeking to confront the escalating scale of the pandemic, is calling for renewed effort in the search for affordable cures, and greater attention paid to overcoming the stigma still associated with its casualties. A two-mile thick cloud of toxic pollution known as the Asian Brown Cloud which is threatening millions of lives from Afghanistan to Sri Lanka appears to have been caused by the burning of the forests of South East Asia. Professor Ibrahim, human rights defender and director of a centre for development studies and women's rights in Cairo, has been sent to jail for seven years for his involvement in a film project questioning democracy and corruption in his country.

Human rights, the inalienable and indivisible rights held by us all, are the basic standards of equity and justice without which people cannot live in dignity and are all around us. And their abuse is a daily and occurrence.

Education shall be directed to the full development of the human personality and to the strengthening of respect for human rights and fundamental freedoms. It shall promote understanding, tolerance and friendship among all nations racial or religious groups, and shall further the activities of the United Nations for the maintenance of peace.
Article 26 (2), Universal Declaration of Human Rights

For my organisation, Amnesty International, which for 40 years has campaigned against violations of human rights across the world, teaching and learning about human rights is not just an aspiration. We see it as a key and practical defence for upholding and protecting rights. The contribution it makes to preventing those rights from being denied or attacked is not supplementary, it is critical. In the USA, Amnesty International's human rights educators network has called its human rights journal *The Fourth R,* suggesting that human rights literacy – teaching and learning about human rights – is of fundamental importance. Rights deserve their place alongside reading, (w)riting and (a)rithmetic.

It may have escaped the attention of many that we are in the middle of the United Nations International Decade for Human Rights Education (1995–2004). During this decade governments, international bodies, non-governmental organisations (NGOs), professional bodies and all sectors of civil society are meant to be concentrating and pooling their efforts to disseminate and promote human rights and fundamental freedoms through education, training and public information. They should be building and developing a universal culture of human rights, promoting understanding, respect, gender equality and friendship amongst all nations, indigenous peoples and racial, national, ethnic, religious and linguistic groups. They should be enabling all persons to participate effectively in a free society and furthering the activities of the UN for the maintenance of peace.

This stimulating primer *Human Rights: An Introduction* has grown out of the exciting and multi-disciplinary courses on human rights that Dr Darren O'Byrne has taught at the University of Surrey Roehampton in recent years – courses in which I have been a privileged participant as a human rights campaigner.

Education about human rights is an empowering process. How it is taught – from school to university – ranges from the provision of information about international law, the history of struggle and the continuing development of ideas of justice across cultures and around the world. It concerns human rights standards and the machinery by which rights are protected. It has to do with the development of attitudes and values that uphold human rights in daily life and in the agendas of nations.

As Dr O'Byrne says in his Introduction, human rights is a topic that will be encountered by students in aspects of their studies of history, psychology, media studies, geography, anthropology, politics, international relations, law, ethics, sociology, philosophy and criminology. However, it does not normally emerge as a discipline in its own right. This volume, however, is unique, because it reflects the pioneering work on new academic programmes in human rights that are starting to be offered, where theory, academic research and the real world of human rights experience and abuse are brought together into an integrated discipline.

The language of human rights has, of course, changed through the years. The eminent sociologist T.H. Marshall famously described the evolution of citizenship rights according to three stages: first, the emergence of *civil rights* such as liberty, freedom of speech; second, the arrival of *political rights*, active involvement in the political process; third, the development of new *social and economic rights* such as welfare, housing and education. Similar distinctions are often made within the debate on human rights. The emphasis of this book is on the first generation of rights – civil and political rights – rather than on economic, social and cultural rights – the second generation of rights – or issues of the emerging third generation of rights, the collective rights to sustainable development, peace and a healthy environment. Dr O'Byrne justifies this by claiming that these rights, and the abuses thereof, remain firmly located within the power of the state. In an age of globalization, in which so many commentators make the claim that the state is no longer important, Dr O'Byrne issues a timely reminder that the state still has considerable power as the centralised means of violence.

This volume examines the classical origins of human rights thinking and the theoretical traditions that underpin human rights and their history – the theories of ethics, philosophy and social practice, politics and democratisation, society, human nature and modernity. The protection of human rights is examined in the second chapter – the history of the regulation of human rights, the UN, human rights and the law, the role of social movements like Amnesty International; the state and its obligations. Subsequent chapters look at and unpick particular contemporary issues and human rights topics in theory and practice: censorship, political prisoners, torture, the death penalty, apartheid, slavery, genocide and refugees, the particular rights of women and children, business and human rights, poverty and globalisation. Each topic is examined in detail with case studies, background information and contemporary thinking.

Although aimed primarily at student audiences, this book is not only accessible to and important for lay readers, but it manages at the same time to have something new and challenging to say even to experienced specialists in the field. *Human Rights: An Introduction* is an invaluable chart for any academic navigator embarking on a journey into the ocean of human rights.

Dan Elwyn Jones MBE
Human Rights Education
Amnesty International United Kingdom Section

ACKNOWLEDGEMENTS

I am grateful to various colleagues for their support and advice. John Eade and Kevin Bales were kind enough to look over my chapters on apartheid and slavery respectively. Garry Marvin has provided helpful comments on the general structure of the volume, and I am always indebted to my friend Sarah Cant. Dan Jones at Amnesty International UK Section has also been a helpful friend and associate, and his assistance in writing the foreword and locating suitable photographs is particularly appreciated. Thanks to Martyn Gregory for allowing me to discuss his documentary 'The Torture Trail'. My editors at Pearson have not only been refreshingly enthusiastic about this project since I first approached them, they have also been mercifully patient as I found myself immersed deeper and deeper in the fascinating research recounted here, with deadlines approaching!

Over the years, my thinking about each of the topics covered in this book, and more besides, has benefited immensely from the wonderful and enthusiastic work carried out by the students who have sat my undergraduate module 'Human Rights in Theory and Practice', upon which this book is based. One of the things required of these students is that they gather in groups and establish fictitious campaigning organisations. They are asked, in effect, to set themselves up as a one-issue human rights organisation and to provide a definitive document which serves two purposes. First, it should be a *resource file* which includes all the relevant historical and contemporary data, legal and political conventions and arguments, journalistic and academic discourse pertaining to their specific area of concern. Second, it should be a *campaigning strategy* which puts the aims and objectives of the fictitious organisation into practice. The diversity of topics chosen by my students has never ceased to amaze me, and the industry and commitment with which they approach their labours is enough to soften even the most cynical of hearts. Many of these students have gone on to write dissertations on specific areas of human rights research, some on slavery or the death penalty, others on more unusual topics such as female genital mutilation and even euthanasia. Many undertook voluntary work in the campaigning sector during their student years, and some have gone on after graduation to work full-time on human rights issues, or to continue their studies at a university which offers postgraduate courses in human rights research. These students have inspired me with their endless commitment to building a better world. They can take credit for the writing of this book and it is to them that it is dedicated. Responsibility for any flaws is mine alone.

Publisher's acknowledgements

We are grateful to the following for permission to reproduce copyright material:

Table I.1 from *The Observer* Human Rights Index, *The Observer*, 28 June 1998, © The Guardian/Observer; Table I.2 from *The Guardian* Human Rights Index, http://www.guardian.co.uk/Tables/4_col_tables/ 0,5737,94899,00.html, © The Guardian/Observer; Table 10.1 from www.unhcr.ch, courtesy the United Nations High Commissioner for Refugees; Table 10.2 from *World Refugee Survey* (2000), courtesy U.S. Committee for Refugees; Table 10.3 © United Nations High Commissioner for Refugees, 2000. Reprinted from *The State of the World's Refugees 2000* by United Nations High Commissioner for Refugees (UNHCR), by permission of Oxford University Press; Table 10.4 © United Nations High Commissioner for Refugees, 2000. Reprinted from *The State of the World's Refugees 2000* by United Nations High Commissioner for Refugees (UNHCR), by permission of Oxford University Press; Table 10.5 from www.unhcr.ch, courtesy the United Nations High Commissioner for Refugees; Table 11.1 from International Labour Organisation, *Guardian Education*, 16 November 1999, © The Guardian/Observer.

Extract on pages 120–1 from *Amnesty International* (UK Section Magazine), May 1997, pp. 6–7; extract on page 149 and on pages 151–2 from www.uib.no/isf/people/amnesty/whatis01.htm; extract on page 173 from *Voices for Freedom: An Amnesty International Anthology*, p. 66; extract on pages 176–7 from *Voices for Freedom: An Amnesty International Anthology*, pp. 58–9, © Amnesty International Publications, www.amnesty.org; extract on pages 286–7 from Kevin Bales, *Disposable People: New Slavery in the Global Economy*, © 1999 The Regents of the University of California.

Every effort has been made by the publisher to obtain permission from the appropriate source to reproduce material which appears in this book. In some instances we have been unable to trace the owners of copyright material, and we would appreciate any information that would enable us to do so.

Introduction

Thinking about human rights

At some point in their higher education careers, many students under-taking degree courses in the humanities or social sciences will probably encounter some aspect of what we might call 'human rights research'. For example, in history they will almost certainly discuss the trans-atlantic slave trade and, of course, the Nazi Holocaust. In criminology they might learn about the death penalty. In media studies they will be introduced to aspects of censorship. In psychology they may be asked to consider the making of a torturer. In anthropology a lecturer may offer a session on female genital mutilation. In philosophy students will be expected to dedicate time to understanding ethics and moral behavi-our. If they take electives in law, international relations, or politics, they will probably be introduced to various human rights legislations and conventions.

So, it would not be fair to say that the academic world has ignored human rights – far from it. However, from the perspective of human rights, disciplinarity brings its own problems. Where censorship is dis-cussed in media courses, the focus is likely to be on censorship as media regulation, rather than as human rights violation. The making of a torturer is likely to be included under the banner of abnormal psychology and thus detached from questions concerning torture as a human rights abuse. Historians will undoubtedly treat slavery and the Holocaust as obscene assaults on human dignity, but slavery and genocide are more than historical issues – they are also contemporary problems. Sociolo-gists have contributed to these debates in various forms, but – as we shall see in Chapter One – the discipline of sociology has shied away from embracing 'human rights' as a general term. It seems particularly odd that sociologists have done exceptional work on *aspects* of human rights – one thinks of Patterson on slavery, Sellin and Radelet on the death penalty, Bauman and Fein on genocide, numerous media socio-logists on censorship – but their discipline has resisted the need to bring these disparate aspects together.

The purpose of this volume is to right this academic wrong, to bring together for the first time the rich studies which have illuminated our thinking about these different aspects of human rights. In some respects, it requires us to leave our preconceptions about disciplinarity at the door. Research carried out in the field of social psychology is as valid as that in political economy – each contributes to our understanding of a given substantive area. If we want to understand a contemporary concern, such as torture or slavery, then we do ourselves no favours by closing ourselves off in secure disciplinary boxes, ignoring material that would enhance our understanding. This is particularly true if we wish to understand such a problem not just as an academic but as a concerned citizen, an activist. And this is where some aspect of disciplinarity returns, albeit in modified form. I want, if you like, to treat human rights *as a discipline in its own right*. It has its own subfields – slavery, genocide, and the various other topics discussed in this book. It has its own rich theoretical tradition, comprised of such luminaries as Kant, Arendt, and Bobbio. It draws on the research carried out within its sibling disciplines, but it utilises this research for its own purpose, in keeping with its own logic. Its logic, of course, is the promotion of human rights awareness and its ultimate goal the eradication of all forms of human rights abuse. Thus, the discipline of human rights is more than a mere *pot pourri* of interests drawn from other, more traditional, fields. It occupies its own space, located broadly within the social sciences but as far removed from the fallacies of value freedom and scientific objectivity as any discipline could possibly be.

Even more exciting, though, are the *possibilities* that arise from this integrated approach. In Chapter Three, which is dedicated to under-standing the problem of censorship, there is considerable discussion of the theoretical approaches provided by such unlikely bedfellows as Popper, Foucault and Habermas, as well as Althusser, Arendt, Adorno and Marcuse. While these major writers may not have concerned them-selves with censorship *per se*, the theoretical traditions that have arisen from their ideas are all in some way applicable to it. For example, the Habermasian paradigm presupposes the possibility of unhindered com-munication as a foundation for true democracy. Working within such a paradigm, we can thus reach a theoretically informed understanding of censorship in the context of its relationship to democracy. Similar applications can be made following Popper's work on the 'open society', Foucault's on surveillance, Althusser's on ideological state apparatuses, Adorno's on authoritarianism, Arendt's on totalitarianism, Marcuse's on the 'closing down of alternatives', and more besides. This is not, it seems to me, a case of poaching from the canon; rather, it would be a serious omission on our part if we were to try to understand censorship *without* considering the possibilities offered by these paradigms. Additionally, how can we even begin to understand political imprisonment within a theoretically informed framework without reference to Althusser and the idea of repressive state apparatuses? These writers and their ideas are not the private property of any one discipline, and it is clear that they have much to contribute to the integrated approach to human rights advocated here.

It is therefore not inconceivable to envisage the emergence of degree programmes dedicated to this logic, and it is certainly true that individual modules have already been established, under the broad banner of one or another 'traditional' discipline, which seek to adopt such an integrated approach to human rights research. Students sitting these modules may, with good reason, feel rather annoyed when they encounter an unfortunate consequence of the dispersed nature of human rights studies – the lack of an integrated textbook which covers most of the ground they will expect to cover in their course. Having devised a module of this kind myself, I am more than aware of the confusion that can arise when students are sent in different directions, to different corners of the library or bookshop, in order to learn more about a specific important study on, say, censorship or torture. While this is understandable, in so far as disciplines have never really needed to make any links between censorship and torture, and publishers, guided by traditional disciplinarity, have never needed to commission volumes which make reference to both, this volume is intended to fill this gap for an emerging academic audience.

But if there is to be a disciplinary logic to the integrated study of human rights, it must reside primarily in its resistance to any separation between academic research and the 'real world' of human rights abuses. The purpose of human rights studies is to utilise this research for the advancement of an overt political and ethical goal, that is, the betterment of human existence. As Herbert Marcuse famously said, the task of a critical theory is to realise that human life is, or should be, worth living, and to identify the conditions that exist to make it less than it should be.[1] Human rights studies is born out of Marcuse's unapologetic call to arms. Thus, this volume is peppered with case studies, past and present. These case studies are intended to remind the reader that the academic discourse should not be treated as abstract because it reflects a harsh social reality. Human rights should be understood both in theory, and in practice.

Before we proceed any further with this introductory chapter, three things need to be said about the volume as a whole:

The majority of this book is dedicated to understanding specific *violations* of rights, rather than the rights themselves. Thus, these rights – freedom of speech, freedom from cruel and inhuman treatment and so on – reappear throughout the book, as appropriate. While it would not have been inconceivable to have drafted this volume according to the rights themselves, I think the format I have chosen is better suited for the purposes of the book. Take the example of the death penalty. This can be understood as a violation of many rights, notably the right to life, and the right to freedom from cruel and inhuman treatment. Rather than scatter the research unnecessarily, I have chosen to keep it together in one chapter.

The violations and rights discussed throughout the bulk of this book pertain to *civil and political rights*. This may constitute a cause for concern among readers who – while aware of the need to research and educate on the gross violations discussed in these chapters – wish to expand the concept of human rights to incorporate economic, social, cultural, collective and environmental rights. I want to make it clear that I agree wholeheartedly with these concerns. Human rights violations do not only take place in the civil and political realms, and are not only committed by state actors. Poverty is a violation of human rights, as are cultural practices such as female genital mutilation. Of course, to include research on everything which might be included under the human rights banner would be virtually impossible. Constraints imposed upon me by space have forced me to concentrate the bulk of the book on this traditional approach to human rights – favoured by many activist organisations because it allows them to target states as perpetrators of the violations. In the Conclusion, I discuss the extended scope of human rights research, and reflect on the criticisms that can genuinely be made of my decision to concentrate on civil and political rights. There is, however, another reason why I concentrate on these rights, and that pertains to the relationship between human rights, social theory and the idea of the state. I will say more about this later in this Introduction.

This volume is a *textbook*. As such, it provides summaries of research carried out on specific issues, and is structured according to the various themes which have generated most intellectual interest. I cannot hope to have done justice to all the rich and varied studies that have been carried out in these fields. I can only provide the signposts which direct the reader to more in-depth study. Where possible, I have kept to a format which should become recognisable to the reader as she makes her way through the book. The first section of each chapter – 'What is X?' – deals, mostly, with definitional matters. The second – 'A brief history of X' – seeks to provide a historical overview. Later sections might include relevant discussions between moral philosophers – 'The theoretical discourse on X'. I have tried to keep my interjections to a minimum, to let the research speak for itself. In the concluding section of each chapter I attempt to bring together what I feel are the key issues raised therein from the point of view of human rights studies. Readers are at liberty to disagree with my sense of direction in each case.

That, then, is the structure of the book. What is its subject matter? Why study human rights at all? Let us turn now to an overview of the human rights situation in the world at what is for many of its inhabitants the turn of a millennium.

Human rights abuses in the world today

When the United Nations introduced the Universal Declaration of Human Rights in 1948, it was seen by many as a sign of optimism, of the possibilities of a better world. Yet, over 50 years later, observers recognise that we live in an age when human rights abuses are as prevalent as they ever have been – in some instances more prevalent. The world is littered with examples of violations of basic rights: censorship, discrimination, political imprisonment, torture, slavery, the death penalty, disappearances, genocide, poverty, refugees. The rights of women, children, and other groups in society continue to be ignored in atrocious ways. The environmental crisis takes the discourse on rights to a different level.

In 1998, as the Declaration celebrated its fiftieth birthday, the *Observer* newspaper in Britain published a poll called the 'Human Rights Index', which it described as 'the World Cup that no country wants to win'. The Index ranked 194 nation-states according to their record on human rights abuses. The results made for interesting reading. Algeria took first prize, ahead of North Korea. The United States featured in 92nd place, the United Kingdom in 141st. Russia was 32nd, while China was 10th. The poll was based on a points system allocated to countries according to their use of torture or capital punishment, their political prisoners and disappearances, and their denials of basic rights. The totals were then adjusted according to the Human Development Index (HDI) which measures countries in terms of their level of economic and social development. Table I.1 identifies the different indicators used and how the ten highest-placed countries scored on each.

Another attempt to rank countries featured on the website of the *Guardian* newspaper (Table I.2). This list featured a slightly different set of indicators, and a slightly simpler ranking system. On this occasion, the Democratic Republic of Congo shared first place with its neighbour Rwanda. Russia and the United States shared 62nd position, the United Kingdom came in joint 126th, while China was 12th.

Both indexes provide only a guide to the state of human rights in the world today – no country can afford to be complacent about its performance on such a scale. Campaigning organisations such as Amnesty International are usually reluctant to rank countries in this way because it detracts from the central issue: it is not how you perform compared to other countries that matters, but the fact that you have violated human rights at all! Nevertheless, the indexes allow us to ponder the enormity of our task as students and activists concerned with human rights. These lists are also informative as much because of what is *not* ranked as for what is. In selecting which topics to include as chapters in this book, I have faced similar problems, as I will discuss in more detail below. What is apparent, though, is that some *types* of human rights abuse are more common in some countries than in others. The United States of America, for example, may consider itself something of a moral guardian of basic civil and political rights, such as freedom of speech, but is regularly criticised for its use of the death penalty. The United Kingdom is frequently targeted for its mistreatment, including arbitrary detention, of refugees and asylum seekers. Disappearances and extra-judicial executions are usually associated with Latin America, apartheid with South Africa, while censorship is of course a major problem in many authoritarian states and most 'liberal' ones as well. Where possible, I will reflect this geographical spread throughout the chapters of this book.

The scope of human rights research

Let us look in more detail at the structure of this volume. The opening chapters attempt to introduce the theory and the practice of human rights. The first chapter, 'Theorising human rights', provides the reader with a survey of the major philosophers and commentators who have contributed to the history of the idea of human rights. As is often the case with theory chapters, this is the longest in the book – but essential in terms of understanding what human rights are supposed to be, so that we might begin to see how those substantive areas which follow can be located within the human rights framework. The second chapter, 'Regulating human rights', provides an overview of some of the major

Table I.2 The *Guardian* Human Rights Index[3]

	DR Congo	Rwanda	Burundi	Algeria	Sierra Leone	Egypt	North Korea	Sudan	Indonesia	Yugoslavia
Extra-judicial executions	3	3	3	3	3	–	1	3	3	3
Disappearances	–	3	2	2	–	1	2	3	3	3
Torture	3	3	3	3	3	3	3	3	3	2.5
Deaths in custody	–	2	3	–	2	2	1	1	–	1
Prisoners of conscience	3	–	–	2	1	2	2	2	3	1
Unfair trials	3	3	3	3	3	3	3	2	2	3

Table I.2 (cont'd)

	DR Congo	Rwanda	Burundi	Algeria	Sierra Leone	Egypt	North Korea	Sudan	Indonesia	Yugoslavia
Detention without charge or trial	3	3	3	3	3	3	3	2	2.5	3
Executions	3	2	–	–	2	2	3	1	–	–
Death sentences	3	3	3	3	3	3	3	1	2	1
Abuses by armed opposition groups	3	3	3	3	3	2	–	3	2	3
Total	24	24	23	22	22	21	21	21	20.5	20.5

legal and political conventions which have been established to safe-guard human rights. It also considers the role of concerned citizens and social movements in securing a world in which human rights are respected.

The bulk of the book, though, is dedicated to analysing specific, sub-stantive issues in human rights research. For the most part, as I stated above, I have focused primarily on *civil and political rights*, sometimes called 'first-generation rights'. These tend to be easier to locate in so far as they usually have a direct relationship with the *state*. Complications arise when we introduce 'second-generation rights' – *economic, social and cultural rights* – and 'third-generation rights' – *collective rights and land rights*. We turn briefly to these at the end, but we begin, appropriately, with two quite general violations of civil and political rights. Chapter Three deals with censorship, and Chapter Four discusses political pris-oners. Both censorship and political imprisonment can be understood as mechanisms of state repression, political practices oriented towards the maintenance of power, and violations of the rights to information and/or expression, and justice respectively. The right to justice is con-sidered to be a civil right, while the rights to information and expression are both civil and political rights. So, these chapters discuss the bedrock of human rights concerns, human rights abuses as *political manipulation*, where the state infringes upon the civil and political rights of its citizens. Similarly, Chapter Five is concerned with torture, a violation of the right to respectful treatment, which in real terms is often inseparable from issues of political imprisonment.

The inclusion of torture is unlikely to stimulate debate, because it is (in principle) universally condemned and illegal. Yet most official definitions of torture actually include corporal punishment (indeed, torture itself has often been used as a form of judicial punishment), and this often does result in disagreements between parties. Nevertheless, human rights abuses can and do occur within the legal system as well as the political system (which is where most of the formal human rights discourse is often directed). Chapter Six focuses on the death penalty. In this chapter we deal primarily with how human rights abuses can actually form part of a legal and judicial system, for the purpose of punish-ing criminals. If the currency of politics is power, then the currency of law is order. 'Enemies' of the law are referred to as criminals, and they need not be political agents. Thus, this chapter constitutes an analysis of human rights abuses as *punishment*, where the law infringes upon our civil rights (to life and respectful treatment) – even though, in its applica-tion, the death penalty clearly has *political* undertones.

Progressively this discourse has extended further beyond the limits of the political realm to incorporate social and economic issues. Chapter

Seven – 'Apartheid' – offers an introduction to the theories of and the institutional politics derived from the practice of discriminating against certain groups within society. Chapter Eight, on slavery, Chapter Nine, on genocide, and Chapter Ten, on refugees, develop the themes introduced in Chapter Seven. These chapters concentrate on human rights abuses as *social exclusion*. Nevertheless, they remain firmly within the framework of civil and political rights because the violations in question are executed or legitimised by the state.

Few people in the human rights field would deny that apartheid, slavery, genocide, and the plight of refugees constitute human rights violations. Actually, the logic behind this is not always clear. It is true that they are forms of *social* exclusion – that is to say, they exist within the social sphere in so far as the *victims* of these atrocities are targeted *not* because they are enemies of the state or because they are criminals, but because of their characteristics *as groups of people*. However, they are condoned, or carried out in the name of, the state and its agents, and they (usually) constitute violations of civil and political rights. Discrimination – the root of many of these evils – is effectively a social problem, although it becomes a legal one when it is formalised as apartheid or segregation. Slavery is another example of how social exclusion becomes formalised in the legal sense, that is, where the *law* pervades *society*. The primary difference between apartheid and slavery is that the former is the legal violation of the right to equality, while the latter is the legal violation of the rights to equality *and* freedom, although boundaries are never really this clear. Quite clearly, the absence of political equality under apartheid necessarily results in a denial of freedom as well. Genocide is often (but not always) explained in terms of similar reasons to apartheid and slavery, although while these violations constitute legal strategies for social exclusion, genocide is quite clearly a political one, which threatens not the right to life, but the right to existence. The problems faced by refugees are also social problems, problems of *belonging*, although once again they tend to be fought out in the legal sphere. That is to say, questions of existential belonging evolve into questions of legal belonging. That we end on the problem of refugees seems apt, since these problems challenge the very assumptions – to sovereignty, legitimacy, and exclusivity – upon which the theory of the modern state rests.

So, clearly, while we have strayed to some extent from our starting point in the political sphere, we have maintained an attachment to some kind of state involvement. Table I.3 lists the various substantive areas covered in this book, locating them within the relevant sphere (that is, the appropriate *rationale* for the violation in question), and, where it is different, the relevant medium (that is, the *arena* through which the

Table I.3 Traditional forms of human rights abuse

Substantive area	Sphere (medium)	Rights violated (type)
Censorship	Political (Cultural/Legal)	Information/Expression (Civil/Political)
Political imprisonment	Political (Legal)	Justice (Civil)
Torture	Political/Legal (Biophysical)	Respectful treatment (Civil)
The death penalty	Legal (Legal/Biophysical)	Life (Civil)
Apartheid	Social (Legal)	Equality (Civil)
Slavery	Social (Legal)	Equality/Freedom (Civil)
Genocide	Social/Cultural (Political)	Existence (Civil/Cultural)
Refugees	Social (Legal)	Citizenship (Political/Civil)

violation is articulated), and identifying the particular *right* which is violated in each case. This should be read as a very rough table, which serves the purpose only of contextualising the chapters in this volume. No single human rights issue is so simplistic as to fit so neatly into any one category, especially if, as intellectuals, we are able to look beyond the obvious and uncover the hidden agendas which may be at work in each case. Nevertheless, it is a useful analytic tool.

Finally, in the Conclusion, we turn to some emerging areas of human rights research. It is true, as I have already indicated, that most of the formal discussion on human rights has been concerned primarily with the political, and to some extent the legal, spheres; that is, *the state*. However, should we always limit our thinking about human rights to these areas? Surely, economic, social and cultural rights also need to be addressed. We need to be aware, at least, of the multitude of human rights violations which occur outside the state sector.

One, very broad, area deals with violations of rights which take place within the cultural sphere, and which have so far been marginalised

Table I.4   Emerging forms of human rights abuse

Substantive area	Sphere (medium)	Rights violated (type)
Poverty	Economic	Welfare/Security (Social/Economic)
Female genital mutilation	Cultural (Biophysical)	Personal autonomy (Civil)
Sati	Cultural (Biophysical)	Life (Civil)
Forced sterilisation	Social (Biophysical)	Reproduction (Biological)
Ecocide	Various (Environmental)	Existence (Civil)

by the mainstream debates. Two such practices are aimed directly at women and justified wholly according to cultural tradition: the practices of female genital mutilation and *sati*. A third violation aimed at women, that of forced sterilisation, is also discussed in the Conclusion, and is an example of how the state seeks to regulate the social dimension through intrusion upon the body. Other topics discussed here are the emerging literature on children's rights, and the debates concerning the relationship between human rights and business. Poverty is also included as a human rights concern, a violation of the right to economic welfare and security, even though it is not always reducible to the state. Mention is also made of the emerging discourse on environmental rights as well as to questions of indigenous land rights. Indeed, in respect of state and non-state concerns, ecocide is even more difficult to locate within a given sphere. Thus, we can include in Table I.3 the additions shown in Table I.4.

Needless to say, I introduce this useful table at this point only to problematise it! It is true that I have stretched the definition of human rights beyond the standard, state-centred model, by including poverty and female genital mutilation. Does this mean that we can, or should, refer now to human rights issues without necessarily relying upon some degree of state involvement? Let us see how such a shift would impact upon four of our other categories, which are recognised as human rights issues. Let us start with slavery. We will see in Chapter Eight that while the popular definition was applicable to earlier forms of this abuse, it is less relevant with regard to modern slavery, much of which is arranged through illegal, private exchanges, not sanctioned by the state or its agents.[4] Furthermore, in so far as modern slavery does not constitute the deliberate targeting of a particular social group, it is no longer even a form of social exclusion – instead, its rationale (sphere) and its arena of contestation (medium) are both *economic*. Does this make modern slavery any *less* of a human rights abuse, simply because it occurs within the economic sphere? Clearly not.

If, then, it is acceptable to include modern slavery in our discussion of human rights, what else is it possible to include? Murders are committed every day, and they are undoubtedly violations of someone's right to life. Yet these are never treated as human rights issues, because they take place between social actors, in the social sphere. Similarly, while torture is clearly a human rights concern, when a man attacks his partner with intense violence, this is considered a crime, and a despicable one at that, but not an issue of human rights, because once again it occurs within the social (indeed, the domestic) arena. If we include modern slavery, how do we exclude domestic violence from our discussion on torture? If not, how, within what arena, is it best articulated?

Similar complications arise when we turn to the cultural sphere. Female genital mutilation has been a recent addition to the discourse on human rights. However, there are many such practices which have not, as yet, been elevated to that status. There is certainly considerable discussion over the extent to which legal or political violations might somehow be related to cultural traditions. An interesting such discussion concerns the extent to which apartheid can be equated to the caste system. Should we include caste within our discussion of human rights? It is useful for us to be aware, as concerned social scientists, of the debates which seek to understand both caste and apartheid as forms of social stratification, so I have referred to it in Chapter Seven, just as I have referred to 'new' slavery in Chapter Eight. Readers are at liberty to critique what they may feel is an arbitrary decision on my part to include these but not to discuss murder or domestic violence (or any other form of social violence) in the chapters on the death penalty and torture. These omissions highlight the difficulties inherent in any discussion of human rights.

Table I.5, then, re-evaluates these four human rights violations in respect of their executions in both the state and the non-state sectors.

These debates – what to include, what not to include – are taking place not only in academic circles, but in activist ones as well. Amnesty International, which is probably the best known campaigning organisation dedicated to human rights issues, has long debated the possibility of expanding its mandate to take into consideration human rights abuses which take place in the non-state sector. There are, though, additional

Table I.5 Taking a closer look at state and non-state human rights issues

State	Sphere (medium)	Non-state	Sphere (medium)
Apartheid	Social (Legal)	Caste	Social (Cultural)
Slavery	Social (Legal)	'New' slavery	Economic
Torture	Political–Legal (Biophysical)	Domestic violence	Social (Social/ Biophysical)
Death penalty	Legal (Legal/ Biophysical)	Murder	Social (Social/ Biophysical)

complications which such social movements have to take into account. The question is not, then, whether 'new' slavery is a human rights issue because it clearly is, regardless of whether or not it is practised by the state. Instead, the question is whether 'new' slavery is an appropriate concern for this organisation. This is a pragmatic, not a philosophical question, which relates to resources, and to organisational structure and profile. At least when human rights abuses occur within the state sector we can identify the target of our campaigns, and utilise our resources accordingly. It is for this reason, more than all others, that human rights have tended to be synonymous with civil and political rights, but this should not exclude economic, social and cultural rights (or environmental ones for that matter) from the philosophical discourse on human rights.

I think it is fair to say, in conclusion, that although human rights violations can and do take place in any sphere, through any medium, the *discourse* on human rights is articulated primarily through the state. The very idea that we have rights *at all* presupposes that we *need* them, and that the machinery exists to *protect* them. The liberal traditions which stem from the philosophies of Hobbes and Locke presume that the state exists in some kind of contract with its citizens. *Both* traditions require us to view this contract as a kind of balancing act of rights and duties. As Hannah Arendt acutely observed, rights are only meaningful in the context of a state that recognises them.[5] This is true whether we advocate a strong state in the Hobbesian sense or a weaker one as conceived by Locke. One of the great scholars of human rights and duties, Immanuel Kant, argued that the only incontrovertible right is freedom – we will discuss the problem of incontrovertibility in more detail in

driving force of history. These hierarchies – which roughly correspond to economic, social, and political action – occasionally overlap, but they are distinct. Weberian conflict theories are therefore interested as much in non-economic (e.g. ethnic) conflict as they are in economic conflict, so it should not be surprising to see them used to help us understand genocide (Kuper), caste/apartheid (Warner), and slavery (Patterson).

3   *Feminism*. While Marxists argue that the driving force which steers society and creates inequalities is capitalism, feminists argue that it is in fact male domination – patriarchy – which is at fault. There are, though, just as many feminisms as there are Marxisms (as we shall see, particularly in Chapter Three, where we contrast various feminist views on pornography).

Theories of ethics

Although there are many theories of ethics, we can group most of them into two camps which provide alternative answers to the question: What makes an act 'good'? The first camp is associated with *moralism*. Moralism (sometimes called deontological ethics) draws on such thinkers as Kant, and it stresses that the value of an act resides in the act itself. Thus, one should not censor, or torture, or execute, because to do so would violate an inherent and universal right. Alternatively, a moralist might argue that one *should* censor certain material, because the material itself is inherently vile, or execute a criminal, because his or her crime was deserving of such punishment.

By contrast, *causalism* (or consequentialism) focuses not on the act but on its consequences. An act is good if it brings about a desired end, or bad if it has undesirable consequences. Causalist approaches often draw on utilitarianism, in so far as the desired end tends to be the 'greatest good' for the 'greatest number'. For the causalist, nothing is inherently evil, it can only be the right or wrong thing to do in certain circumstances. However, few causalists would want to condone such vile acts as torture, so they seek to avoid being subject to relativism by appealing to more abstract notions of the greater good.

Theories of politics

Theories of politics operate at two levels: the level of the state, and the level of international relations. Our concern here is primarily with theories of power – that is, theories of where power is located and what role the locus of political administration, the state, has in managing that power. There are three dominant traditions that we need to address: *realism*, *liberalism*, and *Marxism*.

Realism takes as its point of departure the ontological assumptions of Thomas Hobbes, that is, that humankind is an innately violent species, in need of protection from itself. Hobbesians thus call for a strong state which acts to guarantee the security of its people, in return for which the people surrender a degree of their natural freedom and rights. It is not too difficult to imagine, then, a realist defence of the death penalty (Van den Haag). When applied to the international political arena, the central premise of realism is that the world is made up of competing, self-interested nation-states, and it is with these that power rests. The world of international politics is thus portrayed as an anarchic war of all against all, from which the strongest emerge as dominant.

Liberalism begins by inverting the Hobbesian presumptions about human nature, drawing on the ontology of John Locke. Locke believed that in the 'state of nature' humans are in fact innately peaceful, but competitive. The liberal position, following Locke as well as classical economists such as John Stuart Mill, Adam Smith and David Ricardo, calls for a minimal state that serves only as arbiter on economic transactions, and should not interfere unduly in the lives of private citizens. Liberals such as Karl Popper have written fiercely about the need to defend individual freedom against the tyranny of the state. Unsurprisingly, the liberal school has been the most outspoken on matters of censorship. In the international realm, liberalism adopts a more pluralistic position than realism, maintaining that power rests not only with nation-states but also with individuals (citizens), groups, organisations, and markets.

Finally, the *Marxist* position, which we have already introduced, tends to see the state as a mere functionary, serving the interests of the market. Power in national and international terms tends to reside in the economic system. However, this position has probably caused more debate and disagreement within Marxism than any other aspect of the wider theory.

Theories of modernity

Theories of modernity did not begin with Max Weber, but he is a good point of departure for our purposes here, because he provides a sociological critique of both liberalism and Marxism, and because he grounds his critique in a theory of rationalisation which has influenced subsequent traditions. *Liberal* ideas, which have influenced pluralist and functionalist thinking, tended to adopt an optimistic and wholly *evolutionist* view of progress, that societies were evolving into more 'civilised' states. Some accounts, inspired by Lockean ontology, behavioural psychology, and utilitarianism, presume that human actors are constantly engaged in rational decision making. One such approach, *rational choice theory*, has been applied to the study of slavery as a social relationship (Fogel and Engerman). Most liberal accounts, then, have equated modernity with progress. *Marxist* accounts, by contrast, have tended to equate modernity with capitalism, and have concentrated primarily on the evolution of the economic system – Marx called his method *historical materialism*. However, it was Weber, in his critique of Marx, who presented the definitive pessimistic view of societal rationalisation. Rather than understanding modernity in terms of the emergence of the capitalist system (as Marx did), Weber understood capitalism in terms of the rise of a particular kind of rationality, associated with Protestantism. Indeed, following Weber, one can equate modernisation with rationalisation, in so far as the latter relates to a particular type of bureaucratic, means–end mentality. The manifestation of this bureaucratic rationality is the modern nation-state, which holds administration over a particular territorial space, devises laws which regulate action within that space, and serves as the centralised means of violence. So, Weber not only replaces the Marxist model with a state-centred alternative, he also provides an informed critique of naïve liberal theories of progress. Furthermore, his cultural sensitivity – his commitment to what some might call *historicism* – is a useful alternative to the alleged reductionism of the liberal and Marxist models.

By linking questions of 'rationality' with the role of the state, Weber laid the foundations for a debate which has moved on significantly since his time. Two significant developments – both of which engage with Weber's equation of modernity with instrumental, bureaucratic 'rationality', with the emergence of the state as the centralised locus of violence, one of which is broadly optimistic and the other of which is wholly pessimistic – are *critical theory* and *post-structuralism*.

Critical theory is a blend of Marxist concerns about capitalism and domination with Weberian ones about rationality, together with insights from Freudian psychoanalysis. Devised by members of the Frankfurt School prior to the Second World War, the perspective is primarily concerned with how domination comes about. The task of critical theory is to bring about emancipation, and this can be achieved by stepping outside the system in order to realise one's position within it, and to identify the inherent contradictions in a system which purports to be rational. Critical theory juxtaposes false rationality – associated with the instrumentalist logic of political and economic action which dominates the modern world – with true rationality – associated with human freedom. Thus, critical theorists recognise the bleak picture painted by Weber, but stress that this is only one kind of rationality, and there is always an alternative. The language of human rights is clearly part of this alternative rationalisation. While much of the original Frankfurt School library is either abstract and philosophical or polemical in nature, a second generation of scholars, led by Jürgen Habermas, has sought to develop more sociologically grounded foundations for critical theory.

Post-structuralism is a vague (and unhelpful) term applied to scholars who broke away from structuralism during the 1970s, embracing instead a variety of radical, challenging perspectives concerned with how language, interaction and everyday life are imbued with power relations. These disparate perspectives share a reluctance to accept that grand ideas such as progress, justice, truth, or rationality, are anything but stories. Where critical theorists search for hidden rationalities which might free us from repression, post-structuralists find only subtle techniques through which systems of power operate. The most celebrated writer of this kind is Michel Foucault, whose comments on torture and the death penalty are essential reading. Foucault's writings appear at first glance to be the antithesis of Habermas's. Habermas holds on to a commitment to the (liberal) Enlightenment ideals of progress and freedom. Foucault understands the various practices which many consider to be synonymous with progress (more 'humane' prisons, more 'advanced' forms of medical care) not in respect of some imaginary evolutionary line, but as reflections of social conditions. Superficially, they appeal to some concept of rationality, but really, however well they are disguised, they are just new ways of telling a familiar story, a story of violence and power.

Habermas and Foucault have set the standard when it comes to trying to make sense of rationality, and both have influenced my thinking on these issues. In many of the chapters that follow, I will attempt to contrast, and if possible synthesise, appropriate ideas drawn from these two different but comparable writers. Readers may decide that my attempts at synthesis are unsuccessful, perhaps undesirable. In true Kantian style, it is not, I would say in response, the success which matters as much here as the attempt – the attempt to make the best use of modern and classical social theory in order to make the most sense of the atrocities and acts of violence which occur daily in the allegedly rational and civilised world in which we live.

Notes

1   Herbert Marcuse (1991, original 1964) *One-Dimensional Man: Studies in the Ideology of Advanced Industrial Society*, London: Routledge, pp. xlii–xliii.

2   The Index appeared in the *Observer*, 28 June 1998, p. 10. The top three categories were scored out of 30, the remainder out of 10. The totals were then cross-matched against the United Nations Human Development Index, which ranks countries by their level of development.

3   www.newsunlimited.co.uk/Tables/4_col_tables/0,5737,94899,00.html.

4   Kevin Bales (1999) *Disposable People: New Slavery in the Global Economy*, Berkeley: University of California Press.

5   Hannah Arendt (1949) 'The "Rights of Man": What Are They?' in *Modern Review* 3, 1, Summer; reproduced in Arendt (1951) *The Origins of Totalitarianism*, New York: Harcourt Brace, pp. 290–302.

6   Norberto Bobbio (1996) *The Age of Rights*, Cambridge: Polity Press, p. 10.

7   Consider, for example, the impact of Hobbesian essentialist thought upon the social sciences. Realism in international relations, control theory and 'right' realism in criminology, sociobiology in anthropology, public choice theory in political science, and classical elite theory in political sociology, are all varieties of neo-Hobbesian social science.

8   It would not, of course, be fair to expect the reader of this volume to be familiar with these traditions, and in this introduction space allows only for a 'beginner's guide'. Students wishing to explore the complexities of social theory in more depth are advised to consult George Ritzer (1992) *Sociological Theory*, New York: McGraw Hill.

CHAPTER ONE

Theorising human rights

What are human rights?

In 1948, the Universal Declaration of Human Rights was signed by the member states of the United Nations. For many, that document was the single most important of the twentieth century, for it lays down certain claims regarding the rights of all peoples around the world, and formalises them within the framework of international law, albeit in a suggestive, rather than legally binding, manner. Over 50 years on, however, we are still faced with a world which does not fully recognise the claims made in the Declaration. Human rights abuses continue in nation-states across the globe. Western democracies preach the observance of human rights regulations to non-Western nations whilst blatantly ignoring them at home. The world of international relations is still as chaotic and competitive as it was before 1948; only it has become more hypocritical.

Why this document was signed, what its claims are, and why it has not succeeded in eradicating human rights abuses around the world, are the subjects of the next chapter. Before we discuss any of these, though, we need to understand exactly what we mean when we talk about human rights, a term that is used frequently and understood rarely. Indeed, very often when we hear human rights discussed, we find that what is actually being discussed is *citizenship rights*, or *civil liberties*. To avoid confusion, we should bear in mind that civil liberties are those rights which are not legitimated according to some universal feature of humanity; instead they are rights only in so far as they are allowed by the state, they are 'granted from above'. Citizenship is often defined in terms of a reciprocal relationship between an individual (the citizen) and the machinery of political administration (the state), and the terms and conditions of this relationship – the rights and duties – are enshrined in positive law. Accordingly, they differ across time and space. Human rights, by contrast, come from 'below', from a universal set of ethical principles which seek to ensure the equal worth of each individual life, and which are applicable to all peoples at all times and in all places. Thus, in principle, if not in practice, they are not subject to the whims of any political machinery.

This seems at first glance to be a simple distinction, but as this chapter progresses, it should become clear that it is far from it. I want to divide the remainder of this chapter into the following sections. First, I will offer a brief history of the idea of human rights, partly as an overview and partly as an introduction to some of the major themes and names that will reappear throughout the book. Second, I want to look in more detail at the three claims which are made about the properties of human rights, namely:

- Human rights are *universal*, that is, they belong to each of us regardless of ethnicity, race, gender, sexuality, age, religion, political conviction, or type of government.

- Human rights are *incontrovertible*, that is, they are absolute and innate. They are not grants from states, and thus cannot be removed or denied by any political authority, and they do not require, and are not negated by the absence of, any corresponding *duties*.

- Human rights are *subjective*. They are the properties of individual subjects who possess them because of their capacity for *rationality*, agency and autonomy.

Each of these properties can be analysed in terms of the problems which arise from it. So, the claim that rights are universal has been subject to criticism from those who suggest that universality is too reliant upon the meaningless abstract notion of natural law, as well as from those who argue that it is ignorant of cultural difference. Similarly, the claim that rights are incontrovertible forces us, in the first instance, to devise a hierarchy of rights to overcome any potential conflicts, and also to counter any suggestion that rights always require reciprocal duties. Also, to claim that rights are subjective requires us to consider the thorny topic of human rationality and agency, and then, since active subjects are usually individuals, to assess the charge that human rights betray a Western bias towards individualism.

Third, I want to make the link – an important link if human rights are to be upheld in practice – between the idea of human rights as a moral convention and that of ethics as a social practice.

Fourth, I will discuss the extent to which the current discourse on human rights is interwoven with the discourse on social change, and in particular modernity, which invariably connects this discourse with the development of the social sciences.

A brief history of human rights theory

The *discourse* on human rights may be a relatively modern creation, but the ideas that underpin it can be traced back at least as far as the classics, if not before. Indeed, most ancient religions included codes of practice which might be interpreted as implying certain rights, even if these were largely stratified. Ancient and classical philosophers also contributed to this discourse. The Enlightenment allowed for a renewal of secular moral universalism, and it is from these roots that we can trace the evolution of the idea of human rights recognisable today.

Classical origins of human rights thinking

Although it is not easy to find, in the ancient and classical scholars, a clear precursor to current thinking about human rights which might be recognisable to us, various strands of thought did originate in the philosophical and dramatic writings of these commentators. For example, the playwright Sophocles (495–406 BC) provided an early defence of the individual's right to resist state repression.[1] Plato (427–348 BC) developed an early version of universalism in ethical standards, implying fair treatment to all persons, whether they are citizens or not. Aristotle (384–322 BC) discussed the importance of virtue, justice and rights in accordance with the political community. The Greek Stoics and their Roman counterparts, notably Cicero and Seneca, were keen to talk about being citizens of the world. For these commentators, wise and rational men belonged to a universal community of world citizens. Cicero (106–43 BC) provided the philosophical foundations for later theories of natural law, when he advocated a general set of universal principles which should transcend local civil laws.

Early versions of human rights thinking can also be found in various religious texts. Geoffrey Robertson makes the useful point that one can read the Ten Commandments, which were intended to be applied universally as rules for moral and spiritual behaviour, as implying certain basic rights. For example, 'Thou shalt not steal' seems to suggest the right for individuals to own private property.[2] Much later, the religious universalists such as Aquinas and Augustine talked about the equality of people before God, thus affirming universal laws but again, not explicitly in the context of rights. Thomas Aquinas (1225–1274) believed that human dignity and value are innate properties which are validated according to natural law. Aquinas based this on his understanding of the Christian faith. Similar readings can be offered of other religious texts and credos.

Both traditions – the classical philosophers and the religious universalists – can be understood in terms of their contributions to the history of the idea of world citizenship, which of course is not easily separated from the history of the idea of human rights. However, we should not dwell too much on these contributions in this volume.[3] Instead, we should turn to the more direct origins of human rights thinking, in the works of the European Enlightenment philosophers.

Natural law and the 'state of nature'

In medieval and early modern Western philosophy, much discussion of politics had centred around the divine right of kings. According to this concept, only monarchs held their place in society by nature, and according to the will of God. All other individuals were subservient to the monarch. The only power they had over their own lives was that which was granted them by the monarch. These ideas were articulated, and challenged, via a meticulous analysis of what would constitute a pre-social human nature, by Thomas Hobbes (1588–1679) in his *Leviathan*, published in 1651. Hobbes claimed that humans are, essentially, violent and greedy animals, and that in their natural state they live in a world of anarchy. However, out of a strong desire for self-preservation, in order to protect themselves and ensure their personal security, they come together to establish a set of rules. The King (or indeed the modern state) is the manifestation of these rules. Individuals surrender their personal freedoms to the state in return for the security it offers. Thus, the King (or the state) is granted the *right* to rule, while the needy subjects (or citizens) have a *duty* to obey. This is the basis of what Hobbes (and subsequent writers) called 'the social contract'. Hobbes's work was a masterpiece of political philosophy, although it has received unfair treatment from those who claim that it justifies an authoritarian state. In fact, Hobbes's defence of the King's right to rule was radical because, by appealing to some pre-social conditions and essential human nature, he justified it according to the consent and basic needs of the people. In effect, while Hobbes was arguing for the right of the monarch to rule, he was also claiming that the individual subject has the basic *right to security*, and that the state itself is formed out of a recognition of this basic right. Indeed, the legitimation of the state derives from its ability to ensure the security of its citizens. If it is unable to fulfil this requirement, the people still have the power to overthrow it.

When judging Hobbes's contributions, we should also bear in mind that the political situation in Europe at the time he was writing was nervous and uncertain. The power of the monarch was under attack from parliamentarians dedicated to establishing a system of government guided by the people. Even more significantly, the Dutch jurist Hugo Grotius (1583–1645) made the first significant case for the establishment of international laws to protect all citizens of the world. The laws of each nation-state should, he claimed, be measured against this standard of international law, which should primarily be applied to prevent the proliferation of unjust wars between states.

Hobbes had indicated that humans had an innate right to security from the state. Grotius based his beliefs on a moral commitment to international justice. It was John Locke (1632–1704), still working within this contractarian tradition, who first suggested that there are such things as natural rights: rights which are ours by virtue of the fact that we are human. According to Locke, these rights are shared by all people; they are inalienable, and cannot be removed by any political authority. Locke set himself the task of attacking Hobbes's defence of the legitimate rule of kings, while celebrating the establishment of the Bill of Rights. In his *Second Treatise of Government*, published in 1690, he used the same methodology as Hobbes but inverted his predecessor's conclusions. Rather than rely upon an image of pre-social human beings as warlike, greedy and violent, and in need of a strong state to ensure security, he claimed that in such a state of nature humans are naturally peaceful, free and mercantile. The state emerges, he claimed, solely out of the occasional need for an independent arbiter in any disputes which may arise over trade or property. Clearly, much of Locke's philosophy was provoked by the influence of the Judaeo-Christian tradition, which maintains that the responsibility to protect our rights and those of others, and to better ourselves, falls on us as individuals. He thus used the idea of rights as an attack on the idea of a strong state. Locke's natural rights were threefold: *life, liberty, and property*; he is thus considered to be the founder of modern liberalism.[4]

The Enlightenment and the 'rights of man'

Locke's ideas were *philosophical*, and did not require, in his view, formalisation into law for them to have any power. Also, they appeared to be true in themselves – that is, they were not necessarily observations on the problems of his time. Jean-Jacques Rousseau (1712–1778), the

Swiss philosopher, extended the social contract tradition beyond the simplistic individualism of Hobbes and Locke to incorporate the role of the community in his famous tome *The Social Contract*, in which he argued that the community must represent the general will of the people. Rousseau began his *opus* with the famous observation: 'Man is born free, but everywhere is in chains', and much of his subsequent work was dedicated to exploring the conditions which restricted human freedom. Rousseau believed that freedom could not be achieved through anonymous states, in which democracy meant only occasional participation in the election of representatives, but through smaller communities in which participatory democracy could be practised.

Rousseau was part of a tradition known as the 'French Enlightenment'. The contributions made to the philosophy of human rights by his predecessors and contemporaries also need to be mentioned. For example, Charles-Louise de Montesquieu (1684–1755) is credited with developing the theory of the separation of powers – that is, that in a just and fair state, it is necessary for the three branches of the state: the executive, the legislature, and the judiciary, to be independent from one another. Although Montesquieu was something of a proto-functionalist in so far as he studied society as a total system and thus considered most of its institutions to be there according to nature, he was nevertheless outspoken in his opposition to all forms of despotism, slavery and intolerance. Another leader of this group of *philosophes*, François-Marie Arouet, Voltaire (1694–1778), called for the abolition of torture and degrading punishments, and, famously, attacked censorship by calling for a respect for freedom of opinion and expression, whatever the views or the content in question might be. Also, despite being an advocate of hedonism and the pursuit of happiness, Claude-Adrien Helvétius (1715–1771) considered inequality to be a fundamental social ill and championed the emancipatory and egalitarian possibilities of universal education.

If the French Enlightenment thinkers provided the foundations of the political 'rights of man', it is the German philosopher Immanuel Kant (1724–1804) who is often credited with laying the groundwork for the modern understanding of human rights as ethical practice.[5] Actually, for Kant, the sole incontrovertible right was the right to freedom. Nevertheless, Kant provides a useful and important break with Lockean abstraction by outlining a manifesto for practical moral action, based on the qualitative recognition of a fundamental human dignity, which has subsequently found its way into the core of human rights discourse. Kant based his belief in justice on what he termed the 'categorical imperative' of moral action. According to this, a principle, to be moral, must satisfy three formulae. The first is known as the *formula of universality*. This states that morality must be impartial and non-arbitrary, and affirms that it must involve *equality*. The recommendation for action is that each individual should act towards others in a way they would expect and desire others to act towards them. It is the moral responsibility of all humans to act in such a way, *as if it were a general, or universal, law* – 'Act only on that maxim through which you can at the same time will that it should become a universal law.' The second is the *formula of the end in itself*. This is the idea that humans should always be treated as ends in themselves, and never as means to ends. It thus demands respect for all persons and affirms that morality must involve *justice* – 'Act in such a way that you treat humanity . . . never simply as a means, but always at the same time as an end.' The third is known as the *formula of the kingdom of ends*, which is a principle of autonomy that demands that individuals recognise their responsibilities and their empowerment, thus affirming that morality must involve *freedom* – 'So act as if you were through your maxims a law-making member of a kingdom of ends.'

Kant wanted to make it clear that human rights were distinct from those civil rights accorded to citizens of a state by the government of that state. This is why he proposed a triangular structure of rights: first, the *civil rights* of individuals within their nation-states; second, the *international rights* of states in their dealings with one another; and third, the *cosmopolitan rights* of individuals and states as existing interdependently in a universal state of humankind. Central to his theorising is the essential oneness of the human race. For Kant, people have rights simply because they share the earth's surface. In his own words:

> the right to resort, for all men are entitled to present themselves in the society of others by virtue of their right to communal possession of the earth's surface. Since the earth is a globe, they cannot disperse over an infinite area, but must necessarily tolerate one another's company.[6]

Here, with Rousseau and then Kant, was the beginning of a radical tradition that would take Locke's noble but liberal ideas further. The linkage of Locke's philosophy of natural law and the political constitution of states came with the publication in 1791–2 of *Rights of Man* by Thomas Paine (1737–1809).[7] Paine, a supporter of the revolutions in America and France, was a radical and democratic republican who believed wholly in the sovereignty of the individual person. In many respects he was, like Locke, a classical liberal, in so far as he advocated minimal state intervention and supported free market economics, although he was also an early advocate of the *right* of the people to education and social welfare. *Rights of Man* was written largely as an attack on Edmund Burke, who had previously published a severe condemnation of the revolution in France. Paine, by contrast, celebrated the revolution and the subsequent approval of the Declaration of the Rights of Man and the Citizen on 26 August 1789. For Paine, the formal implementation of rights within the political sphere was essential for the establishment of social justice. Like Locke, he justified his defence of certain inalienable rights – rights of mind and rights of personal happiness and freedom – by returning to a pre-social time, which in his case was the act of Creation. Thus, the two major revolutions of the age, in America and France, were perfectly justifiable for Paine because they represented the awakening of people from their forced slumber, and, more significantly, they both resulted in the signing of formal documents in which individual rights were legally and positively enshrined.

During his colourful life, Paine served as a revolutionary and a writer of constitutions as well as a pamphleteer. More than anyone he sought a marriage between human rights in theory and in practice. He was a charismatic individual and he gathered support from various writers and commentators of the time. Among the members of this circle was Mary Wollstonecraft (1759–1797), who, in 1792, wrote *A Vindication of the Rights of Women*, a book which borrowed from Paine's ideas but focused specifically on the role women played in the emergent human rights movement. While Wollstonecraft was primarily concerned with the importance of education and self-actualisation, she is rightly considered to be a major pioneer of the struggle for women's emancipation. Another writer who, via an engagement with Paine, developed the literature on rights was Giuseppe Mazzini (1805–1872). This Italian philosopher and ardent republican was among the first to struggle with the relationship between an individual's role within a nation-state and within the wider community of humankind. However, Mazzini focused not on the *rights* of individuals within these fields, but on their *duties*. The central argument in Mazzini's *Duties of Man* was that an individual's duties towards humanity represent the ultimate morality.[8] The role of the nation-state was to unite individuals with otherwise diverse identification under one banner so that they could more effectively realise their ultimate duties towards the community of all people.

Not all influential philosophers and writers of the period were as enamoured of the idea of the 'rights of man' (or woman) as those who followed Paine. The various ideas we have so far discussed – notably Locke's reliance upon natural law and Paine's celebration of the 'rights of man', were subjected to considerable criticism from some of their more illustrious contemporaries or interpreters. Chief among these are the *utilitarian* critique of rights made by Jeremy Bentham, and the radical critique of bourgeois individualism espoused by Karl Marx.

Jeremy Bentham (1748–1832)[9] scoffed at the very idea of natural law, and of rights in general, as 'nonsense on stilts' because they are not observable and not enforceable. For utilitarians, as opposed to Kantians, qualities such as goodness or truth can only be measured in context, that is, in specific, real situations, and not against some kind of abstract universal principle. Thus, for the utilitarians, the concept of rights can only be defensible if these rights are seen to have emerged out of the quest for the greatest happiness. Utilitarians adopt a rational choice model, which presumes human action to be the outcome of a deliberative assessment of the relative benefits and disadvantages of a given course of action. According to such a perspective, human rights are not, therefore, abstract pre-social phenomena rooted in natural law, but the products of human decision making. Ever the pragmatist, Bentham was critical of Rousseau's claim that people are born free and of the related claim that they are all born equal in rights. Clearly, he stated, any simple observation of human development, of parental and community bonds, of inequalities in skills, knowledge and life-chances, shows these up to be obscene fallacies. Humans invent these rights out of necessity. Bentham's utilitarian approach is therefore empiricist (that is, based on observable rather than abstract conditions) and positivist (that is, geared towards scientific measurement and explanation), in contrast to the rationalism of his predecessors. However, it should be added that not all utilitarians were as hostile to issues of human rights as Bentham. The Italian criminologist Cesare Beccaria (1738–1794) applied the principles of utilitarian philosophy to the study of punishment, and duly established a critique of the use of torture and the death penalty which is influential even today.

An equally pragmatic critique of the language of human rights was presented by Karl Marx (1818–1883). Aware of the persecution suffered by Jews in Germany, Marx wondered how useful the Declaration of the Rights of Man in France would be in helping Jews like himself in their plight.[10] Marx re-read the Declaration and concluded that it said little other than that humans were bourgeois individuals separated from each other and from their communities. He added that there are no pre-social rights, since we become people only in society. Thus rights are political and social, and are achieved through historical development and struggle. While applauding the possibilities contained within the new discourse on *citizenship* (in so far as it allowed for the individuals to connect to communities and to external conditions), he dismissed the egoism and individualism of the Declaration as insubstantial in terms of true empowerment. Each of the rights contained therein, he stated, with reference to the rights of *equality*, *liberty*, *security*, and *property*, addresses private individuals and not humanity as a species: *society*. It is one thing to be recognised in law as an individual with certain highly individualised rights. It is another to be allowed to develop as a moral person within a set of conditions which are fair and equally accessible for all persons. The Declaration did not, Marx concluded, pay any attention to such true emancipation. Instead, it addressed the *bourgeois* instead of the citizen, 'man' instead of 'men'. *Formal not actual freedom*

Human rights thinking in the contemporary world

After Kant, the discussion of human rights largely shifted away from the philosophical and theological arena towards that of active politics – the space occupied so vociferously by Paine and Marx. There was much discussion of citizenship rights held by individuals within countries, and the increasingly internationalised nature of politics and trade provoked an increasing awareness of the need for international law. As Kant himself said:

> the peoples of the earth have ... entered ... into a universal community, and it has developed to the point where a violation of rights in one part of the world is felt everywhere.[11]

However, Kant's observations about the inevitable globalisation of human rights aside, the twentieth century saw the world plunge into the depths of warfare and gross violations of basic rights which seemed to make a mockery out of the optimism of rationalists such as Kant. Probably the most significant social philosopher to discuss the theory and practice of human rights in the light of these atrocities was Hannah Arendt (1906–1975). Arendt was a political scientist, born in Germany but later an American citizen, who dedicated much of her life as an activist and an academic to understanding the dynamics of totalitarianism, the concept of freedom, and, in effect, of humanity itself. Herself a Jew, she conducted major historical surveys on the relationship between Jews and modern society from the Enlightenment. For Arendt, the 'rights of man' meant very little or nothing at all to refugees, stateless persons, outsiders within the boundaries of an alien state.[12] She pointed out that, for all their noble intentions, these rights relied nonetheless upon the existence of strong political communities capable of enforcing them. Thus, those refugees and displaced persons necessarily found themselves outside the framework of human rights simply because they were not considered the citizens of any nation-state. Arendt questioned the nature of the relationship between these so-called 'rights of man' and the very concept of humanity. Not only are they not in actuality contingent upon an individual's innate humanity, but there are clearly times when these rights are denied, which do not actually constitute human rights *violations* – examples used included the soldier in wartime, denied the right to life, the prisoner denied the right to freedom, citizens in an emergency denied the right to security or the pursuit of happiness. For Arendt, the only fundamental right exists within the political community itself – that is, the right *to have the right* to life, liberty, happiness, and so on. In other words, a right to *citizenship* which is, in effect, the right to be *recognised* as human, to be included. For Arendt, guided as much by the ghost of Aristotle as by her teachers, the German existentialists Heidegger and Jaspers, the political community is the space wherein we *become*; equality is neither innate nor granted, but is achieved through just human organisation – 'We are not born equal; we become equal as members of a group on the strength of our decision to guarantee ourselves mutually equal rights'.[13]

Today, our thinking about human rights is steeped in the language of Locke, Kant, Paine, and others. By effectively bringing together the contributions made by these important thinkers we have devised a language of human rights which is intended to clarify any potential ambiguities, to allow for human rights to be enforced in practice. This is evident if we consider, for example, the 1948 Universal Declaration of Human Rights, which we shall do in the next chapter. However, the incorporation of a language of human rights into a global system of justice has not been without its problems. Arendt was wise to warn against the liberal assumptions of rationalism and of Enlightenment progress. The twentieth century did indeed produce violations of human rights, of basic decency, which constituted atrocities of the highest order. Nevertheless, it seems too simplistic and Manichean a divide to accept that one has to be either an empiricist who, like Bentham and Max Weber after him, believes that any appeal to abstract ideas is meaningless and thus throws the proverbial baby out with the bath water, or a rationalist who, when pushed to provide an explanation of why humans have rights in the first place, has in the last instance to fall back on philosophical generalisations born of faith rather than truth. The contemporary literature on human rights, be it critical or sympathetic, has tended to avoid these extreme positions. The discourse rests largely on problematising the various properties which the classical Kantian tradition appears to presuppose: universality, incontrovertibility, and subjectivity. It is true, of course, that these remain philosophical concerns only, and that we are under no obligation to accept them in order to justify our belief in human rights at a pragmatic level. Nevertheless, many of the criticisms that have been levelled at human rights even as an idea are based to some degree in these philosophical assumptions. It is therefore useful to be aware of them and to understand these problems which arise from them. We will now address each of these properties, and these problems, in greater depth.

Are human rights universal?

The first such property is universality, that is, the assumption that if human rights exist they necessarily belong to each and every one of us. Universality is probably the single most important – and contested – issue in the discourse on human rights, and is essential for their application as much as for their theorisation. Thus, we will spend sufficient time detailing two of the main criticisms levelled at the theory of universality: first, the philosophical criticism of the idea of natural law; second, the charge that universalism is necessarily insensitive towards cultural difference.

The problem of natural law

The idea of human rights is the idea that all people are part of a community that transcends their immediate political community; that they subscribe to a law that is superior to the laws of their states. Of course, neither this 'community' nor this 'law' has any formalised status. Both ideas form part of an abstract, moral, commitment that can be traced back to the philosophy of the classics.[14] The 'community' is the community of *all people*: humankind. The 'law' is *natural law*. Natural law is grounded in a pre-social, universal, state of morality, as opposed to *positive law*, which is grounded in official, binding, constitutional acts and precedents. Nino characterises natural law according to two propositions:

(a) that the principles which determine the justice of social institutions and the rightness of social actions, are valid independently of their recognition by certain individuals or organisations, and

(b) that a normative system, even when actually recognised by organisations with access to the state's coercive apparatus, cannot be deemed legal if it does not satisfy the principles mentioned in (a).[15]

Initially, natural law was a methodological tool used by political philosophers to justify how citizens (or subjects) *should* act on the basis of a philosophical reading of how they *would* have acted *before* the advent of society. It had less to do with the rights of all peoples *per se* than with the relationship between a citizen and a state (or subject and sovereign). This, at least, is how Locke understood natural law. Both Locke and Hobbes were attempting to explain human *essence*, that which humans *are* before they enter into social relationships. They were, therefore, less concerned with providing guidelines for *moral* action than with establishing the philosophical basis for a *political* constitution. Kant, on the other hand, applied the paradigm of natural law specifically to questions of morality and ethics. He wanted to show not only that morality is *universal* but that it is articulated through the behaviour of people towards one another. In this respect, Kantian moral philosophy can be read as a framework for building the 'good society'. Of course, there is a huge difference between advocating a position which sees moral behaviour among individuals as a pre-social condition, and advocating one that claims certain basic rights exist in some invisible, abstract realm beyond and prior to the social.

The concept of natural law is a hugely contested one. To make the claim that certain rights exist before the formation of human societies, that they are right and true in abstraction from people, that they are grounded in some higher spiritual or moral authority, is to invite criticism and controversy. One interesting question to emerge from this debate is: Would I have rights if I lived alone? That is to say, under such circumstances *would I need them*? Are rights created not for our benefit but for the benefit of *others*? We sometimes call this hypothetical situation the 'desert island scenario'. I am alone on a desert island. I am sovereign and have neither rights nor duties. Only when someone else is shipwrecked on my island is it necessary for us to enter into some kind of contract in order for us to live in security and relative prosperity.

In recent years the Kantian position has found itself under attack from two distinct sources, related in the sense that both are relativist (as opposed to universalist), but coming from wholly different directions. The first challenge we can label the *communitarian* challenge (the second is the *postmodernist* challenge). We will discuss communitarianism in greater depth below, because for the most part this tradition critiques the explicit *individualism* of the Kantian project. However, it has also contributed towards a critique of universalism and natural law. For the communitarians, morality exists not in terms of liberal universal principles but in virtues; the ideal of universal morality is replaced by that of the good life, or, more specifically, the 'good society'. While Kant, ever a

Platonist, believed that there is a right way and a wrong way of doing things, communitarians, drawing more on Aristotle, adopt a more pragmatic stance and pay more attention to *context*. The most significant advocate of this *moral contextualism* is Alisdair McIntyre.[16]

So, communitarianism adopts a relativist position on rights because it argues that they only emerge in particular settings. We cannot devise universal rules which we expect to apply in all cases. Instead, we must treat every community, every society, in its own context. Communitarians do not necessarily oppose the idea of rights; merely their presumed universality. The same can be said of social constructionists, such as Malcolm Waters, a sociologist who has been active in establishing a sociology of human rights.[17] For Waters, rights are meaningful (in that the discourse on rights only exists) in social situations, regardless of whether these rights draw on pre-social or inherent human properties. However, the driving force behind this discourse is context, and in admitting this Waters's constructionism falls into the slippery realm of relativism.

Partly in response to these criticisms, a neo-Kantian tradition has emerged that seeks to re-establish the universal foundations of human rights. Among the leading figures in this movement are John Rawls and Jürgen Habermas. These writers have sought to separate the idea of universality from that of natural law. While conceding that we need to be careful when discussing universals, so that we do not privilege one perspective over another, these neo-Kantians argue that universal truths *do* exist and can be found in our actions. The important difference between these writers and the abstract, essentialist universalists such as Kant is that they accept the need to ground these universals in everyday action. They have adopted an approach akin to pragmatism. There is, it would appear, a middle ground opening up. Universalists such as Habermas have taken to pragmatism, and in doing so have met relativists such as Richard Rorty, about whom we will say more below. Rawls coined the term 'moral constructivism' to define this perspective which, loosely, seeks to defend the search for underlying universals (such as those found in natural law) but show how these abstract principles relate to everyday life and are, indeed, constructed and interpreted through everyday action.

Rawls has offered a modified Kantian version of the 'state of nature' arguments which formed the foundations of earlier contractarian thinking.[18] His defence of the idea of a just society based on universally agreed moral principles lies essentially in the idea that in any pre-social arrangement, people, if given the choice, would opt for a society governed by such principles because this would be most beneficial to them all. These principles are grounded in equality and justice.

Habermas locates these universal principles in the practice of every-day communication.[19] He stresses that in this act, which is the most basic and universal of all human practices, we are actually presupposing the existence of a consensus, and the point is to find it. As consensus is possible so, necessarily, is truth, and for Habermas, using a Rawlsian argument, this truth will always, necessarily, lead to a defence of justice against injustice, equality against inequality, and freedom against oppression. This consensus is the attainment of the 'ideal speech situation', but it is dependent upon the act of communication satisfactorily achieving four *validity claims* which are presupposed in the relationship between the speaker and the hearer. To reach consensus (and achieve truth), Habermas says, an utterance must be *comprehensible* (the hearer must be able to understand it); it must be *rightful* (the speaker must be in an appropriate position to make it); it must be *truthful* (the speaker must be speaking with honesty); and it must be *right* (the utterance must be factually correct). Each claim is made against a different set of rules. Comprehensibility is judged in accordance with the rules of language itself. Rightfulness is judged in accordance with the normative or intersubjective world occupied by the speaker and hearer. Truthfulness is judged in accordance with the subjective world of the speaker. Truth is judged in accordance with the objective world of external reality.

Tom Regan, who, as we shall see later in this chapter, extends the Kantian perspective beyond merely rational human actors (moral *agents*) to include animals and other moral *patients*, offers a similar (if less theoretically rigorous) set of requirements for making the 'ideal moral judgement'.[20] These include: *clarity* (of terminology); (access to) *information*; *rationality* (of argument); *impartiality* (of interest); *coolness* (of temperament); and *valid moral principles* (that is, pertaining to judge-ments about behaviour). Regan's, and Habermas's, schema is an attempt to build a bridge between the abstract world of universal morality and the pragmatic world of social action in which ethical choices are made.

Another modified version of the Kantian perspective comes from Norberto Bobbio.[21] Bobbio aims his criticisms firmly at the alleged pre-social essentialism of the natural law perspective. He points out, in rather sharp fashion, that any recourse to 'natural, fundamental, inalienable or inviolable rights may represent a persuasive formula to back in a polit-ical publication, but it has no theoretical value, and is therefore com-pletely irrelevant to human rights theory'.[22] Adopting a more historicist perspective – Bobbio holds that human rights are and always have been *historical rights* – he claims that different rights have emerged at different times as a result of different social conflicts:

Religious freedom resulted from the religious wars, civil liberties from the parliamentarian struggles against absolutism, and political and social freedoms from the birth, growth and experience of movements representing workers, landless peasants and smallholders.[23]

Bobbio would claim that his perspective maintains a commitment to the *universality* of rights, even if it flatly dismisses any suggestion that rights are pre-social properties of natural law. Just because rights emerge at different stages in human history and against the backdrop of basic and fundamental human needs does not render them subject to relativism.

Bobbio, Rawls, Habermas and Regan have all sought to bridge the gap between universalists and relativists from within the universalist camp. Other contemporary universalists have less trouble embracing essentialist presuppositions about the human condition. Ken Booth, for example, has suggested that human rights emerge from 'universal social facts', and that torture and the ill-treatment of others are *wrong* because they contradict or deny basic human *needs* – needs which derive either from our 'natural' animalistic state, or from our social character.[24]

To summarise, there has been no greater controversy within the field of human rights than that concerning questions of universality and natural law. It overflows into all the other controversies which we shall discuss below – individuality, rationality, duty. The critique of essentialism – that is, of the idea that there are some innate, pre-social characteristics that define humanity – has laid siege to the very foundations – quite literally – upon which the human rights discourse was built. Some commentators have sought to separate universality from essentialism. Writers such as Rawls and Habermas have attempted to justify the existence of universals by appealing, in different ways, to the universal characteristics of pragmatic social action, rather than to abstract natural law. Similarly, the likes of Bobbio (and Jack Donnelly) have argued for a historically sensitive approach, suggesting as they do that human rights are constructed according to the conditions of modernity, but maintaining that they nevertheless reflect universal struggles and/or universal human needs. Booth makes the break with essentialism by suggesting that 'we should have human rights not because we are human, but to make us human'.[25]

The problem of cultural difference

As has just been suggested, in contemporary world society, the most common critique of the idea of human rights has been directed at these universalistic pretensions. Beyond abstract theory, the idea of universality 'is central to the problem of international human rights law, which is directly bound up with the issue of universalism and regionalism in respect of the promotion and protection of human rights'.[26] Supporters claim that this universality implies, by its very nature, the inclusion of cultural diversity and regional particularism. Critics, however, suggest that, far from being universal, the rights that we are told we have reflect a Western bias. In some respects this is a fair charge, as it is only in Western political thought that the world is seen as an aggregation of individuals. We will discuss the problem of individualism – a problem that is central to the Kantian tradition – below. Against this charge of Western bias, though, we should note that to various degrees rights are presupposed in many of the world's major religions, not just Western ones. In fact, the alleged universality of rights is less to do with their intent than with their implementation. We should certainly take care that the 'universality' of human rights is not turned into a weapon for Western cultural hegemony, for 'attempting to replicate the United States in other parts of the world'.[27] In truth, the origins of *our way of thinking about* rights may lie in Western philosophy, but the idea of universal human rights is, necessarily, universal and global. For most commentators, the origins of this universality lie not in the abstract Lockean world of natural law but in a modified Kantianism which encourages respect for all people based on the fundamental dignity which is inherent in human beings without distinction or exception. Such a view of universality does not, then, appear to challenge or undermine cultural diversity.

We have already encountered the tradition known as communitarianism. Communitarians have focused their relativist critique of Kantianism primarily on the problem of universal natural law. Postmodernism also comes from a relativist perspective, and is equally damning of Kantian liberalism, but it is also scathing of the idea of the community, or of the 'good society'. For the postmodernists, such values as 'goodness' and 'truth' are necessarily abstract and have no concrete meaning. To suggest that one thing is 'better' than another is to adopt a dictatorial approach. Truth, justice, goodness and so on are merely grand narratives which we have made use of in our construction of history.[28] That very construction comes from a particular point of view (one which is Western, male, middle-class, white, etc.). History is there to be interpreted, but each interpretation will favour something different, because it carries with it its own power interests. Thus, we need to abandon the search for grand narratives and concentrate instead on the world as a constant struggle between plural, competing discourses. Postmodernism is thus opposed to the Kantian discourse on human rights because it considers it to be essentialist, i.e. that it presupposes an essential core. Postmodernism is opposed to all forms of essentialism.

The obvious problem with this radical position, which seeks to emancipate us from the constraints of grand narratives, is that it seems then to dispense with the whole idea of ethics, and slip into an uncontrol- *NO.* lable relativism. If the world is made up of competing narratives, and no one should be favoured over another, then morality becomes a free market. Torture may not be preferable in our society, but it might *NO* be acceptable in others, and their opinions on the subject should be respected and considered equally as valid as ours. We should not criti- *Specific* cise the practice of female genital mutilation because it is an accepted *Cultural* cultural practice. Now, few postmodernists would condone torture or *Context* female genital mutilation. Most come from the Left, and their project *not a* has been to amend the essentialist, Western view of the world that *history* dominates history. Feminists and anti-racists have thus embraced post- *not a* modernism because it allows for new voices to be heard, new stories *Universal* to be told. But their 'anything goes' viewpoint has serious ethical im- *to be* plications. It demands serious attention because it challenges the very *respected* foundations of rights as we have understood them.

Neo-Kantians have taken issue with this charge of Western bias *Identity/* in their attempts to rethink the problem of universalism. Habermas, in *Difference* particular, has taken serious issue with the postmodernists, accusing them of being apolitical at best, conservative at worst. Jack Donnelly *Difference* also defends a universalist perspective when he suggests that human *not finished* *rights* have emerged alongside modernity as the latest in a series of mech- *yet being* anisms devised to safeguard human *dignity* from state oppression.[29] Donnelly lists various other cultures – non-Western – which have similar religious or ethical guidelines aimed at upholding human dignity, if not rights *per se*. For both writers, time spent debating the metatheoretical questions concerning the foundations of human rights (in natural law or whatever) is time wasted.

Richard Rorty has gone some way to bridging this divide from within a tradition which stands closer to the relativist than the univer-salist side.[30] Rorty's position is as follows. First, we need to move beyond epistemological perspectives which claim that we can, somehow through critique or reason, know the social world (i.e. rationalism), as such perspectives are flawed. Second, in keeping with the postmodernist viewpoint, grand narratives are merely stories which are reflections of particular times and spaces. The grand narrative that is human rights has been told, successfully, by liberal democratic societies. Thus, only these societies are equipped to develop arguments for human rights, but this does not mean that any attempt to do so would be an imposition upon the cultural differences of other societies. On the contrary, Rorty claims that contemporary liberals have a responsibility to continue to 'tell the story', and just because only they can *know* the story of human rights does not make that story any less *real*. Here, Rorty is not drifting into essentialism. Rather, he is upholding a *pragmatism* that recognises that in the contemporary world, with the horrors of the twentieth century recent memories, the culture of human rights has become a reality. This is a reality which has been constructed not through a recognition of innate human dignity or reason, but through a shared (but mainly Western) *sentimentality* which has emerged from hearing these stories and has proven to be the new basis for human solidarity. Rorty does not enter so much into a debate on the existence of universal human rights (*ontology*) but on how we obtain knowledge about such rights (*epistemology*).

Rorty, then, has offered a sympathetic critique of postmodern relativism by calling for activists and intellectuals to abandon their pointless quest for universals, and accept that the discourse on human rights is a Western liberal one, but at the same time to recognise that this does not make it any less of a reality, or any less of a good thing. Whichever position one takes, or attempts to take, there are innumerable pitfalls, not least the most curious criticism of all that Ken Booth has made against the postmodern relativists – that by defending localised cultures against the supposed tyranny of universalism, the relativists are themselves falling back upon an essentialist understanding of those cultures, divorced from time and space, unique and exclusive in their own respects.[31] While the charge is more appropriately made against traditional anthropologists, it can equally be made of extreme postmodern relativists, and in this respect perhaps Rorty, in his honest defence of Western liberalism, should be applauded. However, it seems curious that a universalist such as Donnelly is more sensitive to cultural difference than many relativists. Indeed, in suggesting that human *rights* are a modern reflection of a universal respect for human *dignity* – a respect which is found in most world cultures at most points in history and in no way betrays a Western bias – Donnelly has gone some way to upholding a commitment to universalism beyond natural law.

Are human rights incontrovertible?

To suggest that human rights are incontrovertible is to make a claim which is often closely interwoven with the claim to universality but is in actuality quite distinct from it. While *human* rights must (according to the discourse) be both, neither necessarily requires the other. It would not be inconceivable for me to make the ridiculous claim that university lecturers have certain incontrovertible rights which no other member of human society possesses. After all, Baruch Spinoza happily upheld the incontrovertibility of one absolute truth: that is, the right *of the strongest.* If something is incontrovertible it means that it cannot be negated. Citizenship rights, in so far as they are civil liberties granted by the state, *can* be negated, or amended, or withheld. Central to the discourse on human rights is that they cannot, because to suggest otherwise wrongly empowers states and governments to assume control over these rights. So we can appreciate the *need* for incontrovertibility. However, we should also be aware of the *problems* which arise from it. First, we have the problem of assessing *which* rights, if any, *are* incontrovertible. This problem arises from the simple recognition that sometimes, two or more rights might be in conflict with each other. Throughout the history of the discourse on human rights, commentators have taken care to restrict the numbers of rights we allegedly have which are *a priori* and absolute (although they have not agreed on which rights these are). We might refer to this as the problem of devising a hierarchy of rights. Second, we have a problem of understanding the relationship between rights and *duties,* given that these two are often treated as reciprocal concepts, and yet, if we are to believe that failure to respect one's duties cannot negate one's human rights, then clearly within the context of human rights discourse, this relationship is rather more complicated.

The problem of the hierarchy of rights

So, universality does not imply incontrovertibility. It is one thing to say that there are certain fundamental rights which apply to everyone; it is another to say that these rights are absolute, inalienable and incontrovertible. Even if we could agree, as a global community, upon a set of universal rights, we might be reluctant to make the grandiose claim that these rights can never be removed, denied, or negated *in any circumstances.* Indeed, the Universal Declaration of Human Rights includes a number of basic rights that very few people have ever claimed are in any way incontrovertible. It is certainly not difficult to imagine a *conflict of rights.* My right to work as a tree-cutter in the rain forest conflicts with your right to a healthy environment. Do I still enjoy the right to speak my mind if what I say endangers your right to life, security or happiness? Indeed, can even the right to life be incontrovertible given that, because you threaten my life when you aim a gun at me, I may have to deny you your life in order to protect mine? Similarly, it is not difficult to see how, even in everyday situations, certain basic rights are indeed denied. As Arendt points out, few people complain when the prisoner is denied the right of freedom, so long as the prisoner has in fact committed a crime deserving of such punishment.

We seem to use the language of rights a lot, and there is nothing wrong with this as such. We simply have to be careful to make it clear that the rights we are discussing are not necessarily incontrovertible. Most of what we call 'rights', if we consider them carefully enough, are actually arbitrary, either because they conflict with other 'rights', or because they violate the rights of others, or because they can be withheld for some 'greater good'. In this respect, it is curious that the common language of rights remains rooted in utilitarian thinking; rights are still seen as means towards achieving some goal, the 'common good', which inevitably falls back upon the good of the majority.

Of course, it would hardly be a surprise for us to fail to achieve any consensus on what rights, universal though they may be, are incontrovertible rights in the last instance *in themselves*. After all, as Table 1.1 shows, even the major contributors to the historical debate on human rights have suggested different such absolutes.

Norberto Bobbio has stated, with some vigour, that the problems associated with incontrovertibility – essentially, the philosophical need to ascertain which rights are absolute – are ultimately meaningless. Bobbio states that the problem of human rights today is not in their justification but in their implementation, a political not a philosophical problem. Instead of seeking fundamental principles, says Bobbio, we should be trying to understand the various possible principles for each particular circumstance.[32]

If we are to treat rights seriously within a sociological discourse, we need to move beyond the everyday discourse that has appropriated the language of rights in the name of single-issue protest movements. Aware of the problems raised by the possible conflicts and prioritisations of rights, Bryan Turner has suggested that we should devise a

Table 1.1 Summary of 'incontrovertible' rights

Author	Rights
Hobbes	Security
Locke	Life, liberty, property
Kant	Freedom
Paine	Life, liberty, pursuit of happiness
Arendt	Citizenship
Regan[33]	Respectful treatment

'hierarchy of rights'.[34] Accordingly, the first right might be that all individuals have lives which are of equal worth and value. This draws, of
course, on Kant's categorical imperative, but can be interpreted according to whichever theorist one prefers. Similarly, Tom Regan's discussion
of incontrovertible rights indicates that such rights (of which there is
only one – the right to be treated fairly and with respect) are not absolute but *prima facie*.[35] Given that, for Regan, this right applies as much to
moral *patients* (namely, animals) as it does to moral *agents*, he clearly
wants to make this distinction so as to avoid any suggestion that we
should *never* harm or kill animals. In other words, it would be justifiable
to harm animals if they posed some innocent threat or needed to be used
as an innocent shield. We can use a similar argument to explain, following
Arendt's question, why it is considered acceptable to deny a criminal the
right to freedom, or even the right to life in instances where other lives
are under immediate threat.[36]

So, it is possible to see how a right can be both incontrovertible and
pragmatic, although such a right would itself have to be defined in a
sufficiently vague way in order to overcome the inevitable pragmatic
conflicts. Social scientists, however, are in a good position to intervene
at this point, because the debate has moved away from abstract philosophical concerns towards sociological pragmatics. Thus, an understanding of the broader socio-economic climate would allow us, as social
scientists, to show how these rights need not necessarily conflict. If
we return to the earlier example of the tree-cutter, we might claim that
there is no *a priori* conflict between my economic security and your right
to live in a healthy environment. Indeed, the conflict arises because
within the current historical context my basic human needs are in themselves not being met, and what is required is a large-scale redistribution
of wealth.

The problem of duties

Much of the literature – especially that on *citizenship* rights – suggests
that there can be no rights without corresponding duties. Indeed, one of
the arguments sometimes put forward as to why *humans* are blessed
with rights and animals are not is drawn from this. Accordingly,
humans can have rights *because* they can perform the corresponding
duties. Animals cannot be expected to perform these duties and thus
cannot be accorded the rights.

Here, then, is a slight contradiction. After all, human rights are
(allegedly) absolute, *not* accorded by any decision-making body, and are
not relativised against corresponding duties. If they were, then failure to

abide by these duties would imply the negation of these rights, which contradicts the philosophy.

What, then, *is* a duty? There are two varieties:

---

1   Positive duties. These are duties *to perform an act*. So, it might be agreed that in order for you to earn the right to a free health service, you need to abide by your duty to pay sufficient national insurance.

2   Negative duties. These can be defined as *by-products* of rights. In other words, my right to freedom of speech might be relativised according to how I perform my duty to respect freedom of speech in others.

Citizenship rights tend to rest upon the presence of both sets of duties. Human rights, necessarily, do not involve positive duties but, indirectly, presuppose negative duties. In other words, the only duties which correspond to human rights are those which involve respect for those rights. However, even if I fail to respect the rights of others, I cannot surrender, or have taken from me, my own rights as a human. Thus, this question of the relationship between rights and duties is a complex one. According to Locke, the duties which are associated with rights are those to respect the rights of others, for only in doing so are we offering any defence of our own rights. These duties should be respected because only by respecting the rights of others can we attribute value to human life in general. This is called a 'benefit theory of rights'.

Paine, by contrast, argued that rights have corresponding positive duties, involving action rather than Locke's inaction. For Paine, we all have a duty to contribute towards a society so that everyone can enjoy their natural rights fully. Paine argued that respect for such rights leads to a system of *social justice*.

A good discussion of the various positions philosophers have taken on the question of duties is provided by Tom Regan.[37] Regan begins by distinguishing between *moral agents* – who are capable of doing right and wrong – and *moral patients* – who can only be subjected to right or wrong treatment. Moral agents form the 'moral community'. The moral community is not, of course, the human community *per se*. As we will discuss in the section that follows, many humans are excluded on the basis of lacking certain mental capacities.[38] In this respect, they are categorised in much the same way as animals – although there may be a case to be made for certain animals to be included as moral *agents*.

Regan distinguishes between two traditions which share a reluctance to treat those who cannot be construed as being moral *agents* as possessing *rights*, but which nonetheless want to understand our relationship to them within an ethical framework. The *direct duty* views presuppose that moral agents have some kind of responsibility to act in a morally 'acceptable' way, such as not to inflict harm on others. *Indirect duty* views see moral patients as a 'medium through which we may either succeed or fail to discharge those direct duties' we have towards fellow moral agents – that is to say, we have a duty not to them but to ourselves to protect, or not to mistreat, moral patients.[39] Both traditions falter on the complex, and often contradictory, levels of involvement they accord to moral patients.

Regan, clearly, introduces and then critiques these traditions in order to open the door for a third alternative – the argument that moral patients, and more specifically *animals*, have *rights*. To discuss this claim in greater detail would be perhaps to stray too far from our intended course. Nevertheless, it is useful to identify arguments which do not *necessarily* treat rights and duties in reciprocity. It is true to say that the language of civil liberties has usually been couched in terms of a reciprocal relationship with duties, but there is nothing inherent in the concept of rights (or liberties) which requires this to be the case.

Are human rights subjective?

The complexity of our common understanding of the idea of human rights increases with every question we ask. We began this short journey by asking *who* has these rights. The answer, according to the theory of universalism, is that everyone has them. Then we asked *what* these rights are that we all have. Clearly, different writers emphasise different incontrovertible rights. Now we ask another set of questions, which relate to the claim that human rights are carried by individuals, and that these individuals are rational actors, possessing the quality of agency. These questions are drawn from the assumption that human rights are subjective, that is, that they must possess a subject. The question of subjectivity, especially in so far as it relates to questions of agency and rationality, is huge and there will only be sufficient space here to outline some of the debates inspired by it which relate specifically to human rights.

The problem of the rational agent

So, *why* do we, as humans, have these rights at all? What, exactly, is so special about us that makes us worthy of these claims? Answers to this question often resort to the argument of agency. It was René Descartes, the celebrated French rationalist philosopher, who most famously declared that humans are a special form of life because we have consciousness. Descartes began his investigation from a sceptical position, developed it through a recognition of the *dualism* of mind and body, and came to the conclusion that 'I think, therefore I am' (*cogito ergo sum*).[40] Kant added a practical twist to this logic, suggesting that humans deserve to be treated with dignity *because* they have agency. That is, they are active, thinking beings. This forms the basis, of course, of his categorical imperative, that people are capable of being sovereigns in the 'kingdom of ends', to be self-critical. It is claimed that humans all possess the capacity for reason and the ability to make choices about our lives, that is, to exercise sovereignty and autonomy. This is what sets us apart from other animals. Descartes had been rather unkind to other species of animals, declaring them to be no different from machines. In so far as animals are capable of *acting*, Descartes stated, they are so solely due to the effective functioning of their bodies, and not any conscious sensation, will or desire. In distinguishing between humans and other beasts, Kant was only slightly more generous. Humans, he claimed, possess 'a higher order capacity self-critically to evaluate and order their first-order desires'.[41] While animals and humans share the same first-order desires – hunger, thirst, companionship, sexuality – humans are capable of adjusting their relationship to these desires, eliminating some, developing or nurturing others, in a manner which shapes them as complete and unique persons.[42]

This reliance upon human rationality and agency creates severe problems of inclusion and exclusion. *If* humans have rights *because* they have agency, and more specifically the capacity for reason, then it is possible, allegedly, to distinguish between humans and other animals. Accordingly, rights are *not* contained within the individual but within his or her capacity for reason. Animals do not possess the capacity for reason and thus cannot have rights. The suggestion that humankind is superior because of its capacity for reason is dangerous enough in itself – and has been subjected to considerable criticism from sociologists. Even more alarmingly, though, is that the grounding of rights on this claim seems to suggest that individuals who do not possess such a characteristic are somehow less than human, and do not therefore possess these rights.

According to this argument, those creatures endowed with some degree of rationality (or agency, or autonomy) can be termed *moral agents*, that is, they are capable of acting in a way which is 'right' or 'wrong'. Animals, newborn babies, terminally ill patients on life support machines, and so on, whilst undeniably *alive*, cannot be held accountable for their actions because they are not moral agents, they are moral *patients*.[43] Sometimes we, as moral agents, recognise their inherent 'innocence' and uphold our moral *duty* to treat them in a just manner – but does this not imply that they therefore have the *right* to justice? For sure, 'innocence' is a complex term since it seems meaningless when applied to those who cannot, by their very moral nature, be found *guilty*. However, their inability to do wrong cannot negate their right to be treated with protection and justice. We have already discussed this to some extent in previous sections. At this point it is worth, though, making reference to Regan's philosophical justification for animal rights. He does not suggest that animals must necessarily be treated as moral agents – part of this project is to move the discussion of rights away from being the exclusive properties of moral agents. Nor does he say that, in a choice between the two, there should be much discussion as to whether a spare place on a lifeboat escaping a sinking ship should go to a human or a dog – the human gets the spot hands down! What he does say is that all moral agents *and* moral patients should be 'intelligibly and non-arbitrarily viewed as having a distinctive kind of value (inherent value) and as having this value equally. All moral agents and patients must always be treated in ways that are consistent with the recognition of their equal possession of value of this kind'.[44]

Regan's argument does not necessarily contradict human rights arguments. We can accept that all moral agents *and* moral patients (such as animals) have the basic right Regan claims they have, yet still single out *humans* (either because they are moral agents or for some other reason) as deserving of rights *beyond* this. However, if we choose to do so, it is difficult to see how we might continue to justify these additional *human* rights solely on the grounds of the universality of human agency and the capacity for reason (although, one imagines, the *capacity* for reason does not equate to reason *per se*). So where else can we turn? What other 'uniquely' human qualities can we appeal to as evidence of our innate superiority? What, *precisely*, separates humans from other animals to such a degree that we can claim this superiority in the name of rights? The very fact that we are *social* animals is surely not enough – we are not, it seems, alone in that respect. Richard Rorty has, we have already seen, introduced a schema wherein rights form a story which appeals to our sentimentality. Perhaps this could imply that we have rights because of our *capacity for sentiment*, for sympathy and affection. Bryan Turner, the sociologist, has followed a similar path, in so far as he has suggested that rights emerge out of the interplay between *emotions* and *the body* – emotions because, like Rorty, he argues that we are sensitive towards frailty, and the body because we all share the universal frailty of the human body.[45] Thus, while Turner is critical of Rorty for being too much the relativist and the romantic, he shares Rorty's concerns over the extent to which rationality can be a legitimate explanation for human progress, particularly in the light of the Holocaust and contemporary ethnic cleansing. In contrast to Rorty's relativism, Turner offers a corporeal approach which gives a sociological twist to the question of human dignity, and accordingly, hitherto marginalised groups, such as children, are included in his framework. But his approach is somewhat tautological, in so far as it justifies *human* rights on the grounds of a shared frailty of the body, but never actually answers the question: Why the human body? Certainly, bodies are frail. But in this respect, even Descartes recognised no fundamental difference between a human body and that of a dog. Both are, he suggested, merely physical properties in much the same way as a chair, or a table, is a physical property. Turner acknowledges this problem, and ultimately resorts to what he calls a utilitarian position: 'improving animal happiness may contribute to the total sum of human happiness'.[46] His case for separation rests primarily upon *emotion*, but it is not clear how this emotion is distinct from any other form of agency, such as reason.[47]

Another contribution, also from sociologists but which we might wish to describe as a cognitive approach, has been suggested by Vaughan and Sjoberg.[48] These writers emphasise the inalienable right for each individual to possess reflective consciousness, but claim that this right can only ever be realised in a social context. Accordingly, they argue, we have a right to the social conditions of reflectivity. Vaughan and Sjoberg offer a dialectical interpretation, but one which is, perhaps, overly cognitive. As with Kant's reliance upon reason, Turner's upon emotion, or Rorty's upon sentiment, it rests ultimately on some aspect of agency. So far, no attempt to ground rights in agency has succeeded in overcoming the problem of exclusion.

The problem of individuality

That rights are the property of a rational subject – contestable though that might be – necessarily presupposes that they are the property of an *individual*. This assumption is found throughout the literature. For Locke, for example, it is always individuals, not societies or communities, that possess these innate rights, because such rights are part of the essence of each individual person, and thus pre-social in their origins. For Kant, according to the third formula of his categorical imperative, each individual possesses autonomy and should act in such a way as to make his or her actions meaningful. Thus, the Western philosophical discourse on human rights has always emphasised individualism, and advocates of human rights are open to criticism if they continue to base their understanding of rights on Western individualism.[49] It was Karl Marx who stated that:

> None of the so-called rights of man goes beyond egoistic man . . . an individual withdrawn behind his private interests and whims and separated from the community.[50]

With these words, Marx provided a critique not of the concept of rights *per se*, but of (a) the explicit individualism which is integral to their conceptualisation, and of (b) their applicability in the practice and service of liberal democracy. It is fair to say, though, that the two concerns are interwoven, for the discourse on human rights as it has been articulated throughout Western philosophy has indeed been built on a platform of individualism, because individualism is inherent in the liberal democratic tradition. According to this Western tradition, not only are human rights innate properties of individuals, but the whole purpose of upholding human rights is to protect individual freedom against the power of the state.[51] In this respect, individualism is inherently tied up with questions of equality and justice. In so far as equality and justice would constitute important elements of any moral framework, not least one of human rights, a move away from an individualistic perspective on human rights would appear to be problematic. Certainly, the dominant theories of *justice* appear to be based on individualistic premises.[52] *Utilitarianism*, which views justice as the aggregate of individual happinesses, is intrinsically individualistic and also inherently egalitarian (in that it accords equal weight to each individual preference). *Perfectionism*, associated with the likes of Aristotle and Friedrich Nietzsche, is also unmistakably individualistic because it is based on the assumption that some people deserve a greater share of justice, depending on whether they possess, as individuals, certain qualities of 'excellence'. Kant's position – which is based on the inherent value of each individual person, and which we might call *value egalitarianism* – may overcome the populism of the former and the elitism of the latter but clearly not the individualism of either!

The civil rights that dominate the Universal Declaration of Human Rights naturally reflect this Western (Lockean *and* Kantian) bias towards the security and liberty of the person. Critics have gone as far as to suggest that the idea of human rights necessarily upholds the values of market capitalism.[53] However, the potential for human rights does not need to reflect these individualist, capitalist origins, even though Norberto

Bobbio, who supports the Western tradition of rights but is sensitive towards its limitations, argues convincingly that the emergence of a discourse of rights is a consequence of the individualisation which he associates with the process of modernisation.[54]

Non-Western societies, in so far as they conceptualise rights at all, do so through radically different perspectives. When the former Soviet Bloc leaders spoke of human rights, they were talking about rights that did not pre-exist the formation of the socialist state, and that existed only through the state. Following Marx (albeit loosely), they proclaimed that freedom is only possible in a classless society, wherein the individual is truly free to participate in and contribute to the community, and where freedom is regulated by the state.[55] Islam also adopts a collectivist perspective, in so far as the Koran can be interpreted as a manifesto for the building of the 'good society'. Buddhism and Confucianism, meanwhile, understand the concept of freedom solely in the context of a harmonious relationship between the individual and society, which is structured on the family. In Hinduism the concept of individualism takes place solely within a given *caste*, with the reward for a good life being upward mobility in the next one. Many African cultures also prioritise the self-actualisation of the individual through the community, which is manifested in the tribal leader.[56] To talk of human rights and to presume that these rights are *necessarily* carried within the individual, in the Lockean liberal sense, is to misunderstand the debate. By accepting that the *discourse* on human rights has indeed been dominated by a particular individualistic tradition, we are not, necessarily, dismissing human rights as worthless ideologies *per se*. There is much to be gained by expanding our range and developing our Western thinking on rights by incorporating some of these non-Western collectivist traditions.

There is, however, a Western critique of individualism which is not necessarily born out of either the Marxist or the cultural relativist critique, and that is the *communitarian* challenge. Communitarians have attacked Kantianism directly on the grounds of its individualistic bias. Such theories, they claim, assume that rights exist within each and every one of us, and yet are somehow abstracted from us. The communitarians hold that rights can only, in fact, emerge within the context of a community. Various communitarians have drawn on a diverse range of influences – Aristotle, as we have already noted, but also Georg Hegel. Writers in this tradition include McIntyre, Charles Taylor, and Michael Sandel.

Kant, his abstract universalism aside, was, in terms of defining his subject, always an individualist. Hegel, by contrast, focused on grander things than mere individuals. He was concerned with the building of the perfect state. He took a rigorous historical approach to this, stressing that history has always evolved through the clash of opposites, which then come together to form new wholes. This is called the dialectical approach, and it was the most important influence on the younger Karl Marx. But Hegel was no radical. He wanted to defend the Prussian state, with all its conservative values. His major contribution to ethical theory, laid out in his *Philosophy of Right*, is his insistence that individuals are not complete unless they are part of a community (in this case, the nation, but it need not be).[57] Thus, from a communitarian point of view, an individual gives up much of her or his freedom to achieve a greater role within a larger whole. The needs of the community outweigh those of the individual, so the idea of human rights is misleading. Thus, for McIntyre and other communitarians, individual rights in isolation from communities have lost that which gives them any meaning. The criticisms made by Marx are not dissimilar.

In practical respects, this intellectual debate over whether human rights are innate to individuals or developed through communities is irrelevant, but in so far as many more of the world's cultural traditions emphasise collectivism than individualism it is certainly worth bearing in mind. The clear compromise appears to be to accept a dialectical position, that is, to claim that while individuals do possess rights in themselves, paramount among these is the right to exist in a set of external conditions within which these individual rights can be best realised.[58] These conditions could, of course, be interpreted so as to include a healthy environment, the absence of war, adequate social and economic development, and possibly the presence of an efficient system of social security, as well as the existence of healthy, functioning communities. Indeed, the Universal Declaration of Human Rights, which we turn to in the next chapter, includes this additional right, and it has taken on a renewed importance in recent decades as debates over environmental rights, which most of the earlier Western thinkers would not have considered, have taken centre stage.

Ethics and social practice

Kant's project as a moral philosopher was as much about providing a framework for what might constitute ethical social action as it was about tracing the origins of a universal morality. Ethical questions tend to relate to various ambiguous and often misused terms. What is the *right* thing to do? What is a *good* thing to do? What *ought* to be done? Terms such as 'right' and 'good' and 'ought' are clearly difficult to measure, as it remains unclear exactly what they refer to and therefore what they can be measured *against*. Kant, like Plato before him and the moral philosopher G.E. Moore after him, belonged to a tradition known as *intuitionism*, which claims that these terms cannot be measured empirically but can be justified only by appeal to intuition. Intuitionism stands in opposition to *naturalism*, which holds that moral judgements refer to properties or actions that can be understood empirically, such as pleasure, desire, or survival. Notable naturalists include Bentham, as well as Epicurus, John Stuart Mill, and John Dewey. A third tradition is *subjectivism*, which claims that moral judgements are solely strategies of communicating desires and thus not referent to any properties external to the individual.

We know that Kant was a universalist, for whom the 'right thing' to do is always enshrined in abstract but absolute natural law. The first principle of his categorical imperative – the formula of universality – makes this clear even though it is written as a suggestion for behaviour rather than an ontological statement. But he was also an *intentionalist*. Intentionalists place a lot of importance on *motive*. For the intentionalist, the 'right thing' to do depends solely or primarily upon the intentions of the person doing it. Kant insisted that the moral value of any act is contained within its motive. Neither selfish motivation, nor compassionate impulse, nor guilt, are morally praiseworthy motives. Kant argued that the *only* moral motive is that something is done *because it is one's duty to do it*, because it is the *right thing to do*. Thus, the Kantian tradition praises the effort to do what is right as much as, indeed more than, it praises the achievement of that goal. In the Kantian world, the attempt matters, is born out of a recognition of one's duty to make it, and, if made *en masse*, provides the building blocks for the 'good society'.

Kant's blend of universalism and intentionalism thus provides a bridge between his appeal to some abstract sense of truth and his commitment to the practice of moral behaviour. For Kant, ethics are thus embedded in social action. In this respect, human rights are perhaps a macro-structural version of aggregate ethical behaviour. The ethics of everyday social action might reside in a respect for mutual human dignity. Kant would encourage us, for example, to treat others in a way that is fair, and this would involve being respectful towards them *as people*, and not reducing them to the level of their personal misfortunes, their biological characteristics, or their social circumstances.

Clearly, not all theories of ethics make appeals to any such abstract notion of dignity or truth. Bentham's (and Mill's) *utilitarianism* suggests that the 'right thing' to do in any given circumstance is that which brings the maximum amount of happiness to the maximum number of people. It thus operates according to the pleasure principle, but in an aggregate fashion. Utilitarianism is a variant of *pragmatism*. Another form of pragmatism is associated with Dewey and claims that, rather than seeking to measure them against some timeless and spaceless universal law, ethical questions should be understood in their specific context (shades of Aristotle here), and it should be recognised that sometimes the right thing to do is simply that which gets the job done in the most efficient way. A harsher version of pragmatism may even claim that the end can indeed justify the means. Yet another paradigm which problematises the pretensions of universalism is *hedonism*. Hedonism appears to take the pleasure principle to its logical conclusion without recourse to any sense of aggregate happiness. Indeed, it seems to discard ethics (or, at least, separate ethics totally from morality) and measure the 'right thing' to do solely in terms of pleasure; the 'right thing' to do is that which brings happiness to the performer.

If we treat ethics broadly as a set of principles which influence our social actions, and morality as a broad system of codes and conventions, then Kant remains a useful guide in so far as he attempts to build a bridge between the two. Of course, Kant remains convinced that *morality* is universal and absolute. Thus, the bridge that neo-Kantians such as Jürgen Habermas and Tom Regan attempt to build is between this hidden truth and us as social actors, those who somehow *act out* this truth.

A quite distinct, but no less useful, attempt to delineate between ethics and morality has been proposed by the French intellectual Michel Foucault.[59] Unlike the neo-Kantians, Foucault has no time for talk about universal or absolute morality. Foucault recognises that 'morality' has come to mean a set of values and rules of action that are recommended to individuals through social institutions. He calls these conventions *moral codes*. However, 'morality' also refers to the *behaviour* of individuals in relation to these codes – *how* individuals come to comply with or resist them. Foucault calls this the *morality of behaviours*. These are both quite distinct, Foucault says, from the manner in which one conducts oneself – and constructs oneself as an *ethical subject* – *vis-à-vis* these codes. Foucault refers to this as the determination of ethical substance, or *ethical subjectivation*.

> There is no specific moral action that does not refer to a unified moral conduct; no moral conduct that does not call for the forming of oneself as an ethical subject; and no forming of oneself as an ethical subject without 'modes of subjectivation' and an 'ascetics' or 'practices of the self' that support them.[60]

Foucault claims that these distinctions have implications for the way we study history. To study *codes* we must look at comparative systems of rules in any given society and how they are enforced. To study *behaviours* we must consider the extent to which individual actions have been consistent with the prescribed codes. To study the *constitution of the self as an ethical subject* we must look at the different practices which have emerged for the understanding of our relationship with the self and how we might come to transform our mode of being through this relationship. This third research programme Foucault calls a *history of ethics*.

The separation of morality from ethics has proved somewhat useful to the more critically minded signatories to the vague movement known as 'postmodernism'. We have already seen how postmodernists have been sharply critical of Kant for his reliance upon an abstract set of absolute values. Like Foucault, the postmodernists have no time for such grand narratives as 'truth' or 'justice' which have been used by earlier academics as catch-all explanations for the social world. Morality, in the Kantian sense, is dismissed as just another grand narrative. Postmodernists would ask: Who decides upon what constitutes morality in the first place? Whose interests does it serve? Instead, postmodernists celebrate the plurality of competing explanations, competing perspectives. Of course, this extreme *relativism* has left them open to the charge that they advocate, whether explicitly or implicitly, a depoliticised 'anything goes' philosophy of morality. By emphasising historical, spatial, or cultural context, and by respecting difference, they provide no framework for criticising such practices as torture or slavery, no critical guidelines upon which to build a platform for action. The radical tolerance implicit in their perspective has been heavily criticised for its inherent conservatism.

This is a concern that has plagued Zygmunt Bauman, a deeply ethical sociologist who nevertheless wants us to rethink the Enlightenment project with its reliance upon rationality in the light of the Holocaust and other horrors of the twentieth century.[61] According to Bauman, the question of the possibilities of modernity, that people can come together and make rational moral choices, has been answered with an appeal to practice; that is, people quite simply have *not* done this, and furthermore, they have stretched the bounds of reason to extremes with their ambivalence towards the great moral questions associated with modernity and the Enlightenment.[62] But while in some respects Bauman embraces the postmodernist position, in others he stands against it. He insists that an ethical dimension is essential:

> [T]he great issues of ethics – like human rights, social justice, balance between peaceful co-operation and personal self-assertion, synchronization of individual conduct and collective welfare – have lost none of their topicality. They only need to be seen, and dealt with, in a novel way.[63]

Bauman concedes that he can offer no obvious solution to this dilemma, no answer to this question, save that in the 'postmodern' world, beyond Kantian abstractions, we need some kind of an ethics 'without guarantees, without illusions'. Drawing on the writings of Hannah Arendt, Bauman indicates the need to rethink society along the lines of a modified version of the classical *polis*, a political community, which is comprised of, and at the same time cares for, its responsible – in an ethically pragmatic as opposed to morally dogmatic way – citizens. This would involve a reciprocal relationship between the two:

> What may help in this effort is the awareness of the intimate connection ... between autonomous, morally self-sustained and self-governed ... citizens and a fully-fledged, self-reflective and self-correcting political community. Neither is thinkable without the other.[64]

Bauman leaves open the question of whether it is really possible to have a *postmodern ethics*. Yet, of course, if morality is dead, then perhaps ethics is all we *can* have left in a 'postmodern' world. Perhaps ethics are unavoidable, inescapable. The French philosopher Emmanuel Levinas has equated ethics with compulsion, with persecution.

Modernity and democratisation

The idea of human rights might be present in pre-modern, especially classical, thinking, but it is in the modern age that it became central to political debate. 'Modernity' and the 'modern age' are both contested terms within the social sciences. Although it is possible to identify a very rough series of events and transformations which constitute the onset of modernity,[65] theoretical traditions compete over which specific changes form the driving force behind this social change. For example, the three so-called founding fathers of sociology – Karl Marx, Emile Durkheim, and Max Weber – were all concerned with the same basic processes, but they offered wholly different explanations of these because their focus was on different aspects of this social change. For Marx, modernity was ultimately reducible to the transformation in the economic sphere which replaced the earlier feudal mode of production with the capitalist one. For Durkheim, cultural factors were given more weight than economic ones, and the most significant transformation was in the differentiation of social roles, from mechanical solidarity to organic solidarity. Weber, who unlike his contemporaries wanted to avoid presenting a single causal explanation, nevertheless indicated that one of the key factors was a transformation in the political realm, which saw the emergence of a nation-state system based on rational administration and a centralised means of violence.

Norberto Bobbio holds that there is a specific relationship between human rights and the 'modern project'.[66] For Bobbio, human rights reflect the triumph of individualism over the organic model of society associated with pre-modernity. The discourse on human rights is, for Bobbio, inseparable from the discourse on modernity. Modernity has seen the *triumph of rights over duties*. Also:

> Human rights, democracy and peace are the three essential components of the same historic movement: if human rights are not recognized and protected, there is no democracy, and without democracy, the minimal conditions for a peaceful resolution of conflicts do not exist. In other words, democracy is a society of citizens, and subjects become citizens when they are recognized as having certain fundamental rights. There will be stable peace, a peace which does not have war as its alternative, only when there are citizens not of this or that particular state, but of the world.[67]

Bobbio traces the history of human rights throughout modernity as a threefold process:

1   the philosophical doctrine of universal natural law, which, although rooted in the stoics (and other pre-modern writers, a point Bobbio tends to gloss over), emerged as a systematic framework of philosophical analysis with Locke;

2   the concrete assertion of positive rights embedded in the political nation-state as citizens' rights;

3   a combination of the two – rights as both universal and positive, which came about only after the 1948 Universal Declaration of Human Rights.

Curiously, outside the philosophical literature, theorists were largely unconcerned with the discourse on human rights. This is due in no small part to the emphasis placed by most social and political theorists on the nation-state. Max Weber is the theorist most associated with interpreting modernity in terms of the rise of the modern, bureaucratic nation-state. Weber was himself a nationalist, and in his writings he made clear his opposition to such abstract ideas as natural law. Positive law, however, as it related to administrative functions and institutions, was always a different matter. Indeed, Bryan Turner has rightly pointed out that, although in some respects the idea can be traced back to the ancient Greeks, citizenship rights as we understand them have emerged primarily as a result of modernity and, in particular, of the emergence of nation-state administrations and of post-French Revolution democratic ideals.[68] Bobbio makes a similar observation when he suggests that the modern nation-state allowed for the concretisation of otherwise abstract ideals of citizenship into positive law.[69] For Arendt, as we have already discussed, the emergence of the contemporary discourse on human rights is inseparable from the centrality of the nation-state.[70] The state – and by extension the *nation*-state – also plays a central role in Marxist and feminist critiques of the discourse on rights.

The theoretical understanding of modernity drawn from Weber – which locates it within a set of transformations driven by the spread of a particular kind of bureaucratic, instrumental rationality – has been detrimental to a sociological interpretation of human rights. The modifications made to Weber's framework by Jürgen Habermas have been more helpful.[71] Whereas for Weber modern rationality is *only* about the kind of means–end instrumental thinking that is prevalent in the economic and political realms, for Habermas there are dual projects of modernity, each driven by a different kind of rationality. While he accepts much of what Weber says about economic and political modernity, he does not think this is sufficient for us to dismiss modernity in its entirety out of hand. He points out that there has always been a competing modernity, located in the social and cultural 'lifeworld' of human thought and action, driven by a logic of 'true' rationality, self-awareness and human emancipation. It is to this realm that developments in the theory of human rights belong. Thus, for Habermas, human rights quite clearly form an integral part of the modern project.

The political and epistemological upheavals which constitute modernity have undoubtedly influenced the spread of the ideology of human rights worldwide. Bobbio, for example, understands the emergence of human rights in terms of achievements made possible by certain struggles, which are themselves fed by the project of the Enlightenment. To be sure, modernity has allowed for the expansion of the discourse on human rights to take in new claims, and in particular social and economic rights. Just as T.H. Marshall famously discussed the evolution of citizenship rights in terms of a three-tier process, each connected to a distinct set of conditions, so might we understand the development of human rights thinking.[72] For Marshall, the earliest citizenship rights are *civil rights*, such as freedom of speech, opinion and religion, which are protected by a functioning legal system. These are followed by *political rights*, such as the right to vote and be involved in the decision-making process, which are allowed for by the presence of a democratic polity. The third group is *social rights*, such as the rights to welfare, housing, employment, and so on. These are made possible by a working welfare state. While Marshall's ideas are dated and open to a number of criticisms, his model provides a fairly useful framework for understanding the evolution of human rights throughout modernity. Indeed, as we shall see in the next chapter, the 1948 Universal Declaration of Human Rights is itself divided into three sets of rights which correspond to Marshall's categories. Social and economic rights have rarely been included under the banner of human rights, but to reject them from this family would be careless. Inevitably, a fourth family of rights, environmental rights, will become increasingly important as time goes on.

The state and human rights theory

The purpose of this chapter has been to explore some of the major philosophical perspectives that have influenced our thinking about human rights and, in particular, to draw attention to some of the most significant controversies and problematics which the discourse on human rights invokes. We can identify a number of general critiques, not all of which have been discussed in any depth so far. These include:

1   a utilitarian critique of the idea of 'natural law'

2   a Marxist critique of liberalism

3   a communitarian critique of individualism

4   a relativist critique of universalism

5   a feminist critique of state-centredness.

There are, of course, advantages and disadvantages to be found in each of these perspectives, and in each of the critiques. Theoretical

	Ontology	
	Cultural relativism	Universalism
Anti-Foundationalism	Communitarian pragmatism	Cosmopolitan pragmatism
Foundationalism	Traditional communitarianism	Liberal natural rights

Epistemology is indicated at the left.

Figure 1.1 Four perspectives on human rights

assaults are often at the mercy of fashion, and there is, perhaps, still much to be learned from Kant, and perhaps even Locke, even though it may be deeply unfashionable to make such a claim. At the same time, we should not be too quick to disregard the postmodernist critique. If nothing else, postmodernism as a movement in the social sciences has forced us to accept that so much of what we presume to be knowledge has relied exclusively upon highly political foundations, in which ethnic, cultural, gendered, or spatial differences are crushed beneath the weight of a dominant, Western, liberal, middle-class, male, ideology. Nowhere would it be more inappropriate to ignore this critique than in the field of human rights. The question we should ask, then, is not: Can human rights as an idea survive the postmodernist onslaught? but instead: How can we use the postmodern critique to liberate the discourse on human rights from its power-soaked assumptions?

Of course, there is considerable overlap between the viewpoints suggested here. Some earlier writers may have differed on what rights they considered to be natural or universal, and more recent ones may dispute the meta-theoretical, ontological or epistemological arguments which have been used to *ground* human rights, but very few of these writers would be so bold as to overtly *support* human rights violations in the name of respect for cultural diversity, or whatever. Following R.J. Vincent, Dunne and Wheeler outline the various perspectives on human rights through a useful diagram (Figure 1.1).[73]

So, the likes of McIntyre and others who draw upon Aristotelian ideas are included under 'traditional communitarianism', while Rorty can be cited as an example of 'communitarian pragmatism'. Habermas, and perhaps Rawls, belong to 'cosmopolitan pragmatism', while the traditional natural law theorists, Locke and Kant included, would be included under 'liberal natural rights'.

Much of this chapter has been, then, an attempt to provide an overview of the complex philosophical literature which underpins the discourse on human rights. But this is not a volume of philosophy. Instead, the purpose of this text is to discuss human rights issues within a social science framework. However, given that its three most influential early figures, Marx, Durkheim and Weber, all dismissed, or at least paid little attention to, the idea of human rights, it is no surprise to learn that the discipline of sociology developed largely in ignorance of it. From Marx's scientific universalism and his dismissal of rights as 'bourgeois', through Durkheim and Weber's respective nationalisms, to the amoral scientism of positivism and the relativism of postmodernism, the issue has been largely sidelined.

According to Bryan Turner, sociology has suffered from two main biases, to which we can add a third.[74] The first of these is its anti-foundationalism. This is most clearly found in Weber's work. Weber, as we have seen, was an ardent critic of natural law philosophy. From Weber, sociologists have claimed that philosophical attempts to explain things in terms of universal foundations or fundamentals, such as religion, or the abstract morality of natural law, are wholly asocial.

The second bias is towards the nation-state. Sociology has tended to conflate 'society' with 'nation-state', something it inherited in no small part from Weber and Durkheim. Because of this, sociologists have tended to focus more on citizenship rights (which are more legalistic, less abstract, and can be easily situated within political–administrative territories) than human rights. Citizenship has itself been used for the purpose of nation-building, and thus of exclusion (as in the case of refugees, aboriginals, minority groups, children). Of course, it is important to add here that one of the main arguments in the feminist critique of the human rights discourse concerns its *state-centredness*. That is to say, the emphasis on civil and political rights which are exercised or violated within the legal or political spheres (as we discussed in the Introduction) has drawn attention away from non-state violations which occur within the social or cultural realms. Thus, the inability of human rights scholars to embrace such violations as *sati* or female genital mutilation (which we discuss in the Conclusion) because they are located within the *private* realm betrays the gendered nature of much human rights work, which concentrates on the *public* realm. This is therefore a further reason why sociology, if it is going to take rights seriously, needs to delink *state* from *society*.

The third bias, inherited primarily from Durkheim, has been towards collectivism and against individualism. Durkheim may have been a Kantian in many respects, but his emphasis on the *conscience collective*, the moral glue which holds societies together, has been more influential upon sociological thinking than Kant's claim that human beings carry rights *as individuals*.

The decline of the nation-state and the discourse on globalisation have brought human rights to the front line of sociological thinking in recent years. Indeed, some of the writers we have already encountered in this chapter, such as Bryan Turner and Malcolm Waters, have been instrumental in establishing human rights as a topic of sociological inquiry. Three such projects have been discussed in this chapter. One, associated with Vaughan and Sjoberg, is *cognitive*, another, associated with Turner, is *corporeal*, and the third, associated with Waters, is *constructionist*. Underpinning these debates is a recognition of the need to overcome the excessive exclusivity of earlier theories of rights. Turner, in particular, has attempted to move the debate away from its reliance upon rationality because this by its very nature excludes certain members of the human population. However, the preference sociology has shown towards citizenship at the expense of human rights has been equally problematic. As Turner rightly points out, refugees and aboriginals are not so easily located within the discourse on citizenship, but as humans are unmistakably included in discussions of human rights.

But the question remains: Is the study of human rights an appropriate one for social scientists? Before we can answer this question, we have to ask another one: What, precisely, is the scope of sociology? There are many possible answers to this question, and to delve too far into them would be to detract from the purpose of this book, but surely one such answer would be that sociology, the study of the *social*, is concerned with how social *action* is performed, and social *relationships* are established, within the context of certain external *conditions*. Social action is, of course, always relativised in accordance with these conditions, which may be economic (feudalism, capitalism), political (fascism, liberalism), and so on. Given that, at the time of Marx, Durkheim, Weber, and their contemporaries, human rights were of interest to philosophers and activists but had no formal status, and thus did not constitute external conditions as such, we can forgive them their reluctance to treat them seriously. But from 1948, with the emergence of formal and identifiable human rights law, we can safely say that when we contextualise a great deal of social behaviour, we cannot ignore the global significance of the discourse on human rights and its implementation into both international and national legal systems. Human rights have entered the world of objective sociological conditions. Social action can be validated through an appeal to the existence of these norms and standards. Human rights have thus been relocated away from the abstract idealised world of moral universalism and into the pragmatic world of international law. In this respect, there is no doubt that sociologists, who are interested in the conditions of the social world, should take human rights very seriously indeed.

Essay questions

1. Can there be such a thing as 'universal' human rights? Discuss with reference to some of the main arguments in the debate.

2. When, and why, did the idea of human rights emerge?

3. Why should humans have rights and not animals? What makes them so 'special'?

4. Discuss the contribution of Immanuel Kant to the philosophy of human rights.

5. Karl Marx once dismissed human rights as 'bourgeois rights'. What did he mean by this, and was he right?

6. Must human rights always be universal, incontrovertible, and subjective?

Notes

1   Joseph Wronka (1992) *Human Rights and Social Policy in the 21ˢᵗ Century: A History of the Idea of Human Rights and Comparison of the U.N. Declaration of Human Rights with United States Federal and State Constitutions*, Lanham, MD: University Press of America, p. 43, in reference to Sophocles's *Antigone*.

2   Geoffrey Robertson (2000) *Crimes Against Humanity: The Struggle for Global Justice*, Harmondsworth: Penguin, p. 1.

3   On the history of world citizenship, see, especially, Derek Heater (1996) *World Citizenship and Government: Cosmopolitan Ideas in the History of Western Political Thought*, London: Macmillan; Darren J. O'Byrne (2002, forthcoming) *The Dimensions of Global Citizenship: Political Identity Beyond the Nation-State?* London: Frank Cass.

4   Yet these seem to apply in his writings only to white males; he supported slavery and never advocated rights for women.

5   Especially in Immanuel Kant (1959) *Foundations of the Metaphysics of Morals*, Indianapolis: Bobbs-Merrill.

6   Immanuel Kant (1991) *Kant: Political Writings*, ed. H. Reiss, Cambridge: Cambridge University Press, p. 106.

7   Thomas Paine (1992) *Rights of Man*, ed. Gregory Claeys, Cambridge: Hackett Publishing Company.

8   Giuseppe Mazzini (1907; originally written 1840) *Duties of Man*, London: Dent.

9   Jeremy Bentham (1843; originally written 1824) 'Anarchical Fallacies' in *The Works of Jeremy Bentham* Vol. II, ed. John Bowring, Edinburgh: William Tait, pp. 491ff.

10   Karl Marx (1977; originally written 1843) 'On the Jewish Question' in *Karl Marx: Selected Writings*, ed. David McLellan, Oxford: Oxford University Press, p. 54.

11   Kant, *Kant: Political Writings*, p. 107.

12   Hannah Arendt (1949) 'The "Rights of Man": What Are They?' in *Modern Review*, 3, 1, Summer; reproduced in Arendt (1951) *The Origins of Totalitarianism*, New York: Harcourt Brace, pp. 290–302. See also Arendt (1978) *The Jew as Pariah: Jewish Identity and Politics in the Modern Age*, ed. Ron H. Feldman, New York: Grove Press. For an overview, see the 'Introduction' by Peter Baehr in Baehr (ed.) (2000) *The Portable Hannah Arendt*, London: Penguin, p. xiv.

13   Arendt, *The Portable Hannah Arendt*, p. 43, reproduced from *Origins of Totalitarianism*.

14   As stated earlier in this chapter, the stoics, in particular, believed that the citizens, who were the wise and 'rational' members of their societies, belonged to a 'universal society'.

15   Carlos Santiago Nino (1991) *The Ethics of Human Rights*, New York: Oxford University Press, p. 11 (reprinted from Nino, *Introducción al análisis del derecho*, Buenos Aires, Chapter One).

16   Alisdair McIntyre (1981) *After Virtue*, London: Duckworth.

17   Malcolm Waters (1995) 'Globalization and the Social Construction of Human Rights' in *Australian and New Zealand Journal of Sociology* 31, 2; Waters (1996) 'Human Rights and the Universalisation of Interests: Towards a Social Constructionist Approach' in *Sociology* 30, 3.

18   John Rawls (1972) *A Theory of Justice*, New York: Oxford University Press.

19   See, especially, Jürgen Habermas (1990) *Moral Consciousness and Communicative Action*, Cambridge: Polity Press.

20   Tom Regan (1984) *The Case for Animal Rights*, London: Routledge, pp. 127–30.

21   Norberto Bobbio (1996) *The Age of Rights*, Cambridge: Polity Press.

22   Bobbio, *Age of Rights*, p. xii.

23   Bobbio, *Age of Rights*, p. xi.

24   Ken Booth (1999) 'Three Tyrannies' in Tim Dunne and Nicholas J. Wheeler (eds) *Human Rights in Global Politics*, Cambridge: Cambridge University Press.

25   Booth, 'Three Tyrannies', pp. 51–2.

26   Hector Espiell (1998) *Human Rights: 50th Anniversary of the Universal Declaration*, Oxford: Blackwell, p. 525.

59 Michel Foucault (1987) *The History of Sexuality* Vol. 2: *The Uses of Pleasure*, Harmondsworth: Penguin.

60 Foucault, *History of Sexuality*, p. 28.

61 Zygmunt Bauman (1989) *Modernity and the Holocaust*, Cambridge: Polity Press.

62 Zygmunt Bauman (1991) *Modernity and Ambivalence*, Cambridge: Polity Press; Bauman (1993) *Postmodern Ethics*, Oxford: Blackwell.

63 Bauman, *Postmodern Ethics*, p. 4.

64 Zygmunt Bauman (1994) 'New Ethics for New Times' in *New Times*, 3 September, p. 8.

65 Such a list would include: the Industrial Revolution; increasing urbanisation; capitalism; the formation of bordered nation-states; the emerging discourse on democracy; rationality in politics, science, and social life; the Enlightenment in philosophy and science, as a critique of earlier worldviews based on religion or tradition; the Renaissance in the arts; gradual secularisation and the rise of humanism.

66 Bobbio, *Age of Rights*.

67 Bobbio, *Age of Rights*, pp. vii–viii.

68 Turner, 'Outline', p. 177.

69 Bobbio, *Age of Rights*, p. 20.

70 Arendt, 'The Perplexities of the Rights of Man', originally in *The Origins of Totalitarianism*, reproduced in *The Portable Hannah Arendt*, pp. 31–45.

71 Jürgen Habermas (1984) *The Theory of Communicative Action. Volume One – Reason and the Rationalization of Society*, Cambridge: Polity Press; (1987) *The Theory of Communicative Action. Volume Two – System and Lifeworld: A Critique of Functionalist Reason*, Cambridge: Polity Press.

72 T.H. Marshall (1950) *Citizenship and Social Class*, Cambridge: Cambridge University Press.

73 Tim Dunne and Nicholas J. Wheeler (1999) 'Introduction' in Dunne and Wheeler, *Human Rights in Global Politics*; following R.J. Vincent (1986) *Human Rights and International Relations*, Cambridge: Cambridge University Press, p. 152.

74 Bryan S. Turner (1993) 'Outline of a Theory of Human Rights' in Turner (ed.) *Citizenship and Social Theory*, London: Sage.

Further information
Books

Strongly recommended is the excellent collection of readings assembled by
Patrick Hayden in *The Philosophy of Human Rights* (St Paul: Paragon House,
2001), which includes many texts discussed in this chapter. As well as the
major Western contributors – Hobbes, Locke, Paine, Kant, Marx *et al.* – this
reader also includes important contemporary writings and some of the major
non-Western perspectives. It is definitely a handy resource for anyone
interested in human rights.

Locke, Kant and Paine are the key original theorists in the human rights
tradition. Locke's *Two Treatises on Government* and Paine's *Rights of Man* have
been reproduced many times. The best collection of Kant's writings is *Kant:
Political Writings*, edited by H. Reiss (Cambridge: Cambridge University Press,
1991). *Theories of Rights*, edited by Jeremy Waldron (Oxford: Oxford University
Press, 1984) is a useful collection of essays. Carlos Santiago's *The Ethics of
Human Rights* (Oxford: Oxford University Press, 1991) is a more advanced
read, but worthwhile for getting to grips with the Kantian tradition and its
critics. If you are feeling totally advanced, try the wonderful but difficult
collection of essays in Stephen Shute and Susan Hurley's edited volume *On
Human Rights: The Oxford Amnesty Lectures 1993* (New York: Basic Books, 1994),
especially the controversial chapter by Rorty. Finally, although it is by no
means a work of pure philosophy, it is certainly worth mentioning here
Norberto Bobbio's majestic *The Age of Rights* (Cambridge: Polity Press, 1996).
This is a crisp, clear, fascinating survey which I find invaluable and which
many of my students seem to enjoy reading.

Web pages

Again, there are numerous links to writings by or on these key figures.
A good place to start is the Internet Encyclopaedia of Philosophy on
www.utm.edu/research/iep/1 – go through the index to find the links to
Locke, Kant and Paine.

CHAPTER TWO

Regulating human rights

Who protects human rights?

In the last chapter, we said very little about one of the central themes of this book – the state. Most of the theoretical discussion on human rights has been located within a rather abstract framework. However, during the twentieth century, much of this discussion shifted away from concerns with the justification of human rights, towards their protection. In this respect, state institutions, both at national and supernational levels, are crucial. Two of the major theorists of human rights in the twentieth century – Hannah Arendt and Norberto Bobbio – have made claims concerning the protection of human rights which inform the analysis of legal and political institutions in this chapter. Arendt's pragmatic claim that human rights are only meaningful in so far as the state recognises the bearers of those rights is impossible to ignore. Furthermore, Bobbio's suggestion that the 1948 Universal Declaration of Human Rights represented a synthesis of abstract natural law (relating to human rights) and formal positive law (relating to citizenship, embedded in states), provides us with a framework within which to analyse the pivotal role played by political and legal institutions in the contemporary discourse on human rights. Indeed, it would not be too bold a claim to suggest that the 1948 Declaration – for all its faults and limitations – was one of the most significant achievements of the twentieth century simply *because* it allowed for the implementation of these hitherto abstract ideals into concrete, enforceable law.

The development of human rights law has taken place on two levels: first, the level of the nation-state, which has (in many Western democratic societies at least) evolved to accommodate claims to rights under the emerging banner of citizenship; second, the level of international legal and political relations. Both of these levels will be discussed in this chapter. However, they have not always worked in harmony with one another, and one of the major concerns with regard to human rights has been the contradictions which exist between various forms of domestic laws and the various acts and covenants which have been passed into international law.

At the first level, that of the nation-state, the legal safeguards incorporated under the umbrella of 'citizenship rights' have been well documented. Assurances given in law by nation-state governments need not, of course, bear any resemblance to internationally recognised standards associated with human rights. However, in those countries that operate according to written constitutions, such as the United States, there is usually a strong connection between the two. For example, both the US Constitution and the French Declaration of the Rights of Man were born out of the same struggles which laid the foundations for the development of human rights law in the twentieth century. Significantly, both drew heavily upon the philosophical literature in their wording.

In the case of countries without a written constitution, such as the United Kingdom, the rights or civil liberties of *citizens* have taken precedence over those of *humans*. Citizenship has been interpreted in a modern, liberal way as a formalised relationship between an individual and a state. Of course, even in the case of the United Kingdom prior to the implementation of the Human Rights Act in 2000, various avenues of appeal existed beyond the nation-state, the most immediate being Europe.

The purpose of this chapter is to discuss the structures and institutions which serve to regulate human rights. While it will focus on matters associated with *law*, it is not an introduction to human rights law *per se*. Instead it focuses historically and empirically on the emergence of an international (or global) political and legal order. It deals not with cases but with institutions and processes, not with 'hard law' but with extra-judicial rules and global ethical norms, because, as David P. Forsythe correctly says:

> Apartheid was not ended in South Africa by a court case. Communism was not ended in Europe by a court case. Torture was not terminated in the Shah's Iran by a court case. Death squads were not suppressed in El Salvador by a court case. In all these examples, considerable progress was made on human rights through non-judicial action ... through policy decisions – public policy by governments and inter-governmental organizations, and private policy by NGOs, corporations, and even individuals.[1]

Nevertheless, it is widely believed that human rights can only be guaranteed by a meaningful and enforceable international human rights *law*, and that it is the duty of the United Nations to uphold and enforce this. We shall therefore begin with a brief history of rights regulations around the world, focusing primarily on key developments, such as the Magna Carta in England, the French Declaration and the American Constitution, leading up to the development of international law. We follow this with an overview of the theory and practice of international relations, and an examination of such key concerns as national sovereignty and the role of national government. We will then proceed by examining the structure of the United Nations, and discussing its relationship with international law. We will include discussion of the role of other supernational institutions, such as the European Union, which have sought to implement laws and standards pertaining to human rights. After that, we turn our attention to a very different, but no less important, agent of human rights regulation, namely the role played by campaigning organisations and social movements in defending human rights. In the concluding section, we discuss the relative significance of each of these agents in the struggle to protect human rights in what is an increasingly globalised world.

Of course, it is a popular belief among scholars that the issues only touched upon in this chapter constitute the primary area of academic interest in the subject, and are thus deserving of more space than is allocated to them here. There is some mileage in this belief. Certainly, the vast majority of literature on human rights falls under the banners of world politics, international relations, and international law. To discuss that literature in the depth it surely deserves warrants a volume in its own right, and it is not the purpose of this book to serve as a textbook on the structures and institutions of human rights regulation. Forsythe has recently published a magnificent book which does just that, aimed primarily at students of international relations but certainly accessible to the lay audience, and I recommend that students interested in any area of human rights, from any discipline, consult this text.[2] Much of what I say below is developed in far more detail, with far greater scope for scholarly argument, therein, and due acknowledgement will be given to Forsythe's book in the truncated summary I offer here. The purpose of this chapter is merely to highlight some of the main developments in international human rights agreements for the benefit of students who may not otherwise have the opportunity to study them.

A brief history of human rights regulation

The Universal Declaration of Human Rights in 1948 did not emerge from a vacuum. It was presented as the latest in a series of acts, covenants and declarations aimed at securing certain rights for citizens in various countries. These acts, covenants and declarations – which are usually traced back to the English Magna Carta of 1215 – have almost always emerged as strategic responses to social and political upheaval. The Magna Carta was signed by King John merely to serve as a pact between the king and his unhappy barons, and was not in any respect intended to serve as a declaration of rights for all citizens, but its very necessity reflected the uncertainty of the times. The English Bill of Rights of 1688–89 – which was the first document to use the language of 'rights' and which introduced the system of free elections – was merely intended to ensure that royal absolutism was firmly dissolved in favour of the monarch's accountability to Parliament. Thus, the rights it gave were to Parliament, not the people.[3] Nevertheless, these events were significant in so far as they influenced the establishment of the idea of the rule of law.

Of greater significance, perhaps, were the American Declarations of 1776–1789, and the French Declaration of the Rights of Man and the Citizen of 1789. Once again, these historical documents were drafted and signed in the aftermath of great social and political upheavals, bloody revolutions designed to bring to an end colonial rule, in the case of America, and the absolute monarchism of the *ancien régime*, in the case of France. Both Declarations upheld the existence of inalienable rights as an absolute truth, drawing on the philosophies of Locke and Kant, and Rousseau's concept of the general will. As Cassese rightly points out, the language of the American and French Declarations is rooted in a particular model of 'man' and society. 'For those Declarations', he writes, ' "man" . . . is worthy of being called "man" only if he fulfils these conditions: to be free, equal, or have undisturbed enjoyment of his property, not to be oppressed by a tyrannous government and to be able freely to realize himself'.[4] They are based, he suggests, on a model of society comprised of 'free individuals equal with one another . . . and subject only to the law, which in turn is and must be an expression of the general will; political institutions should exist only as a means of realizing the freedom of the individuals and their common good'.[5] However, one important distinction that can be made is that the French Declaration prioritised individual rights, while the American Declarations paid more attention to the 'common good'.[6]

Thus, both the French and American Declarations were attempts to protect the rights of individual citizens according to a set of moral principles which might be applied to *all persons*, whether citizens of those countries or not. It would perhaps be fair to have assumed that, following these Declarations as well as the emerging international relations following the Peace of Westphalia, human rights and international law

co-operative bodies such as the European Union and regional trade co-operatives such as NAFTA.

3   At a meta-theoretical level, realism presumes an historical continuity – it is a variant of that broad perspective in the social sciences which we call 'essentialism'. Conflict between states based on self-interest is an essential trait of the international system. Thus, it is argued, not only is realism an inappropriate paradigm with which to understand world politics today, but it is not equipped to accept that the nature of world politics may have changed at all.

Although these charges made against realism seem fair, it is too early to presume the triumph of liberalism, partly because, despite the increasing significance of non-state actors in world politics, nation-states still retain pride of place. The misnamed United Nations is, after all, comprised of representatives of states. Nevertheless, liberalism offers a more positive response to the question of human rights than does realism. In place of the cynical Hobbesianism, liberalism borrows more from the philosophy of John Locke. Locke, of course, saw the state as a relatively weak actor which serves primarily to uphold the interests of private citizens. If necessary, it arbitrates between interests, and some-times, but rarely, it regulates them. It works to protect the security, freedom and private property of its members. However, the power in this relationship rests with the citizen. In its classical sense, liberalism presumes – following Adam Smith and in a manner not dissimilar to behaviourist accounts – that humans are by their nature economic actors. Thus, the primary interest which requires satisfying is that of the citizen as *bourgeois*. Classical liberalism derives from the ground-breaking texts of Smith and David Ricardo. Smith wrote of the 'invisible hand' of the market which was a driving force in political and social relations, including those between nation-states. Thus, economic activity is paramount and any attempt by the state or any other institution to regulate the economy is damaging to prosperity and progress. According to Hobson, there are three basic premises of the liberal position on the role of the state.[11] First, that the state must adapt to meet the needs of individuals. Second, that in the international arena, states conform to a 'practical rationality' to achieve a world of consensus; states thus have considerable power in the international realm which is a 'realm of possibility'. Third, that there are 'appropriate institutions' capable of carrying out this task. So, while the state is minimal in terms of intervention, it can perform a more positive role as an arbiter of international conflict.[12]

In general terms, liberalism is synonymous with pluralism, in so far as it recognises that there are multiple interests competing for resources and influence in world society. The pluralist perspective necessarily critiques the Hobbesian one, which seems to presuppose that the only political relationship one has is with the state. Individuals can, it points out, exercise their political power through different agencies – as individuals, as members of interest groups such as trade unions, as consumers, and so on. However, liberals have faith in 'appropriate institutions'. In contrast, though, to the realists, liberals like Hedley Bull would maintain that international law is both possible and functional, if it is supported and enforced by states. In other words, when used in pursuit of international justice, war is not a condition of anarchy but a rational and effective state option.

There are, of course, alternative positions within the study of world politics which one needs to take into account. For example, Marxists, like liberals, criticise realists for looking at the state as if it exists in a vacuum, isolated from time and space, uncontextualised in relation to other factors, such as the economy. Traditionally, Marxists have understood the state as a tool of the capitalist economy. They have pointed out that power actually lies with the dominant economic players, and not with the state *per se*. More recently, writers such as André Gunder Frank and Immanuel Wallerstein have used concepts influenced by Marxism to show, *contra* liberalism, that the system of international relations is necessarily a system of inequality, because of the uneven distribution of wealth – some countries are rich *because* others are poor, and vice versa. This is an important position to understand, because it is necessarily born out of a traditional Marxist perspective on human rights; that is, that individual human (i.e. civil and political) rights are meaningless unless they can be exercised within favourable social and economic conditions.

The United Nations

One way of looking at the world which is not strictly realist, in so far as it does not prioritise the nation-state *per se*, not liberal in the specific sense of the word, because its focus is not on individuals, and certainly not Marxist, because it does not locate the economy at the base of its analysis, is what we might loosely describe as a 'federalist', or perhaps 'functionalist' analysis. Such an approach concerns itself primarily with the interconnectedness of nation-states which takes place at a distinct, supranational level. A strong version of federalism might advocate a singular world government, while a weaker version, albeit still largely state-centred, would put its faith primarily in bodies such as the United Nations. It is at this level that the question of human rights is most commonly discussed. We now turn to the United Nations in more detail, before discussing its involvement in human rights regulation.

A brief history of the United Nations

The United Nations was founded shortly after the end of the Second World War in 1945, as a replacement for the defunct League of Nations. The League of Nations had been set up in 1919 by the allied victors of the First World War – the United Kingdom, the United States, France, Italy, and Japan – but it was never a successful venture. Although the idea for the League came from US President Woodrow Wilson, in 1920 the USA voted not to be a member, and the Soviet Union did not join until 1934, so for a long time the organisation was practically powerless. Japan, Germany and Italy all withdrew in the 1930s to form an anti-Soviet alliance, and the Soviet Union was expelled in 1939. Thus, in 1945 the League was disbanded and, on 24 October, the United Nations was established in its place.

Fifty-one nation-states originally came together to form the membership of the United Nations. Its initial charter included a commitment to tackle poverty, war and unemployment worldwide, as well as social development and world economic policy. In practice, as the organisation has evolved, these responsibilities have been passed down to specialist agencies. For example, economic responsibilities have been taken over by such bodies as the International Monetary Fund, the World Bank, and the World Trade Organization, which many critics believe are primarily geared towards serving the interests of the developed world.

Maurice Bertrand has usefully identified a series of phases in the historical development of the UN since its inception, in relation both to its internal politics and to its influence globally:[13]

- 1945–1946 – enthusiasm, with strong support in the West and particularly in the USA

- 1946–1953 – Cold War politics, and the success of the USA in using the UN to support its intervention in Korea

- 1953–1960 – East/West stalemate; invention of peacekeeping operations; crises in the Middle East and Congo

- 1960–1975 – decolonisation; UN assists with liberation struggles and the constitutional concerns of newly created states

- 1975–1985 – UN crisis; USA and its Western allies oppose moves by the majority developing nations to prioritise economic development issues, and also oppose moves by the Arab nations who unite against Israel; the USA and its allies reduce the UN budget and withdraw from certain selective agencies, resulting in a financial crisis

- 1986–1993 – renewed enthusiasm; fall of the Berlin Wall and end of the Cold War, plus dismantling of apartheid in South Africa, prompt people to think about a unified world order; Allied campaign against Iraq in Gulf War receives general support from most world players

We might want to add a seventh phase to Bertrand's list:

- 1993–present – period of uncertainty; initial pessimism and loss of faith in the UN following tragedies in Rwanda, the former Yugoslavia, and East Timor, and the UN's inability to intervene effectively; growing influence of transnational corporations results in increased anti-capitalist and anti-globalisation sentiment; politicians and activists on the political Left and Right express concern with political and legal structures operating above the level of the nation-state, fearing loss of sovereignty and lack of democratic accountability; establishment of permanent International Criminal Court meets with guarded optimism.

The United Nations system

The structure of the United Nations comprises six main organs, each of which, with one exception, is based at the UN headquarters in New York. These are:

- The General Assembly – this comprises representatives from each member state (in 2002, 190 members), each with one vote; important decisions must be carried by a two-thirds majority, others by a simple majority; these decisions are resolutions which are not enforceable by international law.

- The Security Council – this is probably the most powerful of the UN's organs, and is responsible for peacekeeping, interventions, and sanctions against warring or rogue states; we will discuss this in greater depth below.

- The Economic and Social Council – this is made up of 54 members elected for three-year periods to oversee the work of certain specialist agencies (see below) dealing with economic, social and humanitarian issues.

- The Trusteeship Council – this was established to oversee the UN trust territories through to independence and self-government; it is no longer an active body as all such territories had achieved this goal by 1994.

- The International Court of Justice – this court, sometimes called the World Court, is based in The Hague, and its role is to seek to resolve conflicts between states by law rather than by force; states involved in conflict or disagreement can ask for their disputes to be considered by the International Court and abide by its decision; this should not be confused with the International Criminal Court, which we will discuss below.

- The Secretariat – this is the administrative centre of the UN, headed by the Secretary-General, with a staff of around 8,900 from 160 countries.

The structure of the United Nations is far from ideal. It is funded primarily by the most powerful nations, which renders it largely reliant upon those countries. Its annual budget translates into less than $2 per person. This makes more sense if one considers that approximately $150 per person is spent by nation-states on defence. 40 per cent of the UN budget is spent on peacekeeping and emergency aid.

Financial issues aside, a matter of serious concern with regard to the United Nations structure is the power held by the Security Council. Many of the most important decisions are made by this body. The Security Council is dominated by the most powerful nations, who have a tendency therefore only to support policies of which they approve or which might be beneficial to them. The Security Council consists of 15 members. Ten of these are elected by the General Assembly for two years. The remaining five are permanent members. These are the United States, the United Kingdom, France, China (which took the place of Taiwan in 1971), and Russia (which replaced the Soviet Union in 1991), namely, the five leading allied nations victorious in the Second World War. These countries have considerable power. Any one of the permanent members can veto a decision made by the other members of the Council. Between 1976 and 1999, China has vetoed 2 decisions, Russia/Soviet Union 8, France 11, the UK 19, and the USA 60.

The Security Council is empowered to decide whether or not the United Nations should intervene in a particular situation. If it recommends intervention, it can adopt any one of five paths:

- negotiation – the UN can send negotiators to help resolve differences

- observation – the UN can send unarmed representatives to visit a troubled area following a ceasefire

- sanctions – the UN can advise its member states to cease trading with one or both of the warring parties

- peacekeeping – the UN asks its member states to provide troops to monitor a ceasefire, wearing UN colours

- peace enforcement – the UN can send in troops to take a more direct and active role in bringing about a cessation of conflict; this has never actually happened.

Peacekeeping missions are among the more common courses of action. Although the troops operate under the UN banner, they are there solely to police areas of conflict and not for active involvement in the military activities of the area in question. Since their inception, the UN has sent peacekeeping missions to the areas shown in Table 2.1.

Although the principal aims and objectives of the Security Council betray a realist perception of the world, grounded as they are in the maintenance of peace and national security, there is evidence to suggest that since the end of the Cold War it has taken a more active role in promoting human rights standards, blurring the boundaries between state sovereignty and ethical questions of rights.[14] However, the Security Council cannot in all honesty be relied upon to serve as a consistent defender of these standards, which may from time to time conflict with its primary objectives. Other organs of the United Nations are more directly committed to upholding human rights. Indeed, most of the

Table 2.1   United Nations peacekeeping missions

1960–1964	Congo
1973–1979	Sinai
1974	Golan Heights
1989–1997	Angola
1992–1995	Former Yugoslavia
1993–1996	Rwanda
1995–	Bosnia
1995–	FYR Macedonia
1999	East Timor

- Convention Relating to the Status of Refugees 1951 – *102 parties*

- Convention on the Political Rights of Women 1953 – *97 parties*

- Convention Relating to the Status of Stateless Persons 1954 – *37 parties*, followed by the Convention on the Reduction of Statelessness 1961 – *15 parties*

- International Covenant on Economic, Social, and Cultural Rights 1966 – *99 parties*

- International Covenant on Civil and Political Rights 1966 – *95 parties*

- International Convention on the Elimination of All Forms of Racial Discrimination 1966 – *71 signatories, 128 parties*

- International Convention on the Suppression and Punishment of the Crime of Apartheid 1973 – *proposed jointly by Guinea and the USSR in 1971; 91 votes in favour, 4 votes against (Portugal, South Africa, the United Kingdom, and the United States), 26 abstentions; 88 parties, but no signatories or ratifications from Western states*

- Declaration on Protection from Torture 1975, followed by the Convention Against Torture, and Other Cruel, Inhuman or Degrading Treatment or Punishment 1984

- Convention on the Elimination of All Forms of Discrimination Against Women 1979 – *130 votes in favour, none against, 10 abstentions; 103 parties*

- Declaration on the Elimination of All Forms of Intolerance and of Discrimination Based on Religion or Belief 1981

- Convention on the Rights of the Child 1989

- International Convention on the Protection of the Rights of All Migrant Workers and Their Families 1990

The UDHR was adopted by the General Assembly of the UN on 10 December 1948. Although not legally binding, it was to serve as a set of guidelines for nation-states to follow, drawn from shared moral principles. Indeed, despite being promoted primarily by the United States and its Western allies, the UDHR contains not only the civil and political rights traditionally advocated by Western liberal-capitalist democracies, but economic, social and cultural rights as well. Despite the abstentions of Saudi Arabia, South Africa, the Soviet Union, and five other states, there was surprisingly little disagreement on the construction of the Declaration. Forsythe provides a useful overview of this consensus. He points out that in the United States, successive Democratic presidents had been committed to establishing certain social and economic rights, while various non-Western supporters of the UDHR, such as in Latin America and the Middle East, were strongly influenced by Western values.[18] However, the relative ease with which this document was accepted was deceptive. Despite the obviously liberal philosophy underpinning the UDHR, it was introduced into a world dominated by realist politics, not least in respect of the Cold War. It was not until 1966 that the recommendations laid out in the UDHR were introduced into international law, in the shape of the International Covenant on Civil and Political Rights, and the International Covenant on Economic, Social and Cultural Rights, and not until a decade later that these Covenants became legally enforceable.

Human rights and the law

The various acts and covenants listed above constitute some of the principal developments in international human rights law. Thanks, for example, to the 1948 Genocide Convention, genocide is recognised as a crime in international law. The same is true of slavery, as a result of the 1926 Slavery Convention and its 1956 replacement. The 1951 Convention on Refugees and its 1967 amendment clarified international refugee law, and the legal obligation of states to provide asylum for refugees fleeing persecution. These developments have paralleled developments in international humanitarian law pertaining to the laws of war applicable to situations of armed conflict. Gradually, the universal standards laid down initially by philosophers dedicated to promoting human freedom or liberty had, by the last third of the twentieth century, evolved into generally accepted norms or legally enforceable laws that threatened the sovereignty of nation-states. Indeed, the International Tribunal at Nuremberg had decided that if there is a conflict between state laws and international rules which are established to protect humanitarian values, individuals must transgress the state laws.[19]

International humanitarian law

There are two distinct but interrelated components of international law. Whereas human rights law currently lacks adequate provisions for enforcement, the other – international humanitarian law – provides victims of armed conflict with clearly defined protections. The sources of international humanitarian law are the Geneva Convention of 1864, the Hague Conventions of 1899 and 1907, and the four Geneva Conventions of 1949. These four 1949 conventions cover:

- prevention of human rights violations during war (two conventions)
- prevention of mistreatment of prisoners of war
- prevention of mistreatment of civilians during war.

Two additional protocols were added to these in 1977, covering:

- protection of victims of international armed conflict
- protection of victims of non-international armed conflict.

International humanitarian law thus relies heavily upon international human rights standards. For example, in line with other aspects of international (human rights) law, there is a common Article 3 in each of the four conventions, which prohibits 'mutilation, cruel treatment and torture . . . humiliating and degrading treatment' during internal armed conflicts. War crimes are defined as violations of the 1949 Conventions and subsequent additional protocols during international conflict, and include torture, cruel treatment and causing suffering or serious injury. International humanitarian laws also cover other crimes against humanity, such as genocide, slavery, extrajudicial executions and 'disappearances', but as these often occur during peacetime as well as war, they are usually treated under the rubric of human rights law. Of course, this branch of international law is designed to protect not only combatants but also persons not active in the conflict.

As Forsythe points out, despite the huge library of analysis on this particular branch of law, there have been relatively few court cases emerging from it.[20] Forsythe suggests that, instead of utilising traditional judicial processes, international humanitarian laws have been influential through military and political decisions, as well as via agencies such as the Red Cross. As an example, he cites the success of the 1995 Dayton accords in reducing the number of violations of humanitarian law in the former Yugoslavia.

Human rights in European law

The European Convention for the Protection of Human Rights and Fundamental Freedoms 1950 – together with its additional protocols in 1954,

1968, 1970, 1971, 1988, and 1990 – was established primarily to move towards the *collective enforcement* of the UDHR (in contrast to charters established by the UN itself).[21] Subsequently, citizens of European countries have been able to petition directly to the European Commission on Human Rights, which can take cases to the Committee of Ministers of the Council of Europe and (with a two-thirds majority from the Committee) to the European Court of Human Rights which is based in Strasbourg. The European Communities Act of 1972 was designed specifically to override domestic legislation if conflicts were seen to have arisen.

Appeals of this kind are generally made by individuals and tend to take place in cases pertaining to discrimination, for instance on the grounds of gender or ethnicity and in such places as the workplace. The extent to which these appeals, where successful, have sweeping and transformative consequences for domestic law seems minimal. However, on occasion, the European Court has issued rulings which directly challenge not just individual decisions but nation-state policies. A good example is the recent decision that the exclusion of gays from military service, endorsed by successive UK governments, contradicts European human rights law.

In July 1999, France became the first member state of the European Union to be convicted of torture. The European Court found five police officers guilty of unnecessary force, amounting to brutality, against a suspected drugs dealer who was being held for questioning. This amounted to torture under the European Convention on Human Rights, and the claimant was awarded £61,000 compensation. The response from the French interior ministry, while respectful of the decision, stated that the European Court nevertheless had no jurisdiction over the French judges.

The European Convention deals only with matters concerning civil and political rights. The European Social Charter 1961 holds a parallel position in European law with regard to social and economic rights. Another significant addition to European law, continuing the trend of adopting major UN conventions into Europe, has been the European Convention for the Prevention of Torture and Inhuman or Degrading Treatment or Punishment 1987.

International human rights law and its applications

Taken together, the Universal Declaration of 1948 and the two Covenants of 1966 comprise the International Bill of Rights. Effectively, this is the definitive source of international human rights law. However, despite the establishment of the Human Rights Committee and the Committee on Economic, Social and Cultural Rights, whose task it is to monitor the Covenants, the International Bill of Rights has suffered primarily from an inability to reconcile its liberal objectives with realist politics. So long as no court exists which has power to enforce the Covenants and punish violators, international human rights law has relied upon nation-states to promote and uphold it. This situation seems ludicrous – how can a nation-state court pass judgment on issues pertaining to all humanity? The conundrum is similar in many respects to the inclusion of universal human rights in the American and French Declarations. However, towards the end of the twentieth century, universal human rights concerns entered into nation-state laws via a different route. In 2000 the United Kingdom established its Human Rights Act. Of course, this Act was not difficult to write – it was merely a method of including the already existing, and already legally binding, European Convention on Human Rights in UK law, thus directing potential claimants along a less confusing route than that which would have taken them via Strasbourg! Suffice it to add that the European Convention on Human Rights was hardly an original document in terms of its prose; it was largely a method used by the Council of Europe of including the 1966 Covenants in European law. The Covenants themselves were largely expanded from the 1948 Declaration. In this case, and many others like it, international human rights standards have found their way into law by going *from the universal to the particular*.

Another, rather more convoluted, question of law arose from the arrest of the former Chilean dictator, General Augusto Pinochet, in London in 1998. Few observers would deny that Pinochet led a government which was responsible for numerous crimes against humanity, torture, murders, disappearances, and yet for a long time he was a welcome visitor to the United Kingdom. In 1998, while Pinochet was paying such a visit to London, a judge in Spain issued a legal request for him to be arrested and deported to Spain to stand trial for his crimes. Because European law is binding on all member states, there was nothing particularly controversial about the request from one European partner to another. However, international law does not require Pinochet or dictators like him to be held accountable in a neutral country under the laws of that country for atrocities committed against their own citizens – they would only be accountable to the laws of the country in which the crimes took place or to international law. The Spanish request, therefore, was made specifically in respect of charges made that Pinochet was responsible for the deaths of Spanish citizens. Pinochet was indeed arrested in London, and the senior members of the British judiciary and the Home Office contemplated the options available to them. The Chilean authorities demanded that Pinochet be sent back to his own country, pointing out that the Spanish request would interfere with their own process of reconciliation (not to mention their state sovereignty). In the end, Home Secretary Jack Straw agreed to return the former dictator to Chile rather than require him to stand trial in Europe, but made it clear that the only reason for this was Pinochet's medical condition. The subtext was that any subsequent demand by a European partner for the arrest and trial of a visiting human rights violator would be favourably received, sending a warning to dictators around the world, secure in their national immunity, to be careful which countries they choose to visit.

However welcome this judicial warning might be, however welcome the inclusion of these universal standards in national laws, as long as the policing of human rights issues is left to nation-states there is considerable cause for concern. It is precisely this which lies behind the repeated calls for an international criminal court – calls which were finally acknowledged at the United Nations summit in Rome, 1998.

The International Criminal Court

Most students will be aware that after the close of the Second World War, trials were held in the cities of Nuremberg and Tokyo to try the leaders of the German and Japanese forces. In fact, the idea had been tabled much earlier, at the end of the First World War, but it came to nothing. The Nuremberg and Tokyo trials were presided over by the Allied forces, in the name of the world community, although with hindsight we might ask ourselves exactly what these leaders were being tried for: crimes against humanity, or having the misfortune to appear on the losing side of a global struggle. David Forsythe rightly points out that the Allied leaders had on many occasions violated the principles of humanitarian law through the indiscriminate attacking of enemy cities, thus threatening civilians as well as military personnel.[22]

At its inception the UN member states had agreed to create a new system of international justice mobilised around an international criminal court. The UN General Assembly asked the International Law Commission in 1948 to study the feasibility of establishing this permanent court, and in 1950 the ILC responded that such a court was desirable. However, during the Cold War, little or no action was taken, and it was not until 1990 that the UN once again asked the ILC for its recommendations, stating that it was a matter of urgency. A final draft was submitted to the UN in 1994, but there was dissent among its members as to how and when the court could be established.

In the absence of a permanent international criminal court, many human rights violations, which are by their very nature illegal under international law, had gone unpunished. In Argentina in 1991 a presidential pardon was offered and a law citing 'due obedience' as a defence was introduced, which effectively meant that although senior government officials were tried and convicted of human rights violations, the vast majority of those involved went unpunished. Similar situations have arisen around the world. Advocates of an international criminal court suggested that it should be able to intervene where nation-states refuse to take action.

Various *ad hoc* courts – officially referred to as international criminal tribunals – were established in the absence of a permanent body. The two most recent were set up to deal with the tragedies in Rwanda and the former Yugoslavia. The war crimes tribunal for the former Yugoslavia was established in February 1993 to consider cases dealing with serious violations of international humanitarian law committed in this region since 1991. However, it suffered from inactivity on the part of the UN member states, many of whom failed to agree to establish laws ensuring that they would co-operate with the tribunal. In November 1994 an international tribunal was established to try those responsible for genocide, crimes against humanity, and violations of international humanitarian law in Rwanda during 1994. Once again, the vast majority of UN member states did not pass laws ensuring their compliance.

Finally, on 17 July 1998, in Rome, the United Nations voted to establish a permanent court: 120 countries voted in favour, 21 countries abstained, and only seven voted against this proposal.[23] Although the vote was passed with a large majority, the reality remains that the court will not come into existence until it has been ratified by 60 member states, which could be a lengthy process.

One of the biggest problems in establishing the court has been in deciding precisely what model would be adopted. Geoffrey Robertson has, usefully, divided the main arguments into three camps.[24] The first, led by Canada and Germany, wanted a court which had strong prosecutorial powers and acted independently of the Security Council. The second, led by the United States, China and France, would support a court only if it was controlled by the Security Council (and thus unlikely to take action against a Security Council member). The third group, led by India and including a number of Asian and Middle Eastern countries, was fully opposed to the establishment of the court.

In any event, the court, which is based in The Hague, holds jurisdiction over four peculiarly overlapping offences: genocide; crimes against humanity; war crimes; and aggression. Genocide is defined in a way compatible with the 1948 Convention on Genocide, as the attempted or successful destruction of a group on the grounds of its ethnic, national, racial or religious characteristics (see Chapter Nine).[25] Crimes against humanity (a term which surely includes genocide) include various acts of systematic violence or barbarity by a government or governmental organisation against the citizenry, including torture, slavery, apartheid, and extra-judicial executions.[26] War crimes are understood largely as extensions of existing definitions found in the Geneva Conventions, with various additional atrocities taken into consideration.[27] Finally, the UN has yet to reach an agreement on what constitutes aggression, save that it relates to 'crimes against peace'.

While we await the conclusions of these discussions, we also watch with considerable interest, even as this volume goes to press, events unfolding in The Hague following the arrest of the former Yugoslavian president, Slobodan Milosevic. His arrest and trial in 2001 have received easily the most publicity of any matter coming under the jurisdictions of the *ad hoc* tribunals. To date, Milosevic has refused legal counsel and has responded with scorn to the charges against him, stating with due defiance that he does not recognise the legitimacy of the court. This in itself says a great deal about the problems arising from efforts to police human rights violations in a world still dominated by nation-state sovereignty.

Human rights and social movements

One of the most significant transformations in the nature of political action to have taken place over the last 50 years has been the increasing shift away from established political parties and towards issue-based campaigning organisations or social movements; away from nation-state politics towards global politics. It is generally accepted that, before the 1939–1945 war, formal politics only really took place at the level of the nation-state, within the context of a world composed of competing sovereign nation-states, which gave birth to the notion of international relations. The nation-state was, indeed, the defining feature of life in this early modern phase. In democratic nation-states, political action took the form of allegiance to ideologically driven political parties, which competed for power on usually broad platforms and manifestos. Most of the significant desires of the citizenry could be met, theoretically, either by the nation-state government or, through it, at the international level. Most of the major social and political philosophers – Hobbes, Locke, Rousseau, Hegel, Mill, Marx, Weber – took the presence of the nation-state for granted, and accorded it primacy in their writings. Only Kant, with his notion of cosmopolitanism, could be considered an exception.

The experience of 'total war' shook the foundations of these assumptions at the global level. Movements emerged which took as their mandates the achievement of certain goals that transcended nation-state borders. These movements were concerned with such issues as global peace, the global environment, and respect for universal human rights. These issues had largely fallen outside the limited scope of nation-state political parties. While such parties may include as part of their manifestos a commitment to these issues, they have largely lacked the power on their own to enforce any such commitment. These issue-based campaigning movements have thus taken their demands to the global arena. Social movements thus appeal directly to the United Nations, as well as to the governments of individual nation-states.

It is fair to say that the shift away from nation-state-based politics (formal politics) towards these global, issue-based concerns (which are connected to what Anthony Giddens calls 'life politics'[28]) reflects a growing awareness among the citizenry that the things which most directly affect our lives are not, in most cases, those which fall into the restricted (hitherto class-based) politics of the nation-state, but are instead those which transcend these nation-state and class barriers and impact upon the entire globe, regardless of borders. The post-1945 era has seen, for example, a decline in the memberships of established nation-state political parties and a huge increase in those joining campaigning organisations such as Greenpeace, Friends of the Earth, the peace movement, and Amnesty International.

This is by way of an introduction to the role played by these social movements in regulating issues such as human rights concerns on the global scale. When we talk of 'regulating human rights' we cannot simply refer to formal political and legal bodies, such as the state, the United Nations, or the structures and institutions of international law. Non-governmental organisations and global social movements are beginning to form an increasingly important sector, both as spokespersons for citizens' demands, and as respected advisors to policy-makers. This is not to say that nation-state politics or class-based politics are either dead or insignificant. We still pay taxes to nation-state governments; we still expect or make demands pertaining to welfare standards from these officials. It is, nevertheless, in the spirit of the age that global social movements offer an alternative mouthpiece through which to voice our concerns as citizens not just of nation-states but also of the world. Social movements are not political parties; they are not democratically elected and do not have territorial constituencies. They are, however, spokespersons for issues which concern all our futures. Few organisations typify this global spirit more than Amnesty International. We will discuss this particular social movement in depth below, before turning our attentions towards a quite different organisation which has similar practical aims but is driven by a wholly different philosophy – the World Service Authority.

Amnesty International

Amnesty International is a worldwide organisation which acts on behalf of victims of human rights abuses around the world. In 1961 lawyer Peter Benenson read a report in a newspaper about two students in Portugal who had been sentenced to seven years' imprisonment simply for toasting freedom. Noticing that there was a disturbing number of people around the world who were imprisoned not for committing 'crimes' but for having opinions or lifestyles with which their governments disagreed, he wrote an article in the *Observer* newspaper called 'The Forgotten Prisoners', and launched an appeal for amnesty for such political and religious prisoners. Initially, Benenson intended this appeal to last a year, but the response was so enthusiastic that the campaign evolved into the global social movement known as Amnesty International.

Amnesty International's mandate is drawn from the Universal Declaration of Human Rights. In practice, though, it specialises in four particular areas:

1 It calls for the immediate and unconditional release of all prisoners of conscience. A prisoner of conscience is defined as being anyone imprisoned solely because of their religion, ethnic origin, political beliefs, sex, sexuality, language, colour of skin, or lifestyle, who has not used, or advocated the use of, violence in any way. These are individuals who may have stood up for their beliefs, exercising their right to freedom of expression, and suffered the wrath of a government less than tolerant towards their opinions or actions. By raising their toast to liberty, the two Portuguese students were exercising this right, and punished because of it.

2 It demands that all political prisoners be granted fair and prompt trials, as in many countries political prisoners are held for long periods of time without charge or trial. Political prisoners in this sense include those who have used or advocated violence. When it campaigns on behalf of this aspect of its mandate, Amnesty International does not demand the immediate release of prisoners. It calls for governments to respect their right to a fair, prompt, and open trial.

3   It calls for the universal abolition of torture, the death penalty, and all forms of cruel, degrading and unusual treatment towards prisoners, by which it means all prisoners, including those who are imprisoned according to standard (i.e. non-political) criminal law. In addition, Amnesty International thus calls for those responsible for torture to be brought before an international court.

4   It calls for an end to all extra-judicial executions and 'disappearances'. Amnesty demands an investigation into these activities and continues to search for the whereabouts of the 'disappeared'. It also calls for the perpetrators of extra-judicial executions and disappearances to be brought to justice.

The mandate deals specifically with Amnesty International's campaigning work, but in reality this work extends into a number of areas. For example, it works on behalf of refugees. It has been a staunch advocate of the establishment of the International Criminal Court. It campaigns to end the transfer of military, security and policing equipment which may be used for torture or other human rights offences. It also works to promote human rights in all sectors of society through education programmes and outreach groups.

The organisation is funded by donations from its members. It has nearly a million members in some 150 countries worldwide. There are national sections in over 70 countries. It is run from the International Secretariat office in London, and each national section has its own section office.

It receives its information from a number of sources worldwide, such as the international press, broadcasts, government bulletins, reports from experts and fact-finding missions, and letters from prisoners. Delegations are sent by the International Secretariat to investigate the country in question, all the available information is gathered together, and the well-researched reports are then published. Copies of these reports are sent to the relevant heads of state, and to other interested parties, such as the United Nations. It is hoped that bringing to the attention of the world's leaders the human rights violations within a certain country, will make that country feel obliged to respond favourably. Having assembled all the materials required for campaigning, the International Secretariat then passes on the information to all or some of the national sections, which in turn distribute information on various cases to their members, who act accordingly. Some campaigns are entered into by all sections (except, as we shall see, that based within the country in question); others are handled only by one or a few sections.

While Amnesty International is working at the macro-level of pressurising world leaders and encouraging support from international political bodies, its membership is going about a similar operation in a different, but no less important, way. Members are encouraged to write letters – formal and respectful – to the ambassadors and officials of the countries involved, opposing their human rights policies and calling for the release of all prisoners of conscience. Usually this involves writing on behalf of a particular individual whose case the movement has taken up.

National sections are not allowed to take up cases in their own countries. This is partly because of the potential dangers faced by groups who might attempt to criticise their own governments from within. It is also important because it helps Amnesty International maintain impartiality and, therefore, validity of information. The organisation continues to stress its impartiality. It does not concern itself with political ideologies. It criticises governments of all persuasions, whether on the left or the right of the political spectrum, military dictatorships, liberal democracies, or theocracies. Human rights transcend such differences, and Amnesty International is solely concerned with bringing to the world's attention, and to an end, abuses of human rights wherever and whenever they occur. It is partly because of this impartiality that Amnesty International is so successful, because its neutral opinions are respected, and its advice sought, by the international political community. Indeed, Amnesty International stresses that it is a *non-political* organisation. This is somewhat misleading. It *is* an apolitical movement because it does not operate from any particular political – or ideological – standpoint; it is non-*partisan*, but that does not mean it does not act politically. The very act of appealing to governments for changes in their human rights policies is very much a political one. In taking a non-partisan approach, Amnesty International maintains its autonomy and its integrity. It is because of this that it does not seek to receive any money from governments, nor does it offer services to any government in return for payment.

For the same reason – that is, the need to be seen as impartial and therefore to maintain the respect of the international community – Amnesty International does not demand the release of prisoners who have advocated or used violence, and would never support violent action on behalf of its cause. Indeed, its refusal to endorse such violence where it might be necessary forms the basis of a common criticism of Amnesty International's work. One of the world's most famous political prisoners, Nelson Mandela, was not adopted by Amnesty International as a prisoner of conscience because he had advocated violence. However, the movement holds that it can be most effective if it maintains the respect of the governments of the world, and of public opinion. Political activists who have used or advocated violence might be seen by some as freedom fighters, but for others less sympathetic to the cause they are branded as terrorists. Amnesty International cannot be seen to take sides in such issues.

Amnesty International has changed throughout the years. Indeed, the political climate of the wider world has made this inevitable. Debates continue to rage over the nature of direct action, and whether the movement should be more proactive. Some sections have focused more of their energies on human rights education. There has been discussion over possible links with other non-governmental organisations. In a globalised world opposition to human rights abuses is more likely to coincide with other campaigns, for instance, over environmental issues as in the case of Ken Saro-Wiwa and the atrocities in Nigeria involving the Shell organisation. Despite this, Amnesty International must stick to its mandate to maintain its level of success.

Its success, though, is relative. Most of its cases have been closed for the wrong reasons. Even so, the work of the movement is widely respected. Its combination of political lobbying and individual letter-writing has proved to be an effective method of campaigning. A famous quote in support of Amnesty comes from a former prisoner of conscience, Julio de Pena Valdez, who was a trade union leader imprisoned in the Dominican Republic as a result of his activities in 1975. Thanks to Amnesty International's actions, he was subsequently released. He later described his experiences:

When the first two hundred letters came, the guards gave me back my clothes. Then the next two hundred letters came and the prison director came to see me. When the next pile of letters arrived, the director got in touch with his superior. The letters kept coming and coming: three thousand of them. The president was informed. The letters still kept arriving and the president called the prison and told them to let me go.

After I was released, the president called me to his office for a man-to-man talk. He said: 'How is it that a trade union leader like you has so many friends all over the world?' He showed me an enormous box full of letters he had received and, when we parted, he gave them to me. I still have them.[29]

The World Service Authority

Students are likely to be less familiar with the World Service Authority (WSA) than with Amnesty International. One way to introduce the WSA is to compare it directly with AI. First, AI is a membership organisation, while WSA is not. Second, and significantly, AI is a non-governmental campaigning organisation. WSA, which is the administrative arm of a movement known as World Government of World Citizens (WGWC), would deny this label, because to claim non-governmentality would be, in its view, to claim disempowerment. WGWC and WSA are fundamentally liberal movements which proclaim the sovereignty of the individual citizen above and beyond the territorial nation-state. I have discussed this movement, and these philosophical underpinnings, in greater detail elsewhere, and I do not intend to repeat myself here.[30] I make reference to it, though, because it serves as a useful example of how the 1948 UDHR has made a considerable difference in how all actors – not just states – are capable of upholding human rights. WSA provides various documents which identify bearers as citizens of the world. One such document is particularly interesting – the so-called 'world passport'. This document provides a direct, and quite successful, assault on the realist system of nation-states, each of which relies upon a tightly regulated system of border control to maintain its territorial sovereignty. WSA's attack on border controls begins with an interpretation of Article 13 (2) of the UDHR: 'Everyone has the right to leave any country, including his (*sic*) own, and to return to his country.' According to WSA, this Article necessarily upholds travel across borders as a basic human right, and dismisses border control as a violation of that right. Most nation-states require passports and visas to be shown by non-citizens on arrival. Many people fleeing persecution across borders do not have the luxury of time to apply for these documents, and yet without them, their basic human right to travel is frequently and easily denied. The WSA therefore issues its 'world passport' to such needy people. Needless to say, border officials are often confused by this document, so WSA legal specialists are on hand to argue the case in terms of international law. Every time a country recognises the passport for the first time – over three-quarters of the world's nation-states have at some point recognised it – a copy of the entry stamp of that country is taken and used in future cases as evidence of precedent.[31]

No doubt readers will react with scepticism to many of the claims made by WSA, but that does not alter the simple fact that each year, countless people who would otherwise have their basic right to cross borders denied are able instead to exercise that right because of the 'world passport'. Prior to 1948, this passport would have been a symbolic document. However, since the 1948 UDHR and the 1966 Covenants were passed, its role is clearly more pragmatic. Lawyers are able to make the claim that the passport is validated by the combined

International Bill of Rights, to which countries have signed up. WSA's mission is thus born out of the transformation of human rights – identified by Bobbio and others – from theory to practice.

The state and human rights regulation

Throughout this chapter, we have looked at some of the conflicts and tensions which exist between liberal and cosmopolitan concepts of human rights, and the realist image of a world of nation-states. We have seen how different routes have been taken towards the grounding of human rights standards in nation-state laws. The French and American Declarations both adopted the universalist language of human rights. The same language was adopted by the international political community in 1948, and influenced the 1966 Covenants. These have since filtered back into some nation-states, such as the United Kingdom, via European law. At the same time, since 1948, various campaigning organisations have emerged which provide an alternative means of upholding individual human rights. Some, such as Amnesty International, work alongside the existing political structures, while others, such as the World Service Authority, are antithetical to them.

These developments can, of course, be understood in terms of the globalisation of politics. New technologies of mass destruction, as well as new threats to existence, such as ecological damage, have forced us to abandon the simplicity of the Hobbesian model of the nation-state, which could be justified if *in the last instance* it provided security for its people. While the nation-state has faced a crisis of legitimation, individuals have looked elsewhere for ways of expressing their political concerns, hence the rise in memberships of campaigning social movements. At the same time, nation-states have surrendered some of their sovereignty to supranational alliances, of which the United Nations is clearly the most important. The conflict between the UN and the nation-state has yet to be resolved – various forms of protectionism have resurfaced in formal politics while in the US alone numerous anti-UN extremist groups have emerged. For the most part, these tensions take us beyond the mandate laid out in the volume. However, the part played by the state in regulating human rights is clearly crucial, particularly if we agree with Hannah Arendt's views on the subject. Despite the obvious successes which have sprung from the 1948 Declaration (successes attributed primarily to campaigning movements rather than formal politics), it is still uncertain who claims responsibility for upholding human rights. Nation-states appear willing to do so only when it suits their own interests – the USA champions civil and political rights worldwide but continues to execute its citizens. The UN seems to be willing to uphold human rights but lacks the power to translate its enthusiasm into practice. This point has been recognised by Jürgen Habermas:

> The discrepancy between, on the one hand, the human-rights content of classical liberties and, on the other, their form as positive law, which initially limits them to a nation-state, is just what makes one aware that the discursively grounded 'system of rights' points beyond the constitutional state in the singular toward the globalization of rights. As Kant realized, basic rights require, by virtue of their semantic content, an international, legally administered 'cosmopolitan society'. For actionable rights to issue from the United Nations Declaration of Human Rights, it is not enough simply to have international courts; such [courts] will first be able to function adequately only when the age of individual sovereign states has come to an end through a United Nations that can not only pass, but also act upon and enforce its resolutions.[32]

It is uncertain at present whether processes of globalisation enable or disable moves towards tighter regulation of human rights standards. One interesting position has been adopted by the sociologist Leslie Sklair, who, in an important new publication, posits human rights as part of a process of 'socialist globalization', and in direct contrast with the culture-ideology of consumerism prevalent in capitalist globalisation.[33] It is certainly interesting that Sklair locates the logic of human rights within a broadly socialist framework, and thus as antithetical to the individualism it is so often accused of advocating. The globalisation of the ideology of human rights is also central to writers advocating 'globalisation from below'.[34] In my own work I have contrasted these alternative models of globalisation within a broadly Habermasian framework which distinguishes between competing projects of modernity.[35] Once again, the achievement of human rights is firmly understood as part of a project of self-discovery and emancipation associated with the 'globalisation of the lifeworld'. Each of these approaches rejects the crude economism of scholars who equate globalisation solely with the spread of capitalism, and who thus see it as necessarily damaging to human rights protection. Such reductionist accounts completely miss the point – that the ideology of human rights itself needs to be globalised.

Essay questions

1.   How has the language of human rights been used in the political system?

2.   Is the theory of human rights incompatible with realist theories of the state?

3.   What contributions might the International Criminal Court make to the regulation of human rights worldwide?

4.   Show, with reference to two or more human rights campaigning organisations, how different social movements have campaigned on behalf of human rights.

Notes

1   David P. Forsythe (2000) *Human Rights in International Relations*, Cambridge: Cambridge University Press, p. 13.

2   Forsythe, *Human Rights*.

3   Geoffrey Robertson (2000) *Crimes Against Humanity: The Struggle for Global Justice*, Harmondsworth: Penguin, pp. 3–4.

4   Antonio Cassese (1990) *Human Rights in a Changing World*, Cambridge: Polity Press, p. 24.

5   Cassese, *Human Rights*, p. 24.

6   Norberto Bobbio (1996) *The Age of Rights*, Cambridge: Polity Press, p. 80.

7   Forsythe, *Human Rights*, p. 34.

8   Forsythe, *Human Rights*, p. 34.

9   At this point, it is important to point out that there are many variants of realism, and there is certainly an important distinction between classical realism – associated with Edward Carr and Hans Morgenthau amongst many others – and the neorealism of commentators such as Kenneth Waltz. The latter, as opposed to the former, views the state as possessing – in the words of John M. Hobson (2000) *The State in International Relations*, Cambridge: Cambridge University Press, p. 17 – 'high domestic agential power . . . (but) no international agential power to determine policy or shape the international system free of structural constraints'. In other words, neorealists have retained the idea of the state as the central unit of analysis, but have replaced the classical view of the state as the defining political actor pursuing self-interest, with that of the more passive state adapting to circumstances. So, while the classical realist position grants the state full power in the international arena, the neorealist stance comes closer

to a functionalist analysis, in so far as it grants autonomy to the international system of states, within which the individual state is powerless, and to the operations of which it is subject. It is possible that this position overcomes the second of the criticisms which have been directed at the realist perspective.

10 Forsythe, *Human Rights*, p. 48.

11 Hobson, *The State*, p. 64.

12 Of course, as Hobson points out, there are multiple versions of liberalism, which differ from one another in terms of the weighting each gives to the relative positions of individuals, institutions, and the state. While a functionalist-institutionalist like David Mitrany (e.g. Mitrany (1966) *A Working Peace System*, London: Quartet Books) might envisage the desirable withering away of the sovereign state, to be replaced not with an undesirable federal superstate but with a looser form of functional interdependency, a rationalist like Hedley Bull (e.g. Bull (1977) *The Anarchical Society*, London: Macmillan) would view the state as the most appropriate institution to bring about world order.

13 Maurice Bertrand (1994) 'The Role of the United Nations in the Context of the Changing World Order' in Yoshikazu Sakamoto (ed.), *Global Transformation: Challenges to the State System*, New York: United Nations University Press, pp. 463–4.

14 Forsythe, *Human Rights*, p. 62.

15 Each of the following descriptions of the roles and functions of the specialised agencies is adapted from the UN website – www.un.org – and is intended to serve solely as an introduction and not as a critical judgement. Some of these agencies will be subjected to a more critical analysis at appropriate stages throughout this volume.

16 Forsythe, *Human Rights*, pp. 63–4.

17 Robertson, in *Crimes Against Humanity*, wonders whether the Human Rights Commission, which has been largely unsuccessful in monitoring human rights concerns, might be considered a 'permanent failure'. Its record, Robertson reports, 'has been woeful. It has never taken economic or social rights seriously, and has largely confined itself to studying breaches of civil rights in those countries which lack lobbying influence at the UN' (Robertson, *Crimes Against Humanity*, pp. 45–6).

18 Forsythe, *Human Rights*, pp. 38–9.

19 David Held (1989) *Political Theory and the Modern State: Essays on State, Power and Democracy*, Cambridge: Polity Press, p. 234; Antonio Cassese (1988) *Violence and Law in the Modern Age*, Cambridge: Polity Press.

20 Forsythe, *Human Rights*, pp. 13–14.

21 Held, *Political Theory*, p. 234.

22   Forsythe, *Human Rights*, p. 85.

23   The seven countries that voted against the proposal make for unusual bedfellows. Two of them – the United States and China – are permanent members of the Security Council, which raises its own difficulties. The others are Israel, Iraq, Libya, Sudan, and Yemen.

24   Geoffrey Robertson (1999) *Crimes Against Humanity: The Struggle for Global Justice*, Harmondsworth: Penguin, p. 325.

25   Robertson, *Crimes*, p. 334.

26   Robertson, *Crimes*, pp. 335–9.

27   Robertson, *Crimes*, pp. 339–42.

28   Anthony Giddens (1991) *Modernity and Self-Identity: Self and Society in the Late Modern Age*, Cambridge: Polity Press.

29   Quoted in Jonathan Power (1981) *Amnesty International: The Human Rights Story*, Oxford: Pergamon Press, p. 21.

30   Darren J. O'Byrne (2002, forthcoming) *The Dimensions of Global Citizenship*, London: Frank Cass.

31   For more on the 'world passport', see also Darren J. O'Byrne (2001) 'On Passports and Border Controls' in *Annals of Tourism Research* 28, 2, pp. 399–416.

32   Jürgen Habermas (1996) 'Postscript to *Between Facts and Norms*' in Mathieu Deflem (ed.) *Habermas, Modernity and Law*, London: Sage, p. 143.

33   Leslie Sklair (2002) *Globalization: Capitalism and Its Alternatives*, Oxford: Oxford University Press.

34   Jeremy Brecher, John Brown Childs, and Jill Cutler (eds) (1993) *Global Visions: Beyond the New World Order*, Boston: South End Press.

35   O'Byrne, *Dimensions*.

Further information

Books

I have made considerable use of David P. Forsythe's *Human Rights in International Relations* (Cambridge: Cambridge University Press, 2000) in this chapter because it provides a wonderful overview of some of the main concerns, even if its author is unapologetic in his advocacy of a neo-liberal position on human rights. All students of human rights should carry by their sides an accessible collection of the relevant major conventions, declarations and covenants, and one of the best is *Basic Documents on Human Rights* edited by Ian Brownlie (Oxford: Clarendon Press, 1992). Geoffrey Robertson QC is one of Britain's leading specialists in human rights law, and his *Crimes Against Humanity: The Struggle for Global Justice* (Harmondsworth: Penguin, 2000) is both accessible and scholarly. Also, a new textbook has appeared on the market which covers virtually every aspect of the International Criminal Court. Written by William A. Schabas, *An Introduction to the International Criminal Court* (Cambridge: Cambridge University Press, 2001) is an invaluable resource for those interested in legal aspects of human rights regulation.

Web pages

Information about the United Nations can be obtained through the UN's website www.un.org. The Universal Declaration can be viewed in multiple languages either through the UN page – go to www.un.org/Overview/rights.html – or through a 50-years celebratory page, www.udhrfifty.org.uk. Amnesty International's website is www.amnesty.org. Information about the World Service Authority can be found on www.worldgovernment.org/wsa.html.

CHAPTER THREE

Censorship

Everyone has the right to freedom of thought, conscience and religion; this includes freedom to change his religion or belief, and freedom, either alone or in community with others and in public or private, to manifest his religion or belief in teaching, practices, worship or observance.

Universal Declaration of Human Rights, Article 18

Everyone has the right to freedom of opinion and expression; this right includes freedom to hold opinions without interference and to seek, receive and impart information and ideas through any media and regardless of frontiers.

Universal Declaration of Human Rights, Article 19

(I) Everyone has the right to freedom of peaceful assembly and association;
(II) No one may be compelled to belong to an association.

Universal Declaration of Human Rights, Article 20

What is censorship?

Censorship is the vaguest of terms. It takes many forms, ranging from some limited government restriction or regulation on news, information, or performance, to torture or summary execution. Over the years, it has evolved from the duties of the censor and census-taker in ancient Rome, taking careful note of people and possessions and ideas, to the highly technological tools of modern surveillance, carefully hidden from the democracy of the public sphere.[1] In human rights circles, censorship is treated as an affront to individual freedom, a violation of our rights to know, to think, to express ourselves. It is a tool for state repression, for the maintenance of power (the task of any state, whatever colour its rosette may be and whatever it claims for itself), achieved through the manipulation of the cultural sphere – 'the history of censorship belongs to the history of culture and communication'.[2]

Paul O'Higgins distinguishes between six types of censorship.[3] The first is *autonomous censorship*. This is self-censorship brought about by conscious or unconscious motives which lead an individual either to refrain from expressing or to alter his or her views. The second is *social censorship*. This involves the discouragement of the expression of certain ideas, either through socialisation or sanctions, which leads to the emergence of taboos. Censorship is thus a means of protecting the interests of the group. Third is *legal censorship*, the enforcement of restraint by legal institutions such as the police or the courts. This can be either prior censorship, according to which material has to meet certain approved standards, or penal censorship, where no such approval is needed but punishment is at hand for a violation of legal limits. The fourth variety is *extra-legal censorship* – telephone tapping, d-notices, limited release of information about a defendant at trial. Fifth is *voluntary censorship*, where an individual or company, with no legal power, imposes upon others limitations on what they might say or do without sanction. This may be exercised by an institution, such as the Press Council, or by an employer, and is usually based on a shared code of beliefs. The sixth and final form is *subterranean censorship*, where an individual or institution uses powers set aside for another purpose to impose censorship without direct government involvement.

In the last instance, O'Higgins claims, all censorship is reliant upon laws, all censorship – following William Seagle – is political censorship. But it is not always the case that censorship is such a vile and manipulative thing. It is found in varying degrees in all political cultures, and its extent varies in accordance with its setting. Thus, 'part of the history of censorship leads through the Bastille and the gulag, but most of it belongs to the critical zone of cultural contention, where the censor would become a collaborator of the author and the author an accomplice of the censor'.[4]

In this chapter, we will discuss censorship with less consideration for its potential benefit to the artist. We will deal with it as government regulation (the way it is usually dealt with by media commentators), and from this, trace its relationship to various abuses of human rights. Indeed, much of the debate over censorship concerns issues of rights – to freedom of speech, to privacy, and so on – and the debate therefore transcends traditional differences between the political left and right. Even from this starting point, though, the treatment of censorship as a human rights issue is somewhat confusing. For example, opposition to it in its various forms occupies much of the time of social movements such as Amnesty International, and yet nowhere in the mandate of that campaigning organisation is there a mention of it. Groups like Amnesty emerged initially as part of the struggle to uphold certain basic civil rights – those rights which in practice should be defensible by law – against those states which sought to suppress them. So censorship, understood in this respect as the strategies employed by the state for the purpose of suppressing these basic civil rights, is at the heart of Amnesty's project. It represents a denial of freedom of speech, of expression, and of information. Yet the term is more commonly associated with a wide range of government limitations which do not appear to have been raised to the status of human rights issues. In *this* respect, censorship is the *bête noire* not of human rights activists, but of libertarians, who want to extend Locke's minimal state to its extreme position, restricting all state involvement in private life and certainly opposing any practice which restricts individual human freedoms, whether or not this constitutes a human rights violation *per se*. One topic which is often discussed in this context is pornography. This will serve as an example later in the chapter, when we discuss this strange relationship between the state and the individual, the public and the private. The issue of pornography is certainly one which transcends political boundaries. Some on the left are opposed to it because it is degrading, offensive, or dangerous to women, while others celebrate it as a form of sexual liberation, and are opposed to any kind of state interference. Similar disputes take place on the right.

It is probably fair, then, to say that human rights movements are reluctant to include in their documentation a global condemnation of censorship *per se*. It becomes a human rights issue not when it violates individual liberties (as it necessarily always does), because *any* government action, malevolent or benevolent, is going to violate individual liberty in some respect, and the political implication of such an extreme philosophy is the dismantling of *all* forms of authority or government or law. It becomes a human rights issue only when it violates a clearly defined civil right, such as freedom of opinion, freedom of expression, freedom of assembly; when it is used to *target* those whom it seeks to censor; when it is used as an instrument of oppression. But even here there are complications. Consider these four examples:

1   To what extent should the right to freedom of speech be allowed for non-democratic, inciteful, or aggressive organisations (a subject we discuss at length below)? Is there not, in this case, a possible *conflict of rights*?

2   What other conflicts of rights might emerge from these debates? Might censorship not be necessary in order to uphold, for example, the right to privacy, or the right to a fair trial?

3   Related to this, we should bear in mind that some of these 'rights' – expression, assembly, association – are in fact denied *legally* by governments according to international law. Indeed, Article 20 (2) of the International Covenant on Civil and Political Rights states that: 'Any advocacy of national, racial or religious hatred that constitutes incitement to discrimination, hostility or violence should be prohibited by law'. Thus, when campaigning on these issues, activists have to distinguish between those restrictions which are used for repressive purposes, and those which are 'legally acceptable'.

4   How much power should the state legitimately hold in order to act in the 'public good', which may take the form of censorship in areas such as official secrets, video nasties and so on? In respect of this, the question of censorship returns to the fundamental question of political philosophy; that is, the relationship between the citizen and the state.

Thus, in this chapter we will seek to relate censorship to these fundamental questions of power, authority, liberty and democracy. We will address the major freedoms which are often censored, and discuss them in the context of these contested concepts. When we discuss censorship in this respect, we are inevitably drawn to a range of philosophers and social scientists whose work might not otherwise have received much attention in a more limited analysis of the topic: Althusser, Popper, Arendt, Adorno, Marcuse, Foucault, and Habermas all make appearances. Realist and liberal perspectives on the state, moralist and causalist ones on ethics, will be discussed. In so far as these questions inevitably force us to consider the relationship between the public and the private spheres, we will then turn to a specific topic, pornography, because it is useful in an illustrative sense even if it is rarely debated within human rights circles. First, as is the way with each of these chapters, we must immerse ourselves in a historical overview of censorship in order to see where we have been before, and where we are now.

A brief history of censorship

Readers will soon become familiar with the structure of this book – each chapter begins with a brief history of the substantive area under discussion. Of course, in all cases, and some more than others, it is simply impossible to do justice to the history of the topic in such a small space. Censorship is a prime example of this. Where does one begin? Censorship has occurred in some form in almost all known societies. Varieties of censorship existed in ancient Greece, in Rome, in the Far East, among the native Americans. . . . The list is endless. I will, therefore, focus my attentions here on two regional histories: censorship in Europe, beginning with the printing press and the Catholic prohibition, with particular reference to England and France, and, as an example of censorship in the former Eastern Europe, drawing on an interesting account of the structures of censorship in East Germany; and censorship in the United States, where freedom of speech and information is guaranteed under the Constitution.

Censorship in Europe

Since the first Gutenberg Bible was printed in 1455, the spectre of censorship has hung over the cultural world.[5] In 1551, it became an offence according to the Edict of Worms decreed by the Holy Roman Emperor, Charles V, to print, sell, copy, read, even possess, anything written by the reformer Martin Luther. Indeed, in 1564, an index of prohibited books – *Index Librorum Prohibitorum* – was drawn up by the Catholic Church, resulting in the underground sale and exchange of various works considered inappropriate for Catholics. Johannes Kepler's *The New Astronomy*, which proved Copernicus's heliocentric theory, was added to the list upon its publication in 1609, and it was quickly followed, in 1632, by Galileo's *Dialogue Concerning the Two Chief World Systems*.

Censorship laws in (what is now) the United Kingdom can be traced back to the establishment of theatre censorship in 1551, and in 1617 blasphemy was made a crime. During the seventeenth century, though, Enlightenment writers such as Thomas Hobbes and (especially) John Locke spoke in different ways about the rights of citizens in relation to the state. Locke successfully advised the British Parliament to allow the Licensing Act to lapse, leaving only the common law doctrine of seditious libel as a block on total freedom of expression in print. In 1763 the parliamentarian John Wilkes tested this with his paper *The North Briton*, in which he attacked government policy and branded the king a liar. This resulted in a prosecution for seditious libel and expulsion from the Commons. In 1792, a new act, Fox's Libel Act, was passed, which handed the power to decide whether a material is libellous over to the jury. Thomas Paine, whose controversial *Rights of Man* was published the same year, was found guilty of seditious libel, and banished.

Subsequent acts included the Obscene Publications Act of 1857 (strengthened in 1959 and 1964), and the Official Secrets Act, section two, of 1889. One of the most famous cases pertaining to the Obscene Publications Act was the trial and acquital in 1960 of Penguin Books Ltd for the publication of D.H. Lawrence's *Lady Chatterley's Lover*.

Censorship also has a colourful history in France. In an interesting study which compares models of censorship in France during the *ancien régime* and East Germany under communist control, Robert Darnton suggests that in the former, censorship was in part a privilege; however, the administration was rife with contradictions, not least in the matter of censorship:

> When the king first discovered that the invention of movable type could shake his throne, he tried to solve the problem by decreeing in an edict of 1535 that anyone who printed a book would be hanged. That did not work, nor did an edict of 1757 that threatened to punish any author of irreligious or seditious works with death. The system remained relentlessly repressive, in principle. In practice, it became increasingly flexible...[6]

As the Enlightenment encouraged greater critical thinking, various texts were published in defence of liberty. Montesquieu's *The Spirit of the Laws* and Rousseau's *The Social Contract* could both be read as defences of individual rights against state interference, and it was, of course, Voltaire who proclaimed that he would be ready to die for another's right to freedom of expression, however vile the views expressed may be. The Declaration of the Rights of Man in 1789 included a (guarded) guarantee of freedom of thought and speech. Nevertheless, Napoleon made liberal use of censorship in respect of theatre, printed matter, and even private correspondences after 1802. Towards the end of the nineteenth century, the infamous Dreyfus affair attracted much controversy. Dreyfus had been convicted of treason and there was widespread belief that the government had conspired to cover up his innocence. In 1898 Emile Zola wrote an open letter to the government, 'J'accuse', in the newspaper *L'Aurore*.[7]

Censorship issues in Western Europe during the second half of the twentieth century were judged primarily in relation to the European Convention on Human Rights (1953) Articles 9, 10, and 11, which draw, of course, on the International Covenant on Civil and Political Rights. Article 9 guarantees the right to 'freedom of thought, conscience and religion', Article 11 protects the right to 'freedom of peaceful assembly', and, more significantly, Article 10 demands freedom of expression, but in a guarded way:

1   Everyone has the right to freedom of expression. This right shall include freedom to hold opinions and to receive and impart information and ideas without interference by public authority and regardless of frontiers. This article shall not prevent States from requiring the licensing of broadcasting, television, or cinema enterprises.

2   The exercise of these freedoms, since it carries with it duties and responsibilities, may be subject to such formalities, conditions, restrictions or penalties as are prescribed by law and are necessary in a democratic society, in the interests of national security, territorial integrity or public safety, for the prevention of disorder or crime, for the protection of health or morals, for the protection of the reputation or rights of others, for preventing the disclosure of information received in confidence, or for maintaining the authority and impartiality of the judiciary.

Given the extent of the limitations, one could argue that the Article fails to uphold freedom from censorship at all. Nevertheless, this interesting if long sentence mentions various issues – such as national security – which are always raised when one talks of 'freedom of information', and to which we will return later.

This history concerns Western Europe. In the former Soviet Bloc, censorship often involved more direct practices of state involvement in the production and dissemination of ideology. In the Soviet Union, as is well known, leaders such as Stalin were less than tolerant of outspoken political rivals. In flagrant contradiction of any pretence to Marxism – for Marx and Engels, the state, once its job is done, withers peacefully away – the Soviet state became the most dictatorial of censors. The educational and cultural sectors were often rigorously monitored to ensure that they fulfilled their function in the transmission of Marxist ideology. This ideological and political centralisation was far removed from the alleged pre-revolutionary Bolshevik commitment to free speech and civil liberties:

The idea that a socialist state should force every citizen to think the same, let alone to endow its leaders collectively with something like papal infallibility ... would not have crossed the mind of any leading socialist before 1917.[8]

Robert Darnton continues his comparative study with a fascinating account of the dynamics of censorship in East Germany, according to the testimonies of those involved in the process. These sources worked in what was imaginitively named, apparently without irony, the 'head administration for publishing and the book trade', and their job was not to *censor* (they had no time for that term), but to 'make literature happen'.[9] They described their work as 'planning': 'In a socialist system . . . literature was planned like everything else'.[10] This planning would begin with the agreeing of an initial proposal, and proceed into the vetting of the texts of the commissioned books once a manuscript was received, although by this time 'most of the effective censorship had already occurred – in the planning process and in the authors' heads'.[11] However, certain words and phrases would have to be removed or amended, and some even had 'stock replacement' which could be inserted immediately – thus 'opponent of Stalin' would become 'contradictor of his time'.[12] Figure 3.1 shows the structures of censorship in East Germany at the time.

Censorship in the United States

Freedom of speech, press, religion, and assembly are all guaranteed by the First Amendment to the United States Constitution, written in 1787 and ratified in 1791. Thus, the United States has, famously:

> [T]he strongest legal protection for free speech in the world, thanks to the unequivocal wording of the First Amendment: 'Congress shall make no law . . . abridging the freedom of speech, or of the press'.[13]

Nevertheless, various cases have emerged which seem to contradict this guarantee. In Tennessee in 1925, a teacher, John T. Scopes, was tried and convicted for violating a state law prohibiting the teaching of Darwin's theory of evolution.[14] Similar cases have been taken to court since. Also, the more commercial arts were not necessarily free from state intervention: the US Production Code Administration, or Hays Office, existed from 1934 to 1968, and required films to have 'moral' endings, and to restrict the length of time of any screen kiss to no more than three seconds.[15] Even today, conservative authorities attempt to censor what they argue is 'obscene' material, including educational materials about sexual awareness and abortion.

Freedom of information had not been guaranteed by the First Amendment, but the Freedom of Information Act of 1966 made it clear

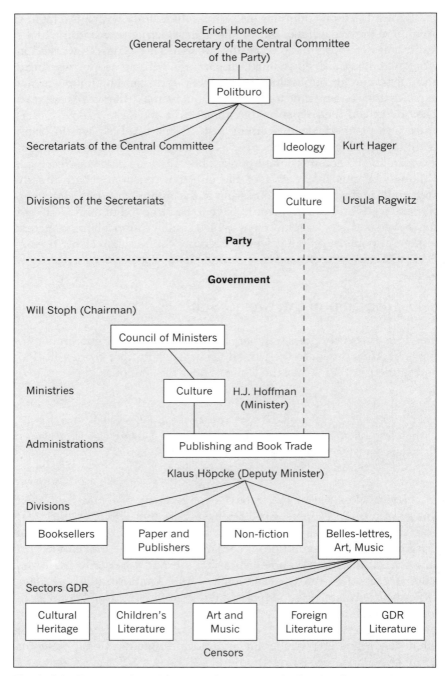

Figure 3.1 The control mechanism for literature in the German Democratic Republic[16]

that, unless government is able to provide a good reason to the contrary, all government documents should be accessible to the public. This may well be the case, but freedom to express ideas and impart information has often been cleverly restricted through immigration control, the refusal of entry either to people or materials on ideological grounds.[17] This was particularly common during the height of the Cold War. More recently, commentators have accused the United States authorities of censoring press information in time of war (the response at home to the war in Vietnam, which was shown liberally on television, clearly sent a message to the authorities that this should never be allowed to happen again). A critical report by Human Rights Watch and the American Civil Liberties Union claims that during the Gulf War control over the information received by the media was tightened. Only carefully selected journalists were allowed to cover the fighting, and reporters were to be accompanied by a military escort at all times. Also, before their release, all dispatches were carefully scrutinised by military officials, and this review went beyond simply military matters and sometimes involved the changing of words.[18]

Censorship and democracy

The purpose of this section is to examine the claim that the very presence of censorship violates the fundamental bases of democratic society. According to the liberal theory of democracy, in such a society power rests with the citizen, who is entitled to certain freedoms (each of which has found its way into the Universal Declaration of Human Rights), including freedom of speech; freedom of information; freedom of worship and belief; freedom of the press; freedom of assembly; freedom to impart educational knowledge, and so on. As we have already discussed, in the United States, unlike the United Kingdom, freedoms of this kind are guaranteed according to the Constitution. Although the UK does not have a written constitution, and thus has no guarantee of free speech,[19] it is a party to the European Convention on Human Rights. In effect, therefore, these freedoms should be universally agreed upon. In reality, of course, they are not. What, then, might this mean for the claim that we live in a liberal democratic society?

I am going to concentrate here on two particular rights from those listed above: freedom of speech, and freedom of information. I appreciate that any number of these freedoms could also be listed. For example, freedom of assembly represents the most basic of human needs, association, upon which society is formed, and to deny freedom of assembly is to deny society itself. My feeling, though, is that the two freedoms I am going to focus on can incorporate these other rights, because they constitute the most basic features of *human* existence, upon which not only democracy but society itself is based, and in respect of which it has adapted: the right *to speak* and the right *to hear*.

Freedom of speech

The dominant voice in the debate over freedom of speech has come from the *liberal* tradition within theories of politics. Liberals – who have favoured minimal state intervention since Locke – have also advocated the concept of the 'marketplace of ideas' since John Stuart Mill.[20] In his groundbreaking treatise *On Liberty*, Mill made four arguments in favour of freedom of speech, which can be summarised as follows:[21]

1   If we suppress an opinion, it may turn out to be true. To assume otherwise is to assume that we are infallible, which is not the case.

2   Even if the opinion is false, it might still contain some truth. So, given that it is unlikely even for a generally 'true' account to be without fault, by listening to other accounts we get closer to a 'total' truth.

3   Even if the true account already is a 'total' truth, it still has to be criticised or challenged, because only by defending an account against criticism or challenge are we able to understand the reasons why it is a true account, instead of just accepting uncritically that it is.

4   Only by challenging an established truth can we keep the vital link between theory and action. People often get complacent otherwise, and this link is broken.[22]

Following Mill and others, it is accepted in the liberal tradition that freedom of speech and of information is an essential part of a democratic society. One scholar who has upheld this belief is Rodney A. Smolla, a professor of constitutional law.[23] According to Smolla, freedom of speech serves five functions which are essential for democratic self-governance. First, it is a means of *participation*, 'the vehicle through which individuals debate the issues of the day, cast their votes, and actively join in the processes of decision-making that shape the polity'.[24] Thus, it enables the fulfilment of the individual as an active citizen. Secondly – following the tradition of the marketplace of ideas – it serves the *pursuit of political truth*. Thirdly, it facilitates *majority rule*. Fourthly, it provides *restraint on tyranny and corruption*, keeping government in check in the best tradition of Locke. Finally, it helps to ensure *stability* by allowing for minority voices to be heard.

Freedom of speech, in the broadest sense, includes freedom of political opinion, freedom of religious belief and worship, and freedom to espouse secular views. However, of course, freedom of speech is often restricted according to the *content* of the speech. For example, there is an on-going debate about whether extremist views should be tolerated. This is especially true in the case of far right movements and parties which preach racial intolerance, but it can also be used to silence political opponents. Thus, in 1988, the United Kingdom government passed a broadcasting ban on the Irish republican political party Sinn Fein so as not to give it the 'oxygen of publicity'.

In a debate which took place in the *Guardian* newspaper in May 1994, two respected columnists, Seamus Milne and Polly Toynbee, discussed the pros and cons of allowing a platform for the British National Party.[25] Milne claimed that the British National Party necessarily violates the rights of a large proportion of the population, and, in a somewhat utilitarian sense which seeks to devise a hierarchy of rights, made the point that by doing so, it surrenders its rights to freedom of speech. He also feared that the 'oxygen of publicity' would encourage the spread of racism. Toynbee, by contrast, suggested that the banning of this particular group might set a precedent by which any group which does not conform to a norm is liable to a similar ban. This would apply to left-wing as well as right-wing groups. According to Toynbee, 'Free speech is not absolute . . . but we must be free to speak our political minds, and listen to the political opinions of others, however nasty'.[26]

Toynbee thus seeks to uphold Voltaire's famous maxim, that while I disagree with what one might say, I will defend her or his right to say it. But she also seems to be upholding the liberal 'marketplace of ideas' thesis – suggesting that truth will triumph in the public arena – and arguing from a position akin to that of the German sociologist and philosopher Jürgen Habermas. Toynbee suggests that, rather than set a dangerous precedent by censoring these dislikeable opinions, we should allow them their platform and trust in human rationality to give them the contempt they deserve. By censoring them, she suggests, we will merely be sending them underground where they can continue unchecked, but by offering them a space we will be giving them a fair trial in the courtoom of public opinion. Only by hearing the arguments can we reach a full understanding so as to come to an informed decision. Where speech is prohibited, then communication is hindered, and consensus impossible. These are the opinions put forward by Habermas in his famous 'theory of communicative action'.[27]

According to Habermas, communication between human actors always involves four validity claims which need to be satisfied in order for a consensus to be reached between the speaker and the hearer. The first of these is *comprehensibility*. Here, the hearer is unknowingly asking of the speaker the question: Is what you say understandable to me? It may well be that the language is muddled, or incoherent, or full of jargon. If so, a barrier exists between speaker and hearer. The rules which govern this validity claim are located within the rules of language itself. The second is *truth*. Here, the question is: Is what you say true? Regardless of intention, the speaker may be making a statement which in reality is not the case and, if so, another barrier is drawn up. The rules governing this claim are found in the *objective world of external reality*, a world which has laws not reducible to human construction. The third such claim is *appropriateness*, or *rightness* – in other words: Are you in a position to say what you say? If a colleague promises me a promotion, she may genuinely think this can happen, and in fact it may actually happen, but the power to make it happen is not hers, and thus she is not in such a position. The laws which govern this are found in the *intersubjective or normative world of rules, expectations, society, culture*. In such a world, we assign certain positions to certain individuals and with those come expectations of appropriate behaviour. The fourth claim is *truthfulness* or *sincerity*. Here, the questioner has to ask: Do you mean what you say? If the speaker is deliberately trying to deceive the hearer, then clearly another barrier is drawn up. This claim operates within the *subjective world of internal reality*, of consciousness and intention.

Habermas would suggest, then, that communication – in so far as it is unhindered and can result in knowledge and understanding – is empowering and emancipatory. The public sphere is indeed the arena where rational people exchange views in the hope of reaching a consensus. It is of course possible to accuse Habermas of a liberal naïveté, of misunderstanding the power relations inherent in all forms of communication and social interaction. Certainly, a Foucauldian perspective would claim not only that language is imbued with power, but that power exists in a complex and inseparable relationship to knowledge. However, it is important to consider Habermas's claims in the context of the *meaning of democracy*. In other words, if one side of a debate cannot speak its views, can we truly say we live in a democratic society? And if certain views are stifled, how is it possible for change to take place? These questions do indeed refer back to the claims made by Mill. We will return to this matter of democracy below.

Readers interested in the issues raised in debates such as that between Toynbee and Milne might want to consult an interesting text called *Free Speech*.[28] This volume includes various debates – literally – on issues related to censorship. For example, two questions debated are: Should unrestricted speech be allowed on college campuses? and: Should there be limits to free speech?

The first of these questions emerged from moves to impose a speech code – banning the use of 'offensive' language – at Stanford University. Among those upholding the First Amendment right to unrestricted free speech on college campuses was constitutional lawyer Gerald Gunther. Gunther presented his case with due recognition of the potential for speech to serve as a weapon of intolerance:

> [S]peech should not and cannot be banned simply because it is 'offensive' to substantial parts of, or a majority of, a community. The refusal to suppress offensive speech is one of the most difficult obligations the free speech principle imposes upon all of us; yet it is also one of the First Amendment's greatest glories – indeed, it is a central test of a community's commitment to free speech.[29]

Gunther was, however, in a minority, and a speech code was introduced. Supporting Gunther's position, the journalist Nat Hentoff pointed out that 'at most colleges, it is the administration that sets up the code. Because there have been racist or sexist or homophobic taunts, anonymous notes or graffiti, the administration feels it must *do something*'.[30] But supporters of speech codes, such as Charles Lawrence, argued that the restrictions reflected genuine demands from students from minority ethnic groups, who had through harassment been denied their right to equality of education.[31] Racism inflicts harm, Lawrence pointed out, before stating, correctly, that examples of restriction on freedom of speech already do exist in the United States, pertaining to obscenity, official secrets, and defamation. If we cannot tolerate the defamation of another's character, why do we consider it acceptable to insult their ethnicity? This is a persuasive argument, backed up by Lawrence's critique of the 'marketplace of ideas' philosophy – '[e]xperience tells quite the opposite'.[32] It seems perfectly plausible to counter the human rights argument in favour of free speech with an even earlier rights-based argument, drawing on Hobbes: the right for a citizen to expect from the state security of person.

Indeed, the question of censorship and free speech gets even more complicated when we bring in an additional factor, the freedom of the press. It certainly seems fair to say, as some have done, that the mass media are now so powerful that the public requires protection from them.[33] If the media are servants of populist democracy (see below), they shift away from their role as the Fourth Estate. They thus become a hindrance upon 'true' democracy, and require reform and, where necessary, government intervention. Thus, we can use the very same theoretical stance we have so far adopted to argue against censorship in order to argue for some degree of intervention and restrictions.

Freedom of expression is denied in different ways in different parts of the world. The following case study relates to a particular anomaly. Article 28 of the Turkish constitution guarantees a free press and derides censorship, but Article 8 of the reformed Turkish Legal Code states that is is illegal to write or publish anything which falls under the broad heading of 'separatist propaganda'. According to Sanar Yurdatapan, whose testimony we will read below, the purpose is to prevent anyone from publishing anything by the rebel PKK leader Abdullah Ocelan, in much the same way as the UK government sought to deny the 'oxygen of publicity' to representatives of Sinn Fein.

In January 1995 our well known writer Yasar Kemal was invited to the State Security Court to be questioned about an article he had written for the German magazine *Der Spiegel* . . . That morning 90 intellectuals turned up to support Yasar. We gathered in the back yard of the State Security Court in Istanbul. We started a signature campaign there and then. We used the famous quote of Voltaire written over 250 years ago: 'I may disagree with your ideas, but I'm ready to die for your right to express them.' Within a month we were able to publish this book, *Freedom of Thought*. In this book we published ten banned articles by different writers, including Yesar Kemal . . . 1,080 intellectuals, artists, writers and publishers added their names to the list of publishers of the book. It was the longest publishers list in the world. And by this act we all became criminals.

We went to the State Prosecutor and gave a copy of our book to him and said, 'Please do your duty.'

Cases were opened against 185 of us under Article 8 of the Anti-Terror Law 3713. The State Prosecutor himself said there was an urgency in this case. He recognised the contradiction that existed between the legislation under which we were being charged and Article 90 of the Turkish so-called 'Constitution'. . . Either the State will have to change all its legislation – unfortunately there are over 500 Articles of the Turkish law which define 'thought crime' – or Turkey will have to remove its signature from the International Conventions to which it is party.

It was a funny sight to see all these intellectual publishers turning up at the Constitutional Court in a long queue with the State Prosecutor sitting on the 4th floor ... The Court is trying to get rid of us by making its deliberations as slow as possible. We are trying to speed it up, and force them to make its decision which we know should be a minimum of 20 months' imprisonment for each of us. What will happen? A minimum of 10 very popular TV programmes will have to be cancelled because their stars or directors are in jail. Five TV soaps will have to find new directors and change their story lines. The media will lose 30 of the best known journalists, popular columns will be left blank, 8 professorial chairs will be left vacant, and whole universities will require new teaching staff, theatres and film studios will need new artists, directors, and musicians. But on the positive side 20 new books about prison life will be added to our literature if everyone writes one.

... [On 12 March we] invited many authors from different countries to publish a new book called *Mini Freedom of Thought*. It contains just one paragraph from each banned article. Here are 144 signatures from all over the world. Here is Harold Pinter's signature. But the State Prosecutor refused to do to them what he had done to us. He said it was impossible to bring them to Turkey to question them and to try them. He said:

'Who prepared this Turkish leaflet? Mr Harold Pinter? Mr Arthur Miller? Mr James Kellman?'

'No, we did.'

'OK, I'll open a case against you! Second, who distributed this?'

'I did,' I said.

'OK, that's another case against you as distributor.'

And, of course, every time he does something like this against one of us, all the others come the next day and sign the same damn thing and participate in the so-called 'thought crime'...

... [W]e wrote to the foreign authors again and asked them to come to Istanbul. Well 19 of them did come from 12 different countries ... And we went all together in front of the door of the Court again. But the State Prosecutor again closed the doors. He didn't want to hear us, and refused to take the petition we gave him ... If the State Prosecutor and the Turkish State have not taken action within the 60 days, we will take out a case against them for violating the State Constitution: first for breaching the principle of equality, and second for refusing to take the petition. And within 60 days if no answer has come from the higher Commission of the State Prosecutors and judges – the last legal step in the Turkish legal process – the road opens to Strasbourg. We go there.[34]

Freedom of information

Freedom of information is, of course, inseparable from freedom of speech. If a speaker cannot express a view, then a hearer cannot receive information. Necessarily, then, the consequences of censorship for democracy outlined above are applicable with regard to restrictions on freedom of information. Toynbee's views on whether the extremist BNP should be given a platform to speak, with their quasi-Habermasian leaning, are not dissimilar to those put forward by the media analyst Adrian Wilkes.[35] Wilkes seeks to uphold the 'right to know' in the context of the legitimacy of democracy. Beginning with the liberal defence of freedom of information as essential in a democratic system, Wilkes suggests that, without full access to information, the right to vote – the cornerstone of democracy – is limited, and that such measures as the United Kingdom's Official Secrets Act 1911 deny this. This Act (and subsequent Acts of 1920 and 1939) places often ludicrous restrictions upon the civil servants, politicians, and others who have signed it. Furthermore, it is an offence according to this and related legislation for any official or contractor to make any disclosure relating to matters of security, intelligence, politics, diplomacy, or so on. As a result, Wilkes claims, the public is kept in the dark about many issues, the public service is no longer accountable to the people, and public opinion itself becomes unreliable.

The Official Secrets Act is not the only block on the public's 'right to know' in the UK. Three potential threats include the Terrorism Bill, the Local Government Bill, and the Regulation of Investigatory Powers Bill. The Terrorism Bill makes it a crime *not* to report any suspicions about terrorist activities, but with a definition of terrorism so vague that a journalist might be expected to inform on a large range of campaigning activities. It also makes it an offence to support any armed struggle outside the UK. The Local Government Bill threatens to remove existing rights to information about local authority decision making, while the Regulation of Investigatory Powers Bill threatens the confidentiality of journalistic sources, and allows state officials to intercept private e-mail and telephone communications.

The position adopted by Habermas and his supporters necessarily demands an open and communicative democracy. According to such a position, democracy cannot be reduced to mere public opinion. Simple referenda among citizens are often hailed as fundamental tools of democracy, but the kind of democracy they uphold is the utilitarian or populist variety, which espouses majority rule. Open or communicative democracy sets such opinion polls in context. If consensus can only be reached through unhindered communication, what structural constraints exist to restrict that possibility? How can these be overcome? Further problems

Table 3.1 Countries with Freedom of Information Acts

Sweden	1766	New Zealand	1982
USA	1966	Hungary	1992
Denmark	1970	Republic of Ireland	1997
Norway	1970	Thailand	1997
Netherlands	1978	South Korea	1998
France	1978	Israel	1998
Australia	1982	Japan	1999
Canada	1982	United Kingdom	2000

associated with public opinion polls of this kind will be discussed in the chapter on the death penalty. In that case, as in all others, a rational (and therefore politically meaningful) decision can only be made if one has access to all relevant information pertaining to the debate.

The United Kingdom government has introduced a Freedom of Information Act which creates a statutory right to access official information about public authorities and government. The UK thus joins a relatively small list of countries, as outlined in Table 3.1, to have such an Act.

In democratic countries, freedom of information – whatever the extent to which it is, in practice, denied – goes hand in hand with those other basic civil and political rights (equally inconsistent in their application), such as voting rights, and the right to join political movements. They are the building blocks of democracy. In non-democratic countries, where there is not even the pretence that power is held by the people, freedom of information, in the form of access to government activity, is hardly a matter for discussion. But a different form of the censorship of information is certainly worth considering. Repressive governments fear an *educated* populace because knowledge breeds insurrection. So, while restrictions placed upon freedom of information pertaining to government operations may result in a tarnished, incomplete form of democracy in some countries, in others, one risks death even by daring to educate, whether the information imparted is political or not. Consider the following case, known to Amnesty International:

Wednesday 28th February 1989, Antioquia Department, Colombia...
Like other nuns in the community, Sister Teresa taught literacy to the peasants and had become involved in the peasant marches of the early 1980s organized to protest against poverty and violence in the region. When the security forces had tortured these peasants, she had stood by

them and denounced the crimes. She feared there would be more reprisals.

Later that Wednesday, as she was teaching a class of children, two men knocked on her door and came into the classroom asking for some paper and pencils. As Sister Teresa turned to get some the men took out their guns and shot her eight times in front of the children. Sister Teresa was taken to hospital in San Roque but was dead on arrival.

In Colombia hundreds of teachers like Sister Teresa have been murdered by the death squads and thousands have received death threats (often in the form of *sufragios* – invitations to their own funeral). Harassment, detention and torture by the security forces are not uncommon. The government appears to have done nothing. Leaders of the Colombian Federation of Teachers … believe this is because of a shift in policy in the early 1980s, when union members started to challenge educational policy instead of confining themselves to labour demands.

'Teachers began to extend their role as educators to the entire community, instead of keeping it closed up in the classroom … Along with students and parents, teachers began to investigate, question, analyse reality as a means of changing it. In [Colombia] critical thinking and this type of teaching, are considered subversive.'

To be considered subversive in Colombia is to be one step away from the grave. According to [the teachers' federation] the situation is not improving: 47 teachers have been killed since the beginning of 1991 and more than 400 have received death threats.[36]

'In Colombia, critical thinking and this type of teaching, are considered subversive.' Should we be surprised? From Gramsci through the Frankfurt School to modern scholars of ideology, commentators have written on how the state manipulates its public into consensus in order to maintain the status quo. All areas of public life – science, the arts, politics – are becoming one-dimensional, warned Herbert Marcuse; they are conforming to a singular instrumentalist logic, accepting uncritically a particular scientific form of rationality.[37] This *appears* to be good, to be beneficial, to be progressive, but this appearance is superficial and serves to cover up the falseness of the rationality. True rationality is achieved only in human freedom, and freedom means the freedom *to think differently*. Marcuse summoned us to adopt a critical approach, to deny this false rationality, to step outside the system and see ourselves from an objective position, to realise its falseness, to imagine a world which is different. Only then can the repressive state be brought to its knees. Foucault, though similarly critical, would find this recourse to some hidden rationality which the public might at some point 'achieve' wholly problematic. The repressive state will always act to control the means of knowledge (and not just the means of violence, which earlier sociologists such as Max Weber concerned themselves with; the instruments of repression once again conform to Althusser's ideological and repressive state apparatuses) because of the symbiotic relationship between knowledge and power. It may be easy for us to see how a more overtly repressive government would fear an educated populace; commentators such as Foucault (and Althusser, and Marcuse, in their different ways) would apply the same paradigm to Western 'democratic' countries.

Perhaps it is with this in mind that we should think about those cases so often brought to Amnesty International: the arrest and torture of biology lecturer Dr Faruk Mohamed Ibrahim in Sudan in 1989 for teaching the Darwinist theory of evolution 'in contradiction of the principles of Islam'; the murder of sociologist and anthropologist Myrna Mack in Guatemala in 1990, possibly for her work with displaced persons; the imprisonment for eight and a half years of postgraduate student Bonar Tigor Naipospos in Indonesia in 1990 for attempting to 'undermine Indonesian state ideology' by participating in a study group.[38]

The theoretical discourse on censorship

As with other areas of research covered in this volume, the ethical and theoretical discourse on censorship operates at two general levels: those opposed versus those in support, and those who adopt a *moralist* position versus those whose views are influenced more by *causalism*. As we discussed in the Introduction, moralism bases its arguments on the inherent value (or lack thereof) of the material or act itself, while causalism (which is sometimes called consequentialism, and is often associated with utilitarianism) passes judgement according to the implications or consequences of the material or act. So, when applied to censorship, the debate can be summarised as shown in Table 3.2.[39]

According to the moralist position, the value of something is contained within itself. Therefore, the author's intentions should not matter. However, some moralists would suggest that the opposite is true – the author's intentions are *all* that matters when judging the 'good' or 'evil' of a particular material or act. From a causalist position, though, only the consequences matter, so the author's intentions are irrelevant. While this is only a general model, and in most cases arguments for or against something shift between moralist and causalist stances, it is worth

Table 3.2   Moralist and causalist perspectives on censorship

	Pro-censorship	Anti-censorship
Moralist	the material or act should be censored because it is offensive to some	censorship is wrong because it is a denial of the basic right to free speech
Causalist	the material or act should be censored because it is likely to incite people to behave in anti-social ways	censorship is wrong because it denies people the opportunity to encounter different views, and thus impedes innovation

considering that public opinion on matters such as censorship appears to be moving away from the moralist and towards the causalist position; that is, we as a public appear to be less concerned about whether something is necessarily 'good' or 'bad' and more about what possible good or harm it might do.[40]

We can apply these positions to the debate between Toynbee and Milne. In supporting the censoring of the British National Party, Milne falls back on both moralist and causalist arguments. He makes it clear that he finds the material itself deeply offensive. However, he is also concerned with the consequences of giving this extremist party the platform to speak – that is, giving them the 'oxygen of publicity'. This is clearly a causalist line. Toynbee, who opposes censorship in this case, is more broadly moralist, because she wants to defend the universal right to freedom of speech. However, there is an interesting causalist subtext to her argument. She points out that the rational consequence of providing a platform to such a political voice is that the public will be able to ridicule it. So, for Toynbee, the best way to destroy an undesirable idea is not to brush it under the carpet but to air it in public.

Pornography and obscenity

No chapter on censorship would be complete without some reference to the debates concerning pornography and matters of obscenity and public decency. In many respects, the study of pornography illustrates some of the complexities and ambiguities inherent in the wider discourse on censorship. For example, it is quite difficult to break down the various perspectives according to traditional boundaries. With regard to the *politics* of pornography, the issue divides both left and right into liberal (more often termed 'libertarian') and realist (or 'control') factions. With regard to *ethics*, it divides both further into moralist and causalist positions. The traditional conservative critique usually takes a moralist position, while the left critique tends to be more causalist (focusing on the harmful effects rather than the amorality of the material itself).[41] However, the right libertarians' position is also moralist (in defending a neo-liberal market system per se) while left libertarians oppose censorship more in causality terms (such as civil liberties). So the classical conservative argument sees pornography as a threat to the 'moral order' and stability, and sees the material itself as disgusting. This is the position associated in the United Kingdom with the National Viewers and Listeners Association, and in wider terms with the Catholic Church, and most senior politicians. Of course, this 'moral order' may itself be a patriarchal one. The classical liberal position, by contrast, has sought to uphold individual freedoms and oppose state interference, although an alternative liberal wing holds that sexual repression is itself more damaging than sexual openness.

Just as there is no singular conservative or liberal line on pornography, there is also no generalisable feminist response. Traditionally, feminists supported the liberal cause, celebrating the need to discover the body and sexuality. In the 1970s, though, realist feminists emerged who stressed that pornography was not only damaging to women's status in society, but it was also dangerous to their safety. Thus, commentators such as Andrea Dworkin have suggested that pornography not only provides the foundations for, but also *is*, violence against women.[42] These realist feminists have thus sought to locate a largely moralist stance (the representation of women in this way is inherently wrong) within a causalist argument (the main concern being the consequences of the material for men's behaviour and women's safety). While critics might find naïve the assumption that men are naturally misogynstic, many feminists have drawn on this position (including Catherine McKinnon, Anna Mayne, and Dworkin herself) to stand in opposition to censorship in general, but at the same time to move the debate over pornography away from the problem of censorship, towards that of (women's) human rights. Indeed, the term 'realist' is not out of place here, because the argument that Dworkin and others are making is not dissimilar to that which Lawrence makes regarding restrictions on racist speech: pornography, like racist abuse, violates the fundamental right to security of an entire section of the citizenry. The right to expect protection from the state is a fundamental right upheld in the writings of Hobbes, the 'founder' of realism. The realism of Hobbes is based on a sociobiological foundation – that people are intrinsically violent. The realist feminists adopt a similar view with regard to men. Dworkin writes, in recognition of the literal meaning of pornography (i.e. writing about whores):

Whores exist to serve men sexually. Whores exist only within a framework of male sexual domination . . . Men have created the group, the type, the concept . . . The debasing of women depicted in pornography and intrinsic to it is objective and real because women are so used.[43]

Reacting against this realist or cultural feminism, writers such as Avedon Carol have claimed that women are suppressed not because of pornography but because of censorship.[44] Wendy McElroy has warned that anti-pornography legislation might result in a backlash against feminism[45] – indeed, the points she makes are not dissimilar from Toynbee's warning that denying freedom of speech to the racist right opens the doors to similar measures targeted at other non-conformist groups. In addition, American feminist writers and academics such as Betty Friedan, Nora Ephron, and Erica Jong have suggested that anti-pornography legislation merely allows for a convenient scapegoat to explain male violence. Jean Seaton has suggested that the realist femin-ists run the risk of losing touch with the roots of feminism, in the civil liberties and emancipatory movements, in their haste to present their understandable anger.[46] Others, such as Melissa Benn, argue that the problem is one of structural sexism, and that censoring pornography would not itself solve the problem.[47] Instead, anti-sexist laws need to be established. From such a perspective, pornography is seen to mirror sexism in society, but does not create it.

Benn's position takes us along the lines of structuralist analysis – not dissimilar in some respects to Althusser's, save that the dominant ideo-logy for Benn is not capitalism but patriarchy. McElroy's position attacks the realist feminists from a different angle altogether, sharing much in common with the liberal critique of the state, albeit with a healthy dose of feminist criticism:

The final irony is that it is the state – not free speech – that has been the oppressor of women. It was the state, not pornography, that burned women as witches. It was 18th century law, not pornography, that defined women as chattel. 19th century laws allowed men to commit wayward women to insane asylums, to claim their wives' earnings, and to beat them with impunity. 20th century laws refuse to recognize rape within marriage and sentence the sexes differently for the same crime. It is the state, not pornography, that has raised barriers against women. It is censorship, not freedom, that will keep the walls intact.[48]

However, the question of pornography as it has traditionally been discussed within (American) legal circles has involved the relationship between the public and the private; that is, the debate over privacy and civil liberties, over the extent to which private behaviour should be exempt from state interference. In the United States, it has been upheld as a constitutional right according to the First Amendment to enjoy a private life free from unnecessary state surveillance. Supreme Court justice Thurgood Marshall has stated that if the First Amendment means anything at all, 'it means that a state has no business telling a man, siting alone in his own house, what books he may read or what films he must watch'.[49] In the United Kingdom, the 1959 Wolfenden Report upheld this liberal fundament, stating that 'private behaviour should be free from public control'. Dissenting from this view, Patrick Devlin, a noted conservative jurist, complained that the law should be inseparable from morality, and thus immoral acts, even in private, undermine the authority of the law. Such a perspective has been echoed not just by moralists such as Mary Whitehouse, but also by radical libertarians such as Germaine Greer, who famously claimed that 'to fuck . . . is to fuck the system'.[50] However, liberals such as Herbert Hart defended the Report, arguing for a separation of private and public spheres based on the rights of individuals. Even in an increasingly conservative climate, and – if we were to once again adapt the brilliant observations of Foucault to our surroundings – in a world increasingly characterised by hidden surveillance the liberal position is still dominant in political circles.

The state, censorship and human rights

Society, I have claimed, is based upon the principles of sociality, to speak and to hear. To put it another way, societies exist because of language – we recognise each other, we know we are not alone, we communicate, and from this communication comes knowledge, and from this, change. Societies can only adapt because of communication, debate, and learning. The Colombian example cited above serves as a reminder that understanding is dissent. The teachers were not killed for their views; rather, they were killed so that others are denied the chance to hear them.

I have said that societies are based on speaking and hearing, but I have also said that they have *adapted themselves in respect* of speaking and hearing. The state, or perhaps capitalism, or maybe the uncontrollable juggernaut of 'rationalisation', depending on your view, has gone to great lengths to suppress communication. Why? Have we reached a level where the very foundations of sociality need to be kept in check? Did our ancestors in the mythical state of nature invent the state to serve as a balance to society? Is the authority of the state legitimate?

From a social scientific point of view, then, one of the key concerns in respect of censorship clearly harks back to early debates in political philosophy about the relationship between the citizen and the state. As we discussed in Chapter One, the two dominant, and opposing, views on the nature of this relationship come from Thomas Hobbes and John Locke. Hobbes argued that in return for protection from the state, the citizen must surrender some of his or her liberties; thus, the state has the rights, and the citizen has duties to abide by the state's laws. Many feel, perhaps unfairly, that Hobbes was an early advocate of an authoritarian state. More accurately, Hobbes inspired the theory of politics (and the state) known as *realism*. Contrary to this, John Locke defended the weaker state. He felt that the state was there merely to act as arbiter and overseer of the public and private transactions of individual citizens. Locke thus defended a *liberal* position in politics, and this position has been the most articulate in the debates concerning censorship.

One of the most strident defenders of the liberal position has been Karl Popper. Popper was an Austrian-born philosopher of science and political commentator who warned, in *The Open Society and Its Enemies*, that any attempt to plan or regulate society would result in a reduction of human freedom.[51] Opposed to grand-scale, historical theorising, Popper attacked such writers as Hegel and Marx as enemies of freedom. He advocated an approach to society which viewed it as a forum for individuals engaged in debate, critique and conjecture. The future is made by such free individuals, he claimed, and not predetermined by historical cycles. For Popper, authoritarianism is a great social evil because it stifles the human potential for shaping the future.

So, according to the liberal theory, authoritarian control is not a natural state at all. If this is true, then how does it persist in spite of society? How does authoritarianism come about? One answer to this question was provided by the historical sociologist Barrington Moore. In his book *The Social Origins of Dictatorship and Democracy*, Moore identified three distinct routes to modernisation.[52] One route requires the emergence of an influential bourgeois class challenging from below the existing social relations. This route leads to *capitalism*. A second route, the inverse of this, begins with a weaker bourgeois class and thus requires modernisation from above, enforced by an already-dominant political group. This route leads to *fascism*. A third outcome, resulting from a situation where neither of these conditions is present and peasant solidarity has remained strong, is *communism*. Moore argued that in the twentieth century Germany and Japan were examples of fascist authoritarianism.

The suggestion that fascism (or authoritarianism in any form) can be explicable according to historical routes would be dismissed by Popper, the anti-historicist, for obvious reasons, but it would be equally anathema to the political philosopher Hannah Arendt. In attempting to understand *The Origins of Totalitarianism*, Arendt delinked not only the nation from the state (the atrocities of the Holocaust could in no way be reduced to some aspect of German culture), but also the problem of totalitarianism from any specific kind of nation-state.[53] Elements of total-itarian control were present in most, or all, societies (notably France dur-ing the Dreyfus affair), be they liberal democratic, fascist, communist, or whatever. Totalitarianism comes about not because of specific routes to modernity but because of *modernity itself.*

It is Arendt's work that links totalitarian, authoritarian regimes specifically with human rights issues. Arendt writes at length about *how* the authoritarian leaders manipulate and transform the state, and, whether through ideology or coercion, the people. There are similarities between Arendt's account of the rise of totalitarianism in modernity and Herbert Marcuse's discussion of repression in modern societies. There are also some similarities with the work of Adorno *et al.* on *The Authoritarian Personality.* Perhaps what is most chilling about these accounts is the notion that elements of totalitarianism are omnipre-sent. Marcuse, for example, sees little more than superficial differences between liberal-democratic and Soviet societies, and relates them both to authoritarianism.[54] Although approaching the subject from a differ-ent perspective, Louis Althusser's theory of state repression is equally informative, in so far as Althusser distinguishes between those arms of the state concerned with coercion (*repressive state apparatuses*) and those concerned with consent (*ideological state apparatuses*).[55] Althusser included the media, religion, the family, and the education system, as examples of ideological state apparatuses; they reproduce the dominant ideology of society through the control of information. For Althusser, censorship is not carried out by individuals, or classes; it is an operation which is performed unconsciously by the system itself, in which it is inherent.

Althusser's position may have been subject to criticism for its reduc-tionism and its determinism, but his legacy has been profound, not least upon Foucauldians keen to move beyond liberal assumptions about censorship as agency. Sue Curry Jansen makes the not unreasonable point that the 'triumph' of liberalism I refered to earlier, with its belief in the rightful power of the individual citizen above that of the state, did not, in fact, abolish censorship – it merely sent it underground.[56] State governments – even liberal democratic ones – do not need to impose too many legal restrictions upon what their citizens can or cannot read, or discuss, or think. In liberal democracies today, censorship takes the form of surveillence – we may be 'free' to do as we wish, but the state is always there, closely watching our movements.

Perhaps such a Foucaldian perspective is overly cynical. Perhaps it is guilty of misunderstanding – or at least adopting too broad an understanding of – censorship. But perhaps also it has something to add to the discussions, because, as we have sought to make clear throughout this chapter, censorship is intrinsically linked to questions of *freedom* – freedom to speak, to learn, to believe, to gather and discuss. Can these freedoms mean anything if our bodies are not free to exercise them? Curry Jansen points out that: 'A state which carries out its routine operations behind closed doors is not a democracy.'[57] No, it is not. She adds, convincingly:

> If censorship is ever justified in a democracy, it is only when its groundings are open to public scrutiny. Liberal critical traditions have discouraged us from asking fundamental epistemological questions about the relationship between power and knowledge.
>
> The essential question is not, 'Is there censorship?' but rather 'What kind of censorship?' Posing this question is not an affirmation of darkness but an invitation to enlightenment. To expand the boundaries of human freedom, we must first identify them.[58]

This is true. In this respect, there are clear similarities between the Foucauldian project, and the spirit of critical theory espoused by Marcuse and Habermas, as discussed in this chapter. Both would be critical of the liberalism of a Popper, for they would all argue that liberal democracies contain their own contradictions. Both perspectives would look beneath the surface to uncover the hidden rationalities and irrationalities. Of course, Foucault would call for an intellectual deconstruction which, a critic might point out, is abstracted from political reality, while Marcuse would demand that we abstract ourselves from the reality in which we live to identify its repressive irrationality, thus ensuring that theory precedes practice and duly carving out a role for intellectuals as vanguard in the revolution. Habermas's position would seem tame by comparison, but it may also be the most realistic, and the most sociologically rigorous.

Let us consider, briefly, how this perspective might help us understand the role of censorship. We can summarise the argument very quickly. The Habermasian position prioritises the role of *knowledge*, not only in respect of censorship, but also of democracy and freedom in general. Knowledge allows for informed debate. Informed debate allows for consensus. Consensus results in truth. Truth allows for freedom. I admit, this is not exactly as straight a line as I have presented it here. It is more complex, both in the writings of Habermas and of those who have followed him. At first, the Habermasian position appears to be a contemporary development of the 'marketplace of ideas' thesis championed by Mill and other liberals. For sure, there are similarities, and Habermas is certainly locatable in this tradition. But the classical liberal tradition has very little to say about the role of the state, save that, as with economics and other areas of social life, the marketplace of ideas must be left to its own devices, free from external interference. Habermas is more cautious, more concerned with the power of the state, mainly because, while liberals see the state as an autonomous social construction, created to serve the interests of the citizenry, critical theorists such as Habermas locate it within wider projects of rationalisation. The development of the modern state is closely allied to the development of modern capitalist rationalisation, and thus serves interests not always in tune with the interests of human freedom and social and cultural rationalisation. The exchange of views and information in the public sphere is a necessary part of this emancipatory process, but where the agents of the public sphere (the media) lose their autonomy and become dependent upon either the state (in more overtly repressive regimes) or the capitalist market (in allegedly democratic ones), then the transmission of ideology becomes inevitable, and, instead of opening up debate, the media in fact serve to close down access to information and freedom of expression. Thus (shifting from a liberal position to a social democratic one), media reform seems necessary – but who reforms the media? The state itself? Clearly this would be a self-defeating exercise; what would be required (shifting now from a social democratic to a more radical tradition) would be a fundamental overhaul of the state and the social structure to allow for free and competitive media engaging in public debate, regulated by the logic of communicative action.

Whichever theoretical or ideological tradition we locate ourselves in, the problem of censorship will never be an easy one to grapple with. As with so much in this wide field of rights, a great deal of sense appears to be spoken by both sides of the various debates, on racist speech, on pornography, and freedom of information and public security, and so on. How do we, as concerned citizens, even begin to make informed decisions on such complex matters? Certainly, the debates themselves require a public airing. What is most complicating, though, is that in each of the debates, both sides can, and do, appeal with some conviction to the language of human rights to make their case heard.

Essay questions

1. How might the presence of institutional censorship contradict the principles of democratic society?

2. Contrast moralist and causalist approaches to the ethics of censorship.

3. Can an act be deemed immoral if it is performed in private, between consenting adults?

4. Is freedom of speech really an incontrovertible human right?

Notes

1   Sue Curry Jansen (1991) *Censorship: The Knot that Binds Power and Knowledge*, Oxford: Oxford University Press.

2   Robert Darnton (1995) 'Censorship, A Comparative View: France, 1789 – East Germany, 1989' in Olwen Hufton (ed.) *Historical Change and Human Rights: The Oxford Amnesty Lectures 1994*, New York: Basic Books, p. 129.

3   Paul O'Higgins (1972) *Censorship in Britain*, London: Nelson.

4   O'Higgins, *Censorship*, p. 130.

5   Much, but not all, of the following chronology is drawn from a Channel 4 television information sheet, 'Banned', published in association with the British Film Institute and *New Statesman and Society* in 1990 as a companion to a documentary series shown at the time.

6   Darnton, 'Censorship', p. 112.

7   Examples drawn once again from 'Banned'.

8   Eric Hobsbawm (1994) *Age of Extremes: The Short Twentieth Century 1914–1991*, London: Michael Joseph, p. 388.

9   Hobsbawm, *Age of Extremes*, p. 113.

10   Hobsbawm, *Age of Extremes*, p. 115.

11   Hobsbawm, *Age of Extremes*, p. 123.

12   Hobsbawm, *Age of Extremes*.

13   Human Rights Watch/American Civil Liberties Union (1993) *Human Rights Violations in the United States*, New York and Washington: Human Rights Watch and American Civil Liberties Union, p. 149.

14   Examples once again taken from 'Banned'.

15 Examples both taken, once again, from 'Banned'.

16 Adapted from Darnton, *Censorship*, p. 114.

17 HRW/ACLU, *Human Rights Violations*, p. 150.

18 HRW/ACLU, *Human Rights Violations*, pp. 159–61.

19 O'Higgins, *Censorship in Britain*.

20 For a decent overview of the 'marketplace of ideas' theory, and some applications in the American context, see C. Edwin Barker (1992) *Human Liberty and Freedom of Speech*, New York: Oxford University Press.

21 John Stuart Mill (1987, original 1859) *On Liberty*, Harmondsworth: Penguin, Chapter 11.

22 See Nigel Warburton (2001) *Freedom: An Introduction with Readings*, London: Routledge, Chapter 4, for a good discussion of these claims.

23 Rodney A. Smolla (1994) 'Free Speech is Essential for Democratic Self-Governance' in Bruno Leone (ed.) *Free Speech*, San Diego: Greenhaven Press. Originally from Smolla (1992) *Free Speech in an Open Society*, New York: Alfred A. Knopf.

24 Smolla, 'Free Speech', p. 151.

25 Seamus Milne and Polly Toynbee (1994) 'Fear in the Airing' in the *Guardian* Monday, 2 May.

26 Milne and Toynbee, 'Fear in the Airing', p. 14.

27 For a good introduction to the complexities of Habermas's argument, see William Outhwaite (1994) *Habermas: A Critical Introduction*, Cambridge: Polity Press.

28 Leone, *Free Speech*.

29 Gerald Gunther (1994) 'All Speech Should Be Unrestricted on College Campuses' in Leone, *Free Speech*, p. 76; originally 'Is There Ever a Good Reason to Restrict Free Speech on a College Campus? – No', in *This World*, 9 September, 1990.

30 Nat Hentoff (1994) 'Campus Speech Codes are Incompatible with Free Speech' in Leone, *Free Speech*, p. 81; originally 'Speech Codes on the Campus and Problems of Free Speech' in *Dissent*, Fall 1991.

31 Charles Lawrence (1994) 'Racist Speech Should be Restricted on College Campuses' in Leone, *Free Speech*, pp. 104–5; originally 'Is There Ever a Good Reason to Restrict Free Speech on a College Campus? – Yes' in *This World*, 9 September, 1990.

32 Lawrence, 'Racist Speech', p. 106.

33   See Judith Lichtenberg (ed.) (1990) *Democracy and the Mass Media*, Cambridge: Cambridge University Press. See also Claudia Mills (1994) 'Regulation of the Press is Needed' in Leone, *Free Speech*, p. 126; originally 'Freedom and Fairness: Regulating the Mass Media' in *OO: Report from the Institute for Philosophy and Public Policy*, Fall 1986.

34   The testimony of Sanar Yurdatapan was presented to the 1997 Annual General Meeting of Amnesty International UK Section in Belfast, and reproduced in *Amnesty International*, May 1997, pp. 6–7.

35   Adrian Wilkes (1986) 'Freedom of Information' in James Curran, Jake Ecclestone, Giles Oakley and Alan Richardson (eds) *Bending Reality: The State of the Media*, London: Pluto Press, p. 229.

36   From Michael Crowley (1992) 'Thought Crimes' in *Amnesty*, December/January, pp. 18–19.

37   Herbert Marcuse (1991, original 1964) *One-Dimensional Man: Studies in the Ideology of Advanced Industrial Society*, London: Routledge.

38   Crowley, 'Thought Crimes', p. 19.

39   This table is adapted from Rajeev Bhavan and Christie Davies (1978) *Censorship and Obscenity*, London: Martin Robertson, p. 22.

40   Bhavan and Davies, *Censorship*.

41   See Nettie Pollard (1993) 'The Modern Pornography Debate' in *Media, Law and Practice*, Vol. 14, No. 4.

42   For example, see Andrea Dworkin (1979) *Pornography*, Harmondsworth: Penguin. Similar views are discussed in Catherine Ibzin (ed.) (1992) *Pornography: Women, Violence and Civil Liberties*, Oxford: Oxford University Press. For an overview of the debates, see Gillian Rodgerson and Elizabeth Wilson (eds) (1991) *Pornography and Feminism: The Case Against Censorship*, London: Lawrence & Wishart.

43   Andrea Dworkin (1994) 'Pornography Debases Women and Should Be Censored' in Leone, *Free Speech*, p. 169; originally in Dworkin (1979) *Pornography*.

44   See Alison Assiter and Avedon Carol (1993) *Bad Girls and Dirty Pictures: The Challenge to Reclaim Feminism*, London: Pluto Press.

45   Wendy McElroy (1994) 'Censoring Pornography Endangers Feminism' in Leone, *Free Speech*, p. 188; originally 'The Unholy Alliance' in *Liberty*, February 1993.

46   Jean Seaton (1986) 'Pornography Annoys' in Curran *et al.*, *Bending Reality*.

47   Melissa Benn (1986) 'Campaigning Against Pornography' in Curran *et al.*, *Bending Reality*.

48   McElroy, 'Censoring Pornography', p. 198.

49   *Stanley vs Georgia* (1969), cited in McElroy, 'Censoring Pornography', p. 193.

50   Germaine Greer (1984) *Sex and Destiny*, London: Chatto.

51   Karl Popper (1966; original 1943) *The Open Society and Its Enemies*, London: Routledge.

52   Barrington Moore, Jr (1966) *Social Origins of Dictatorship and Democracy: Lord and Peasant in the Making of the Modern World*, Harmondsworth: Penguin.

53   Hannah Arendt (1951) *The Origins of Totalitarianism*, New York: Harcourt Brace.

54   Marcuse, *One-Dimensional Man*.

55   Louis Althusser (1972) 'Ideology and Ideological State Apparatuses' in B.R. Cosin (ed.) *Education: Structure and Society*, Harmondsworth: Penguin.

56   Curry Jansen, *Censorship*, p. 16.

57   Curry Jansen, *Censorship*, p. 24.

58   Curry Jansen, *Censorship*, pp. 24–5.

Further information

Books

There is no shortage of books covering different aspects of censorship. The collection of debates gathered by Bruno Leone (ed.) *Free Speech* (San Diego: Greenhaven Press, 1994) is rather repetitive, and focuses primarily on civil liberties in the context of the United States Constitution, rather than on human rights, but it is still an entertaining read. Students interested in aspects of the censorship debate may find themselves shifting back and forth across the library, from constitutional law to moral philosophy by way of media studies. From a media studies perspective, a number of useful articles on the relationship between the media and the state, with reference to such topics as freedom of information and the debates over pornography, can be found in James Curran, Jake Ecclestone, Giles Oakley and Alan Richardson (eds) *Bending Reality: The State and the Media* (London: Pluto Press, 1986).

Web pages

The Campaign for Freedom of Information can be accessed on www.cfoi.org.uk. Feminists against Censorship can be contacted on www.fiawol.demon.co.uk/FAC. The widely respected journal *Index on Censorship* also has a homepage, found at www.indexonline.org. There's also Article 19, the British-based campaigning organisation for freedom of expression and information, which is found on www.article19.org. Before accessing any of these, though, the interested reader – whether she is intellectually curious, or simply in defiant mood – should check out the Freedom Links page on censorship at www.mathaba.net/www/censorship. This contains a vast list of web pages related to censorship. Some are academic or activist sites, some are government sites, while others are geared towards consumers searching for banned material. Feminism, freedom of information, banned music, and (of course) censorship of the Internet all get a mention.

CHAPTER FOUR

Political prisoners

> All are equal before the law and are entitled without any
> discrimination to equal protection of the law. All are entitled to equal
> protection against any discrimination in violation of this Declaration
> and against any incitement to such discrimination.
>
> *Universal Declaration of Human Rights, Article 7*

> No one shall be subjected to arbitrary arrest, detention or exile.
>
> *Universal Declaration of Human Rights, Article 9*

> Everyone is entitled in full equality to a fair and public hearing by an
> independent and impartial tribunal, in the determination of his rights
> and obligations and of any criminal charge against him.
>
> *Universal Declaration of Human Rights, Article 10*

What is a political prisoner?

It is commonly held to be a feature of advanced democratic societies that
a clear separation exists between politics and the law, or the executive
and judiciary. Indeed, legal autonomy is often regarded as an essential
check on political power. Articles 9 and 10 of the Universal Declaration,
cited above, clearly state that the judiciary and its agents, such as the
police, cannot perform their duties in any manner that might be partial
or arbitrary. A trial, for example, must be fair, and for it to be fair the
judicial process must be free from interference from the executive.

This presupposes, of course, that the prisoner is even brought to
trial. Despite the wording of these Articles, international law still permits
governments to exercise administrative detention, or internment, in
emergency situations where it is considered the best possible option.
Administrative detention can be described as 'detention by the executive

branch of government without a judicial warrant, without the filing of any criminal charge and without the intention of bringing the detainee to trial'.[1] Each of these three clauses appears to violate the principles of justice.

Article 9 is admirably to the point. Its intentions are presented in more detail in the International Covenant on Civil and Political Rights, Article 9, the European Convention on Human Rights, Article 5, and the American Convention on Human Rights, Article 7, each of which lists the rights due to anyone who has been arrested or detained. These rights include the right to be informed of the reasons for the arrest and of the specific charges being made; the right upon detention to take the matter to court so that the court may decide upon the lawfulness of the arrest; and the right to compensation for wrongful arrest. Article 9 of the Political Covenant ends with the demand that 'no one shall be deprived of his liberty except on such grounds and in accordance with such procedures as are established by law'.[2] The consequences of this demand are that the powers of the executive are duly curtailed, and that 'not every policeman (or other state functionary) is entitled to decide at his discretion, and on his own responsibility, who can be arrested, why and how'.[3] In so far as detention is permissible, it must therefore be 'in accordance with law but also in conformity to the principles of justice'.[4] These principles of justice are further secured through Article 10, which clearly lays out the conditions within which any judicial process is permitted to take place – it must be *fair* (impartial) and *public* (open to public scrutiny).

This chapter is dedicated to charting how, in various ways, legal systems have served as mere agents of political systems, how political agendas have manipulated the law. The noble idea of justice is the idea that the law is there to protect us all. In the wrong hands, though, the law is a dangerous weapon that can be, and often is, directed against those who pose the greatest threats to the political regime. The sanction of the law – the power of imprisonment – can take many forms. An Amnesty International report from 1980 provides a chilling introduction:

An estimated 15,000 people 'disappear' in one country and, in another, 25,000 people are seized, 'disappear' or are killed . . .

In a third country, the wife of an imprisoned nationalist leader serves out another 24 hours of a 'banning' order, the latest in a series that has ruled every day of her life for the past 16 years . . .

In a fourth, a trade unionist is detained by the police for the 24th time in two years . . .

> The vast majority of these people, political prisoners – the cases of thousands of them documented in detail by AI – have been subjected to some kind of imprisonment that falls outside the usual sense of the word – that is, confinement in some official place of detention for a specified period.
>
> They are victims of different 'faces' of imprisonment; in these cases: 'disappearance'; 'banning'; house arrest; internal exile; repressive short-term detention.[5]

We could probably say much more on each of these types of imprisonment and more besides. We could ask, as social scientists, what constitutes a prison, in the context of seeking an understanding of 'house' arrest. 'Disappearances' are discussed in this chapter as the most extreme form of political imprisonment, of punishment without trial. Torture, which is omitted from the above list but is nevertheless closely associated with political imprisonment, is discussed in the next chapter. Indeed, although I have called this chapter 'Political prisoners', we should bear in mind that political *imprisonment* is not a human rights violation *per se*. It is included here because it is associated with certain other violations – arbitrary arrest and detention, unfair trials, torture, 'disappearances'. In other words, the primary human rights concern is *how certain governments deal with – or dispose of – their political opponents*. In this chapter I will treat imprisonment not as a condition but as a process, and thus dedicate time to the various stages of this process, and various aspects and types of detention and types of detainee, specifically:

1 the *policing* process; including policing strategies and arbitrary arrests;

2 the *trial* and *imprisonment* stage as applied to political prisoners;

3 the specific group of political prisoners known as *prisoners of conscience*;

4 types of imprisonment not involving conventional prisons, such as house arrest, exile and banishment;

5 'disappearances' as the ultimate form of political imprisonment.

I will tentatively suggest how theorists might want to try to make sense of these, perhaps using Max Weber's account of the rationalisation of the modern state, Louis Althusser's theory of 'repressive state apparatuses', or Niklas Luhmann's contributions to the sociology of law. To put these into perspective, however, we should use as our starting point Emile Durkheim's distinction between 'religious criminality' and 'human criminality'.[6] The former applies to acts which are considered disruptive to the moral order of the community, the social structure. These acts of sacrilege are carried out not only against formal religion but also against the various institutions of civil religion, namely, the state and its agents. Given the severity of these offences against the social order, and the insignificance of the offender *vis-à-vis* the target of the offence, harsh, violent punishments seemed appropriate. In an analysis which was to have a huge influence on the work of Michel Foucault, Durkheim suggested that the progress of modernity saw the attention shift away from these acts of treason towards human criminality: crimes carried out against individuals. However, traces of this demarcation remained embedded in the legal systems of most countries. For example, the death penalty has been kept on the statutes of many nation-states for political crimes long after it has been abolished for ordinary crimes. In all respects, political prisoners constitute a wholly different group from ordinary prisoners. In truth, political action is about the achievement and maintenance of power, and thus, from the point of view of the state, no crime is greater than that which threatens this agenda. Governments are willing to resort to extreme methods to silence their enemies. In our discussion of 'disappearances' we will come across a fascinating and disturbing consideration: that for a government to go to such lengths to cover up its atrocities, it must be aware of the evil of its actions; it is, therefore, clearly driven not by an ideological commitment to its cause, but by the desperate need to maintain power, at all costs.

Before I address these different stages in the process, I will provide a brief history of political imprisonment.

A brief history of political prisoners

Search with only minimal industry throughout the historical texts and it will soon become apparent that history is littered with references to political imprisonment. They appear throughout classical history and mythology, and throughout biblical and post-biblical history and literature; these narratives are rife with tales of how enemies of one king or another, or heretics or blasphemers, are imprisoned and, in most cases, executed for their views. Philosophers who dared to question conventional wisdom suffered for their beliefs. Christian theologians may remind us that Jesus was persecuted, imprisoned and arrested for expressing his views, which were considered dangerous by the state and its agents. Medieval history contains many tales of the ransom of kings, captured during one or another expedition into foreign lands. Indeed, wars were often financed through the capture of kings or noblemen. In cases such as these, political prisoners were prisoners of honour, of nobility. Exiles and banishments were also common throughout this period of history. English kings and queens of the later middle ages kept political prisoners in the Tower of London, not a place for ordinary criminals. Elizabeth, to take one example among many, imprisoned her sister Mary. Conspirators, revolutionaries and would-be assassins were also imprisoned and tortured behind these dark walls. In France, one of the most celebrated cases concerns Lieutenant Alfred Dreyfus, a Jew in the French army who, in 1864, was arrested, court-martialled, imprisoned on Devil's Island, and, in 1899, finally pardoned, in respect of charges of passing military secrets to the Germans.[7]

And yet, despite this rich history of political imprisonment, there is little mention of the term 'political prisoners' in most of the major encyclopedias of world history. Perhaps it is easy for us, with hindsight, to recast these celebrated historical cases in this light. Indeed, the idea of a 'political crime' emerged primarily during the nineteenth century; 'prior to the French Revolution, most crimes against political rulers were defined as "treason" or . . . crimes against sacred authority'.[8] Such offenders were usually punished using the most extreme, painful methods, as Michel Foucault points out in his vivid description of the execution of Damiens, the regicide.[9] However, as sensitivities changed in the nineteenth century, so did the image of the political criminal, who was seen as increasingly noble, motivated 'neither by private avarice nor by vindictiveness', and punishable by more lenient and political treatment than would apply to ordinary criminals.[10] In Britain, especially, political prisoners were treated with considerable respect. All of this changed in the twentieth century. From the First World War onwards, attitudes towards political criminals became increasingly negative and punishments became harsher; 'the "political criminal" was transformed into the "arch-criminal"'.[11] Our appreciation of the plight of political prisoners in the here and now – and in other parts of the world – is a relatively recent development, and there is little doubt that a lot of it is due to the post-war concern with human rights and with the work of campaigning organisations like Amnesty International.

As we saw in Chapter Two, Amnesty International was first established because one man took an interest in the plight of three students, each of them sentenced to seven years' imprisonment in their native Portugal for toasting freedom. Peter Benenson, the concerned man in question, was inspired by this atrocity to write his article in the *Observer*, 'The Forgotten Prisoners', which first made use of the phrase 'prisoners of conscience'. Benenson concentrated on eight such prisoners in his article, each from a different background, each espousing a different cause or belief. Agostino Neto was a doctor and poet imprisoned without trial by the Portuguese authorities in Angola because of his beliefs and his healthcare work. Constantin Noica had been sentenced to twenty-five years' imprisonment by the Romanian authorities for allegedly spreading anti-communist propaganda. Ashton Jones, a minister, was imprisoned in America's segregated Deep South for demanding equality for blacks. A Spanish lawyer, Antonio Amat, had been imprisoned for three years without trial for his political activities. The Czechoslovakian authorities had imprisoned Archbishop Josef Beran of Prague for non-criminal reasons. A white South African, Joseph Duncan, was in prison because he spoke out against apartheid. The primate of Hungary, Cardinal Mindszenty, had been a prisoner and was now a political refugee, trapped in the American embassy in Budapest.

This is a diverse list. Today, it is believed that over half of the member states of the United Nations still hold political prisoners. This is, of course, a vague term, and not always useful in helping us understand the issues at stake. Some political prisoners are also criminal prisoners, in so far as they have broken the law. Many are terrorists. The United Kingdom holds a number of political prisoners – mostly IRA soldiers – in its Maze facility in Northern Ireland. Others, though, are prisoners of conscience, who have been imprisoned solely because of their political or ideological beliefs or their social or physical characteristics.

It is not unreasonable to suggest that in respect of political imprisonment China has one of the world's worst records. Much of this is to do with its treatment of Tibetans and those who advocate Tibetan independence. According to the International Campaign for Tibet:

> During the anti-rightist campaign of the late 1950s, tens of thousands of Tibetans were sent to labor camps for criticizing communism or the Communist Party and for the ideological crime of "local nationalism". Thousands more were imprisoned because of their social or economic status during the revolts against Chinese rule, which swept Tibet from 1956 until 1959. During the Cultural Revolution tens of thousands of Tibetans were also sent to labor camps for aiding or sympathizing with the revolts. During and after the demonstrations of 1987–89, Tibetans were detained for long periods without charge or were sentenced to prison for peacefully advocating Tibetan independence.[12]

The same report goes on to suggest that while the number of political prisoners in Tibet has declined in recent years – approximately 300 documented political prisoners in 2001 – the situation is far from ideal. Arbitrary arrest, arbitrary detention, denial of access to legal counsel, and torture are all common policing tactics against 'counter-revolutionaries' who commit such dreadful crimes as flying the Tibetan flag or singing protest songs. At present, the average prison sentence among these dissidents is 8 years, 8 months.

I have highlighted the case of Tibet because it is well documented, but these human rights violations – arbitrary arrest, arbitrary detention, unfair trials, and so on – are by no means limited to any one part of the world. In most cases, the capture and imprisonment of political prisoners and dissidents is left not to the ordinary police but to special units and death squads. Let us turn now to the issue of political policing.

Political policing

Political interference in the machinery of 'justice' takes place on various levels and at various stages. Indeed, it cannot be reduced to a simple matter of internal politics. The sociologist Martha Huggins has conducted an extraordinary study of United States involvement in internal policing structures and strategies in other countries.[13] Huggins points out that although US Congress abolished programmes aimed at assisting foreign police forces in 1973/1974, by the early 1990s there were still at least 125 such programmes in operation which were considered exempt from the ruling.[14] Although these are justified on 'legitimate' grounds, Huggins notes that there is a rich history of US involvement in the internal policing affairs of other nation-states, aimed primarily at securing allies to combat perceived threats and carry out strategic military and economic ends.[15] This is especially true in Latin America. Thus, through police assistance and training, foreign policy is transformed into an extension of domestic policy:[16]

In other words, as the United States trains foreign police, it can establish intelligence and other social control infrastructure for protecting and strengthening its position vis-à-vis the recipient country and maximise its position within the international world system. This makes foreign police assistance – whether publicly recognized or not – fundamentally political, although of course this has not usually been a publicized motive behind U.S. assistance to foreign police.[17]

Huggins concludes that the logic and rationale behind overseas police training is riddled with contradictions and inconsistencies. However, these are in some respects reflections of an inherent tension in the relationship between policing and politics. The police has always been held up as a democratic servant of the people, separated from the political structures of the state. However, clearly, increasing *professionalisation* has always been more about developing more efficient means of social control than about improving police skills or accountability. The twin myths of democratic professionalisation and political neutrality have allowed the police to act as an agent of social control in a more covert manner – its role in protecting class interests and institutional hierarchies is obscured through a public perception of autonomy.[18] Huggins understands this within a theoretical framework informed in part by Weber's theory of bureaucratic rationalisation. If this is the case in 'democratic' countries, then it is hardly surprising to learn that these inconsistencies are even more apparent in overseas training programmes. If the ostensible intention has been to 'democratise' the policing structures and strategies of the recipient country, the actual result has been an increasing *authoritarianisation* and *militarisation* of the recipient force, which has duly become less humane, less respectful of citizens' rights:

> "[M]odernization" and "professionalization" have unintended (or sometimes intended) consequences that contradict the assumption that the processes always lead to greater constraint on police toward legality and justice.[19]

Huggins describes at length the strategies employed in Brazil following the 1964 coup to make efficient use of the police in the new government's systematic clean-up of the country. This of course involved the purging of the country of communists or other potential insurgents. Processes of centralisation and devolution and the application of systematic violence were developed; the hitherto regionally appointed police became a centrally controlled resource, and from this centralisation came the devolution of the force into specialised units which became the death squads.[20]

Political prisoners and just punishment

As we have already seen, briefly, in Chapter Two, the campaigning organisation Amnesty International works for fair, prompt, and open trials for all political prisoners, and demands the immediate release of all prisoners of conscience. One of the problems faced by organisations like Amnesty International is actually defining who is, and who is not, a political prisoner, and, related to this, distinguishing between prisoners of conscience and other political prisoners. For example, students learning about the organisation are often surprised to hear that Nelson Mandela, during his long years of captivity in South Africa, was never adopted by Amnesty as a prisoner of conscience, and so they never campaigned for his release. They did, of course, highlight his case as a political prisoner and called for him to be treated accordingly. However, his former wife, Winnie Mandela, was adopted as a prisoner of conscience. So what is the difference, and does the distinction actually matter?

What does it mean to say that one is imprisoned on political grounds? First, we must be clear about the meaning of 'political' in this context. It cannot be reduced to a strict definition based on political affiliation. That is to say, it does not merely mean the imprisonment of those who belong to different political movements. It is more to do with political action, or rather the *politicisation of identity*. Thus, activists who campaign on behalf of their ethnicity, gender, sexuality, religion, or so on, are duly politicising their respective cultural or gender identifications. This is clearly a contested point, but identities only become politicised when they are situated *vis-à-vis* structural conditions. 'I am a woman' is a statement of gender identity, but 'I am a woman *within a system of patriarchy*' situates that gender identity within a political framework.[21]

In other words, we must distinguish between an institutionalist definition of 'politics' and a more general one. In respect of the latter, the insights of Michel Foucault are particularly useful. According to Foucault, the development of structures of power is tightly interwoven with the development of cultural discourses. So, the definition of 'political prisoners' necessarily relies upon the discursive construction of the 'political'. Of course, such a perspective necessarily understands the entire system of legal and punitive structures as political institutions, because they serve to reinforce the structures of social control (in much the same way as Althusser understands political and legal institutions as repressive state apparatuses which police the reproduction of ideologies).

Let us consider three scenarios which may involve political prisoners. First, according to both the institutionalist and the Foucauldian definitions, you would certainly be a political prisoner if you were arrested whilst campaigning for equal rights for women within a patriarchal society. How you choose to campaign – that is to say, whether you choose to operate within or outside the law – is at this stage irrelevant. You may have committed a crime, but that crime was committed not in or for itself but as part of a particular political project. But you would also be a political prisoner if you were arrested without having taken part in any such campaign, simply because you happened to be a woman. In a society where women are arrested arbitrarily for no other reason than because they are women, basic human rights are clearly being violated. Clearly, the Foucaldian perspective would incorporate this passive definition of political prisoners, and, in so far as the prisoner cannot be labelled an 'ordinary' criminal, so would the institutionalist definition.

So far, so good. But what if you were arrested whilst committing, say, a burglary? Let us assume at this point that you are not a political activist of any sort, that you have no interest in involving yourself with anti-patriarchal protest. In most cases, the fact that you are a woman is irrelevant – you are a burglar, your burglary is not intended to be some kind of political gesture, you have been caught and convicted. It is a simple case of criminal law. But what if, in this patriarchal state, you were sentenced to 15 years' imprisonment instead of the usual five? Do you become a political prisoner because you have been a victim of the structural inequalities within the judicial system?

If so, we already have three distinct types of political prisoner. The first is arrested first and foremost because of their political activities (a man on the anti-patriarchy demonstration may suffer the same treatment). The second is detained because the state has decided to treat their views, or personal characteristics, in much the same way as it would treat ordinary criminal activity. The third is clearly arrested as an ordinary criminal, but then indirectly becomes the victim of inconsistencies in the system. Should we treat them all the same? While they are all subject to the political whims of a particular ideology, there are important differences between them, which has implications for campaigning strategies. In the case of the burglar, we would not condone her criminal occupation but we might feel obliged to campaign for the reduction of her sentence, and also to campaign for a change in the law of that country. In the case of the second example, we would probably ask what crime this person had committed. None, would be the answer. In the name of justice, then, we would find it extremely difficult to justify their continued imprisonment and we would demand their immediate release. The same would probably apply to the first example, if the political activities were demonstrably peaceful and lawful. However, activists very often resort to extreme measures to get their point across; violence, or its advocacy, is not uncommon. How are we to treat people who knowingly break the law in order to make a political point? In this section we will concentrate on two extreme types of political prisoner: those labelled 'prisoners of conscience', and those labelled 'terrorists' or 'freedom fighters'.

Prisoners of conscience

The term 'prisoners of conscience' was first used by Peter Benenson, the founder of Amnesty International, in his *Observer* newspaper article, 'The Forgotten Prisoners'. Today, it is widely used to describe those people imprisoned not for having committed a crime but for who they are and what they believe. A useful summary and definition can be taken from the Amnesty website:

> In many countries people are detained for trying to exercise their rights to freedom of expression, association, assembly, or movement. Some are imprisoned because they or their families are involved in political or religious activities. Some are arrested because of their connection with political parties or national minority movements that oppose government policies. Trade Union activity or participation in strikes or demonstrations is a common cause of imprisonment. Often people are imprisoned simply because they questioned their military service on grounds of conscience. Others are jailed on the pretext that they committed a crime, but it is in fact because they criticized the government. People who are imprisoned, detained or otherwise physically restricted because of their political, religious or other conscientiously held beliefs or because of their ethnic origin, sex, colour, or language and who have not used or advocated violence are considered by Amnesty International to be prisoners of conscience.
>
> Prisoners of conscience are held by governments in all regions of the world; in countries with diverse political and social systems. Some prisoners of conscience are held for actions undertaken as individuals; others are part of a group or a movement. Some have spoken in direct opposition to the government in power or the established system or government; others have taken care to work within their countries' political system but have been imprisoned for their beliefs or peaceful activities nonetheless.[22]

© Amnesty International Publications, www.amnesty.org

This definition actually includes a number of different types of prisoner. There is, for example, a considerable difference between people who are imprisoned because of their political (using the term in its broadest sense) activities – marking them as 'enemies of the state' – and those who are imprisoned because of their pre-social characteristics, such as Jews imprisoned by Nazis *simply because they were Jewish.* In respect of the former group, China, as we have seen, is known to be a consistent offender, liberally imprisoning peaceful activists who demand independence for Tibet. One report suggests that, by the end of 1997, some 1,216 known Tibetan prisoners of conscience and political prisoners were being held in Chinese prisons in Tibet.[23] Among them, the report lists three people arrested in 1996 for possessing photographs of the Dalai Lama, as well as five nuns – aged between 21 and 29 – who have been sentenced for periods ranging from 12 to 17 years for recording songs and poems whilst imprisoned. Other 'crimes' include displaying the Tibetan flag, distributing pamphlets, and posting 'Free Tibet' posters on walls. Ngawang Phulchung, a monk, was sentenced in 1989 to 19 years' imprisonment for producing 'counter-revolutionary' literature, including a Tibetan translation of the Universal Declaration of Human Rights.

With regard to the second group, to imprison someone on the grounds of their pre-social characteristics, rather than for their criminal activities, seems antithetical to any system of law, but what, precisely, is a *crime*? If one treats law solely as *positive law*, isolated from morality, then a crime is whatever is defined as a crime by the agents of the state. To understand such imprisonment we must return to the origins of contemporary human rights theory in *natural law*. To say that I am worthy of punishment because of some pre-social characteristic, such as the colour of my skin, is as ridiculous as to declare that from now on blood must be pumped from the liver and not the heart. Such things are beyond my power to control, and so I cannot be held responsible for them. This seems wholly logical, and yet it can only make sense in practice if positive law is grounded in natural law. If we understand the development of legal systems in modernity along the lines of Niklas Luhmann's theory of 'hyper-differentiation', we begin to make some theoretical sense of the separation of law from morality. Law thus becomes an autonomous instrument of power, to be appropriated by the dominant agents of the state. And if law becomes subject to such relativism – a social construction – so, too, does humanity itself, or those to whom the law applies. As Zygmunt Bauman – following Hannah Arendt – has observed, the Nazis reconstructed the accountability of their Jewish victims by redefining guilt, by claiming that it is possible for someone to be guilty at birth. In other words, the Jews were 'guilty' not of committing a 'sin' but an 'evil'.[24]

If one adopts an extreme realist perspective, this separation of the law from morality could be justified in the interests of national security. Despite Hobbes's natural law approach, subsequent realists have usually taken a more pragmatic, consequentialist stance, rejecting appeals to abstract ideals such as morality in favour of empirical observations and rational calculations. Legal positivists also maintain that the law must be treated separately from morality.

As we have seen, there are various types of prisoner of conscience, and because of the often complicated conditions inherent in this definition (e.g. the grey area of what constitutes violence), it is not always easy to locate them all within a general framework. For example, as a pacifist, I may object to my country requiring me to undergo national service or even to play an active part in warfare. As a conscientious objector, am I a prisoner of conscience if I am punished for such refusal? Here is Amnesty International's response to this question:

A conscientious objector is understood to be a person liable to conscription for military service who, for reasons of conscience or profound conviction arising from religious, ethical, moral, humanitarian, philosophical, political or similar motives refuses to perform armed service or participate directly or indirectly in wars or armed conflicts.

Amnesty International considers such a person a prisoner of conscience if his or her imprisonment arises from any of the following:

- The legal code of a country does not contain provisions for the recognition of conscientious objection and for a person to register his or her objection at a specific time;

- A person is refused the right to register his or her objection;

- The authorities' recognition of conscientious objection is so restricted that only some and not all of the above grounds of conscience are acceptable;

- A person does not have the right to claim conscientious objection after being conscripted into the armed forces;

- He or she is imprisoned for leaving the armed forces without authorization for reasons of conscience developed after being conscripted if he or she has tried to secure his or her release by lawful means or if he or she did not use those means because he or she had been deprived of reasonable access to the knowledge of them;

■   There is no right to service outside the 'war machine';

■   The length of the alternative service can be seen as a punishment for conscientious objection.

A person who is not willing to state the reason for his or her refusal to perform military service is not adopted as a prisoner of conscience, unless it can be inferred from all the circumstances of the case that the refusal is based on conscientious objection. Nor is someone considered a prisoner of conscience if he or she is offered and refuses comparable alternative service outside the 'war machine'.[25]

© Amnesty International Publications, www.amnesty.org

These conditions are fascinating in many respects, because they throw up many of the complexities associated with defining someone as a prisoner of conscience. The first situation concerns the legal *structure* of the nation-state in question. The second concerns the possible abuse of that legal structure. The third is almost philosophical in nature, charging the legal structure with a non-universalist conception of rights. The fourth and fifth recognise the transient nature of opinions, and plainly demand that an individual not only has the right to refuse to join, but also has the right to resign, at any time, from her or his military service. The fifth, interestingly, recognises this right to resign, but makes it clear that simple desertion is only acceptable under certain circumstances, and that the objector should make every effort to work within the system. It also returns us to the issue raised in the previous chapter about access to information. The final two points recognise the need for a fair alternative to military service – the 'war machine'. The objector should not be required to play any part in this machinery – the distinction is not between active service in the field and a comfortable job behind a desk or in a factory. The 'war machine' is the very structure of the means of violence. How – especially in times of war – is one ever not part of it?

'Terrorists' and 'freedom fighters'

Prisoners of conscience represent one type of political prisoner. However, many political prisoners cannot be termed 'prisoners of conscience' because they have, to some degree, used or advocated the use of violence. Clearly, not all such prisoners can be labelled 'terrorists'. Nevertheless, terrorists are an extreme, and interesting, type of political prisoner. At the heart of the problem of terrorism is the problem of determining what might be 'justifiable violence' for a 'legitimate cause'. According to Baljit Singh, terrorism can be described as:

> ... [T]he result of a conscious decision by ideologically inspired groups to strike back at what their members perceive as unjust within a given society or polity.[26]

Terrorists, then, are engaged in what we might call 'private wars' against an unjust state. The violence itself is often seen as a last resort, and in many cases justified as a necessary reaction to *state* violence. McLaughlin is right to pose two closely connected questions regarding the use of violence against the state.[27] First, can violence ever be treated as a legitimate means of achieving a political end? Second, how do we deal with those criminals who have used violence for such a purpose?

The first question leads us frustratingly into a sea of other uncertainties. Must we always obey the law, however unjust it may be? Clearly not, for most political philosophy – even that attributed to so-called 'authoritarians' such as Macchiavelli and Hobbes – stands firm in its belief in the importance of a benevolent state and in the ultimate power of the citizen and subject to overthrow a malevolent one. But is violence ever the *only* means of changing the system? Some writers, committed to a belief in human rationality and the power of the better argument, would say no, and urge protestors to make use of the public sphere in mobilising public opinion. Hannah Arendt and Jürgen Habermas would both belong to this camp. Others would defend the right of an individual or group to use violence, in so far as it is used for legitimate ends, because it is a way of achieving immediate change, of overhauling the structural inequalities in a social system. Karl Marx might be included in such a group, as would critical theorists such as Franz Fanon and Herbert Marcuse, for whom violence is justifiable as a necessary means to an end and as a psychological cleansing force, restoring the self-respect of the oppressed peoples.[28]

In the end, 'terrorism' as a term is socially constructed: there are 'many historical examples of officially defined and labelled "terrorists" becoming rehabilitated as "freedom fighters" and, eventually, reborn as peace-makers and respected leaders of nation-states; and of successful "terrorist" campaigns being redefined and remembered as wars of liberation or independence'.[29] Terrorism is thus a loose and flexible concept, all things to all people. At the beginning of the twenty-first century, public attitudes towards terrorists are at their most negative. Opinion polls continue to show that the vast majority of British citizens favour the re-introduction of the death penalty for terrorists. After the events of 11 September 2001, the American people, under the leadership of President Bush, have entered into a 'war against terrorism'. Scholars of international law advise caution, warn the President that one can only wage war on another nation-state, and that terrorists are not soldiers but criminals and must be taken before a court of law. What punishment, though, is appropriate for the terrorist? Penological theory suggests that prisons serve to protect wider society (by incarcerating the criminal) while providing the criminal with an opportunity for rehabilitation and atonement. Are these theories applicable to political as well as criminal prisoners?

Exile and house arrest

Let us turn now to some of the other kinds of imprisonment – those which rarely apply to ordinary prisoners – mentioned in passing at the beginning of this chapter.

Imprisonment is, by its very nature, a denial of freedom. If Kant believed that freedom was our absolute right, then Arendt was clearly correct in pointing out that we violate it liberally whenever we legitimately send a criminal to jail. Imprisonment, however, is also a denial of *home*. Philosophers might wish to debate whether a sense of belonging is inherent in human nature. For sure, there are plenty of happy nomads wandering through this life without attachments. Most of us, though, probably consider ourselves homely creatures. Home represents the warmth and security we crave, our escape from the outside world. Home is familiarity, structure, routine, control. Home might be a house or an apartment, it might be a town or a city, it might be a region or a country. When criminals are sent to prison they are removed from this familiar world and relocated in one not of their own making. The same is true of political prisoners.

However, two alternative methods of political imprisonment take this denial of home to opposite extremes, and are certainly worthy of our consideration as social scientists. On the one hand, strategies of exile and banishment are, in contrast to imprisonment, *not* denials of freedom – they are quite overtly denials of home. On the other, house arrest strips home of its meaning by turning it *into* a prison.

Of course, the study of what constitutes home is a vast and complex labyrinth, and one not suitable for inclusion in these pages. Needless to say, it will make a further appearance later in this book, when we discuss the plight of refugees. In the social sciences, discussions of 'home' usually take in broader theoretical discussions of identity, memory, collective history, nostalgia. They usually draw on discussions of existential and ontological need. To be 'homeless' – in this broader sense – is to be dislocated from fixity, disembedded from the structures and institutions of modernity; to experience disenchantment, *anomie* and alienation. Some commentators might go so far as to suggest that such 'homelessness' is the quintessential modern condition.[30] It is no coincidence that the journalist John Simpson, in the introduction to his anthology of exile, confesses to the reader how from time to time, while collecting his entries, he found himself working on an anthology not of exile but of alienation.[31]

If this brief analysis applies to exile, what, then, of house arrest? This clearly takes us to a different but comparative level of analysis. Political prisoners are very often placed under house arrest, denied freedom of movement, denied also freedom from surveillance, but in a familiar space. One of the most famous examples of a political prisoner being placed under house arrest in recent years has been the case of Aung San Suu Kyi in Burma. The leader of the National League for Democracy and the legitimate leader of that country – her party won 80 per cent of the national vote during the 1990 election – she was placed under house arrest for six years by the military junta who refused to recognise the results. What, if any, are the sociological implications of the transformation of the home into a prison? Nothing less, one would imagine, than the ultimate denial of security, of a place of refuge, of privacy, of personal decency and autonomy. House arrest is the violation of personal space, and the stripping away from the prisoner of her or his sense of self-identity. Personal space extends, of course, beyond the home. Since Aung San Suu Kyi was released from house arrest, her movements have been severely restricted. If imprisonment in the traditional sense restricts freedom to a specific space, exile and house arrest both serve to transform the very meaning of our space and how we relate to it.

'Disappearances' and extra-judicial executions

The purpose of this chapter has been to show how political imprisonment constitutes a violation of the rule of law. The autonomy of the law is dissolved by the state, and the concept of justice is lost in the wilderness. All the agents of the law can be involved – the police, the courts – so political imprisonment can be understood as a process of selection and victimisation aimed at those who are considered 'enemies of the state'. But what happens when the state bypasses its legal system; when it targets and discriminates against its enemies without even a superficial recourse to the judicial process? This is what is at stake when one talks of 'disappearances' and 'extra-judicial executions'.

'Disappearances' necessarily bring together some of the worst kinds of human rights violations: arbitrary arrest, detention without trial, inhumane and degrading treatment, torture, murder, and the secret disposal of bodies.[32] Indeed, 'disappearances' might be viewed as a kind of politicide involving careful as opposed to indiscriminate targeting (we discuss politicides in Chapter Nine). The origins of 'disappearances' appear to lie with the Nazis' 'night and fog' decree, the spiriting away of suspected threats during the night.[33] The earliest recorded 'disappearances' took place in Guatemala in the 1960s.[34] In 1973, the practice of 'disappearing' one's political enemies – in practice, anyone thought to espouse liberal or left-leaning views – was adopted by General Augusto Pinochet in Chile, who killed some 4,000 people using this method.[35] Pinochet then initiated 'Operation Condor', effectively a gathering of leaders of Latin American dictatorships with a recommendation to extend the practice throughout the continent. It was adopted most notoriously by the Argentinian *junta*, which came to power in 1976, and later spread to parts of Africa and Asia.[36]

'Disappearances' are carried out by a secret police, which is established to work outside of the law, but in parallel with the official forces such as the police and the army. Many of the members of this secret police were former police officers or soldiers. They were often based in a series of secret locations and detention centres. Their primary function was to adopt extreme tactics to deal with the threat of left-wing insurrectionists.[37] Part of their mandate was to torture subversives for information, but their role was also to spread fear amongst the population.[38] They would kidnap their targets, often wearing masks to cover up their identities, and then take the hostages to their secret locations. Because they had no idea where they were being taken to, nor who their persecutors were, nor why they were even there, the victims of these kidnappings were facing the slow dismantling of their identities; cut off from the outside world, they barely knew they were even still alive.[39] The victims were tortured, then murdered, then buried in some unmarked grave. When relatives inquired about their whereabouts, the courts were powerless to do anything, the military did not care, and the government denied any knowledge of the 'disappeared'. These people had, quite simply, vanished into thin air![40]

As Antonio Cassese points out, the actions of the military dictatorship indicated a return to practices incongruous with modern rationality:

One of the characteristics of the Western-type modern state is that every individual, as well as having a name, surname, and proof of residence, is identifiable in his movements. If he has an accident, relatives and friends are 'activated', and the authorities carry out enquiries. In theory, the individual is not alone (at least externally) nor isolated from other members of civil society. Even if he is imprisoned in a place of detention, both relatives and the authorities keep track of his existence and his actions. Certificates, attestations and documents testify to his life and personal circumstances. Even the final event of his human existence, death, leaves its formal, external trace: certificates, stamps, markers of the death remain, a cross or some other symbol on a tomb, serve to indicate that a 'person' – having been materialized for a specific period of time in a specific place – has run his earthly course.

All of this was negated in Argentina by the simple decision of a group of generals. The external 'certainty' of the existence of people was 'cancelled out'. A 'subversive' could disappear into nothingness: for civil society and the state, it was as if he had never been born or existed. If our world, our real and interior world, is an immense labyrinth which in theory offers thousands of people pathways . . . then in Argentina in those years of horror, even the labyrinth disappeared . . . They were offered only cancellation from the 'register', annihilation of body and soul, and almost always, final 'disappearance'.[41]

What is a person if she is not even recognised by the law? This is the kind of question Hannah Arendt would ask. Indeed, it is a crucial one, for even where the legal system is merely a tool of a corrupt state, it is at least there to provide an insulting justification for the state's actions by *recognising* the individual in question as an 'enemy of the state'. We have already discussed some of the ways in which the state infiltrates and manipulates the judicial system to meet its own ends. Why, then, would the state deem it necessary to develop a practice which operates outside the law, rather than simply amend the law to make such a practice legitimate, or to find other ways to deal with one's opponents? Partly, the answer lies in the extremity of the methods adopted, so far beyond legitimation that no legal or military code would be allowed to endorse them.[42] Indeed, we might see the emergence of the practice of 'disappearances' as being a frightening consequence of the global awareness of human rights – things would have to be done in secret, because to do them openly would be to invite the disgust of the global political community.[43]

What does this tell us about the logic behind these atrocious practices? We should bear in mind that, by resorting to extra-legal methods, countries such as Chile and Argentina defied the trend associated with the modern nation-state: the trend identified by Weber towards bureaucratic rationalisation.[44] Such a trend demands that individuals' lives are ordered by laws, and subjected to meticulously detailed examination and monitoring. The Nazis in Germany and the South Africans under the apartheid regime were typical of this obsession with legalistic scrutiny. The South American dictatorships operated in total contradiction to this trend, but why? Cassese makes the important point that in those historical instances where extreme measures have been taken by the authorities – the Inquisition, the atrocities carried out in Nazi Germany and South Africa under apartheid – the perpetrators of these violations had no need to worry about the records they were keeping, or the actions they were taking, because they were driven by ideology, convinced that their actions were right and good.[45] From this, we might deduce that the authorities in Chile and Argentina carried out their kidnappings and tortures without any such delusion; they did so *despite* knowing that their actions were indefensible, and this makes them all the more terrifying.[46]

There is still much to be done with regard to reparation of the atrocities committed under the military *juntas*. One landmark decision was made, though, by the Inter-American Court in 1988, in the *Velasquez Rodriguez Case*, where the court held that the Honduran government could be held liable for the disappearance of a student activist and ordered to pay reparations to his family.[47]

The state, political prisoners and human rights

Does it seem natural to us, viewing it as we are from our particular place in time and space, that justice involves due process, accountability, and equality, and is achieved through an open legal system? As Foucault points out, in most European countries until the middle of the eighteenth century, trials were usually held in secret.[48] Even the accused was often unaware of the specific details of her or his case. This intense secrecy was in marked contrast, of course, with the openness of the punishment, which was a public spectacle. Little or no attention was given to the question of prisoners' *rights*. 'Innocent until proven guilty' is a comparatively recent statement of jurisprudence. The imposition of the *Miranda* ruling was met with hostile opposition from conservative forces in America who felt that, by granting suspects certain rights, the law was effectively restricting the powers of the police to carry out its duties. Small wonder that the ruling was followed by a wave of reactionary films that celebrated violence and individualism among police officers who refused to play by the rules and to surrender to bureaucracy, such as *The French Connection* and *Dirty Harry*.

Our concern, though, is not only with the extent to which a system of law-enforcement can be *accountable*, but also with the intrusion of an ideological, *politicised* rationality into the 'neutral' territory of the law. Has the law *ever* been neutral? Can it ever be neutral? While advocates of the theory of autonomous, hyper-differentiated, autopoietic social systems developed by Niklas Luhmann may view the law as an independent system operating and evolving according to its own internal dynamics, most commentators would treat this position with scepticism.[49] The object of politics is the maintenance of power in a given space, with a secondary aim being the expansion of power beyond its immediate territory. The object of law is the maintenance of social order. Historically, both have been defined territorially in terms of *nation-building*. For sure, a number of laws are drawn up from existing (non-political, often religious) sources – thus, murder becomes a criminal offence because it violates a holy Commandment. But how can one explain the emergence and proliferation of 'victimless crimes' or of crimes against abstract entities such as morality, the state, or the sovereign? Clearly, such laws are carefully devised political constructions aimed at enhancing the political project of (territorial) nation-building.[50] Indeed, there is some mileage in seeing, as Huggins does following Charles Tilly, the state as a kind of protection racket which creates a threat against which it uses its own resources to 'protect' the people, thus legitimising and strengthening its role as the centralised means of violence and control.[51]

Of course, in so far as political policing and imprisonment represents the overt operations of the repressive state apparatuses, it cannot be divorced from other concerns, notably torture and executions, which are dealt with in subsequent chapters of this book. Where repression is used liberally and openly, it might follow that its *actual* use declines, in part because the *threat* of it causes a degree of self-policing amongst the population. In other words, society itself becomes organised like a prison.[52] Needless to say, that is not to condone the use of extreme politicised policing techniques as a means of minimising the use of torture – far from it! It should, though, be kept in mind that there is, perhaps surprisingly, no tradition *per se* which might be called the 'social science of political imprisonment'. Foucault's critique of the *meaning* of the 'political' offers us a possible way in to this field. Recently, social science interests have – following the 'cultural turn' – evolved to incorporate an appreciation of *performance*. In other words, one cannot simply box prisoners into categories – criminal, political, and so on – without reference to how these labels are performed by those concerned. Political prisoners appear to have quite different relationships with their place of incarceration, their jailors, and their fellow inmates, and with the justice system as a whole, from non-political prisoners. These relationships are acted out in a series of performances ranging from overt forms of resistance (such as hunger strikes) to subtler bodily expressions. The mass media also play a part in this process, by narrating these stories of resistance and by defining (and redefining) in the public arena the constitution of a political prisoner. These are all interesting observations, and there is certainly scope here for a fascinating programme of research, but these are only suggestions for future developments, not empirical statements. In reality, political imprisonment is often considered within a broader framework associated with questions of the state and punishment in general, and, most significantly, the question of torture. In this chapter we have deliberately shied away from specific mention of torture and executions as repressive state strategies. This is because we now turn to these specific human rights violations in greater detail.

Essay questions

1. How might the presence of prisoners of conscience contradict the principles of law and justice?

2. Discuss the various strategies employed by states to disarm their political opponents.

3. Discuss the charge that the seedbed of terrorism is an unjust and violent state.

Notes

1   Scoop Cowley (1990/91) 'Mandate Review: Against Freedom' in *Amnesty*, 48, p. 21.

2   Richard B. Lillich (1984) 'Civil Rights' in Theodor Meron (ed.) *Human Rights in International Law: Legal and Policy Issues*, Oxford and New York: Oxford University Press.

3   Yoram Dinstein (1981) 'The Right to Life, Physical Integrity and Liberty' in Louis Henkin (ed.) *The International Bill of Rights: The Covenant on Civil and Political Rights*, New York: Columbia University Press, pp. 114, 130; cited in Lillich, 'Civil Rights'.

4   Lillich, 'Civil Rights'.

5   Originally from the Amnesty International newsletter, November 1980, reproduced as 'Different Faces of Imprisonment' in Amnesty International (1986) *Voices for Freedom: An Amnesty International Anthology*, London: Amnesty International Publications.

6   Emile Durkheim (1899–1900) 'Deux lois de l'évolution pénale' in *Année Sociologique* IV, pp. 65–95; English translation 'Two Laws of Penal Evolution' in Mike Game (ed.) *The Radical Sociology of Durkheim and Mauss*, London: Routledge.

7   For a good introduction to the Dreyfus affair, see David L. Lewis (1975) *Prisoners of Honor: The Dreyfus Affair*, London: Cassell.

8   Eugene McLaughlin (1996) 'Political Violence, Terrorism and Crimes of the State' in John Muncie and Eugene McLaughlin (eds) *The Problem of Crime*, London: Sage/Open University Press, p. 277.

9   Michel Foucault (1991; original 1975) *Discipline and Punish: The Birth of the Prison*, Harmondsworth: Penguin.

10   McLoughlin, 'Political Violence', pp. 277–8.

11   McLoughlin, 'Political Violence', p. 280.

12   International Campaign for Tibet, Position paper #2, updated June 2001, www.savetibet.org/background/paper_prisoners.html.

13   Martha K. Huggins (1998) *Political Policing: The United States and Latin America*, Durham, NC: Duke University Press.

14   Huggins, *Political Policing*, p. 1.

15   Huggins, *Political Policing*, p. 3; her book provides an illuminating and accessible history of Western – and especially US – interference in Latin American policing which I am unable to summarise here, but which is without a doubt worth consulting, particularly in so far as it locates these interventions within the wider framework of changing priorities in US foreign policy.

16   Huggins, *Political Policing*, p. 4; following Hannah Arendt (1951) *The Origins of Totalitarianism*, New York: Harcourt Brace, p. 421.

17   Huggins, *Political Policing*, p. 4.

18   Huggins, *Political Policing*, pp. 8–12; following Paul Chevigny (1995) *Edge of the Knife: Police Violence in the Americas*, New York: New Press; David Bayley (1990) *Patterns of Policing: A Comparative International Analysis*, New

Brunswick, NJ: Rutgers University Press; Maureen Cain (1979) 'Trends in the Sociology of Police Work' in *International Journal of the Sociology of Law* 7, pp. 143–67.

19   Huggins, *Political Policing*, p. xi.

20   Huggins, *Political Policing*, Chapter 7.

21   See Darren J. O'Byrne (2001) 'The Construction of Political Identity' in Paul Kennedy and Cath Danks (eds) *Globalization and National Identities: Crisis or Opportunity?* Basingstoke: Palgrave.

22   www.uib.no/isf/people/amnesty/whatis01.htm.

23   The Government of Tibet in Exile, www.tibet.com/Humanrights/HumanRights97/hr97-3.html.

24   Zygmunt Bauman (1989) *Modernity and the Holocaust*, Cambridge: Polity Press, p. 72.

25   www.uib.no/isf/people/amnesty/whatis01.htm

26   Baljit Singh (1977) 'An Overview' in Yonah Alexander and S.M. Finger (eds) *Terrorism: Interdisciplinary Perspectives*, New York: John Jay Press, p. 15.

27   McLaughlin, 'Political Violence', p. 277.

28   Herbert Marcuse (1991, original 1964) *One-Dimensional Man: Studies in the Ideology of Advanced Industrial Societies*, London: Routledge; Franz Fanon (1967) *The Wretched of the Earth*, Harmondsworth: Penguin.

29   McLaughlin, 'Political Violence', p. 299.

30   Peter Berger, Brigitte Berger and Hansfried Kellner (1974) *The Homeless Mind: Modernisation and Consciousness*, Harmondsworth: Penguin.

31   John Simpson (ed.) (1995) *The Oxford Book of Exile*, Oxford: Oxford University Press, p. viii.

32   Geoffrey Robertson (2000) *Crimes Against Humanity: The Struggle for Global Justice*, Harmondsworth: Penguin, p. 245.

33   McLaughlin, 'Political Violence', p. 289.

34   Robertson, *Crimes Against Humanity*, p. 245.

35   Robertson, *Crimes Against Humanity*, p. 41.

36   Robertson, *Crimes Against Humanity*, p. 245. During the 1980s, the United Nations Working Group on Enforced or Involuntary Disappearances, founded in 1980, dealt with reports from 38 countries: Angola, Argentina, Bolivia, Brazil, Central African Republic, Chad, Chile, Columbia, Cyprus, Dominican Republic, El Salvador, Ethiopia, Guatemala, Guinea, Haiti, Honduras, Indonesia, Iran, Iraq, Lesotho, Lebanon, Mexico, Morocco, Namibia, Nepal, Nicaragua, Paraguay, Peru, Philippines, Seychelles, South

Africa, Sri Lanka, Syria, Togo, Uganda, Uruguay, Vietnam, Zaire. See Nigel S. Rodley (1988) 'United Nations Action Procedures Against "Disappearances". Summary or Arbitrary Executions, and Torture' in Peter Davies (ed.) *Human Rights*, London: Routledge.

37 Antonio Cassese, (1990) *Human Rights in a Changing World*, Cambridge: Polity Press, p. 121.

38 Cassese, *Human Rights*, p. 122.

39 Cassese, *Human Rights*, p. 123.

40 Cassese, *Human Rights*, p. 123.

41 Cassese, *Human Rights*, p. 125.

42 Cassese, *Human Rights*, p. 122.

43 Robertson, *Crimes Against Humanity*, p. 245.

44 Cassese, *Human Rights*, p. 126.

45 Cassese, *Human Rights*, p. 126.

46 Cassese, *Human Rights*, p. 126.

47 Robertson, *Crimes Against Humanity*, p. 251.

48 Foucault, *Discipline and Punish*.

49 Luhmann's position is outlined in his 1995 volume *Social Systems*, Stanford: Stanford University Press.

50 R.I. Moore (1987) *The Formation of a Persecuting Society*, Oxford: Blackwell; cited in Huggins, *Political Policing*, p. 196.

51 Huggins, *Political Policing*, p. 197; Charles Tilly (1985) 'War Making and State Making as Organized Crime' in Peter Evans, Dietrich Rueschemeyer, and Theda Skocpol (eds) *Bringing the State Back In*, New York: Cambridge University Press.

52 Huggins (*Political Policing*, pp. 159–60) borrows this idea from the Foucauldian analysis of torture in Iran developed by Darius Rejali (1994) *Torture and Modernity: Self, Society, and State in Modern Iran*, Boulder, CO: Westview Press.

CHAPTER FIVE

Torture

> No one shall be subjected to torture or cruel, inhuman or degrading treatment or punishment.
>
> *Universal Declaration of Human Rights, Article 5*

> The evil that exists in these people resides in their impunity. They didn't have to explain anything to anyone. They didn't have to account for anyone, not even their own consciences. The person being tortured was absolutely at their mercy.
>
> *Victor Basterra, on torturers in Argentina[1]*

What is torture?

Very few violations of international human rights standards are met with such emotional response as torture. The practice of inflicting pain, often excruciating in its severity, is an ancient one, and yet nothing seems to contradict the human pretensions to rationalisation and 'civilisation' more. However, according to Jonathan Power, torture has become more prevalent in spite of, and has evolved side-by-side with, 'civilization'.[2] As we will discuss in the course of this chapter, in the last hundred years, torture methods have become more clinical, more technical, torture equipment has become a commodity to be bought and sold on the market, governments have exchanged tips on successful torture techniques – all of this in spite of the fact that torture has become illegal according to international law.

Torture, however, is not altogether easy to define. Traditional definitions view it as the imposition of physical suffering upon others through violence, for various reasons usually pertaining to the extraction of information or confession of guilt, but possibly simply for the pleasure of being cruel. Power describes it as 'the systematized use of violence to inflict the maximum amount of pain in order to extract information, to break resistance, or simply to intimidate'.[3]

It is common to view torture in this way, as an extreme means of furthering some state project. However, the noted Italian criminologist Cesare Beccaria was adamant in claiming that torture was not only morally wrong, but it was also an inappropriate means of achieving its purported end.[4] Torture, it seems, is more than simply a tool for the extraction of information. Clinical psychologist Lindsey Williams states that:

> There are two common misconceptions about torture. The first is that the primary purpose is to inflict pain; the second is that the purpose of the pain is to elicit information. In reality, researchers have concluded that pain is used as a means to a different end, that end being the destruction of the individual as a person. Any information elicited is usually no more than a side benefit: often the victim has no information to give.[5]

'Torture is used as a tool of power', writes one expert on the subject.[6] For Williams, in agreement, 'torture is less to do with pain than absolute humiliation and domination'.[7] Jean-Paul Sartre, the French philosopher, had come to a similar conclusion:

> The purpose of torture is not only to make a person talk, but to make him betray others. The victim must turn himself by his screams and by his submission into a lower animal. in the eyes of all and in his own eyes. His betrayal must destroy him and take away his human dignity. He who gives way under questioning is not only constrained from talking again, but is given a new status, that of sub-man.[8]

Torture is full of complexities and contradictions. The government, the torturer, even the public, may justify its use in certain circumstances, while civil society condemns it as barbaric, evil, and archaic. How is it that such 'evil' is justified? Governments might answer this with stock responses, such as 'national security'. But torture, like political imprisonment and its most extreme form, the death penalty, is an extension of censorship; its task is to deny speaking and hearing. The purpose of torture has never been so eloquently described as it has by Israeli psychiatrist and human rights activist Ruchama Marton:

The declared purpose of using torture is to force the enemy, the outsider, to talk and reveal secrets. This revelation is supposed to forestall the killing of insiders, members of the group. This way of reasoning is so facile and simplistic that it is readily and uncritically accepted. Presenting the issues in this manner provides validity and justification for torture.

But further examination of torture beyond this simplistic presentation exposes its speciousness. The victim's confession is useless. The torturer knows that the victim's words are worthless. A tormented person will tell the torturers what they want to hear – empty, mute speech, which does not accomplish the declared purpose of revealing secrets. In fact, the real purpose of torture is silence: silence induced by fear. Fear is contagious and spreads to the other members of the oppressed group, to silence and paralyse them. To impose silence through violence is torture's real purpose, in the most profound and fundamental sense.[9]

Clearly, then, traditional definitions – and state justifications – of torture are flawed in so far as they place too much emphasis on the directly instrumentalist purpose of extracting information or confession. A second problem is that many definitions seem to apply solely to physical violence. Clearly, as evidence from the cruel twentieth century has shown us, psychological torture is as useful a means of achieving any of the overt or covert ends – information, confession, humiliation, suffering, silence – as physical torture. Indeed, the World Medical Association, in its Tokyo Declaration of 1975, which otherwise adopted a rather traditional definition of torture, saw fit to make mention of 'mental suffering' as well as physical. However, as philosophers might want to point out, if mental torture is included in our definition, then torture as a whole is far more commonplace than we could ever imagine, for it may include all manner of everyday experiences. In order to qualify this definition slightly, commentators have considered such factors as the *amount of suffering* experienced by the victim, or the *length of time* for which the suffering lasted, but these have proved inadequate.

One other point which needs to be made is that torture has, historically, straddled the divide between the *legal* or judicial sphere, concerned with the maintenance of order, and the *political* sphere, concerned with the maintenance of power. Most uses of torture in the modern world are *illegal*, therefore they are used in a more clandestine way to serve the political interests of those in power. (It would be correct to say *all* forms of torture are illegal, as torture is illegal according to international law, but that does not mean torture is not used occasionally for judicial as opposed to political ends.) However, historically, torture was commonly used for judicial purposes, against non-political criminals, as a form of punishment. We can, therefore, make a distinction between *torture* (the infliction of pain for reasons suggested above), and *corporal punishment* (the infliction of pain for purposes of punishment). This is not, it should be clear, a wholly useful distinction, especially since most forms of corporal punishment have now been condemned by the international political community as constituting 'cruel and inhuman treatment' – effectively, as constituting torture. In its general comments on the Covenant on Civil and Political Rights, the United Nations made it clear that the definition of torture must extend to corporal punishment. In this chapter we will deal with 'corporal punishment', then, under the more general banner of torture.

Two documents, the Declaration on the Protection of all Persons from Being Subjected to Torture and Other Cruel, Inhuman or Degrading Treatment or Punishment, in 1975, and the Convention Against Torture and Other Cruel, Inhuman or Degrading Treatment or Punishment, in 1984, clarify the United Nations' position on torture. It must involve pain or suffering, physical or mental. This must be inflicted upon the victim for an express purpose, and with the involvement of a public (i.e. state) official. The suffering must be severe, intentional, and unjustifiable in the circumstances.[10]

In this chapter, we will discuss how, despite the establishment of international standards and safeguards and in the face of apparent universal condemnation, torture is a more common practice in the world today than at any other point in history. We will also consider various social psychological perspectives pertaining to the making of a torturer, we will discuss various torture methods, and we will look at how specific types of torture are used against specific population groups, especially women. We will also consider the treatment of torture victims, and conclude by asking whether we can develop a sociology of torture and pain within the framework of the sociology of the body. Throughout this investigation, we will encounter some horrific testimonies. We should take care, though, to keep in mind that a sociological understanding of torture would not reduce its subject matter to the whims of violent individuals:

Torture does not occur simply because individual torturers are sadistic, even if testimonies verify that they often are. Torture is frequently part of the state-controlled machinery for suppressing dissent. Concentrated in the torturer's electrode or syringe is the power and responsibility of the state.[11]

A brief history of torture

Most of us may agree that brutality as practised by one person against another is a timeless thing, and that any attempt to provide a history of it is pointless. However, Power is right to state that torture as a practice is a product of 'civilisation'. Our definition of torture goes beyond the practice of simple brutality and involves intent to punish or dehumanise. He points out that:

> Primitive man (sic), like other animals, followed his instincts and killed his enemy as swiftly as the job could be done. Archaeologists, who have dug up prehistoric skeletons, have found no evidence of torture. Even human sacrifices were made without prolonged suffering.
>
> Man for several hundred thousand years existed without using torture; only in the last few thousand has it become a weapon of state.[12]

As social scientists, then, we should be interested in torture:

1 because as a practice it is a social construction and not a pre-social, biological or behavioural one; and

2 because its emergence as a practice seems closely connected to the emergence of political institutions such as the centralised state.

Torture in the pre-modern world

In Ancient Greek law, torture was prohibited against citizens, but permitted against slaves and others as a means of obtaining information.[13] Indeed, Power adds that in Athens, the testimony of a slave was not considered reliable unless he had been tortured. Roman law extended this sanctioning of torture to include citizens, and this influenced the laws of many European countries built on Roman law.[14] However, Christians had suffered considerably under Roman rule, such that for the thousand years following the collapse of the Roman Empire, the Church succeeded in abolishing torture from its lands. Only in the thirteenth century, under Pope Innocent IV, did it resurface, as a means of extracting confessions from suspected heretics during the Inquisition. Various torture methods were used liberally during this dreadful period of history, and magistrates were on hand to observe the techniques and record the methods and instruments used, the length of time, and the confessions extracted. Subsequently, European societies influenced by Roman law (such as France) treated torture as a natural part of questioning and a useful means of securing information. English common law, though, derived primarily from Anglo-Saxon (as opposed to Roman) law, and it recognised only one use of torture: where suspects refused to offer a plea of guilt or innocence, such a plea could be extracted using the *peine forte et dure*.[15]

After the Inquisition, the use of torture once again declined. It was abolished in England by law in 1640, although suspected witches were still subjected to various forms of it. The use of torture became a capital offence in France after the 1789 revolution. Russia and the German states abolished it in the early nineteenth century. Most of the major imperial powers sought to use their influence upon the colonised nations to extend the abolition to other parts of the world.

Torture in the modern world

The well-respected writer Victor Hugo remarked in 1874 that 'torture has ceased to exist'.[16] It is true that the legal, judicial sanctioning of torture in Europe was all but abolished, but in reality the practice was still alive in parts of the world, and set to make a dramatic comeback. During the twentieth century, the use of torture as a political practice became even more widespread. In Italy, Mussolini's fascist government became the first to instigate torture as a state policy, soon followed by Franco's government in Spain, and Hitler's in Germany. Post-colonial dictatorships routinely used torture to silence opponents in Africa and Latin America.

This resurgence of torture as a political tool is despite the passing into international law of various covenants and declarations which strictly forbid the practice of torture in all cases. The Geneva Conventions, which relate to the treatment of prisoners of war and of civilians during wartime, prohibit in absolute fashion the cruel and inhuman treatment of captives. The 1929 Geneva Convention, cloaked within the language of the 'laws of humanity', was the first to prohibit various forms of corporal punishment and cruel treatment against prisoners of war.[17] Through its location within this framework, torture was treated, in much the same way as genocide, as a crime against humanity, and thus under the jurisdiction of the Allied tribunals during and following 1945. When the Universal Declaration of Human Rights in 1948 prohibited all forms of cruel, inhuman or degrading treatment, it inspired the inclusion of similar articles in various subsequent declarations, acts and covenants. Torture was universally outlawed according to the

International Covenant on Civil and Political Rights (ICCPR) in 1966, and opposition to it is standard practice for the United Nations General Assembly, the European Union, and other regional and national administrative bodies. Article 7 of the ICCPR adopts the same wording as the UDHR, with an added clause prohibiting medical and scientific experimentation. In 1975, the United Nations General Assembly adopted the Declaration on the Protection of All Persons from Being Subjected to Torture and Other Cruel, Inhuman or Degrading Treatment or Punishment. In 1984, the United Nations Convention Against Torture provided a more detailed interpretation of 'cruel, inhuman or degrading treatment'. However, this Covenant states explicitly that it does not 'consider it necessary to draw up a list of prohibited acts' because 'the distinction depends on the nature, purpose and severity of the treatment applied'.[18] Nevertheless, this document, which came into force in 1987, did make clear the inclusion of such ambiguous treatments as various forms of mental cruelty, and excessive corporal punishment. It also allowed for the establishment, in 1988, of the United Nations Committee Against Torture. A Special Rapporteur on Torture, answerable to the United Nations Commission on Human Rights, has been in place since 1985, whose job it is to liaise with governments on the measures they have taken to prevent the use of torture.

However, there remains a noticeable bridge between United Nations and related covenants and sanctions, and the responsibility of nation-state governments to enforce those standards within their own borders, or with regard to their foreign policies.[19] As a result, practices which clearly violate these norms have been identified in scores of countries from year to year. Amnesty International reports regularly suggest that almost half the countries of the world practise some form of torture. More than 40 United Nations member states routinely practise torture, including a number which have ratified the Convention Against Torture, while others practise it on a less frequent basis.[20] As well as torture, examples of police and prison brutality and inhuman prison conditions have been well documented.[21] In parts of Latin America and Asia, the use of torture has been so well documented that the issue for governments is not so much concealing the torture but causing confusion over who might be responsible for it.[22]

Torture practices continue to be tolerated, in some cases sanctioned, not only in repressive regimes but in supposedly democratic ones as well. In Israel, the report of the judicial Landau Commission in 1987 justified the use by security forces upon suspected terrorists of 'moderate physical pressure'. Needless to say, this is an elastic term, and agents of the state have stretched it to considerable lengths. On at least three occasions in 1996, the Israeli Supreme Court passed decisions justifying the use of physical force during the interrogations of suspected terrorists.[23] In Western European terms, the United Kingdom has also been a persistent offender. A recent report highlighted the excessive use of police brutality upon prisoners. The UK has also been criticised for its use of torture techniques in respect of the treatment of political prisoners in Northern Ireland. In 1972, after a public investigation, the Conservative government stated that certain interrogation techniques would be discontinued. These included: (i) hooding; (ii) 'white-sound' treatment (subjection to consistent high-pitched noise); (iii) forcing prisoners to stand for long periods against a wall; (iv) deprivation of sleep; and (v) deprivation of diet.[24] Some allegations – that prisoners had been attacked by Alsatian dogs, badly beaten, made to run over obstacle courses littered with broken glass, and threatened with being thrown from helicopters – were excluded from the report. The Irish government brought a case against the UK to the European Commission on Human Rights in Strasbourg, which found the UK guilty of 'torture, inhuman and degrading treatment' which constituted an administrative practice. The word 'torture' was dropped after an appeal by the UK government. France became the first European Union member state to be convicted of torture when the European Court of Human Rights upheld a charge of extreme brutality made against five police officers in 1999. A 1998 Amnesty International report found that prison conditions in the United States often amounted to torture, including instances of severe brutality and cruelty.

Torture methods

When does torture begin and end? Inge Genefke rightly points out that torture is a *process* rather than an act, and that this process begins with the arrest, which is usually violent and usually occurs at night. This is followed by a 'softening phase' – a few days of violence and humiliation designed to weaken the victim – and then by the more systematic use of violence. This lasts many days: prisoners should not be broken too quickly.[25]

Almost anything can become a weapon of torture. The most innocent household appliance can, in the wrong hands, become a lethal and savage tool of violence. While certain famous torture methods use equipment specifically designed for that purpose, others make effective use of whatever is around. In this section, we will discuss how torture in the twentieth century has become increasingly clinical and sophisticated. We will also turn to one specific form of torture which is rightly receiving considerable attention, as it challenges many earlier definitions:

rape. In both instances, the text will be supported by disturbing testimonies and case studies. A lengthy passage from Inge Genefke, worth quoting in full, serves as a disturbing but effective introduction to the various methods adopted:

> They can include the application of electric shocks to the most sensitive areas of the body; the suspension of the victim by an arm or by a leg, which can last for hours; the immersion of the victim's head under water until the point of suffocation; the burning of the victim's skin with cigarettes or red-hot iron rods; beatings aimed at specific parts of the body, such as under the feet until the soles are badly damaged. Sexual abuse is common, particularly against women, though men are also sometimes harmed in their ability to function as men; dogs can be trained to rape both men and women. Sanitary conditions in detention are usually extremely poor, any request for visiting the toilet becoming a pretext for torture; the victim is kept alive with filthy food and drinking water; freedom of movement is limited, with prisoners often packed so closely as to force them to sleep in turns.
>
> Physical torture is complemented by acts of psychological torture. Methods such as sleep deprivation, blindfolding and isolation invoke a deep sensation of fear and helplessness and can also provide hallucinations. Total isolation can be maintained for years, in which time the victim is uncertain of their fate, and their family is ignorant of their condition and whereabouts. Many victims are coerced to say or do things which violate their ideology or religious convictions, the purpose of which is to destroy fundamental parts of the victim's identity related to their self-respect and self-esteem. Political and ethical values are attacked by techniques such as the coercion to sing songs which praise the very things which the victim is against. Mock-executions lead the victim from a sense of reality into a nightmarish state of almost suspended animation.
>
> The breaking down of the victim's personality begins with their arrest. Names are replaced with numbers. Personal belongings are removed, including glasses, life-saving drugs, etc., and are replaced with ill-fitting uniforms.[26]

Torture in the twentieth century has been carried out using more and more sophisticated methods. While medieval methods included the rack, the thumb screw, and the iron maiden, all designed specifically to exact extreme physical pain, more subtle methods of dehumanisation and individual demoralisation began to emerge. The Italian fascists would pump a prisoner full of castor oil to 'purge him of the will to exist'; the Nazis kept their prisoners in appalling conditions, herded together and kept like animals, in concentration camps. In Rwanda, prisoners have been subjected to the *cachots noir*, black cells devoid of light in which victims have been held for as long as a year. In the former Soviet Union, opponents of the state were sent to psychiatric hospitals and subjected to pain-inducing drugs. In many countries, prisoners have been denied sleep and food to weaken their senses. The following, disturbing account took place in Rhodesia, now Zimbabwe, in 1968, and it describes the torture of Desmond Francis, a South African Indian schoolteacher:

[He] spent 17 days in an infested cell, chained by leg irons and severely beaten. His head was held under water to make him confess to corrupting African detectives and when he refused to comply, he was smothered by a canvas bag and beaten on his testicles with a copper finger-printing pad.

[O]n the fifth day of this interrogation, [he] tried to commit suicide by plunging a broken bottle into his chest.

While still in Rhodesia, Francis was burnt repeatedly with a hot iron on the thigh and lighted matches held against his body. His pubic hair was singed off in this manner. To relieve the pain he was given two aspirins and placed in solitary confinement.

On the 18th of January, 1968, he was taken by car to South Africa... For the next 13 months, he was held in solitary confinement in Pretoria Central Prison where, he said, 'I was beaten all over with fists and an inch-thick cane; one blow broke my right cheek-bone. I was then handcuffed and blindfolded with a wet cloth. I had to sit with a stick under my knees and over my arms. Electric terminals were applied to my ears and the current was turned on. This was a terrible experience. My whole body shook and my head seemed full of vibrations. My teeth chattered so that my tongue was cut to ribbons.'

It took over two weeks to extract a statement from Francis. The torture was kept up by rotating shifts of police using every conceivable method. Eventually he signed a statement – with a rough canvas tool bag over his head and his nerves shattered by the firecrackers the police were throwing at him. A week later, Francis was finally granted medical attention. He had been vomiting and excreting blood almost without stop. The prison doctor's diagnosis was bleeding piles.[27]

© Amnesty International Publications, www.amnesty.org

It is true that the infliction of physical pain is still used, such as the *falanga* or *falaka* used frequently in the Middle East, where the soles of feet are beaten repeatedly. Increasingly, though, direct means of inflict-ing bodily pain have been aimed at the sexual organs: electrodes in the testicles, bottles pushed into the anus, rape as a means of torture. In Syria, the 'black slave' has been a common torture technique: a heated metal skewer is inserted into the victim's anus. These are all aimed at inducing a sense of degradation and self-loathing. Williams notes how one victim:

> [R]eported that he withstood the pain, terrible though it was, but that he broke down when a guard demonstrated his contempt by forcing open the victim's mouth and urinating into it.[28]

The testimony of Ayse Semra Eker, who was tortured in Turkey in 1972, has similarities with that of Desmond Francis in Rhodesia. Mrs Eker's horrific account includes 'old-style' beatings, plus the use of elec-trical and sexual torture:

> My eyes were covered by a special black band and I was forced into a minibus. I was then taken ... into a rather spacious room ... After a short while they forced me to take off my skirt and stockings and laid me down on the ground and tied my hands and feet to pegs. A person by the name of Umit Erdal beat the soles of my feet for about half an hour ... Later, they attached wires to my fingers and toes and passed electric current through my body. At the same time they kept beating my naked thighs with truncheons ... After a while, they disconnected the wire from my finger and connected it to my ear. They immediately gave me a high dose of electricity. My whole body and head shook in a terrible way. My front teeth started breaking ... After a while I felt dizzy and could not see very well. Then I fainted. When I came to myself, I found out I was lying half-naked in a pool of dirty water. They tried to force me to stand up and run. At the same time they kept beating me with truncheons, kicking me, and pushing me against the walls. They then held my hand and hit me with truncheons in my palms and on my hands, each one taking turns. After all this my whole body was swollen and red and I could not stand on my feet ... They tried to penetrate my feminine organ with the end of a truncheon. As I resisted they hit my body and legs with a large axe handle. They soon succeeded in penetrating my sexual organ with the truncheon with the electric wire on, and passed current. I fainted ... Then they untied me, brought me to my feet, and took me out of the

room. With a leather strap, they hanged me from my wrists on to a pipe in the corridor. As I hung half-naked, several people beat me with truncheons...

During the whole time I was in Istanbul, my hands were tied to chains. Because of this and because my tongue was split, I could not eat. A doctor would occasionally come to look at me and suggest first aid...

During the ten days... the same torture, insults, threats, and pressure continued.[29]

As with the death penalty (which we cover in the next chapter), contemporary torture techniques have become more clinical, and highly technological, in part to distance the torturer from any feeling of direct involvement. With such methods, no direct physical force is required; merely the pressing of a button.[30]

Paulo Schilling describes the experience of electrical torture in his *Theory and Practice of Torture in Brazil*; it creates a mental and physical sense of confusion and pain, along with convulsive shaking, loss of muscular control, and a sense of loss. A stimulation is caused in the muscle identical to that in the nerves, causing uncontrollable movements similar to epileptic fits. In the midst of this, the screaming victim clings on to any sense of balance available. The sensation is so overpowering that any alternative pain would be a welcome relief:

He tries to cause himself pain by beating his head repeatedly on the ground. But generally he is tied, hanging on the 'parrot's perch' and not even that resource is available to him.[31]

The passing of electrical convulsions through the brain can, if repeated regularly, cause such severe cerebral disturbance as to render the victim demented and incontinent. Another method of torture used in Brazil is the holding cell itself – known as the *geladeira*, or 'refrigerator', a windowless room five foot square with loudspeakers and strobe lighting, and heating and cooling mechanisms to alternate the temperature. Martha Huggins notes how officials 'commonly used the geladeira to manipulate a victim's sense of time, essential for quick extraction of information. Captives were isolated from any outside stimuli and administered high-technology attacks on their senses'.[32] She describes it as 'the ultimate ... rationalized positivistic panopticon or observation room':[33]

> Oxygen was introduced only through tiny holes in the walls. For the first five days of incarceration, the prisoner was nude and hooded, his or her arms tied behind the back. Food was withheld and no sleeping was allowed. The captive had to defecate and urinate on the floor of the cell; every movement was monitored through closed-circuit television...
>
> During the day, the victims faced beatings – especially the 'telephone' torture, in which objects were smashed with great force against the ears. The captors administered electric shocks...[34]
>
> The torturers subjected their prisoners in the geladeira to cycles of heat and cold, noise and silence...

Sensory deprivation techniques of this kind are widely used. They are designed to break down the victim's defences, and can result in total nervous breakdowns. These can also result in anxiety, hypochondria and hysteria, and possibly phobias, depression, emotional fatigue, and obsessive-compulsive disorder. Physical consequences can include stomach, heart, and genito-urinary problems.

The following account was received by Amnesty International from a torture victim in Brazil:

> They ordered me to strip completely; I obeyed. They made me sit down on the ground and tied my hands with a thick rope. One of the six or seven policemen present put his foot on the rope in order to tighten it as much as possible. I lost all feeling in my hands. They put their knees up to my elbows so that my bound hands were on a level with my ankles. They then placed an iron bar about eight centimetres wide between my knees and elbows and suspended me by resting the two ends of the iron bar on a wooden stand so that the top part of my body and my head were on one side and my buttocks and legs on the other, about three feet from the floor. After punching me and clubbing me, they placed a wire on the little toe of my left foot and placed the other end between my testicles and my leg. The wires were attached to a camp telephone so that the current increased or decreased according to the speed at which the handle was turned. They began to give me electric shocks using this equipment and continued to beat me brutally both with their hands and with a *palmatoria* – a plaque full of holes – which left a completely black haematome, larger in size than an outstretched palm, on one of my buttocks. The electric shocks and the beatings continued for several hours... Each time that I fainted, they threw water over me to

increase my sensitivity to the electric shocks. They then took the wire from my testicles and began to apply it to my face and head, giving me terrible shocks on my face, in my ears, eyes, mouth and nostrils. One of the policemen remarked, 'Look, he is letting off sparks. Put it in his ear now...'

The torture was so serious and long-lasting that I thought I would die. I began to feel completely drained; my body was covered in a cold sweat; I could not move my eyelids; I was swallowing my tongue and could only breathe with difficulty; I could no longer speak... I think I eventually lost consciousness. When I came to, they had lowered the bar and laid me out on the ground. They tried to revive me with ammonia but I didn't respond. They struck me on the testicles with the end of the stick; they burnt my shoulders with cigarette stubs; they put the barrel of a revolver into my mouth saying they would kill me. They threatened me with sexual abuse.[35]

One of the most documented developments in torture techniques over recent decades has been the increase in use of rape as a weapon of torture. Rape and other forms of violence against women held in custody under state jurisdiction or by private individuals in the domestic sphere remain widespread due to the underreporting of these crimes, either out of fear of retribution by the perpetrators, fear of social stigma, or ignorance. The use of rape and other forms of violence against women as torture clearly violates – in addition to Article 7 which denounces torture in the generic sense – Articles 10 and 17 of the International Covenant on Civil and Political Rights. Article 10 states that: 'All persons deprived of their liberty shall be treated with humanity and with respect for the inherent dignity of their person.' Article 17 demands that: 'No-one shall be subjected to arbitrary or unlawful interference with his (sic) privacy.' In 1992, the United Nations Special Rapporteur on Torture stated:

Since it was clear that rape or other forms of sexual assault against women in detention were particularly ignominious violations of the inherent dignity and the right to physical integrity of the human being, they accordingly constituted an act of torture.

However, police torture and sexual abuse against women detainees seem to be committed with virtual impunity. Despite these public declarations of recognition, international law appears to have largely ignored the suffering of women through torture techniques such as rape, and this has resulted in 'a profoundly gendered portrait of the torture victim as a male prisoner of conscience'.[36] In some countries, such as Pakistan, there is an additional absurdity which makes it even less likely that the victim will file a complaint – women who report rape may find themselves charged with adultery. Some statistics suggest that 72 per cent of the population of women in Pakistan taken into police custody are physically and sexually abused – and 75 per cent are charged with adultery under the Zina Ordinance. In the United States in 1997 the Justice Department sued the states of Michigan and Arizona for failing to protect female prisoners from sexual assaults.[37] In 1998, the Federal Bureau of Prisons settled a lawsuit brought by three women who had been beaten, raped, and sold by guards to male inmates for sex. They were awarded $500,000.

Rape in times of war is not a new phenomenon, but the use of rape as a weapon of war, as a form of torture, has become disturbingly common during the second half of the twentieth century. In 1993, testimonies from perpetrators and victims of rape in the Balkan conflict suggested that some 20,000 women and girls had been raped by the Serbian soldiers.[38] A European Community report has suggested that such rapes are committed in 'particularly sadistic ways to inflict maximum humiliation on victims, their families, and on the whole community'.[39] The following account is given of one such victim:

For 28-year old Senka, the horror began late one night in April 1992 when 10 Chetniks (Serbs) barged into her apartment in Gorazde as she was sitting talking to some friends. 'At the moment they entered', she recounts, 'they began to curse our "Muslim mothers", saying "You sent your husbands to fight but you will see, we will do to you everything we know and we will take you to the concentration camps after that".'

She and another young woman were dragged to a bedroom and repeatedly raped: 'They ripped off all my clothes till I was naked. Two of the Chetniks held me and two of them had intercourse with me. After those two had raped me, the others did the same. My friend was raped in the same room by the same soldiers. I recognized two of the Chetniks as my former neighbours from Gorazde.'

In the morning at about three o'clock, Senka came to her senses. She heard noises from the sitting room and realized that the soldiers were raping her other friends. She ran into the bathroom and managed to escape through the window. Shortly after the rape she realized she was pregnant and had to go to Sarajevo to have an abortion.[40]

So far, we can identify at least two distinct developments in torture techniques. One, that methods have become increasingly *rationalised* and *sanitised*, thanks to technological developments. Two, that they have become increasingly *personal*. Rape and other forms of sexual and bodily abuse engender strong feelings of self-loathing designed to destroy the personality of the victim. A third disturbing way in which modern torture differs from its medieval ancestor is that torture techniques have become *commodities*, and an information economy has been established between nation-states which exchange details of different methods and their effects. Amnesty International states how a French priest, serving in Algeria as a reserve officer, had been forced to attend a course on 'humane torture',[41] while in 1969 various army officials were sent to a similar course on torture techniques in Rio de Janeiro, Brazil, where:

> Techniques were explained, advice given on the use of different instruments, and the effect on the prisoner was demonstrated – partly by lantern slides, but also on living objects: political prisoners.[42]

The torture economy is not merely an information economy. Torture equipment is bought and sold freely at arms fairs around the world. The award-winning documentary *The Torture Trail* followed the journey of various instruments of torture and oppression from their manufacture in the UK, through their sale and export, to their use in the hands of brutal regimes. Recently, there have been damaging revelations concerning the export of arms to Indonesia. We will discuss this trade in torture later in the chapter.

The theoretical discourse on torture

Can torture ever be justified? This appears to be one of the classic dilemmas often posed by philosophers of ethics. Strangely, it features far less in textbooks and student guides on practical ethics than, say, capital punishment, abortion, euthanasia, war, civil disobedience, and vegetarianism. Nevertheless, the debate, such that it is, generally takes place between deontologists, or Kantians, and utilitarians. Kantians tend to adopt what we have already introduced as a moralist perspective, which argues that torture is *in itself* evil, while utilitarians adopt a *causalist* approach which is concerned more with the consequences of the act. The debate, put very simply, concerns three important questions.[43]

First, is torture universally wrong? That is, can it be *absolutely* proscribed? From a moralist point of view, it is *always* wrong to torture someone, regardless of the reasons (as ends must never justify means, in true Kantian style). It is thus absolutely proscribed. Causalists, however, suggest that it is *possible* for situations to arise in which torture becomes a necessity (although only ever as a last resort). One famous dilemma asks: If a terrorist has planted a bomb in a building full of people, and refuses to confess where the bomb is hidden, given that there is no time to search the building nor to get all the people out to safety, is it acceptable to torture the terrorist in order to obtain that information?

A second, related question concerns the nature of the torturer. Crude moralists would dismiss the torturer as an innately evil person, but causalists might add that a person's character is defined as much by omission (the observer who allows things to occur) as by act (the torturer). Thus, an omission to perform an act, even one as evil as torture, might be as wrong as committing the act itself if the consequences of a failure to carry out the torture result in greater harm to others.

Thirdly, the more general question asks: Why is torture wrong? Here, causalist utilitarians delight in critiquing the abstract philosophy of the moralist Kantians. For the utilitarians, it is the agony suffered by the victim which makes the torture wrong, and not the denial of an abstract fundamental right to dignity which the moralists would seek to uphold as central in this matter.

These and related questions occupied the minds of French intellectuals and commentators during the Algerian war of independence from France, which took place between 1954 and 1962. France, which had adopted a role as a champion of liberties and rights, frequently resorted to torture during this war. As one commentator suggests, this led to heated discussions and bizarre justifications. The French military commander in Algiers claimed that torture and other extreme methods were essential because the Algerian rebels were fighting with such savagery, and were themselves using torture techniques. Others turned instead to culturalist and colonialist justifications based upon France's 'mission' to bring 'civilisation' to Algeria, which was clearly so important it meant that even torture could be forgiven. As Maran says:

> The avowedly benevolent ideology of the civilizing mission was the mechanism by which the doctrine of the 'rights of man' was contorted in order to encourage and justify the practice of torture.[44]

Understanding torturers

Who, then, are the torturers? Is there a specific psychological type which can be employed to perform this task, or are we all capable of doing it? From different perspectives, a number of psychologists have sought to show how the capacity to inflict pain on others exists within each of us. The classical version of this model is drawn from psychoanalysis. The human subconscious is divided into the life instinct (*Eros*) and the death instinct (*Thanatos*). Thus the impulse for aggression and destruction is part of a basic human instinct. Subsequent theories, inspired in part by the psychoanalytical drive, have sought to challenge this simplistic account.

The assumption that there is a natural impulse for aggression and destruction clearly borrows heavily from the essentialist paradigm which reminds us that, in the last instance, the human being is still an animal, albeit a socialised one. Many attempts to explain the making of a torturer – such as Adorno's theory of the 'authoritarian personality', Milgram's theory of obedience, and Festinger's theory of cognitive dissonance – seek to do so using social categories. Zimbardo's famous experiment conducted at Stanford University in 1971 is perhaps the closest such study to the essentialist, or sociobiological, position.[45] Zimbardo gathered some college students and asked them to take part in a role-playing exercise, either as prison guards or prisoners. The 'guards' were given only three general rules: to maintain law and order, to prevent prisoners from escaping, and to refrain from physical violence. He subsequently observed how the behaviour of those playing the role of guards regressed to violence and inhumanity, reporting sadistic instances, some of which took place during the night when they were not even being observed. The intensity of this regression, and the dehumanising effect it had upon those playing the prisoners, resulted in the two-week experiment being cancelled after only six days. It appeared that the roles assigned to the students allowed them to break free of the conditioning of socialisation and regress to a 'natural' (Hobbesian) state of conflict and violence.

Social psychologists after the Second World War sought to understand how and why people allowed the Holocaust to take place. In a major study carried out by a team led by the noted critical theorist and Frankfurt School member, Theodor Adorno, it was suggested that such atrocities could only have been carried out if enough citizens shared as a personality trait an unquestioning obedience to authority, and thus legitimated the actions of their governments. They dubbed this the 'authoritarian personality'.[46]

Dr Mika Haritos-Fatouros, a clinical psychologist, has also conducted research into what makes a torturer (with special reference to those under the Greek dictatorship between 1967 and 1974). She has found that torturers are not sadistic, but ordinary people who have been remoulded, refashioned, by the state, through intense programming, into torturers.[47] Her point is that, as the Adorno study showed, those who participate in these actions do have a predisposition towards accepting authority (many torturers she interviewed were obedient sons from strict families, or former army officials). Worryingly, in general, our potential for mutual concern and humanity is not strong enough to dominate our obedience to authority.

If a torturer is – regardless of his or her dispositions – primarily the product of state machinery, a social construction, then how is she or he constructed? Behaviourist and phenomenological studies have both offered answers to this question. One of the most important behaviourist studies was carried out on the willingness of people to inflict pain upon others. It is common for torturers on trial to justify their actions as merely the carrying out of orders. Society establishes a kind of hierarchy into which we are all placed, and we often find ourselves deferring to the better judgements of so-called 'experts'. The classic study by Stanley Milgram in the 1970s (reported in his landmark book *Obedience to Authority*) involved the setting up at Yale University of an experiment in which volunteers were asked to administer a short memory test to another person who was hidden behind a screen.[48] If the examinee failed to answer correctly, the volunteers were told to inflict electric shocks. The authority figure assured the volunteers that these shocks, though painful, were not fatal, and would help to improve the scoring on the tests. Although the shocks were fictional, the actor behind the screen would scream in pain as the volunteer pressed the button. 60 per cent of the volunteers continued to administer the shocks despite these obvious signs of pain, and despite their own feelings of stress. The volunteers comforted themselves in the knowledge that whatever they had done was not their responsibility but that of the scientists in white coats. Milgram himself said: 'Although the subject performs the action, he allows authority to define its meaning.' Milgram concluded that the violence carried out by the individuals could not be explained according to some primordial animal nature. It was constructed through normative rather than biological means: 'The ordinary person who shocked the victim did so out of a sense of obligation – a conception of his duties as a subject – and not from any peculiar aggressive tendencies.'

While behaviourists such as Milgram focus on the conditions within which we learn our roles, the phenomenological perspective looks at how the active, creative human actor constructs her or his social world.

This often takes the form of a series of negotiations and interpretations. In this vein, Leon Festinger has offered a more detailed account of the personality conflicts which result in the carrying out of an act of torture.[49] He calls this his theory of 'cognitive dissonance', and it involves a belief that torturers need to distance themselves from their actions, because a tension inevitably occurs between a recognition of the cruelty of torture, on the one hand, and a belief in one's own sense of moral decency, on the other. This is offered by Festinger as a general theory – we all experience discomfort when we are faced with inconsistencies in our cognitions, so we change our thoughts in order to make these seem more consistent. Various strategies or techniques are used to help us rationalise these conflicts. Of course, deference to authority is one such technique of dissonance. Authority figures often reassure their servants that, in the last instance, all responsibility for their actions will fall on their leaders. Himmler and Hitler used this reassurance to successfully secure the co-operation of their troops.

Another is the derogation, devaluing and dehumanisation of the victim. Nazi propaganda succeeded in convincing many in the German army that Jews, gypsies, homosexuals and others were incurably sub-human, and that inflicting pain on them was no worse than inflicting pain on an animal. This was supported by the conviction, again perpetuated by ideology, of the innate superiority of the Aryan race.

Where this dehumanisation cannot be brought about by racial distinctions, the individual victim can be devalued through a process of blame-shifting. The torturer might convince him- or herself that the victim is an enemy of the state, a criminal, and, thus, it is his or her own actions which have resulted in the need for torture. He or she may genuinely come to blame the victim for forcing them to learn and perform such grotesque acts.[50] In a similar vein, as Martha Huggins has pointed out in reference to Brazilian torturers and their United States sponsors, these agents of the state 'approached their work with a kind of religious mission, as "true believers" who equated social turmoil with Communism and saw force as a legitimate method for eliminating Brazilian disorder'.[51] Former torturers have stressed that they saw themselves at first as playing a vital role in a 'war'. In Argentina, former torturers active during the 'dirty war' have spoken of their initial enthusiasm – they were convinced they were serving their country, fighting a war.[52] Huggins suggests that this has affinities with Weber's theory of rationality, indicating that while the commitment to a larger goal resembled Weber's *wertrational* mentality, the goal (of ensuring 'security' at any cost) soon became an absolute value in its own right, Weber's *zweckrational* instrumentalism, which necessarily distances the actor from any external considerations pertaining to the possible consequences of the act.[53] Weber's interpretative approach to social action – his emphasis upon *verstehen* – has affinities with the phenomenological perspective.

According to the theory of cognitive dissonance, torturers might consciously distance themselves from their victims through a process of social closure. They may set themselves up as an elite group, dedicated to one another. They are kept apart from outside influences which may damage their commitment. This group mentality is established through rigorous training sessions. As with much army training, it involves, ultimately, the breaking down of the individual, and the submission of all members of this group to the 'group will'. Above all, the torturer should feel no affinity with the victim, regardless of how this is achieved. One former torturer has conceded that the only concern he felt was not for the victim but for the victim's wife, at home terrified because her husband had not returned on time, uncertain what had become of him. His own wife had once told him that she lived in fear of the telephone call informing her of his death.[54]

Medical involvement in torture

In this section, we will discuss how doctors are involved in the torture process. One type of involvement is benevolent and commendable – the treatment of victims of torture. However, our image of the torturer is as likely to involve a man in a white coat as it is to involve a military general. The singer Peter Gabriel expressed it well: 'Loaded questions from clean white coats/Their eyes are all as hidden as their Hippocratic oath'.[55] Doctors have played their part in the practice of torture.

Doctors as torturers

The World Medical Association has emphasised, in its Tokyo Declaration of 1975, that 'no crime, of which a person might stand accused, justifies medical involvement in maltreatment of that person'.[56] The doctor serves only the commitment to heal, and should never become an agent of the state. The Declaration was made with the express purpose of condemning such atrocities as were committed by Nazi doctors during the Second World War, and affirming the demand of the Geneva Declaration of 1948 (the International Code of Medical Ethics) that medical knowledge is never used 'contrary to the laws of humanity'.[57] Nevertheless, approximately 20 per cent of torture victims claim medical professionals were in some way involved in their mistreatment.[58] Furthermore, it is widely known that many authoritarian regimes – particularly in Latin America – have made use of doctors and other medically trained staff in their 'special' forces, whose task it is to ensure 'national security' at any cost. Psychiatrists in hospitals in the former Soviet Union were responsible for administering the pain-inducing drugs to their political prisoner patients. Indeed, despite the Tokyo Declaration, doctors appear to be present throughout the horrific torture process. The remarkable Ruchama Marton presents this in poetic fashion:

> The white coat passes like a shadow through the interrogation centres which include 'the coffin', 'the refrigerator', 'the banana knot', and the terrifying darkness of being hooded. The doctor is in the background, behind every torturer/interrogator. A doctor performs a pre-torture examination. He provides medical approval granting 'fitness for interrogation'. A doctor monitors the torture process. A doctor examines and takes care of the prisoner following the infliction of torture. A doctor writes a medical opinion or a pathologist's report.[59]

The British Medical Association lists the following ways in which medical professionals may be involved in torture:[60]

- assessing torture techniques
- training others in techniques
- assessing detainees' fitness
- monitoring torture
- administering punishment
- reviving detainees
- helping torturers disguise the effects of torture
- providing treatment after torture
- providing certificates/reports
- failing to denounce known examples of torture
- assessing people who claim to have been tortured
- rehabilitation of survivors.

In places such as Israel – a country in which medical professionals appear to be so closely involved in the process of torture that a conference and subsequent edited volume have been put together for the purpose of exposing and condemning it – doctors appear torn between their duties to their patients and their medical ethics, and towards the state. Doctors and other health professionals – whether employed by the state or not – are often placed under considerable pressure, particularly when confronted with such deceptive expressions as 'the interests of national security'.[61] Like everyone else involved in the process, doctors often seek comfort in rationalisations – that they are actually helping the victim, that the victim finds the awful ordeal more bearable *because* a medic is at hand – and these may actually be true. But what possible justification could there be for the careless handling by doctors of torture victims such as Hassan Bader Abdallah Zbeidi, treated by Ruchama Marton and the Association of Israeli-Palestinian Physicians for Human Rights after spending a month in detention in Israel? Marton writes:

> He arrived home in a seriously catatonic condition; he was unable to establish contact with the outside world. He recognized nobody, not his wife or children, nor his parents. He did not respond or talk spontaneously, and he was incontinent. He had an empty, frozen stare, and his body was stooped and shaking. He would remain frozen in the position in which he was placed.[62]

Zbeidi, it seems, was one of many prisoners taken in for interrogation, detained for weeks, and released disabled. At least one prisoner there at the same time as Zbeidi died under interrogation. Yet, the physician who saw Zbeidi during his incarceration wrote, in his report, that the patient was 'calm', had 'clean' lungs and a 'clear' heart, had 'no pathological findings' in the head, neck, arms and legs, and, according to the psychiatrist, had 'no clearly defined problem'. No medical supervision was deemed necessary, and the patient was returned to interrogation. The doctor's diagnosis was that the patient was 'malingering', and his recommendation was to treat with a placebo. The doctors who treated him after his release confirmed that he was suffering from a serious psychosis which none of the four prison doctors who had seen Zbeidi saw fit to raise. Such blatant disregard for medical ethics is confounded by the apparent acceptance of torture as an interrogative technique. Marton reproduces the assessment form doctors must complete concerning patients under interrogation. It requires the doctor to state if the prisoner's medical condition places limitations on the prisoner being

chained, hooded, blindfolded, or prolonged standing. It even asks
whether a prisoner has any physical injuries *before entering interrogation*:

> What are we to make of this? That now the one being investigated is
> prepared for sleep deprivation, starvation, exposure to intense heat, to
> freezing cold, to pain from blows, being tied in painful positions for long
> periods of time, being forced to stand for long periods, having one's
> head covered by a stinking and suffocating sack, being humiliated,
> sexual exploitation and having his spirit broken by prolonged solitary
> confinement?[63]

Another victim, from Argentina, describes how doctors play dual
roles during the torture process – the good and the bad. During her
ordeal, doctors had been present supervising the torture. Briefly, she
had been left alone by her tormentors, at which point another doctor
entered the room, claiming he was there to help her, asking her if she
was cold, if she was comfortable. This merely served to prepare her for
the next period of torture.[64]

The one outstanding question, which lends itself to the title of a
chapter by Mamdouh Al-Aker, is: Where are the medical associations
when all of this is going on? James Welsh lists a number of instances
where national medical associations, usually after receiving independence from state control or upon their re-establishment following
changes in policy, have embarked upon human rights promotion
schemes – Chile, Uruguay and Turkey are cited – but these have been
balanced out by instances of failure.[65] One of the worst examples is
cited by Al-Aker, who cites the case of the Israeli Medical Association.
Upon receiving a request from a Palestinian human rights organisation to investigate the alleged involvement of doctors in the torture of
Palestinian prisoners, the response of the IMA was to hastily denounce
the organisation.[66]

The treatment of victims of torture

As one astute commentator has stated, 'the effects of torture do not stop
when the doors of the torture cells are opened. Another torture follows:
memories, depression, sleeplessness, nightmares, apathy and helpless-
ness. This is the "torture syndrome"'.[67] In recognition of this, rehabilitation centres have been set up around the world to assist victims of
torture. The International Rehabilitation Council for Torture Victims has

contacts in well over 100 countries.[68] In 1986, Helen Bamber – a survivor of Belsen concentration camp – set up the Medical Foundation for the Care of Torture Victims. There are a number of similar centres or organisations scattered around the world dedicated to the care of victims of torture and their loved ones – it is worth pointing out that the victims' families and friends are often in great need of counselling and care. An interesting article by Lone Jacobsen and Edith Montgomery – who have themselves worked for some time at the Rehabilitation and Research Centre for Torture Victims in Copenhagen – lists the experiences and needs of victims.[69]

Drawing on their experience with clients, the authors suggest that the initial reaction is the most disabling – the feeling of *having one's personality changed*, from having perhaps been an extrovert character to being more insular and insecure. *Anxiety, sleep deprivation* and *nightmares* are other common symptoms. The authors suggest that torture victims often try to suppress their anxiety, albeit unsuccessfully. It is also not uncommon for the victim to feel a sense of *guilt*, blaming themselves for having survived the ordeal while so many others did not. They might also feel *shame* and self-loathing, particularly if they have experienced some form of sadistic humiliation, or sexual abuse, akin to those we have discussed above. Other mental reactions include decreased memory and lack of concentration, and an inability to control their aggression. Psychotherapy and counselling are thus required to help the victim cope with this 'demoralisation'. Torture victims who are refugees often experience a deep sense of guilt as well as loss, while those who undergo treatment in their homelands live in fear of renewed violence.[70]

These mental reactions are, of course, in addition to the physical disabilities experienced by the victims, few of whom receive any treatment for their suffering whilst in prison.[71] According to one study, the majority of victims suffer long-term damage to the musculo-skeletal system and to the central and peripheral nervous systems, as well as constant pains in the face and head and around the heart, difficulty in breathing, and gastro-intestinal problems.[72] It is thus important, say the authors, for the physical examination of the victim to include a variety of medical specialisms, including examinations by a nurse, a general practitioner, a rheumatologist, an ear, nose and throat specialist, and a dentist.

The authors go on to suggest that, as well as the victims themselves, *children* of torture victims are particularly prone to suffering, either because of their own experiences of violence, or because of the separation they have experienced from important family members, or because of the impact of torture upon parental responsiveness. Children of torture victims are thus prone to anxiety, psychosomatic pain, and emotional imbalance.[73]

The authors proceed to list some of the principles of rehabilitation of torture victims to which they adhere, and which form the basis for the treatment. These include:

- the need to avoid any procedures that may remind the victim of the torture
- that the treatment must cover physical and mental aspects
- that physiotherapy is an important part of the physical treatment
- that nursing care is important for co-ordinating and health educational reasons
- that social conditions must be taken into consideration and supported by counselling
- that treatment must include the victim and the victim's family.

These, though, are based only on the medical needs. One of the greatest existential needs is surely justice, and so long as torturers and their political masters are able to claim impunity, this remedy seems tragically out of reach.

The trade in torture equipment

In 1995, the Channel 4 documentary series *Dispatches* commissioned an important and controversial film, *The Torture Trail*. In it, reporter Martyn Gregory posed as a British contact working for a fictional Lebanese buyer, looking to purchase electro-shock batons. Since 1988 it has been illegal for companies to sell these batons to a UK market, but not to export them.

The film uncovered some disturbing secrets. It became evident that the purchase of 15,000 items of electro-shock equipment – even by representatives of countries with poor human rights records – was easy. Various companies were incriminated in the sale of torture equipment disingenuously labelled 'internal security' or 'riot control' equipment. A Birmingham-based firm, Hiatt and Company Ltd, which had been unmasked by a national newspaper some years before for selling leg-irons to brutal regimes around the world, continued to operate via its US-based distributor.[74] Another legitimate corporation, ICL Technical Plastics, based in Scotland, backed by senior officials in business and the police, knowingly sold batons to South Africa during the era of apartheid, to various Middle East regimes, and to China – only a year after the 1989 Tiananmen Square atrocities. Export to China had been banned after 1989, but these deals were made, allegedly, with the blessing of the Department of Trade and Industry. Indeed, the company's executive was about to tour South America on a sales trip paid for in part by the Scottish Office and sanctioned by the DTI. It was also revealed that Royal Ordnance, then part of the Ministry of Defence, sold 100 anti-riot guns to one of the world's most notorious terrorists (albeit unknowingly). Royal Ordnance was subsequently privatised and taken over by British Aerospace, a representative of which informed the undercover reporters that even without a licence to trade in electro-shock batons, deals could be made using contacts in the UK police and overseas. British Aerospace offered to sell the 15,000 items of electro-shock equipment to the fake buyers for $3.62 million, via distributors in the US and Germany.

The British Aerospace spokesperson warned his clients that this was a 'covert business'. The reporter also gained entry to the Covert and Operational Procurement Exhibition – COPEX – held in Surrey every year. This legal but secretive arms fair attracts security and intelligence agencies, government ministers, and arms dealers from around the world, and not only from allied countries but from states known to employ torture methods, such as Iran, China, Colombia, and Saudi Arabia. Sales to Iran are technically illegal but the Iranian delegation moved around the arms fair without hindrance.

After the film was shown, all of the companies incriminated denied that they had ever been involved in selling illegal equipment, and the Conservative government defended the companies against the allegations. Indeed, the film-makers successfully sued the government for libel. While it was revealed that none of the companies had government backing for their deals, it did become apparent that the government knew about the trade in electro-shock batons, and had sanctioned the sale of such equipment to dangerous states. An Amnesty International investigation revealed that in 1995, following the government's 1993 statement that arms sales to Nigeria would be restricted, 30 licences were granted to sell to the Nigerian police and army 'firearms, rubber bullets, CS gas, spare parts for weapons and military vehicles'.[75]

One year later, in *Back on the Torture Trail*, the team of journalists revealed that nothing had changed. British companies were still ready and willing to sell torture equipment to representatives of governments with poor human rights records, and quite capable of circumventing UK law on the export of such equipment by using distributors in other countries.[76]

How might we make sociological sense of these covert activities? First, we should bear in mind the seminar in torture techniques discussed above. Torture information and equipment are valuable items in the marketplace of terror, in which the state – a legitimate political actor – plays an important role. Torture has not only become commodified, it has also adapted itself to suit the needs of global capitalism. Under globalised conditions, the eyes of the world may be watching the rogue states, monitoring their activities, so where better to hide than in plain sight? Economic globalisation makes such exchanges easier, in so far as it reduces the role of the state to act as arbiter in the marketplace, thus distancing it from blame. The contemporary global capitalist economy is in every respect an economy of violence.

The state, torture and human rights

If we have learned nothing else from the remarkable, harrowing accounts of torture discussed in this chapter, we should at least remember the following points. Firstly, that torture is a form of censorship. Its purpose is not to extract information, but to silence, to violate the rights to speak and to hear. It is a denial of personhood, of humanity. Secondly, that the 'official' justifications for the use of torture are used to conceal this hidden purpose, the silencing of a people. Where torture was once justified in moralist terms, as an appropriate punishment for crimes, modernist sensitivities turned away from moralism towards causalism, and these official explanations are wholly causalist. The purpose of this book, of course, is to unite areas of human rights research. How can torture not be treated in the same context as censorship, or the death penalty, or genocide? Executions, like torture, are explained in causalist terms, such as 'deterrence', but in fact their real purpose serves a different, hidden agenda – far beyond moralism or causalism – which is quite political.

Few commentators have described these contradictions as well as Haim Gordon, who talks of 'legalised' and 'concealed' sadism. 'Today's evil political leaders', observes Gordon, 'outwardly reject sadism for pragmatic reasons. For them, sadism is not wrong or evil; it is an approach that can endanger the realization of their political goals.'[77] So instead, sadism is concealed, or called by a different name, given a different function. Sadists are employed to carry out these tasks of the state, and they are driven by an inherent contradiction: on the one hand, they want to dehumanise their victim, but on the other, they want to see their victims as free agents whose confession or testimony is given as an act of submission to the superiority of the torturer. Indeed, contradictions and anomalies are in abundance in the ritual of torture. As Gordon says, guilt is presumed and innocence must be proven, ends become means and means become ends, and (in the case of Israel following the Landau Report) the actions of the sadist, hitherto concealed, could now be performed with the blessing of the law.[78] By its very nature, the process of torture destroys all involved, the victim, the soldier, the doctor, robbing them of their dignity, and their 'humanitarian impulses'.[79]

Torture, like genocide, is a crime of the state. As with the other abuses of human rights discussed in this volume, its greatest contradiction lies precisely in the fact that the authority responsible for punishing crimes is guilty of the worst violation.

Essay questions

1. How have various social psychological perspectives sought to explain the making of a torturer?

2. Contrast moralist and causalist approaches to the ethics of torture.

3. The global trade in torture equipment and information about torture methods clearly shows how modern capitalism is an economy of violence. Discuss.

4. To what extent have torture methods become more clinical and more personal?

Notes

1 Unofficial translation of an interview taken from the Channel 4 documentary, *The Roots of Evil*, Programme 2: *Torturers*.

2 Jonathan Power (1985) *Amnesty International: The Human Rights Story*, Oxford: Pergamon Press.

3 Power, *Amnesty International*, p. 35.

4 Cesare Beccaria (1764) 'On Crimes and Punishments'. Reproduced in Richard Bellamy (ed.) *On Crimes and Punishments and Other Writings*, Cambridge: Cambridge University Press.

5 Lindsey Williams (1995) 'Through the Eyes of a Torturer' in *Amnesty*, May/June, p. 10.

6 Inge Genefke (1998) 'Challenges for the Future' in Basil Duner (ed.) *An End to Torture: Strategies for Its Eradication*, London: Zed Books, p. 252.

7 Genefke, 'Challenges', p. 252.

8   Jean-Paul Sartre, Preface to Henri Alleg (1958) *The Question*, London: John Calder, p. 24.

9   Ruchama Marton (1995) 'Introduction' in Neve Gordon and Ruchama Marton (eds) *Torture: Human Rights, Medical Ethics and the Case of Israel*, Atlantic Highlands, NJ: Zed Books, p. 4.

10 Love Kellberg (1998) 'Torture: International Rules and Procedures' in Duner, *An End to Torture*; Nigel Rodley (1987) *The Treatment of Prisoners Under International Law*, Oxford: Oxford University Press.

11 Amnesty International (1986) *Voices for Freedom: An Amnesty International Anthology*, London: Amnesty International Publications, p. 169.

12 Power, *Amnesty International*, p. 35.

13 Egon Larsen (1985) in Power, *Amnesty International*, p. 35, citing research carried out by Egon Larsen.

14 Leonard D. Savitz (1986) 'Torture' in *Encyclopaedia Americana*, international edition, vol. 26.

15 Savitz, 'Torture'.

16 Quoted in R. Maran (1989) *Torture: The Role of Ideology in the French-Algerian War*, New York: Praeger, p. 4.

17 See Kellberg, 'Torture'.

18 Quoted in Kellberg, 'Torture', p. 11.

19 See Katarina Tomasevski (1998) 'Foreign Policy and Torture' in Duner, *An End to Torture*.

20 Genefke, 'Challenges', p. 252.

21 See Antonio Cassese (1996) *Inhuman States: Imprisonment, Detention and Torture in Europe Today*, Cambridge: Polity Press.

22 Eric Sottas (1998) 'Perpetrators of Torture' in Duner, *An End to Torture*, p. 69.

23 Sottas, 'Perpetrators of Torture', p. 67.

24 On which, see T.P. Coogan (1980) *On the Blanket: The H Block Story*, Dublin: Ward River Press, especially Chapter 11, 'Torture, Politics and Censorship'.

25 Inge Genefke (1995) 'Evidence of the Use of Torture' in Gordon and Marton, *Torture*, p. 99.

26 Genefke, 'Evidence', p. 100.

27 Amnesty International, *Voices*, p. 66.

28 Williams, 'Through the Eyes', p. 10.

29 Power, *Amnesty International*, pp. 37–8.

30 Amnesty International, *Voices*, p. 64.

31   Cited in Amnesty, *Voices*, p. 68.

32   Martha K. Huggins (1998) *Political Policing: The United States and Latin America*, Durham, NC: Duke University Press, p. 166.

33   Huggins, *Political Policing*, p. 166.

34   Huggins, *Political Policing*, p. 167.

35   From a letter written by Brazilian torture victim Marcos Settamini Pena de Arruda to the Vatican on 4 February 1971, reprinted in Amnesty International, *Voices*, pp. 58–59.

36   Lisa M. Kois (1998) 'Dance, Sister, Dance' in Duner, *An End to Torture*, p. 105.

37   Amnesty International (1998) *United States of America*, London: Amnesty International Publications, p. 62.

38   Angela Robson (1993) 'Rape: Weapon of War' in *New Internationalist & Amnesty*, June.

39   European Community (1993) *The Warburton Report*, cited in Robson, 'Rape', p. 13.

40   Robson, 'Rape', p. 14.

41   Amnesty International, *Voices*, p. 63.

42   Amnesty International, *Voices*, p. 64.

43   R.G. Frey (1992) 'Torture' in Lawrence C. Becker and Charlotte B. Becker (eds) *Encyclopedia of Ethics*, Chicago and London: St James Press.

44   Maran, *Torture*, p. 2.

45   Philip Zimbardo *et al.* (1974) 'The Psychology of Imprisonment: Privation, Power and Pathology' in Z. Rubin (ed.) *Doing Unto Others*, Englewood Cliffs, NJ: Prentice-Hall. For more on Zimbardo's work on abnormal psychology, see also Zimbardo (1969) 'The Human Choice: Individuation, Reason, and Order versus Deindividuation, Impulse, and Chaos' in D. Levine (ed.) *Nebraska Symposium on Motivation*, Lincoln: University of Nebraska Press.

46   Theodor Adorno, Else Frenkel-Brunswick, Daniel J. Levinson, and R. Nevitt Sanford (1950) *The Authoritarian Personality*, New York: Harper.

47   Mika Haritos-Fatouros (1979) *The Official Torturer: Learning Mechanisms Involved in the Process. Relevance to Democratic and Totalitarian Regimes Today*, PhD dissertation, University of Thessaloniki; J.T. Gibson and Mika Haritos-Fatouros (1986) 'The Education of a Torturer' in *Psychology Today* 20, pp. 50–58; Mika Haritos-Fatouros (1988) 'The Official Torturer: A Learning Model for Obedience to the Authority of Violence' in *Journal of Applied Social Psychology*, 18, pp. 1107–20.

48   Stanley Milgram (1974) *Obedience to Authority*, London: Tavistock.

49   Leon Festinger (1957) *A Theory of Cognitive Dissonance*, Evanston, Ill.: Row-Peterson; see also Festinger (1980) *Retrospections on Social Psychology*, New York: Oxford University Press.

50   See an interview with a former torturer in Argentina, shown on the documentary *Roots of Evil*, Programme 2: *Torturers*.

51   Huggins, *Political Policing*, p. 173.

52   See the documentary, *Roots of Evil*, Programme 2: *Torturers*.

53   Huggins, *Political Policing*, p. 173.

54   Again, see *Roots of Evil*, Programme 2: *Torturers*.

55   From 'Wallflower'; words and music by Peter Gabriel.

56   British Medical Association (2001) *The Medical Profession and Human Rights: Handbook for a Changing Agenda*, London: Zed Books, p. 56.

57   James Welsh (1995) 'The Role of Codes of Medical Ethics in the Prevention of Torture' in Gordon and Marton, *Torture*, p. 49.

58   BMA, *The Medical Profession*, p. 65.

59   Ruchama Marton (1995) 'The White Coat Passes Like a Shadow: The Health Profession and Torture in Israel' in Gordon and Marton, *Torture*, p. 33.

60   BMA, *The Medical Profession*, p. 69.

61   See Hernan Reyes (1995) 'The Conflict Between Medical Ethics and Security Measures' in Gordon and Marton, *Torture*.

62   Marton, 'The White Coat', pp. 35–6.

63   Marton, 'The White Coat', p. 37.

64   From an interview included on the documentary, *Roots of Evil*, Programme 2: *Torturers*.

65   Welsh, 'The Role of Codes', pp. 56–7.

66   Mamdouh Al-Aker (1995) 'Where is the Israeli Medical Association?' in Gordon and Marton, *Torture*, p. 63.

67   Anna Craven (1992) 'Can You Recover from the Effects of Torture?' in *Amnesty Student*, Autumn, p. 3.

68   Genefke, 'Evidence', p. 102.

69   Lone Jacobsen and Edith Montgomery (1998) 'Treatment of Victims of Torture' in Duner, *An End to Torture*.

70   Helen Bamber (1995) 'The Medical Foundation and Its Commitment to Human Rights and Rehabilitation' in Gordon and Marton, *Torture*, p. 127.

71   Jacobsen and Montgomery, 'Treatment of Victims'.

72   Lone Jacobsen and K. Smidt-Nielsen (1999) *Torture Survivor: Trauma and Rehabiliation*, Copenhagen: IRCT.

73   Among various studies listed by the authors detailing children's experiences, see Edith Montgomery, Y. Krogh, A. Jacobsen and B. Lukman (1992) 'Children of Torture Victims: Reactions and Coping' in *Child Abuse and Neglect* 16, pp. 797–805.

74   For more on this, see Brian Wood (1991) 'Iron Trade' in *Amnesty*, 52, August/September, p. 20.

75   Amnesty International (1996) 'If It Sells . . .' in *Amnesty*, 80, November/December, p. 15.

76   For more information on the sale of electro-shock batons and other potential weapons of torture, and on the UK's involvement in the trade, see Amnesty International (1997) *Arming the Torturers*, London: Amnesty International Publications, and Amnesty International (1997) *Made in Britain: How the UK Makes Torture and Death Its Business*, London: Amnesty International Publications.

77   Haim Gordon (1995) 'Political Evil: Legalized and Concealed Torture' in Gordon and Marton, *Torture*, p. 11.

78   Gordon, 'Political Evil'.

79   Gordon, 'Political Evil', p. 18.

Further information

Books

Two volumes which have been frequently cited in this chapter stand out as essential reading for anyone concerned about these issues. One is the collection by Basil Duner (ed.) *An End to Torture: Strategies for Its Eradication* (London: Zed Books, 1998). This volume is particularly strong in analysing torture from the point of view of structures and institutions – the role played by the United Nations, by non-governmental organisations, by truth commissions, by national foreign policies, and so on. The other is Neve Gordon and Ruchama Marton (eds) *Torture: Human Rights, Medical Ethics and the Case of Israel* (Atlantic Highlands, NJ: Zed Books, 1995). While it is true that this volume is country-specific, there is more than enough in its content that is applicable more generally, and its various contributions – short conference deliveries – are presented with feeling. Chapters cover not only medical involvement, but the role of lawyers, the psychology of torturers, and the muted responses of wider society.

Videos

The Roots of Evil, Programme 2: *Torturers,* a documentary made by Channel 4 in the United Kingdom, makes for compulsive and disturbing viewing, as it highlights case studies of torturers and their victims in various parts of the world. *The Torture Trail* and *Back on the Torture Trail,* both made by Channel 4's *Dispatches* series, have already been discussed, and provide a revealing insight into the sale of torture equipment.

Web pages

There are many useful websites dedicated to aspects of torture. The Association for the Prevention of Torture, based in Switzerland, can be accessed on www.apt.ch, while the World Organisation Against Torture can be found at www.cmct.org. Essex University provides an 'activists' guide', the Torture Reporting Handbook, at www.essex.ac.uk/torturehandbook. Various associations concerned with the treatment of torture victims have websites, including the Medical Foundation for the Care of Victims of Torture at www.torturecare.org.uk, the US-based Center for Victims of Torture at www.cvt.org, and the International Rehabilitation Council for Torture Victims at www.irct.org.

CHAPTER SIX

The death penalty

Everyone has the right to life, liberty, and security of person.

Universal Declaration of Human Rights, Article 3

[Capital punishment is] the most premeditated of murders to which no criminal's deed, however calculated, can be compared. For there to be an equivalence, the death penalty would have to punish a criminal who had warned his victim of the date at which he would inflict a horrible death on him and who, from that moment onward, had confined him at his mercy for months. Such a monster is not encountered in private life.

Albert Camus

All the men and women I have faced at that final moment convince me that in what I have done I have not prevented a single murder.

Albert Pierrepoint, former British hangman

What is the death penalty?

This chapter will present a general survey of the arguments for and against the death penalty, and of the use of the death penalty in practice, with particular reference to the United States of America. It is worth pointing out that, as a matter of human rights, the death penalty sits in an uncomfortable position. Unlike slavery, torture and genocide it is not (even in principle) universally condemned. Indeed, it is a practice that is used liberally in a variety of nation-states with different cultural and religious traditions. The lack of universal condemnation is due in no small part to the fact that the punishment is endorsed by, among others, the United States, Japan, and most countries adhering to Koranic law. As a human rights issue, though, it clearly contravenes two important norms, pertaining to the right to life, and the right to be free from cruel, inhuman and degrading punishment.[1] However, it is worthwhile reiterating an important theme that has run throughout this volume. To understand the death penalty within the context of human rights it should not matter that, for the most part, it is not a (directly) political form of oppression, used to silence enemies of the state and maintain power. For sure, it is sometimes used for this purpose, and there is certainly a politics to it. However, it is primarily a *judicial* institution, located within the legal sphere, which serves the primary task of maintaining *order* and which punishes enemies not of the state but of the law, namely, *criminals*. This is a very difficult and often arbitrary distinction, but it is one that has served to keep the topic of executions outside the agenda of human rights from the perspective of many governments. Of course, human rights campaigners have had little problem in including it, often arguing (rightly) that it is naïve to assume that the law is easily separated from politics; in many cases the law is little more than an agent of the state.

From a social scientific point of view, the death penalty is a particularly fascinating object of study. There are, in my opinion, three main reasons for this. First, the various issues which are at the centre of the *political* debate about capital punishment (the question of deterrence, economic and racial inequalities in the process of capital punishment) are also at the heart of the *academic* debate, and have been subjected to rigorous empirical analysis. Secondly, there is a philosophical underpinning to these issues which is also of crucial importance to social scientists, that is, the question of *the nature of the relationship between the state and its citizens*. Thirdly, as we shall see, the death penalty is not an event but a complex, multi-layered *process* which lends itself to scrutiny from any number of theoretical and methodological positions.

To elaborate on this third point, there is much to be gained by understanding the death penalty process from an eclectic position. Many of the major theoretical traditions in the social sciences can be used to illuminate our knowledge of different levels of the death penalty process. For example, quantitative empirical analysis is helpful in providing statistical information on the death penalty as it is used in practice, death row populations, public support, and so on. Ethnomethodology allows us to look at the process by which a crime is defined as 'capital' and thus to uncover the power relations inherent in the capital decision-making process. Phenomenology offers ways of understanding the experiences of a person under sentence of death, while Goffmanian dramaturgical analysis provides a framework for viewing death row as the ultimate total institution, and thus exploring ways in which inmates maintain or lose a sense of self. Psychoanalysis suggests ways of understanding the 'need for revenge' on the part of the victims' loved ones, and also of making sense of the experiences of those who have witnessed executions. Marxism provides a means of locating the power relations between the authorities and the inmates within a wider economic structure, and, in its Gramscian variety, allows us to consider the role played by independent state agents in reinforcing the state's view. Foucauldian post-structuralism goes beneath the official view of the death penalty to reveal the multiple hidden reasons for it, reflecting power relations and the way the process becomes a spectacle, part of the public gaze. Foucault, along with Weber's rationalisation thesis and Elias's civilisational analysis, assists us in tracing how changes in the methods of execution, the sanitisation of the process, are in keeping with wider societal and cultural changes. Finally, Frankfurt School-inspired critical theory is extremely useful for understanding the tension between rational authoritarianism and its antithesis in modern societies. In fact, to borrow from Marcuse, the death penalty can be seen to be a wholly irrational system that appears to be rational.[2] This is a distinction between false needs and true needs. We can use this to examine the philosophical arguments that offer support for the death penalty, such as retribution, and how people come to take them for granted. According to critical theory, the only way to realise the inherent irrationality of the system would be through objective understanding, which requires education, and unhindered public discourse and debate.

These theoretical traditions will resurface throughout the chapter. We also need to outline some of the reasons people have for claiming to be opposed to or in support of the practice of the death penalty. Many argue that it is *racist*, or unfavourably biased against some other group in society which lacks full access to political and economic resources. Many also point out that there is always a danger of executing the innocent. Both of these criticisms, which certainly appear to be legitimate, are focused on the death penalty *in practice*. A moralist counterpart, which focuses on the death penalty *in principle*, would stress that the death penalty is a violation of the basic, universal right to life, as well as being a violation of human dignity. I would like to propose two alternative criticisms which are perhaps more *sociological*. First, that it is *unnecessary*, serving as it does no purpose that could not be otherwise, and better, served by an alternative punishment. Second, that it is an intrinsically *irrational* system, containing its own contradictions, in that it actually creates more harm to the social order, and leaves itself open to abuse from the powerful against the powerless. Taking these two criticisms as our starting point, we need to explore why, in the face of empirical evidence and so-called 'rationalisation', the death penalty is still practised. We will discuss these issues concerning the nature of power in modern society in the conclusion.

I have just described one argument as 'moralist'. Elsewhere in this volume I have introduced the perspectives of moralism and causalism (or consequentialism). Moralist claims are made in accordance with various qualitative principles, pertaining to notions of justice and right. They tend to be ethical in nature, and understand an issue with regard to absolute principles or inherent values. Causalist (or consequentialist) claims are made in accordance with the effect or consequences of a particular act or omission. So, while a moralist critique of the death penalty would view all killing as inherently *wrong*, or uphold the universal right to life, a moralist defence would be based on *retribution*. A causalist critique of the death penalty would focus on its effects upon society, such as *brutalisation*, while a causalist defence would rely heavily upon the theory of *deterrence*. What unites these perspectives is that they are primarily located within the realms of jurisprudence and penology. They are general theories of justice or punishment which focus specifically on the aims of a justice system. In this respect, they can be distinguished from those perspectives which either oppose or justify the death penalty on the basis of some factor which is *outside* that system, such as religion, politics, or economics. These arguments, which are often (but not exclusively) *populist* in their nature, reduce the role of the justice system to some other factor in the wider social structure. We will discuss all these perspectives in greater depth below. First, we need to look at the practice of the death penalty throughout recent history.

A brief history of the death penalty

The death penalty has been practised in some form or another since the earliest recorded times, and in virtually every society around the world. There is no space, therefore, to provide a thorough history of its use here. I shall instead focus on certain key trends and dates in a very summary fashion, drawing data liberally from Peter Hodgkinson and Andrew Rutherford's excellent global survey, *Capital Punishment: Global Issues and Prospects*. Students wishing to learn more about the death penalty in the various regions of the world are strongly advised to consult this collection.

The death penalty in Europe

In England and Wales, executions had formed part of the 'bloody code' which for a long time defined the legal system. For example, between 1770 and 1830, some 36,566 death sentences were passed, resulting in between 6,322 and 7,713 executions.[3] However, after 1861, these numbers declined, and murder and treason were, in practice, the only remaining capital offences. The Murder (Abolition of the Death Penalty) Act of 1965 officially abolished it for all but the 'exceptional crimes' of piracy and treason (following the UK's last execution in 1964), and this was confirmed by a free vote in 1969. Total abolition for all crimes was finally agreed in 1998.

Indeed, the abolitionist trend, reflecting an inherent incompatibility between the death penalty and some notion of civilisation, is most clearly apparent in the case of Western Europe. Although some countries had already led the way with abolition for ordinary crimes (Portugal in 1867; the Netherlands in 1870; Sweden in 1921; Denmark in 1930), it was the experience of 'total war' which encouraged others to do the same. Italy started the trend, abolishing it for ordinary crimes in 1947, although, like most other countries, it retained the punishment for certain special crimes. West Germany abolished the death penalty for all crimes after its last execution in 1949 (total abolition extended to all Germany after reunification). The Netherlands had done away with the punishment for ordinary crimes as long ago as 1870, and for all crimes in 1982. Meanwhile, Spain, where the last execution was in 1975, abolished the death penalty for ordinary crimes in 1978 and, for all crimes, in 1995, while France (last execution 1977) agreed upon universal abolition in 1981.[4] Belgium is the only Western European country to retain the death penalty, although, having ratified the EU conventions which oppose the practice, this is more of a nominal retention. Although Portugal is the only member of these nation-states not to have executed someone in the twentieth century (its last execution being in 1849), most of the Western European nations performed their last state killing immediately after the war, in the late 1940s or early 1950s. Only France, Greece and Spain have carried out executions since 1970, and all are now fully abolitionist. In addition, Israel – not technically part of Europe at all but closely culturally allied to it – carried out its first, and last, state execution in 1962, when the Nazi leader Adolf Eichmann was hanged following a famous trial.

As elsewhere, the death penalty was imposed liberally and often ruthlessly in Eastern Europe from the dawn of statehood, in some cases as early as the ninth century.[5] It was introduced in Russia in 1397, but during the eighteenth century it was all but abandoned, and between 1826 and 1906 there were only 170 executions.[6] However, after the 1905 revolution the number increased dramatically, and some 1,500 people were executed in the following three years. Although the practice was debated and even periodically abolished after the 1917 Bolshevik revolution, it was hastily reinstalled out of necessity.[7] Events following the collapse of the Berlin Wall in 1989, and various legal reforms implemented in Russia by Gorbachev after he came to power in 1985, and carried forward by Yeltsin, ushered in a new hope for democracy and in many, but of course by no means all, of these independent states, the punishment has either been abolished or its use severely restricted. This is by and large in keeping with international standards on the subject, and with the worldwide trend towards abolition.

The death penalty in the United States of America

American criminal law developed directly from the English 'bloody code' of the seventeenth century, when hanging was used liberally.[8] After the Civil War, during the period of reconstruction, the federal laws concerning capital punishment were relaxed, and during the subsequent period of progression, many states abolished it. This reform did not last, however, and by the 1920s many states had reimposed the punishment. It was only during the 1950s and 1960s, during a period of increasing discontent with the formal legal or political structures, that abolition once again became an important issue. The numbers of executions had declined steadily since the peak years of 1935 and 1936, when the USA executed 199 prisoners, and 1967 effectively saw the beginning of a moratorium on capital punishment, which lasted ten years. During this time, the Supreme Court further contributed to the argument for abolition with its decision in *Furman v Georgia* (1972).[9] *Furman* is one of the two most significant cases with regard to the legal history of the death penalty in the United States, the other being *Gregg v Georgia* (1976).[10] It was in *Furman* that the Supreme Court submitted a final ruling which led to the official suspension of the death penalty. In fact, the nine senior judges who comprised the Supreme Court at the time submitted nine separate opinions, ranging from abolitionist, through neutral, to strict retentionist. For Justices Marshall and Brennan, the death penalty constituted 'cruel and unusual punishment contrary to the Eighth Amendment'.[11] For Brennan, it was degrading and immoral *per se*. He argued that if a punishment is 'unusually severe' and can be 'inflicted arbitrarily', and that if there is 'no reason to believe that it serves any penal purpose more effectively than some less severe punishment', then it necessarily violates the Eighth Amendment. Marshall, however, saw it as achieving only two possible ends: retribution, which he saw as an illegitimate goal, and deterrence. Marshall would have supported the death penalty as a deterrent if statistics showed this to be the case, but they did not. It served, he argued, 'no purpose that life imprisonment could not serve equally well'.

The Furman decision, five votes against four against the death penalty, did not actually abolish the death penalty; it simply banned it, stopping all executions due to take place. Decisions were made by judges, not legislators, and thus based not on the morality of the death penalty *per se* but on its permissibility with regard to the Eighth Amendment. This was overturned in 1976, in *Gregg v Georgia*, and in a number of subsequent cases.[12] New judges sat in the Supreme Court, and the more conservative administration was less likely to retain the ban on the death penalty if it was on constitutional grounds (i.e. those in the judges' power). The Supreme Court voted seven to two that the death penalty was indeed constitutional so long as a separate sentencing hearing took place in which mitigating and aggravating circumstances could be heard, after the jury had returned a verdict of guilty in the guilt phase. The first post-*Gregg* execution took place in Utah in 1977, of Gary Gilmore. Gilmore had volunteered to die, thus forcing the state into carrying out the punishment laid down in its laws. This set the wheels of the system in motion and the trend, though initially inconsistent, reached dramatic heights in 1995, as Table 6.1 clearly shows. The level of executions rose from 5 in 1983 to 21 the following year; it hovered around the 20 mark for a few years, but by 1992 it had reached 31, and the following year a high of 38. In 1995, 56 people were executed, and in

Table 6.1 Number of executions in the USA since 1976[13]

Year	Number	Year	Number
1976	0	1989	16
1977	1	1990	23
1978	0	1991	14
1979	2	1992	31
1980	0	1993	38
1981	1	1994	31
1982	2	1995	56
1983	5	1996	45
1984	21	1997	74
1985	18	1998	68
1986	18	1999	98
1987	25	2000	85
1988	11	2001[14]	42

Table 6.2   US executions since 1976 by state[15]

State	Number	State	Number
Texas	249	Indiana	9
Virginia	82	Utah	6
Florida	51	Mississippi	4
Missouri	51	Maryland	3
Oklahoma	44	Nebraska	3
Louisiana	26	Pennsylvania	3
South Carolina	25	Washington	3
Arkansas	24	Kentucky	2
Alabama	23	Montana	2
Georgia	23	Ohio	2
Arizona	22	Oregon	2
North Carolina	17	US Federal	2
Delaware	13	Colorado	1
Illinois	12	Idaho	1
California	9	Tennessee	1
Nevada	9	Wyoming	1

1997 a staggering 74. The number climbed as high as 98 in 1999. By 17 July, 2001, the United States had executed a total of 725 people.

Thirty-eight of the 50 US states – plus the military and the US federal jurisdiction – have the death penalty on their statutes, with the majority of executions concentrated primarily in the South (589 of the total number have been in Southern states). Of these, 31 states, plus the federal jurisdiction, are 'active', in so far as they have carried out executions since 1976.[16] As Table 6.2 suggests, Texas has been the most active state in its use of the death penalty.

With regard to the United States, though, one needs to remember that the death penalty is only applied to cases of *capital* murder.[17] This usually means murder with an underlying felony, such as murder in the course of a robbery, a rape, a kidnapping, and so on. It also includes the murder of a law-enforcement officer by someone serving life imprisonment. The term 'capital murder' is vague at best. It is usually a discretionary matter as to whether a prosecutor wishes to seek a capital murder charge. This depends very much on whether the prosecutor is confident of winning a conviction, and the factors which influence this decision will be discussed in greater depth below. Another unusual feature of the American capital system is that it is administered mainly at state level, and only very rarely in federal matters.

The death penalty around the world

Although it would be ludicrous in this space to offer a generic world history of the death penalty, complete with constitutional and legal references, a few points are worthwhile. One is that, even though the death penalty is no longer employed in the United Kingdom, it is still used in a number of Commonwealth territories in the Caribbean, and for a number of these, the Judicial Committee of the Privy Council in London remains the final court of appeal.[18] Similarly, in Commonwealth Africa, political independence did not lead to radical transformations in the penal system, and very few countries responded favourably to the trend towards abolition.[19]

Worldwide, in 1994, 2,331 prisoners were known to have been executed in 37 countries. 1,791 of these were in China, 139 in Iran, and over 100 in Nigeria. Several hundred executions were alleged to have taken place in Iraq, but investigators have been unable to confirm these. In 1998, there were 1,625 confirmed executions in 37 countries, with 3,899 people known to have been sentenced to death in 78 countries. There were 1,067 in China, over 100 in Congo, and – again – hundreds unconfirmed in Iraq. Table 6.3 shows the number of confirmed executions (in countries that were known to have executed at least ten people) in 1998. As of 1 April, 2001, the countries of the world could be divided as shown in Table 6.4.

Table 6.3 Execution figures by country, 1998[20]

Country	Number	Country	Number
China	1,067	Saudi Arabia	29
DR Congo	100	Singapore	28
USA	68	Sierra Leone	24
Iran	66	Rwanda	24
Egypt	48	Vietnam	18
Belarus	33	Yemen	17
Taiwan	32	Afghanistan	10

Table 6.4 International breakdown of death penalty users

Abolitionist for all crimes	75
Abolitionist for ordinary crimes only	13
Abolitionist *de facto*	20 (minimum)
Retentionist	87

Towards abolition?

As is the case with torture, the practice of the death penalty has under-gone various, often conflictual, transformations in the light of processes of modernisation and social rationalisation. On the one hand, the global trend appears to be towards its abolition. The earliest recorded case of abolition was in Tuscany, where the Grand Duke Leopold abolished the practice allegedly after reading Cesare Beccaria's 1764 book *On Crime and Punishment*. Indeed, Beccaria earned a reputation as a travelling celebrity for the abolitionist cause, and one can trace the origins of the modern movement to him and his work. Venezuela was the first mod-ern nation-state to abolish the death penalty for all offences in 1863, but it was not until the years following the Second World War that the ques-tion of worldwide abolition was taken seriously. The abolitionist cause has been taken up by an unusual alliance of intergovernmental organisa-tions such as the United Nations and the Council of Europe, religious bodies such as the Catholic Church, and non-governmental organisa-tions such as Amnesty International. Now, for many, not only is the death penalty considered to be a 'cruel and unusual punishment' in violation of the various UN and related covenants, but it is also held to be incompatible with the allegedly civilised character of late modernity. The latest country to abolish the practice is Chile, whose Justice Minister described it following its abolition on 3 April, 2001, as an 'irrational and inhuman law'.

However, on the other hand, we can see how, in practice, this trend towards abolition is not reflected in the numbers of individual execu-tions. The increasing number of executions in countries such as China, Iran, Nigeria, Saudi Arabia, and the United States makes for worrying reading. The United States remains a curious case, given the trend towards abolition in other Western countries. Considering the possib-ility of abolition in the USA, Zimring and Hawkins have suggested that this would only be possible if the death penalty was recognised as a *national*, as opposed to local, problem, if political leaders took a stand against growing public support for it, and if there was some assurance that it would be kept as a fall-back for exceptional crimes.[21] But these are unlikely conditions.

Social rationalisation appears to be on the side of abolition. The 'civilising process' already allows us to look back at the burning of witches at the stake with disgust, and abolitionists can take heart from this fact.[22] However, rationalisation is a two-sided coin. It does not merely refer to the appeal to 'genuine reason', but also to the intensi-fication of bureaucracy and the popularisation of democracy. In the USA, for example, it seems wholly unlikely that abolition will take place so long as such a large majority of the people appear to be in favour of it. Politicians and judges, as elected representatives, serve not the people but public opinion.

Execution methods

Nothing appears to exemplify the concern expressed by writers such as Weber and Foucault about the absurd consequences of rationalisation more than the transformation in methods of executions, for this represents little more than the sanitisation of the grotesque. Even a populist country such as the USA cannot be seen to be surrendering too much to the rule of the mob. Executions cannot be seen to be the grotesque practices they are. As a result, methods of execution have become more clinical, more sanitised. The electric chair was introduced because it was believed to produce the quickest and most painless death. Quite obviously, this did not prove to be the case. The gas chamber was introduced later for the same reason, and with the same results. The most recent innovation is the lethal injection. This is supposed to be the ultimate form of sanitisation; putting someone to death is akin to putting them to sleep before an operation. Executioners have taken advantage of all the developments in medical science available to them in an attempt to legitimate their practice. This is the kind of rationalisation Weber and Foucault have so often concerned themselves with in their writings – society as a machine. Unfortunately for the executioners, the machine still goes wrong a lot. Even death by lethal injection is not quick or painless – far from it. We will turn to these methods of execution in more detail now. One way of beginning this discussion is with a passage from Foucault's *Discipline and Punish*. In the opening few pages, Foucault describes the execution of Damiens, the regicide, in Paris on 2 March 1757, who was to be brought to the place of execution holding a torch of burning wax, the flesh torn from his breasts, arms, thighs, and calves with red-hot pincers, his right hand burned with sulphur, molten oil, resin, wax and sulphur poured onto his skinless body, and, finally, drawn and quartered by four horses before his body was cremated. The gruesome account spares the reader nothing of the image of a man in indescribable pain.[23]

Foucault's point is that the transformation from such a grotesque spectacle of punishment as this to a rigid system of incarceration actually reflects a shift in the societal interpretation of the nature of crime and punishment, away from the *punishment* of the body of the individual towards the *regulation* of time, space, and body. Where the individual is punished in a bodily fashion, it reflects the seriousness in which the transgression of that individual against God or the state is held. The prison system serves a different kind of rationality.

Clearly, the particular method favoured in executions is usually dependent upon the country, a remnant of some aspect of that country's culture or history. Biblical tales include references to stoning, and this method is still practised in some countries today. Iran, for example, demands death by stoning, and its penal code clearly states that 'the stones should not be too large so that the person dies on being hit by one or two of them; they should not be too small either that they could not be defined as stones'.[24] A barbaric curiosity in respect of stoning is that it usually allows the punishment to be carried out *by the people* rather than by the state officials. This would appear to uphold a penal code which is written in the name of the 'good society' rather than the state or the individual; crimes are crimes *against the people* and thus punishment is meted out by the people as well.

Historically, beheading has been a popular method of execution in many countries. While the *guillotine* is a famous symbol of the French Revolution, a number of Middle Eastern countries still carry out (often public) beheadings using a sword.

Execution by hanging has a long history, initially as a slow death by strangulation (still recorded in some countries). A more modern form of hanging was introduced in the United Kingdom in 1888 as a supposedly humane means of execution, designed to ensure speedy and painless death. The cause of death is fracture to the cervical vertebrae with crushing to the spinal cord, which is supposed to cause immediate unconsciousness and the impossibility of resuscitation due to the impossibility of breathing. However, this is not always the case. Amnesty International reports from Thailand that one man took nine minutes to die because his neck was not broken due to his slight build. He eventually died of suffocation.[25]

Shooting is still used in many parts of the world. Death by a single shot to the back of the head is probably the quickest and most efficient method of execution. This type of execution is carried out with alarming frequency in China, almost always without safeguards for judicial error. However, death by firing squad, which is more commonly practised, adds some degree of regimental ceremony to the occasion. Nevertheless, this method is, by virtue of the distance involved, by no means guaranteed to result in immediate death.

In 1888, while the English were busy developing a more efficient means of hanging, the Americans were introduced to the electric chair. Designed by a dentist, the chair induces death by cardiac arrest through electrocution. Electricity is passed through the body of the condemned, in a manner intended to be humane and quick. In actual fact, the electric chair has become a symbol of the barbaric nature of execution:

> Electrocution produces visibly destructive effects as the body's internal organs are burned; the condemned prisoner often leaps forward against restraining straps when the switch is thrown; the prisoner may defecate, urinate, or vomit blood. Eye-witnesses always report that there is a smell of burned flesh.[26]

Amnesty International has recorded numerous examples of the barbaric cruelty of death by electrocution. One man executed in Indiana in 1985 endured 17 minutes, and five charges of electricity, before he was officially dead. Another example is taken from the state of Alabama, where a condemned man, John Louis Evans, experienced the following death in 1983:

> [I]t required three separate charges of 1,900 volts over 14 minutes before he was officially dead. During the first electrical charge, the electrode on his leg burned through and fell off; prison guards repaired it after doctors had said he was not dead. During the second charge, smoke and flames erupted from his left temple and leg. The third jolt was given after doctors had put a stethoscope to his chest and said they were still not certain he was dead.[27]

Noted criminologist Michael Radelet provides the following account of the execution by electrocution of Jesse Joseph Tafero in Florida in 1990:

> During the execution, six-inch flames erupted from Tafero's head, and three jolts of power were required to stop him from breathing. State officials claimed that the botched execution was caused by 'inadvertent human error' – the inappropriate substitution of a synthetic sponge for a natural sponge that had been used in previous executions. They attempted to support this theory by sticking a part of a synthetic sponge into a 'common household toaster' and observing that it smoldered and caught fire.[28]

Drafting of the UDHR. © **Amnesty International**.

Eleanor Roosevelt holding the UDHR. © **Amnesty International**.

Peter Benenson, 1991. © **Amnesty International**.

A young Chinese protestor pleads with army officers to stop the killing in Beijing. © **Amnesty International**.

Military personnel in Columbia. © **Amnesty International**.

Relatives of the disappeared protest every Saturday in Istanbul. © **Amnesty International**.

Demonstration marking the sixth anniversary of mothers/grandmothers of the Plaza de Mayo's weekly marches to demand information about their 'disappeared' relatives. © **Amnesty International**.

Legcuffs produced by the UK company Hiatts. © **Amnesty International**.

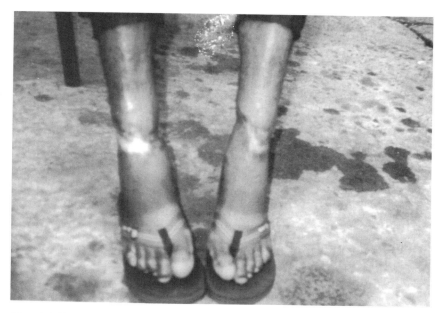

Wounds inflicted on prisoners forced to wear leg irons. © **Amnesty International**.

Execution of 10 people convicted of armed robbery, Calabar, Nigeria. © **Amnesty International**.

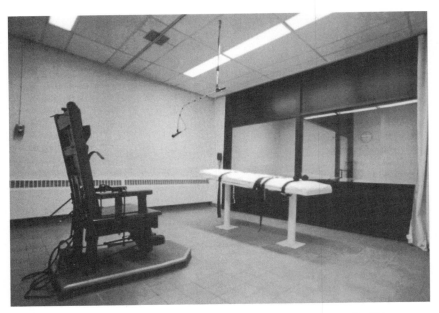

Death chamber and witness room, Southern Ohio Correctional Facility, Lucasville, Ohio.
© **Amnesty International**.

Young children protesting the death penalty in Houston, USA. © **Amnesty International**.

The gates of Auschwitz. © **Amnesty International**.

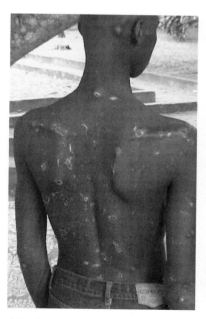

A freed slave displaying his whipping scars. **Courtesy Kevin Bales.**

Cambodia's killing fields. © **Amnesty International**.

An ethnic Albanian walks between two rows of corpses as he tries to identify his relatives. © **Amnesty International**.

A young woman attends a candlelight vigil in Central America to call attention to violence against women. © **Amnesty International**.

On the face of it, there is little difference to be found between these accounts and the tale of Damiens's execution so vividly recollected by Foucault, except that Evans died in 1983, Tafero in 1990, over two hundred years after Damiens. An equally violent method was introduced in the 1920s: gassing. Here, the condemned prisoner dies by asphyxiation once lethal cyanide gas is passed into a chamber, where the prisoner sits tied to a chair or gurney. Whether death is instantaneous depends greatly on the speed with which the gas reaches the vital organs, and is slowed down when the prisoner struggles by trying not to breathe. One inmate, Jimmy Lee Gray, executed in Mississippi in 1983, convulsed 'for eight minutes and gasped 11 times, striking his head repeatedly on a pole behind him'.[29] Observers were asked to leave the room, at which point they were uncertain whether the inmate was yet dead. It was later revealed that the executioner was drunk at the time. In 1992, Donald Harding was put to death by lethal gas by the state of Arizona. Radelet offers the following account:

> Death was not pronounced until $10^{1}/_{2}$ minutes after the cyanide tablets were dropped. During the execution, Harding thrashed and struggled violently against the restraining straps. A television journalist who witnessed the execution, Cameron Harper, said that Harding's spasms and jerks lasted 6 minutes and 37 seconds. 'Obviously, this man was suffering. This was a violent death . . . an ugly event. We put animals to death more humanely.' Another witness, newspaper reporter Carla McClain, said, 'Harding's death was extremely violent. He was in great pain. I heard him gasp and moan. I saw his body turn from red to purple.' One reporter who witnessed the execution suffered from insomnia and assorted illnesses for several weeks; two others were 'walking vegetables' for several days.[30]

In 1977, the United States experimented with an even more calculated method of execution, lethal injection, which was to become the standard means of killing condemned prisoners. Approved by many medical specialists as genuinely humane, this method is akin to putting down an unwell pet. However, any number of errors can be made which could lead to the slowing down of the process, which would result in a painful death. Drug users are particularly at risk, as are those with collapsed veins. In some cases, the prisoners themselves have had to assist the technicians to locate a usable vein. There are also numerous examples of technical failure. In 1984, a Texas inmate, James Autry, took about ten minutes to die, during which time he was conscious and in considerable

Judaism and Christianity hold similar views. Judaism rarely demands the use of the death penalty even though it is famously called for in the Old Testament. Christianity has distanced itself from the use of the death penalty (although not, in all cases, officially). Non-violence is a central philosophy of the Buddhist and Hindu faiths.

In terms of organised opposition to the death penalty, the major Catholic, Protestant and Jewish bodies in the United States have for some time been opponents of the practice, despite the rise of fundamentalist Christian groups which support it.[34] In the mid-twentieth century, after providing the theoretical justification for the practice for centuries, the Church of England finally came out in opposition to it, and in 1969 the Archbishop of Canterbury and 18 other bishops voted in favour of total abolition. In America, the campaign to abolish the death penalty is supported by the leaders of most of the major religious bodies.

Religious arguments justify the use of the death penalty according to the dominant cultural traditions of a given society. They thus appeal to a 'higher' code of ethics, the law of God. Sometimes, political justifications adopt similar means of legitimising executions, except that the appeal to religion is replaced with one to *ideology*. If politics is about establishing power, then the death penalty can, of course, be an important instrument in maintaining that power. Here, the state is established as the administrative arm of the people, working on behalf of the 'public good'. The message sent out by the very presence of the death penalty is one of 'zero tolerance' for those who threaten the established order. Advocates of this position might suggest that a certain amount of freedom must be sacrificed for the good of society. This position is held by, amongst others, neo-Macchiavellians and neo-Hobbesians, who argue, in different ways, that the state must be allowed to conduct its affairs without unncessary interference from citizens, so long as it works in the interests of such citizens. This is a liberal interpretation at best. Essentially, while this argument has been used by conservative tendencies within liberal democracies, it is more commonly associated with authoritarian regimes. While the rhetoric may be about the 'good society', the reality is usually more about the maintenance of order. Karl Marx saw the death penalty as incompatible with a socialist system, in that it assumes authority from above; that is, it assumes that the state has the right to execute one of its citizens. But in Marx's name, executions have been considered necessary means of ridding 'socialist' societies of enemies of the state and of the people. This is the line used by the likes of Josef Stalin to justify his use of execution as a political tool. We return to this crucial question – that of the role of the state – in the concluding section of this chapter.

Political-economic conditions of the death penalty

One argument often used in liberal democracies to support the death penalty is concerned with public opinion. This is especially true in the United States, where much importance is placed on the 'will of the people'. As C. Wright Mills has said, 'in the standard image of power and decision, no force is held to be as important as The Great American Public. This public is thought to be the seat of all legitimate power'.[35]

Proponents of the death penalty point out, often by way of an alleged defence of the principles of democracy, that studies constantly show a majority of people, both in the USA and also in Britain, to be in favour of its use. There would appear to be a number of flaws in this line of reasoning. One obvious criticism is based on the ambiguous nature of *statistics*. Studies also show how this support would be reduced to below 50 per cent if it was made clear that life imprisonment as an alternative to death *meant* life imprisonment without parole. Also, in some US states, studies show that the support would drop dramatically if life not only meant life, but the inmate would be expected to work so as to raise money for the victim's family. According to research carried out in California, the 82 per cent which supported the death penalty at first dropped to only 26 per cent once these two factors – life to mean life, and some degree of restitution – were introduced.[36] In a poll held in Japan in 1967, the superficial finding was that some 71 per cent of respondents agreed with the death penalty. However, when one delved further into questions pertaining to the deterrent effect (or lack thereof) of capital punishment, or to the alleged rise in violent crime in Japan at the time, only 26 per cent ended up opposing a temporary suspension of the practice pending further investigation.[37] Similarly, an American study claimed that the percentage of supporters would drop from 70 per cent to 55 per cent if there could be a guarantee that the homicide rate would not increase.[38]

A second criticism of this argument pertains to the *autonomy of law*. The argument assumes that the law should be subservient to politics; that the political whim is the voice of the people, and that this outranks any moral or ethical argument. It also goes against the whole principle of an autonomous, neutral legal system. In the United States, where senior judges are elected, such populism might result in the law becoming nothing more than a political plaything.

A third criticism pertains to the *meaning of democracy*. The public opinion argument presumes that democracy must be of the utilitarian kind, which holds the will of the (majority of the) people to be sovereign, and thus to outweigh the wishes, and rights if necessary, of the minorities. According to such an argument, literally *anything* could be made legal so long as the public demanded it! However, public opinion clouds other arguments, and the public is not always the best judge of society because it does not always have access to the relevant information, or indeed the appropriate knowledge to make those decisions. Democracy need not be based on utilitarian assumptions. It could instead be based on *communication* as the rational exchange of knowledge and as a means of achieving consensus and truth.[39] Victor Hugo famously pointed out that most people are indifferent on the matter of the death penalty because they do not have experience of it, and thus are not in possession of the facts. Once a person observes, or in some other way comes to experience, an execution, then he or she will necessarily come to a more informed decision about its merits. Hugo, an opponent of the death penalty, certainly hoped that people's capacity for reason would steer them in the direction of opposition rather than support. A 1975 random study of adults in a US town compared attitudes towards the death penalty before and after being given access to information on the subject. At first, 51 per cent of the sample supported it, 29 per cent opposed, and 20 per cent were unsure. After reading an essay outlining some of the key arguments in the debate, only 38 per cent were in support, while 42 per cent were now opposed, and 20 per cent remained uncertain.[40]

For some supporters of the death penalty, the justification is not so much political as *economic*. It is, they point out, becoming increasingly expensive to keep prisoners in jail. Tax payers' money goes towards their food and accommodation, regardless of peripheral issues such as the extent to which prisoners should be allowed certain pleasures. These people argue that it would be far cheaper to execute serious offenders. And of course, in one respect, they are right – provided one were to take the offender aside after trial and perform a summary execution there and then. However, it is generally accepted that there is some need for safeguards to ensure that the prisoner is indeed guilty. As Barry Nakell points out, capital trials, driven by this need to ascertain guilt, are usually longer and more complicated, and defendants usually plead not guilty, thus ensuring they require a jury, and more expert witnesses, especially in mitigation, whose expenses must be met.[41] This also means that rigorous and often lengthy appeals processes and possibly retrials are required. According to one report, the cost of the trial and first stages of appeal alone would be double that required for life imprisonment.[42] In the meantime, the prisoner must be kept under maximum security conditions. In the United States, this appeals process has been known to last so long that sometimes prisoners are kept on Death Row for 20 years or more. Added to this is the cost of employing medical practitioners and of producing the necessary chemicals required for lethal injection or gassing. When all this is considered, the cost of executions exceeds that of lifelong imprisonment.

The theoretical discourse on the death penalty

Jeffrey Reiman and Ernest van den Haag are, I think, quite right to point out that even if one opposes the death penalty in *practice*, one may still support it in *principle*.[43] Concerns over arbitrariness, discrimination and wrongful executions are based not on the rightfulness of the death penalty as a punishment but on faults within the criminal justice system. Although there are many arguments which are often used to either defend or oppose the practice of executions in principle, the two major ones, which we turn to now, are *deterrence* and *retribution*.

Is the death penalty a deterrent?

The theory of deterrence suggests that, necessarily, the presence of a death penalty, being the ultimate punishment, will cause potential killers to refrain from killing through the fear of punishment. As such, it is a causalist defence of the death penalty, concerned not with its morality *per se* but with its effect upon the crime rate. Those who advocate deterrence theory tend to assume that the primary function of a punishment system is to protect the 'greater good', and that this can be achieved by making examples of those who commit crimes. It is thus grounded in utilitarian theory. John Stuart Mill, a founder of this movement, believed that the death penalty should be supported as long as it could be argued that it served the greater good by acting as a deterrent. He added that abolition of the death penalty would lead to a general contempt for death, and that such a fear of death is a necessary and healthy virtue of society. A similar justification for the death penalty has been advanced by the conservative criminologist Ernest van den Haag.[44] For van den Haag, necessarily, 'the threat of 50 lashes deters more than the threat of 5; a $1,000 fine deters more than a $10 fine; ten years in prison deters more than one year in prison'. Accordingly, death must be the ultimate deterrent.

The first criticism that can be made of deterrence theory is a moral one. That is, by sacrificing one individual for the benefit of others, it reduces human life to a means–end calculation, thus violating Immanuel Kant's famous maxim to treat humans always as ends and never as means to ends. Countering this opposition, Jeffrey Reiman has developed a *functionalist* defence of the theory of deterrence.[45] It is not the individual act of punishment which deters, Reiman argues, but the *existence of a functioning punishment system*. Such a system, he claims, benefits society *as a whole*, even those punished by it, because they also gain protection through the deterrence. However, Reiman's argument, whilst logically plausible, is, like that of his erstwhile opponent van den Haag, open to a charge of ignoring the normative basis of a punishment system. Both Reiman's functionalist account and van den Haag's Hobbesian realist one can be used to legitimise any action, however severe, so long as it could be shown to function as a deterrent. Indeed, van den Haag has admitted that he would support the use of torture if he believed, which he does not, that torture had any deterrent effect.[46]

The second criticism is a psychological and philosophical one. Thorsten Sellin has argued that the theory of deterrence is necessarily based upon an assumption that life is precious and worth saving at all costs.[47] But for this deterrence actually to take effect, there would have to be a genuinely realistic chance that one might be endangering one's life. In countries where the death penalty exists but is rarely carried out (statistically speaking, when considering the number of possible capital murders compared to the number of executions, the USA fits into this category), the threat does not seem real. Besides, what is so special about the death penalty that it *necessarily* deters more than, for example, life imprisonment? If we accept the deterrence theory in principle, we would agree that any heavy punishment would deter more than a light one. For the most serious crimes, we should have the most serious punishment, but this need not be death.

A third criticism, related to this, is also a psychological one, which claims that proponents of deterrence theory misunderstand human behaviour. They assume that people act in a rational, calculated way. Most killings, in fact, are crimes of passion, and a number are committed by people unable to grasp the complexities of the law. That is to say, if over 50 per cent of all murders are committed by people who are close to the victim during a moment's lapse of reason, then deterrence is not a factor. Many murders are committed due to the influence of drugs or alcohol. This is also likely to cloud the potential murderer's capacity for reason. Many others are committed because the offender is suffering from either diminished responsibility or some form of mental illness. Even murders that do not fit into these categories are not necessarily susceptible to deterrence. A study of 145 murderers in Japan concluded with the observation that none of them gave any consideration to the possibility of them facing the death penalty, even though they were aware of its presence, because most of them were focused solely on the present.[48] Meanwhile, recidivists who know and understand the law remain undeterred. For example, terrorists and other such 'professional murderers' are unlikely to be deterred where their dastardly plans are driven by some political passion, or by the power of their own commitment to their chosen profession. This claim has been supported by, amongst other things, interviews with terrorists. So, killers are not deterred. Van den Haag, who defends the deterrence theory, has accepted that certain groups will not be deterred, but maintains that the value of deterrence is in the prevention of other people from becoming criminals. He also points out that deterrence does not require a rational calculation to take place every time a criminal activity is made available – the deterrent effect acts upon the opportunities for individuals to commit crimes.[49]

A fourth criticism is perhaps the most convincing to many people in so far as it is based on statistical evidence. That is to say, studies continue to show that the death penalty *does not deter*. For example, a study in 1983 of 14 countries which had abolished the death penalty showed that over half had experienced a decline in homicides.[50] In Nigeria, the murder rate continued to rise despite the presence of the death penalty, while incidents of armed robbery rose quite dramatically after it had been declared a capital offence in 1970.[51] In Canada (where abolition took place in 1976) the murder rate dropped from 3.09 per 100,000 to 2.79 per 100,000 between 1975 and 1983. These findings have, by and large, been replicated by other studies.[52]

An interesting counter-argument to deterrence theory is provided by Bowers and Pierce. They argue that, in fact, the very presence of a death penalty might result in the glorification of violence, which in turn might produce an increase in homicide rates. They point out that in New York between 1907 and 1963 an additional two murders occurred in the month following an execution.[53] According to the authors of this influential study, the effect is *brutalisation*, not deterrence. Bowers goes on to suggest that this is the real reason why executions – despite their apparent deterrent effect – are no longer public events. They are kept from those who are most in need of deterrence because they are grotesque spectacles which might result in violence.[54] Jonathan Glover, who claims to be a neo-utilitarian, has also suggested that the death penalty does more harm than good to wider society, because, he claims, of the side effects which result from it, such as brutalisation and psychological torture.[55]

An earlier counter-argument came from Cesare Beccaria.[56] The deterrence argument is, as stated above, based upon a causalist, utilitarian perspective, but Beccaria adopted a wholly utilitarian argument to oppose the use of the death penalty. The purpose of punishment for Beccaria was always the protection of the majority, and thus deterrence. Beccaria based his critique of the death penalty on three principles, the first two of which are utilitarian, the third of which is contractarian.

1   It is not the cruelty of the punishment which is the basis for its deterrence value, but the likelihood of the punishment being carried out.

2   Further to this, it is not the intensity of the punishment but the duration of it which deters; thus the lifelong loss of liberty would necessarily deter more than the immediate removal of life.

3   In the social contract, through which civil society emerged from the state of nature, there is no reason why persons would volunteer to the state control over their lives.

Beccaria could see no reason why the death penalty served any purpose. Given that a utilitarian is concerned more with the causes of an act rather than the act itself, then such an argument would need to consider the suggestion that the death penalty in fact leads to an increase rather than a decrease in human suffering, and thus oppose it. In place of the existing theory of deterrence, he proposed a theory of prevention, based around a recognition that deterrence is not simply a consequence of the existence of a punitive system, but also of these other factors.

Before moving on to discuss another important issue in the debate, we should remember a different kind of deterrence, which raises its own interesting questions. While it may be true that the death penalty does not actually dissuade others from committing similar heinous crimes when we execute an offender, then, if nothing else, we are at least preventing her or him from killing again! Thus goes the argument for incapacitation, or individual deterrence. For example, Marcel Normand has listed numbers of killers who have escaped execution only to kill again. Normand's point is an ethical one: the sacrifice of one criminal life is necessary for the protection of the innocents in society. By refusing to execute, the state is risking the lives of those innocents for the sake of that one criminal.

The problems with this approach are twofold. The first is a matter of jurisprudence. Surely, we might say, no one would advocate a legal system whereby we punish offenders not for the crime they have just committed, but for a crime they might commit sometime in the future. Such a system would make a mockery of the whole idea of legal justice. The second problem is statistical. Most offenders would not kill again. Many murders are committed in moments of passion. Annually, this accounts for the majority of murders. Others occur under the influence of drugs or alcohol. Many murderers have psychological problems and require medical help. In some cases, these people would be spared the death penalty for just this reason.

Even if we knew an offender was going to kill again, why should we kill him or her, rather than keep them locked up for the rest of their life? If we had a time machine, and could predict a future scenario where the offender would kill again – assuming it was legally admissible to do so, surely we could prevent that scenario just as effectively by keeping the offender in maximum security detention. Of course, we have no such device, and the point appears moot, but in fact it is another example of how arguments in support of the death penalty often rely on emotion, and when studied carefully are exposed as fraudulent in so far as they offer no justification specific to the *death penalty* at all.

Justice and retribution

Retribution involves punishing an act because it is morally wrong, and duly balancing out a level of social justice. Plato offered an early justification for the death penalty as the 'law of nature', using essentially retributivist claims. These were developed by Immanuel Kant and Georg Hegel, and more recently have been advanced by Jeffrey Reiman. Bobbio sums up the Kantian position succinctly:

> The function of punishment [is] purely as legal redress and not the prevention of crime. In other words, the punishment had to correspond precisely to the crime... He argues that the state had a duty to apply the death penalty, and this was a categorical imperative, not a hypothetical imperative based on a relationship between means and ends.[57]

The state's duty is clearly performed in the name of the people. Thus, the state must be seen to balance out the loss and suffering endured by the victims. Hegel took these ideas even further. He argued that the idea of punishment according to crime is the only way not only of redress but also of redemption. Indeed, it is an honour, and the prisoner has a right to expect it. Hegel's case is extreme, but the retributivist argument has many defenders. Reiman has defended the claim that retribution is the function of a punishment system by suggesting two ways in which it re-establishes equality.[58] First, he argues, equal suffering by an offender forces the recognition of suffering and vulnerability to it. Second, it reassures society that every person's suffering is a tragedy, thus reaffirming equality between offender and victim.

These suggestions are open to considerable questioning. Taken to its extreme, in the old adage 'an eye for an eye', retribution implies not only that all murderers should be executed – instead of the strategically selected proportion which is – but that all rapists should be raped, and so on. Also, how can retribution enhance respect for the value and equality of life, when clearly the state, in taking a life, is rendering it worthless? How also can social justice suddenly be 'balanced' when the state kills someone? By committing this 'immoral' act itself, it legitimates murder. And if the taking of a human life necessarily requires the loss of one's life, then who is there to take the life of the executioner? Indeed, the death penalty as it is practised in many countries around the world might rebuke its own retributivist argument. Some might go so far as to say that it actually creates more harm to the social order, not just in the taking of the life but in the subsequent effects upon any loved ones. It should also be remembered that the need for an often lengthy appeals process means that prisoners are kept in what are usually the worst conditions of all for long periods of time, prior to their execution. Rather, then, than offering 'an eye for an eye', the state in fact in practice responds to murder with imprisonment, torture, and murder.

However, there is nothing particular about retribution which requires 'an eye for an eye'. John Conrad defends the idea that retribution is the primary goal of punishment, but duly opposes the death penalty.[59] Following Emile Durkheim, Conrad argues that, in a rational society, rewards and punishments are necessary to maintain order. Guilt must therefore meet with appropriate punishment. But Conrad dismisses the Kantian position which requires the punishment to be proportionate to the crime. Instead, he argues that punishment is *itself* retribution, and that retribution is about the balance of justice. Murder is a more serious crime than theft. Hence the murderer should be given a harsher punishment than the thief. Life imprisonment instead of a year, or whatever. This argument, which is heavily indebted to Durkheim's moralistic theory of justice, is referred to as the 'scales of justice' argument, and suggests a useful retributivist critique of the death penalty which is both moralistic and sociological.

'Race', class and the death penalty

However one feels about the appropriateness of the death penalty *per se*, the major concerns stem from its use in *practice*. Various charges are made against it. Of course, for many people, the most striking such charge is that it is irrevocable, and that, given that a perfect, faultless legal system has yet to be defined, there will always be the danger of executing innocent people. Even as celebrated an executioner as the

French revolutionary, Maximilien-François-Marie-Isidore de Robespierre, opposed the death penalty on the grounds of its irreversibility and of the possibility of judicial error. According to the criminologist Roger Hood, approximately 350 innocent people were convicted of capital murder in the United States between 1900 and 1985, of whom 23 were executed.[60] Indeed, for many opponents of the death penalty, following Robespierre, the very fact that there is *always* a *possibility* of wrongful conviction is *in itself* sufficient reason not to have any punishment which cannot be reversed if necessary.

Questions of guilt or innocence aside, the practice of the death penalty is also riddled with demographic inequalities, which should be of particular interest to social scientists. Statistics show that the vast majority of those sentenced to death belong to the poorest socio-economic category. Also, a hugely disproportionate number are black. In this section we will discuss some of the research which has been carried out on the death penalty in practice, particularly as it relates to these evident inequalities in the punitive system.

Racial discrimination and capital punishment

The chances of a black defendant being given the death sentence for murdering a white victim, in the USA, are phenomenally higher than the chances of it being sought against a white offender. Even before the moratorium in 1967, race played a major factor in determining who died. According to an Amnesty International report, between 1930 and 1967 two-thirds of those executed were black.[61] Studies suggest that between 40 per cent and 62 per cent of the inmates on Death Row are black, even though blacks make up only 12 per cent of the US population.[62] Similarly, 84 per cent of those executed since 1977 were convicted of murdering white victims, even though the ratio of white people murdered compared to black people is roughly equal. According to one study, there is a 40-times-greater chance of a death penalty being sought against someone convicted of killing a white person than of killing a black person.[63] Thus, the death penalty has been accused of being a racist system in the USA. But this racism is not unique to the American system. In many non-Western countries, the death penalty is primarily sought against foreigners, refugees, or internal 'Others'. These tend to be among the most powerless groups in the society.

Racial discrimination can take place at any stage of the capital decision-making process, and each stage reflects and exploits some inherent racism in the wider system.[64] It can begin with the initial arrest and indictment, run through the prosecutor's method of jury selection, which would clearly influence the outcome of the trial, and influence the possibility of a fair appeal. At the outset, the decision – which is at the discretion of the prosecutor – to seek death, is clearly racially unbalanced.[65] One Georgia politician wrote a report claiming that, during the 1980s, blacks were the victims of some 70 per cent of homicides in the state, but only once did the District Attorney seek a death sentence in a case involving a black victim.[66] But there are other factors which influence the prosecutor's decision in this respect. He or she will be keen to secure a conviction, and to do so, such factors as the location of the trial, and the selection of the jury, come into play. A prosecutor is allowed to 'strike' 12 jurors without reason, and in the case, for example, of a young black male accused of killing a white woman, she or he will usually use those strikes to exclude black candidates and ensure an all-white jury. Given that the vast majority of judges are also white, the race factor is very significant when the defendant may be the only black person involved in the case!

Executing the poor: the role of trial attorneys in deciding who dies

If these statistics are damning, then those pertaining to socio-economic status are even more revealing. Well over 90 per cent of those on Death Row come from the lowest socio-economic group. These statistics actually reflect not only the discriminatory but also the arbitrary nature of the death penalty in practice. It is often used as an instrument of political power, and it is invariably the weakest and most powerless members of society who will suffer. In the United States, for example, the death penalty will only be sought against those who are poor and marginalised. Such people would be those unable to afford a decent defence, and would require the assistance of court-appointed lawyers who, in most cases, are not able to combat the skill and resources of the state officials.[67] These lawyers are poorly paid, and usually lack the facilities to perform a thorough investigation. Some are recent graduates from law school, while others are lawyers of a more seasoned vintage unable to practise in any other capacity. One study found the following trends to be common across the six American states – Texas, Louisiana, Mississippi, Alabama, Georgia and Florida – that constitute the 'death belt'.[68]

1   Over half of court-appointed defence counsel were handling their first capital case.

2   Capital trials are often completed in one or two days.

3 Fees paid to the counsel are often so low that it is impossible for lawyers to carry out decent investigations.

4 On appeal, incompetence of trial lawyers has been dismissed as 'harmless error' and not seen as sufficient reason to merit a retrial.

The trial process itself is comparable to a game that is biased in favour of the experienced campaigner. The relationship between law and politics in the USA is such that prosecutors are reluctant to risk their reputations by trying a capital case that they may not win. In other words, your chances of receiving a death sentence rely less upon what you may have done than upon who you are in the context of socio-economic conditions. Financial security allows the offender a greater chance of overcoming the system. It is always the powerless who suffer, because they make easy targets for the state, as they cannot afford decent legal representation, and make do with makeshift court-appointed lawyers who botch their cases. Skills at striking jurors so as to ensure a sympathetic panel are necessarily better employed by the experienced state attorneys than by inexperienced or incompetent defence lawyers. Should the state successfully obtain such a jury, this would virtually ensure a conviction and an execution, assisting the prosecutor with his or her political career and satisfying a public bloodlust, regardless of the facts. If they cannot, or if they are up against a wealthier or more resourceful defendant, they are unlikely to seek the death penalty. If they do seek the death penalty and achieve a guilty verdict, the inexperience of their opponents once again works in their favour. Studies indicate that over 40 per cent of defence counsel have confessed to being under-prepared for the penalty phase of a trial following a guilty verdict, while 27 per cent did not call for character or expert witnesses.[69]

These charges are not aimed solely at the US system, nor are they solely contemporary. They manifest themselves in methods as well as processes of execution. While the most notable example is the racist and arbitrary application of the system in the USA, in truth the severity of a punishment has always reflected issues of status and class. Historically, even methods of execution have differed between those in diffferent class groups. In ancient Greece, freemen were treated to a quick death by poison, while slaves were beaten or stoned. In ancient Rome, citizens were either stoned or thrown off the Tarpeian Rock, while slaves and non-citizens suffered crucifixion. In medieval England, the gentry were beheaded, while others were hanged. By understanding the death penalty in practice, and its arbitrary use therein, we are better able to understand its hidden agenda, and its use as a political (rather than a solely ethical-legal) instrument. In this respect, we may wish to return to the earlier chapters on censorship and political imprisonment. In these chapters, we discussed the theories of Louis Althusser.[70] While we have focused in this chapter primarily on the death penalty as a violation of human rights which is exercised within the *legal* sphere, it is clearly open to manipulation by the political sphere, and as such can be understood as a *repressive state apparatus*. Also, it is often argued that the harshness of a punishment reflects not the crime itself but the extent to which the crime has captured the imagination of the public. Punishment thus becomes nothing more than a means of securing political support by responding to the public mood. It can also be used arbitrarily to reflect wider cultural divisions within societies.

The experience of Death Row

As we have seen, Ernest van den Haag, a supporter of the death penalty, nevertheless criticises aspects of its practice in the United States. Van den Haag opposes the additional element of psychological torture which, he claims, results from being imprisoned for possibly ten years or more; a theft of hope which is not, he claims, inherent in the nature of the death penalty itself.[71] Arguing from a different perspective, Robert Johnson agrees that the manner in which the system is played out in the USA amounts to an additional torture: on Death Row, prisoners are 'warehoused' in appalling conditions, and 'dehumanised' through experiencing the uncertain wait for death.[72] An Amnesty International report claimed that an average US Death Row cell, located in the Maximum Security Unit of the state penitentiary, is 5ft × 7ft (1.5m × 2.2m) or 6ft × 9ft (1.8m × 2.8m), with minimal light, all of which contravenes the American Correctional Association's minimum standards.[73] Similar, often more inhumane, conditions are attributed to other nation-states' prisons.

It was not until various legal actions were filed in the late 1970s and early 1980s that condemned prisoners had rights at all. Prior to this, prisoners in Georgia had no right to exercise, and in states such as Alabama and Missouri prisoners spent all but one half-hour a day in their cells. In most cases these cells were dark, dirty and bug-infested, and in many cases meals were taken there, the last one coming as early as 2.30 p.m. There was no dental care and little medical care. Although, thanks to various actions, the situation has improved, it is far from tolerable. Haas and Inciardi claim that Death Row inmates suffer 'enforced idleness, unnecessarily repressive custodial restrictions, intentionally sub-standard living conditions, and mind-numbing isolation from ordinary human contact'.[74] Cells are 'cramped, windowless, and arranged in tiers with little or no natural light'. Inmates also suffer poor plumbing, low ventilation, and restrictions on food, medicine, hot water, and bedding. Many states deny contact visits. These conditions vary dramatically across states, with no obvious geographical or cultural reason why.[75] While the noted psychiatrist Herbert E. Thomas once claimed that any inmate who spends three years or more in a maximum security unit is in danger of suffering from a deteriorating ability to function in a free society,[76] the reality for Death Row inmates is that rehabilitation – turning the prisoner into a 'good citizen' – is not a consideration. Instead, as Robert Johnson points out, human conditions on Death Row are not feasible because the purpose of confinement is dehumanisation.[77]

Johnson interviewed 45 of the 47 inmates on Death Row in Alabama, and he found, among other things, that inmates suffered from a morbid obsession with their seemingly inevitable eventual fate. Thoughts of the execution itself, and of the mechanics of death by electrocution and its impact upon the human body, began to dominate their minds. They thought about how they would feel during their walk to the execution chamber, about how much pain they would experience and for how long, and about how the experience might affect their loved ones. These thoughts often led to nightmares. At the same time, other considerations, thought of as healthy under normal conditions, deteriorated. Family relationships began to seem futile, as inmates suffered a feeling of abandonment, what Johnson calls a 'death of the personality'. Common conditions included depression, apathy, loss of any sense of reality, and physical and mental deterioration. On Death Row, unlike other institutions of confinement such as penal colonies, labour camps and prisoner-of-war camps, there is little or no sense of hope for release. The dominant feeling is one of finality, a living death.

The slow process of dehumanisation carries on until the end. Although the process of preparing for the execution differs from state to state, most of these differences concern times rather than deeds. The inmate is nearly always moved prior to the execution to an isolation cell next to the death chamber for the 'death watch'. His or her few remaining possessions are taken away, and the prisoner is placed under special observation. This stripping away of dignity and humanity is used in part to assuage any feelings of guilt or loss on the part of the guards and others involved in the execution. The inmate is then usually allowed a last contact visit with loved ones, and a last meal, both of which serve in part to make the process seem almost civilised, while at the same time adding to the finality of the occasion.

Medical involvement in the death penalty

The death penalty is not so much an event as a *process*, and at each stage of this process, 'experts' are called in to assist with its execution. Police officers, lawyers, and prison officials of course play key roles, but the active involvement of medical professionals has received by far the most controversy and notoriety. Physicians and psychiatrists often testify on behalf of the state, either to show that the defendant could be held accountable for his or her crimes, or – absurdly – to guarantee to the court that he or she is physically or mentally fit enough to be executed. Medical professionals are also required during the administration of death by lethal injection.[78] This involvement contravenes all known medical ethics, which stipulate that the doctor's commitment is to the preservation of life. National and international medical associations, starting with the American Medical Association in 1980, supported the following year by the World Medical Association, have spoken out in condemnation of physician participation in all aspects of the death penalty process except the certification of death.[79] The AMA now bars its practitioners from even attending executions. These professional bodies have thus become an integral part of the anti-death penalty movement.

However, there are still grey areas in respect of medical involvement. Doctors and correction officials widely accept that it is not too difficult to bypass the AMA's regulations. When Daniel Morris Thomas was executed in Florida in 1986, the physician in attendance and his medical assistant were among seven men who brutally subdued the inmate and forced him into the restraints. The very fact that so many clearly mentally ill prisoners are executed is testament to the extent to which the state, and not the defence, is capable of mobilising medical experts to serve its ends. Dr James Grigson has earned himself the nicknames 'Dr Death' and 'The Hanging Shrink' for his eagerness to assist the state of Texas win death sentences. Radelet notes with caution how the eagerness of medical associations to condemn involvement by a doctor in assessing an inmate's fitness for execution would necessarily bar those same professionals from playing a crucial role in possibly preventing the execution. 'As with other decisions on the road to execution', writes Radelet, 'the ethical burden is heavier for those whose professional involvement leads to the death of others'.[80] This area is full of double standards and inconsistencies. Should, for example, a medical professional who has determined that a condemned prisoner is medically unfit for execution, then be required to *treat* that inmate so that she or he might become fit?[81]

In a recent survey, the British Medical Association has outlined the various guidelines which distinguish 'acceptable' from 'unacceptable' forms of participation by physicians, and has noted that a third category, 'controversial' forms of participation, remains.[82] Those forms of involvement which are deemed 'acceptable' according to the BMA are:

- providing forensic expertise and evidence

- examining the prisoner and presenting evidence at trial

- provision of routine medical care during the pre-execution period

- attention to psychological and psychosomatic crises

- examination of the corpse and certifying death after it has clearly occurred.

The following forms of involvement are widely considered 'unacceptable' by the medical community:

- facilitating execution, e.g. finding suitable veins for administration of lethal poison

- tranquillising or restraining the prisoner

- witnessing the execution

- examining the prisoner during the execution to pinpoint the moment of death

- recommending further applications of lethal agents if the prisoner has not died.

Finally, these forms of participation are considered 'controversial', which is to say, there is no agreement among medical associations over whether they can be justified. While in some cases there may be benefits either to the prisoner or to wider society, involvement in them might set an undesirable precedent in respect of the process of capital punishment:

- attempting to predict an individual's future dangerousness when this is a deciding factor in whether a person should be executed

- assessing competence in order to establish fitness for execution

- providing treatment in order to make the prisoner fit for execution.

We should remember, of course, that it was a physician, Guillotin, who, in search of a more humane means of execution, devised the machine – perfected by another doctor, Antoine Louis – that bears his name, and that the electric chair was invented by a dentist, Alfred Southick. Indeed, the presence of a medical professional often adds some degree of authority and, necessarily, 'cleanliness' to the otherwise gruesome occasion of an execution. Pro-euthanasia spokesperson Dr Jack Kevorkian has argued that doctors should be legally required to administer the lethal injection because it is clearly the 'best' form of execution – despite the case studies we have already encountered and with apparent disregard for the obvious parallels one can make between his statements and those of the Nazi physicians during the Second World War.[83]

Kevorkian has, in fact, advocated the use of lethal injection instead of electrocution on another 'humane' ground. There is a history – still in operation in parts of Asia today – of physicians benefiting from executions by receiving the organs or corpses of the deceased.[84] In most respects, the use of body organs with the consent of the donor for the purpose of saving the life of another is, of course, laudable. However, in China, where executions involve a bullet to the head and thus cause no internal damage, there is a considerable trade in organs, which benefits the state and its allies and often takes place without consent (Chinese officials have denied accusations to this effect). The issue of organ donations has also been debated time and again in the United States, with Kevorkian among those supporting the practice.[85]

The state, the death penalty and human rights

In this chapter, we have paid attention to the death penalty *in principle* (that is, to the arguments used to support or oppose the punishment), to the death penalty *in practice* (that is, to the issues which arise from how it is carried out), and to the *experience* of Death Row. Running throughout and between the three debates are a series of contradictions and inconsistencies which appear to betray an inherent irrationality. Governments often justify the use of capital punishment by appealing either to deterrence or to retribution. Very little intellectual rigour is needed to provide a criticism of the deterrence argument – empirically, it has been disproved by countless statistical surveys; theoretically, it appears to be based on wholly inaccurate premises. This leaves the argument of retribution, which is an *a priori* argument and cannot be disproved empirically or theoretically. However, it is only an *a priori* argument if it involves a simple relationship, free from additional factors. The practice of the death penalty is, however, inseparable from such additional considerations, notably the length of time spent waiting for the punishment to be carried out, a consideration which is inherent in the punitive system itself. Because of the need to establish guilt, death sentences usually involve a lengthier process of review and appeal than other sentences. This often takes years. Meanwhile, the offender is being kept in appalling conditions, all the time not knowing whether he or she will be dead soon. This amounts to torture. The retribution argument duly falls flat here, because the punishment is greater than the crime. Thus, from such a perspective, the death penalty is necessarily self-defeating and irrational.

At one level, this appears to be true. Nevertheless, it would be unwise to dismiss the continued use of capital punishment solely on the basis of such generalisations. Perhaps there *is* a bizarre rationality to it, which is not readily apparent. Perhaps, in some respects, the presence of the death penalty is *wholly* rational, if not to society *per se*, then to the dominant system. Perhaps, if we delve beneath the obvious, the empirical, we can detect possible hidden justifications which offer a more credible explanation. Necessarily, such an investigation would require us to pay careful consideration to the role of the state as an agent of repression. Above all others, it is Michel Foucault who has brought these alternative readings to our attention.[86]

One such reading points out that the death penalty is far more than a punishment. It is also, for example, a form of ritual. Many legal and punitive systems are steeped in traditions that turn punishment into a bizarre ritual. In many countries these are religious rituals. Indeed, the death penalty for secular crimes only emerged in the West with the development of the modern state. Still, the ritualistic element remains. Consider such things as the last meal for condemned offenders. Are these ways of pacifying the prisoner, or of detracting from the horror of the situation by locating it in some time-honoured, and thus apparently functionally necessary and normal, tradition? This is not to say that tradition is itself a justification for the death penalty. However, it can be subtly interwoven with other arguments and is essentially a means of maintaining state power in the form of the status quo. It is thus repressive and a means of preventing change in society.

In the past, the death penalty has also served as a kind of spectacle, appeasing the populace in much the same way as television does today. According to Foucault, punishment ceased being a spectacle in the early nineteenth century, when this element was replaced with less emotive, more rationalised applications. Public executions had often excited the public imagination and were seen as festive occasions. That punishment became a more secretive process may reflect sinister intentions on the part of the state. It has been argued that executions ceased to be public when it was realised that the public itself might recognise the condemned person as a victim of state tyranny, and thus have cause to protest. Why, for example, are executions in the United States not shown, when, if their aim is deterrence, the deterrent effect would be better served if it was visible to people? Indeed, some opponents of the death penalty have requested executions to be televised, in the hope that opinion would change once people see the process for themselves. Victor Hugo, as was stated earlier, believed that people would be forced to make a rational decision about the death penalty if they actually experienced an execution. In some Islamic countries, meanwhile, beheadings are still public, stressing the importance of being seen to carry out the demands of the religious code.

Whether the execution is public or secret, it is important to bear in mind that, by its very nature, capital punishment is inflicted upon the individual offender. As Foucault says, punishments against the body, such as torture, beatings, and executions, originally reflected an emphasis on the punishment of the individual. The hidden agenda of such a process may have been to strip away the person's humanity (in the form of the body), rendering that person as a non-human. Even today, control over the body is seen as a means of maintaining power over individuals in society. While this perspective is useful when analysing Western cultures, it is not so easily applicable to other regimes. Is it possible, we might ask, to draw up an accurate assessment of the practice of capital punishment in two countries as different as the United States and China? Foucault's analysis appears to suit the American case because it allows us to look beyond the surface rationality and uncover the subtle power relations at work. Foucault provides a powerful counter-argument to liberal theories of modernisation and civilisation. The application of punishment in Western culture has been altered to suit the changing role of the state in an era of democracy and capitalism; it has not become more civilised, it has simply gone underground, reflecting the more covert ways in which the state enters into private life. The use of the death penalty in a country such as China is not afflicted with these subtle manipulations, these superficial appeals to public opinion, these claims to rationality and efficiency. In this case, the death penalty is used far more overtly as a means of maintaining social order, a tool for control, or, to use Althusser's phrase, a repressive state apparatus. However, there are common factors. By emphasising its strength, the state – whether in its totalitarian form or in the form of an alleged representative of the people – is duly emphasising its superiority, and thus repressing individual freedom.

In any case, the purpose is to place the blame for the crime very much at the feet of the offender. Accordingly, capital punishment can allow the outraged public its 'pound of flesh'. Of course, as a consequence, focus is detracted from structural questions which pertain to the reasons for the offence, or the conditions in which it took place. This is different from simple retribution, although it feeds off it. Retribution is about a moral condition, a matter of 'right' and 'wrong'. The release of crowd anger serves a hidden, political, project as well. It affirms the power of the state.

Punishment is affirmation of justice being done, and being seen to be done. While dictators such as Stalin and Hitler have overtly used executions as a means of affirming power, Foucault's argument suggests that they necessarily serve this end. By carrying out its punishments, the state is asserting its authoritative position over its citizens. In all these forms, we can see how the application of punishment reflects the interests of the state. The neo-Marxists, Rusche and Kirchheimer, sought to locate forms of punishment firmly within the logic of forms of economy.[87] While corporal punishments were rife at an early stage of capitalism, the growth of mercantilism and the expansion of liberal capitalism brought with it a need for newer forms of punishment which reflected the work ethic and the rationalisation of time. Once again, we locate the evolution of capital punishment within the logic of an inherently *irrational* form of social rationalisation associated with money, power, and expansion.

Essay questions

1. Does the state, in contemporary society, have the right to take the life of one of its citizens?

2. Contrast moralist and causalist approaches to the ethics of the death penalty.

3. In America, capital punishment is reserved for those without the capital. Discuss.

4. Does the death penalty violate the moral and legal dictum that a punishment should be neither cruel nor arbitrary?

Notes

1   William A. Schabas (1996) 'International Legal Aspects' in Peter Hodgkinson and Andrew Rutherford (eds) *Capital Punishment: Global Issues and Prospects*, Winchester: Waterside Press, p. 18.

2   Herbert Marcuse (1964) *One-Dimensional Man: Studies in the Ideology of Advanced Industrial Society*, Boston: Beacon Press.

3   V.A.C. Gatrell (1994) *The Hanging Tree: Execution and the English People, 1770–1868*, Oxford: Oxford University Press; cited in Peter Hodgkinson (1996) 'The United Kingdom and the European Union' in Hodgkinson and Rutherford, *Capital Punishment*.

4   This information is also taken from Hodgkinson's survey of 'The United Kingdom and the European Union'.

5   Stanislaw Frankowski (1996) 'Post-Communist Europe' in Hodgkinson and Rutherford, *Capital Punishment*, p. 215.

6   Ger Pieter van der Berg (1996) 'Russia and Other CIS States' in Hodgkinson and Rutherford, *Capital Punishment*.

7   Van der Berg, 'Russia'. N.B. Marx was actually an opponent of the death penalty.

8   See Hugo Adam Bedau (ed.) (1967) *The Death Penalty in America: An Anthology*, Chicago: Aldine Publishers, Chapter One, for a general introduction.

9   *Furman v Georgia* 408 U.S. 238 (1972).

10   *Gregg v Georgia* 428 U.S. 153 (1976).

11   The Eighth Amendment of the US Constitution holds that, among other things, 'cruel and unusual punishment (shall not be) inflicted'.

12   Especially *Proffit v Florida* 428 U.S. 242 (1976) and *Jurek v Texas* 428 U.S. 262 (1976). The Supreme Court further upheld the constitutionality of the death penalty in *McCleskey v Kemp* 107 S.Ct. 1756, 1767 (1987).

13   Figures taken from Death Penalty Information Center at www.deathpenaltyinfo.org

14   Until 17 July, 2001.

15   Figures taken from Death Penalty Information Center at www.deathpenaltyinfo.org

16   Seven states – Connecticut, Kansas, New Hampshire, New Jersey, New Mexico, New York, and South Dakota – plus the United States military, have the death penalty on statute but have not carried out any executions since 1976. The remaining 12 states – Alaska, Hawaii, Iowa, Maine, Massachusetts, Michigan, Minnesota, North Dakota, Rhode Island,

Vermont, West Virginia, and Wisconsin – plus the District of Colombia have abolished the punishment.

17 In *Coker v Georgia* 433 U.S. 584 (1977) the Supreme Court ruled that the death penalty was unconstitutional for rape.

18 See Edward Fitzgerald (1996) 'Commonwealth Caribbean' in Hodgkinson and Rutherford, *Capital Punishment.*

19 John Hatchard and Simon Coldham (1996) 'Commonwealth Africa' in Hodgkinson and Rutherford, *Capital Punishment.*

20 Death Penalty Information Center statistics, drawing on Amnesty International 1999 Report.

21 Franklin E. Zimring and Gordon Hawkins (1986) *Capital Punishment and the American Agenda*, Cambridge: Cambridge University Press.

22 The analogy is not mine – it was made by the lawyer Clive Stafford-Smith during an address to the organisation 'LifeLines'.

23 Michel Foucault (1991; original 1975) *Discipline and Punish: The Birth of the Prison*, Harmondsworth: Penguin, pp. 3–4.

24 Islamic Penal Code (*Hodoud* and *Qisas*) Article 119; cited in Amnesty International (1989) *When the State Kills: The Death Penalty v. Human Rights*, London: Amnesty International.

25 Amnesty International, *When the State Kills.*

26 Amnesty International, *When the State Kills*, p. 57.

27 Amnesty International (1987) *United States of America: The Death Penalty*, London: Amnesty International, pp. 117–18.

28 Michael Radelet, 'Post-*Furman* Botched Executions' on the Death Penalty Information Center website.

29 Amnesty International, *When the State Kills*, p. 58.

30 Radelet, 'Post-*Furman* Botched Executions'.

31 Amnesty International, *United States of America*, p. 119.

32 Radelet, 'Post-*Furman* Botched Executions'.

33 H. Potter (1993) *Hanging in Judgment: Religion and the Death Penalty in England*, New York: Continuum, p. 16.

34 National Interreligious Task Force on Criminal Justice (1978) *Capital Punishment: What the Religious Community Says*, New York: NITFCJ; cited in Hugo Adam Bedau (1996) 'The United States of America' in Hodgkinson and Rutherford, *Capital Punishment.*

35 C. Wright Mills (1959) *The Power Elite*, New York: Oxford University Press, p. 298.

36   William J. Bowers, Margaret Vandiver and Patricia H. Dugan (1994) 'A New Look at Public Opinion on Capital Punishment: What Citizens and Legislators Prefer' in *American Journal of Criminal Law*, 22, 77.

37   Cited in Amnesty International, *When the State Kills*.

38   Kenneth Haas and James A. Inciardi (1988) 'Lingering Doubts about Capital Punishment' in Kenneth Haas and James A. Inciardi (eds) *Challenging Capital Punishment: Legal and Social Science Approaches*, Newbury Park, CA: Sage.

39   Drawing, of course, on the theories of communicative action, discourse ethics, and discursive democracy devised by the German social philosopher, Jürgen Habermas.

40   Austin Sarat and Neil Vidmar (1976) 'Public Opinion, the Death Penalty, and the Eighth Amendment: Testing the Marshall Hypothesis' in Hugo Adam Bedau and Chester M. Pierce (eds) *Capital Punishment in the United States*, New York: AMS Press; cited in Amnesty International, *When the State Kills*.

41   Barry Nakell (1978) 'The Cost of the Death Penalty' in *Criminal Law Bulletin*, 14, 1, pp. 68–80.

42   Report from the New York State Defense Association to the Senate Finance Committee and other sections of the legislature on 'Capital Losses: The Price of the Death Penalty for New York State' (April 1982).

43   Jeffrey Reiman (1988) 'The Justice of the Death Penalty in an Unjust World' in Haas and Inciardi, *Challenging Capital Punishment*; Ernest van den Haag and John P. Conrad (1983) *The Death Penalty: A Debate*, New York: Plenum Press.

44   Van den Haag and Conrad, *The Death Penalty*.

45   Reiman, 'The Justice of the Death Penalty'.

46   Van den Haag and Conrad, *The Death Penalty*.

47   Thorsten Sellin (1959) 'Death and Imprisonment as Deterrents to Murder' in *The Death Penalty*, Washington: The American Law Institute.

48   Sadataka Kogi (1959) 'Etude Criminologique et Psycho-Pathologique de Condamnés à Mort ou aux Travaux forcés à perpétuité au Japon' in *Annales Médicopsychologiques*, 117, 2, 3.

49   Van den Haag and Conrad, *The Death Penalty*.

50   Dane Archer, Rosemary Gartiner and Marc Beittel (1983) 'Homicide and the Death Penalty: A Cross National Test of Deterrence Hypothesis' in *Journal of Criminal Law and Criminology* 74, pp. 991–1013.

51   A.A. Adeyemi (1988) 'Death Penalty: Criminological Perspectives; The Nigerian Situation' in *The Death Penalty: Travaux de la Conférence Internationale tenue à L'Institut Supérieur International de Sciences Criminelles,*

Syracuse-Italie, 17 au 22 Mai 1987, Revue Internationale de Droit Pénal, 58, 3 and 4.

52 For example, Reckless (1969) 'The Use of the Death Penalty' in *Crime and Delinquency*, 15, 1, pp. 43–56; Thorsten Sellin (1967) *Capital Punishment*, New York: Harper and Row; Schuessler (1952) 'The Deterrent Effect of the Death Penalty' in *Annals* 284, pp. 54–62. Some studies have shown there to be some short-term deterrent effect, but remain unconvinced by any long-term argument. See, for example, Leonard Kavitz (1958) 'A Study in Capital Punishment' in *Journal of Criminal Law, Criminology and Police Science* 49, pp. 338–41; David Phillips (1980) 'The Deterrent Effect of Capital Punishment: New Evidence on an Old Controversy' in *American Journal of Sociology* 86, pp. 139–47.

53 William Bowers and Glenn Pierce (1980) 'Deterrence or Brutalization: What is the Effect of Executions?' in *Crime and Delinquency* October, pp. 453–4; Bowers (1988) 'The Effect of Executions is Brutalization, Not Deterrence' in Haas and Inciardi, *Challenging Capital Punishment*.

54 Bowers, 'The Effect of Executions'.

55 Jonathan Glover (1977) *Causing Death and Saving Lives*, Harmondsworth: Penguin.

56 Cesare Beccaria (1764) 'On Crimes and Punishments'. Reproduced in Richard Bellamy (ed.) *On Crimes and Punishments and Other Writings*, Cambridge: Cambridge University Press.

57 Norberto Bobbio (1996) *The Age of Rights*, Cambridge: Polity Press, p. 131.

58 Reiman, 'The Justice of the Death Penalty'.

59 Van den Haag and Conrad, *The Death Penalty*.

60 Roger Hood (1989) *The Death Penalty: A World-wide Perspective*, Oxford: Clarendon Press.

61 Amnesty International (1987) *United States of America: The Death Penalty*, London: Amnesty International Publications.

62 Marc Riedel (1976) 'Discrimination and the Imposition of the Death Penalty: A Comparison of the Characteristics of Offenders Sentenced Pre-*Furman* and Post-*Furman*' 49 TEMP.L.Q.261, cited in David Baldus, George Woodworth and Charles Pulaski (1990) *Equal Justice and the Death Penalty*, Boston: Northeastern University Press.

63 William Bowers and Glenn Pierce (1980) 'Arbitrariness and Discrimination under Post-*Furman* Capital Statutes' in *Crime and Delinquency* 26, 4, October, pp. 563–635.

64 See, for example, the important study by Baldus, Woodworth and Pulaski, *Equal Justice*.

65   Studies which make this claim include: William Bowers (1984) *Legal Homicide: Death as a Punishment in America, 1864–1982*, Boston: Northeastern University Press; Michael Radelet and Glenn Pierce (1983) 'Race and Prosecutorial Discretion in Homicide Cases', Paper presented to the American Sociological Association meeting, Detroit.

66   Statement of Senator Gary Parker, Georgia State Senator, Fifteenth Senatorial District, regarding 'Crime in the Black Community and the Death Penalty' to the Sub-Committee on Civil and Constitutional Rights Committee of the Judiciary, United States House of Representatives, 9 May 1990.

67   See, for example, Marcia Coyle, Fred Strasser and Marianne Lavelle (1990) 'Fatal Defense: Trial and Error in the Nation's Death Belt' in *National Law Journal*, 11 June; Stephen B. Bright (1990) 'Death by Lottery' in *West Virginia Law Review*, 92, 3.

68   Coyle *et al.*, 'Fatal Defense'.

69   Coyle *et al.*, 'Fatal Defense'.

70   Louis Althusser (1971) 'Ideology and Ideological State Apparatuses' in *Lenin and Philosophy and Other Essays*, London: New Left Books.

71   Van den Haag and Conrad, *The Death Penalty*.

72   Robert Johnson (1981) *Condemned to Die: Life Under Sentence of Death*, London: Elsevier.

73   Amnesty International, *United States of America*.

74   Haas and Inciardi, *Challenging Capital Punishment*.

75   John L. Carroll (1988) 'Death Row – Hope for the Future' in Haas and Inciardi, *Challenging Capital Punishment*. 'Texas and California', writes Carroll, 'treat death-sentenced inmates in their worst classifications better than states like Ohio, Pennsylvania, Louisiana and Arkansas treat everyone.'

76   Herbert E. Thomas, M.D. (1973) 'Regressive Behaviour in Maximum Security Prisons: A Preliminary Communication', Report dated 6 January.

77   Johnson, *Condemned to Die*.

78   See Kim Marie Thorburn (1987) 'Physicians and the Death Penalty' in *The Western Journal of Medicine* 146, May, pp. 638–40.

79   Amnesty International, *When the State Kills*, pp. 78–9.

80   Michael Radelet (1996) 'Physician Participation' in Hodgkinson and Rutherford, *Capital Punishment*, p. 252. The British Medical Association report on which he is commenting is contained in British Medical Association (1992) *Medicine Betrayed: The Participation of Doctors in Human Rights Abuses*, London: Zed Books.

81   Radelet, 'Physician Participation', p. 253.

82   British Medical Association (2001) *The Medical Profession and Human Rights: Handbook for a Changing Agenda*, London: Zed Books, pp. 178–84. The bullet points are lifted verbatim from the BMA source.

83   BMA, *The Medical Profession and Human Rights*, p. 177.

84   Radelet, 'Physician Participation'.

85   Radelet, 'Physician Participation', pp. 244–7.

86   Foucault, *Discipline and Punish*.

87   G. Rusche and O. Kirchheimer (1939/1968) *Punishment and Social Structure*, New York: Columbia University Press.

Further information

Books

For an introduction to various issues in the debate as they apply to different parts of the world, the edited volume by Peter Hodgkinson and Andrew Rutherford, *Capital Punishment: Global Issues and Prospects* (Winchester: Waterside Press, 1996) is highly recommended. Roger Hood's *The Death Penalty: A World-wide Perspective* (Oxford: Oxford University Press, 1989) is also useful. For a thorough account of the practice in the United States, Hugo Adam Bedau's *The Death Penalty in America: Current Controversies* (New York: Oxford University Press, 1997) is unsurpassable. The Amnesty International report, *When the State Kills: The Death Penalty v. Human Rights* (London: Amnesty International Publications, 1989) is also excellent for an overview of the issues from the point of view of an ethically oriented organisation. Accounts of the death penalty process provided by those involved in it are also excellent, especially Joseph Ingle's remarkable *Last Rights: 13 Fatal Encounters with the State's Justice* (Nashville: Abingdon Press, 1990) – Ingle is a Christian activist and anti-death penalty campaigner. Worth reading also is the beautiful testimony of personal doubt and ultimate conviction provided by the former governor of California, Edmund 'Pat' Brown, *Public Justice, Private Mercy: A Governor's Education on Death Row* (New York: Weidenfeld & Nicolson, 1989).

Documentaries

The award-winning Channel 4 documentary, *14 Days in May*, tells the story of the last two weeks in the life of Edward Earl Johnson, who was executed in Mississippi in 1987. As a film of insight, it is thoroughly revealing. As a personal account, it is savagely powerful and heart-breaking, at times disturbing and even terrifying but never exploitative, never anything but sincere. An equally useful, but quite different, film is Channel 4's *When the State Kills*. This 1995 documentary is more of an academic piece, and it provides a thorough overview of the historical and sociological features of the death penalty.

Web pages

The Death Penalty Information Center is very useful, and can be found on www.deathpenaltyinfo.org.

CHAPTER SEVEN

Apartheid

Everyone is entitled to all the rights and freedoms set forth in this Declaration, without distinction of any kind, such as race, colour, sex, language, religion, political or other opinion, national or social origin, property, birth or other status.

Universal Declaration of Human Rights, Article 2

What is apartheid?

Apartheid is segregation, the legal and political endorsement and institutionalisation of discrimination. The term derives from the Afrikaans word for separateness. It involves the assigning of an individual at birth into one or another class of citizen. In the case, for example, of the apartheid regime in South Africa, this classification depended on skin colour, and four classes existed – white, coloured, Asian, and black. Indeed, in the South African case, this distinction was made before birth, in so far as pregnant women could only be treated by doctors of their own skin colour.[1]

In this chapter, we will, of course, discuss the literature on apartheid in South Africa, as well as its most obvious contemporary, racial segregation in the American South. However, we should not delude ourselves into thinking that these are the only examples of apartheid which might be mentioned, nor that apartheid only targets black populations in countries with white majorities. Discrimination and prejudice are characteristics of many countries, and it is only the extent of the institutionalisation of that discrimination which results in some countries being labelled as segregationist. Here, we will seek to expand our definition to include the anthropological and sociological literature which seeks to relate these forms of racial discrimination with such cultural systems as *caste*. Thus, we will be entering a heated debate between those who seek to differentiate between the two systems, and those who view them both as forms of social stratification based on status. While it will become apparent that there are obvious differences between the two forms of social differentiation – a point made abundantly clear by Oliver Cromwell Cox and Louis Dumont – we will ask not whether segregation can be understood as a form of caste (as some neo-Weberians have suggested) but whether caste constitutes a form of apartheid. This neo-Weberian pre-occupation with status actually takes us into another debate, concerning the role of women in the political sphere. In this chapter we will argue that it is not stretching the definition of apartheid too far to include situations where access to full citizenship is denied to certain members of a society on the basis of their gender. Finally, by way of a conclusion, we will consider the idea of equality as a human rights concern, and ask what relationship it might have with the idea of the state.

A brief history of apartheid

We could find any number of instances of apartheid, using the term in the broader sense advocated here, to make reference to in this history section. History is rife with examples of social exclusion, of the political or spatial separateness of certain groups in society. I will concentrate, though, on the two most famous examples of segregation: the Jim Crow laws in post-Civil War America, and apartheid in South Africa.

Segregation in the United States

In 1865, after the conclusion of the American civil war, slavery was officially abolished in the United States by the 13th Amendment to the Constitution. This was quickly followed by the 14th Amendment of 1868, which guaranteed equal protection for all people under the law, and by the 15th Amendment of 1870, which guaranteed voting rights for all people. However, during the postwar reconstruction, many former slave-owning states experienced difficulties in adjusting to the different legal circumstances now allotted to those who had so recently been denied not only citizenship but basic freedom. Indeed, in many states, these former slaves made up the majority of the population. Agriculture and industry were also troubled by the sudden denial of their labour force. This matrix of uncertainties resulted in the passing of various laws in some of these states – called 'Jim Crow' laws – designed to segregate the white and non-white populations. Initially, these laws – named after a derogatory term used by whites to refer to blacks – applied to rail transport, but in a short time they had been extended to most areas of economic, political, and social life. In 1896, a challenge to these laws – the case of *Plessy v. Ferguson*, in which the charge was made that the laws violated the Constitution – was heard by the US Supreme Court. In making its majority decision of seven against one (with one abstention) on this case, the Supreme Court made the infamous claim that, while the Constitution guarantees equality, the Jim Crow laws were not about inequality, but separateness, about being 'separate but equal'.

Of course, in practice, black people were treated as both separate and unequal. Public facilities were divided among white and black, access to political resources, to education, even to police protection, was constantly denied. Black people may have earned their equality in some legal sense, but they were still unable to reach positions of influence or authority because of the many other obstacles placed in their way. They could vote, but were discouraged from doing so, often through threat of violence, and few possessed a formal education. Assemblies of black people were monitored carefully by the white power structure, which feared dissent through association. Not only was equality denied, but freedom as well. These were the issues Homer Plessy, who had been arrested for sitting in a whites-only train carriage, made when his case reached the Supreme Court – that a 'separate but equal' policy violated legal equality by legitimising the belief in the inferiority of blacks. These obvious consequences of the Jim Crow laws were clearly recognised by the one dissenting member of the Supreme Court, Associate Justice John Marshall Harlan, a former slave-owner from Kentucky. His objection is famous for its clarity and conviction:

In the eyes of the law, there is in this country no superior, dominant, ruling class of citizens. There is no caste here. Our constitution is colorblind, and neither knows nor tolerates classes among citizens. In respect of civil rights, all citizens are equal before the law. The humblest is the peer of the most powerful ... The arbitrary separation of citizens on the basis of race, while they are on a public highway, is a badge of servitude wholly inconsistent with the civil freedom and the equality before the law established by the Constitution. It cannot be justified upon any legal grounds.[2]

Nevertheless, it was over 50 years before the decision made by the Supreme Court in *Plessy v. Ferguson* was finally reversed, in the land-mark decision in *Brown v. Board of Education*, 1954. In judging this case, the Supreme Court made it clear that, in so far as separateness equates with unequal treatment of persons, then the Jim Crow laws were indeed in violation of the Constitution. At the same time, the civil rights movement was emerging as a major vocal opponent of all forms of segregation. Spearheaded by such charismatic leaders as Rev. Martin Luther King, Jr, the movement reached out to a global audience and raised awareness of the plight of black people in these Southern States of the USA. Segregation was ultimately prohibited in all its forms through a series of acts centred around the Civil Rights Act 1964.

Despite the official termination of the practice of segregation on racial grounds, it is still very much a problem in the United States. In respect of education, housing, employment, and voting procedures, there are still instances where the United States finds itself in violation of the International Covenant on Civil and Political Rights.[3]

Apartheid in South Africa

If institutional discrimination has been common throughout the world and takes many forms, it is the apartheid regime in South Africa which has probably attracted the most attention. Blacks, who on average constituted about 74 per cent of the population, were systematically and legally denied basic rights to participate in society or politics.[4] Voting and political membership were denied, and where they ate, what transport they used, and even what toilet facilities they could make use of to relieve themselves, were all restricted by law. They had to live in out-of-town settlements called 'townships'. As one expert observes, during the apartheid regime, one could venture out at night in a major South African city and find oneself in a whites-only zone, 'no longer in Africa but in a piece of Europe'.[5]

The South African Union was formed in 1910 out of four provinces: Cape Province, Natal, Transvaal, and Orange Free State. No sooner had the Union been formed than various legislations were being enacted which laid the foundations for the system of apartheid.[6] The Mines and Works Act 1911 initiated institutional racism in the country by restricting certain jobs to white people only. In 1913 the Land Act prevented black people from buying land outside of certain areas, a form of territorial segregation which perverted an existing system, implemented by the British, devised apparently to protect native groups from colonial interference.[7] Political institutions were separated along racial grounds through the Native Affairs Act 1920, and segregation extended into the cities with the Urban Area Act 1922. After the Second World War, the National Party, dominated by Afrikaners, came to power, under the leadership of Dr D.F. Malan, whose intention was to use apartheid as a means of building a white Christian state. Three levels of apartheid would soon be introduced: *grand apartheid*, designed to ensure that the political and institutional power of whites was maintained; *urban apartheid*, or spatial segregation; and *petty apartheid*, designed to prevent socialisation between whites and non-whites. At each of these levels, the National Party soon began to formalise apartheid through various laws which restricted even the most mundane form of social interaction according to skin colour, such as the Prohibition of Mixed Marriages Act 1949.[8] The Population Registration Act of 1950 demanded that all people be catalogued as belonging to a specific group, and that this categorisation was unchangeable.[9] The Group Areas Act 1950 formalised territorial segregation. The Suppression of Communism Act 1950 was used to prevent any possible insurrection. The Native (Abolition of Passes and Coordination of Documents) Act 1952 forced all adult blacks to carry an identity document which marked them off as members of an 'inferior group' and allowed for government surveillance of their movements.[10] Segregation now existed with respect to territory, political involvement, economic and industrial life, and social interaction. It even existed after death. As A.J. Christopher observes, 'the ultimate aspect of separation in social contact was the maintenance of segregated cemeteries'.[11]

Internal resistance to apartheid was divided at first.[12] A joint campaign was established in 1952 but Indian and black communities made uneasy allies. The subsequent abolition of the Communist Party, and the relocation of its members and ideologies into the African National Congress, resulted in the establishment of the rival Pan-Africanist Congress in 1959. Both the ANC and the PAC organised demonstrations against the apartheid laws. However, tensions reached boiling point when 69 black protestors were shot dead by police during demonstrations in Sharpeville. A state of emergency was called, both opposition movements were banned but continued their operations illegally, and, in 1963, the ANC leaders were arrested and imprisoned on Robben Island. The violence continued, and notable historical events included the Soweto riots of 1976, and the 1984 and 1985 states of emergency.

The response of the international political community to this was muted. Between 1946 and 1951, the United Nations only discussed apartheid in respect of discrimination against Asians.[13] From 1952 it was discussed in terms of a fundamental violation of human rights. On 21 March 1960, 69 anti-apartheid protestors were killed by state officials in the Sharpeville massacre, and the UN began to look more closely at the situation. In 1963 a voluntary arms embargo was commissioned.[14] However, for the decades that followed, the condemnations fell short of the obvious action, which was economic sanctions, because many of the leading nation-states, notably the United States, Israel and the United Kingdom, maintained considerable economic investments in South Africa, and for the Americans, it represented an important strategic military location in the Cold War struggle against the Soviet Union.[15] Thus, for much of this time, such sanctions that existed were gradual and specific to certain areas, or were imposed only by countries with few links to South Africa, and ignored by the dominant economic players. In 1973, the International Covenant on the Suppression and Punishment of Apartheid was adopted, which defined apartheid, for the first time, as a crime against humanity.[16] In *theory*, this empowered UN states to punish those responsible for apartheid, but it was hampered by two main problems:

1   It was binding only on those who ratified it, a list which included various Soviet Bloc states, various African states, and a handful of Western states with little direct interest in South Africa. It was effectively powerless in so far as it was not ratified by the major Western powers;[17]

2   Article 3 of the Convention states that all individuals involved in the practice of apartheid are guilty of a crime, which seems ludicrous in so far as this would involve the majority of the South African citizens at the time. (Noticeably, postapartheid South Africa did not add its name to this well-meaning but unworkable document.) Thus, no prosecutions were ever made in its name.[18]

Despite these flaws in the document, it at least showed that the United Nations was not willing to tolerate apartheid as an institutional practice, and thanks to the long-term planning of the United Nations, various changes did take place within and outside of South Africa during the 1980s which paved the way for the ultimate dismantling of the apartheid system.[19] In retrospect, this historical event was brought about by a combination of forces, some external to South Africa but impacting directly upon it – ostracism from the international community, economic sanctions, some military action – and some internal pressures, economic and political.[20] Indeed, multinational corporations, perhaps spurred on by public opinion against the regime, began to withdraw their assets and investments from the republic.[21] Inevitably, perhaps, President F.W. de Klerk announced and set in motion the dismantling of apartheid early in 1990; by March 1992 he stated that it was now a thing of the past.

Apartheid may have ended in South Africa in 1992, but its ghost would still haunt not only that country but the international political community as well. The legacy bequeathed to the ANC government was one of poverty, illness, violence and desperation. Meanwhile, the United Nations had to realise that apartheid was a global problem in need of legal sanction. The problem with its adoption as a crime against humanity was duly corrected, so that the 1998 Statute of the International Criminal Court qualifies the definition of apartheid (as a crime) by specifying its relationship to torture, murder, or the enslavement of peoples, effectively locating it within the existing boundaries of international law.[22]

Understanding apartheid
The individual capacity for racism

What causes a person to possess racist attitudes? At the level of the individual, biological, psychological, and sociological perspectives are in competition. *Biological* explanations tend to rest upon a sociobiological foundation – that is, that people are genetically predisposed to distrust 'outsiders'. *Psychological* explanations usually adopt a behaviourist position, stressing the importance of environment and learning processes through socialisation. *Sociological* explanations develop these culturalist themes but pay more attention to the social and historical conditions within which a personality develops. So, racist attitudes may be influenced by family structure, or by feelings of nationalism and conservative attitudes towards tradition. In any case, whether the propensity for racism is genetic or environmental, it is certainly maintained and reproduced through the stereotypes which are perpetuated structurally. Religion has often served as the foundation of racist doctrine; science, the mass media, and other belief-systems have also contributed to its reproduction.

Racist attitudes attained scientific credibility in the nineteenth century through the influential doctrine of social Darwinism. Evolutionary biologists had already classified the animal world into species, subspecies and so on. Some scientists thought it only natural to apply the same logic to the human world. It is only a small step from classification, in the name of science, to establishing a hierarchy of types, in the name of politics. If one 'sub-species' of the human race can show itself to be at an 'advanced' stage of 'civilisation' compared to another 'subspecies', then it can seek to justify its superiority in the form of some perverted account of Darwinian struggle. Wars, colonialism, and the massacres of entire peoples were justified on the grounds of 'racial superiority', that the victims were 'subhuman'. These beliefs are so absurd they hardly warrant mention in this volume, and they probably would not have been included if it were not for the fact that some researchers are still trying to appeal to genetics, albeit in a more toned-down way, to explain levels of educational and social development. Additionally, from a social scientific point of view, we should recognise that arguments which seek to explain racism solely in terms of genetic propensities are as crude and limited as those which attempt to define 'race' in this way.

The structural conditions of apartheid

Individualistic explanations of racism are useful in some respects, but any insights gained from them are better understood within a wider framework which understands racism as a structural problem. A considerable library of theoretical analysis has been devoted to understanding and explaining the structural conditions of apartheid. Early accounts belong to a liberal tradition which begins with individualistic theories of racism and transfers them to the structural level. These liberal theories overlap in many respects with more complex Weberian accounts. Marxist accounts have also been important, in so far as they shift the debate away from ideology and towards economic and class relations. Feminists have also contributed to the debate.

Liberal accounts are largely ideological. Their general starting point is the development of a unified identity among the Afrikaner and Boer descendants of the European settlers, of which the maintenance of certain pre-Enlightenment beliefs, including racial distinction, was a key factor. These ideas are expressed in a number of key liberal texts, notably C.W. de Kiewiet's seminal 1941 manuscript *A History of South Africa*.[23] Liberal thinking has come under considerable attack, primarily from Marxist accounts, which shift the responsibility for apartheid away from racist ideologies towards capitalist profitability (we will discuss these accounts below). The significance of racial and segregationist ideology has been restated by important scholars of South African history, such as Saul Dubow and Hermann Giliomee.[24]

Racial conflict, in any part of the world, cannot be understood solely in terms of individual attitudes. One has to consider the material conditions within which this conflict takes place, and, in particular, the inherent inequalities in the struggle for scarce resources. According to the Weberian sociologist John Rex, racial conflict arises out of the interlinking of three preconditions:[25] a plural society in which resources are unevenly distributed; identifiable boundaries between the conflicting groups; and a cultural system which presumes a link between difference and superiority, and thus allows for discrimination to be justified. Thus, a culture of difference and of inequality precedes apartheid and segregation. This may have its origins in any number of individualistic explanations, but these often become lost as the institutionalised racism becomes the norm. Many people may take it for granted that racist attitudes are merely reflections of ignorance, and dumbed-down versions of social Darwinist assumptions about biological difference. In fact, the processes which give rise to institutionalised racism are more subtle than this. In South Africa, justifications for apartheid were rarely, if ever, founded on biological arguments. Instead, they were based on appeals to a sense of cultural superiority, social difference, and tradition.

Given the general acceptance among the international political community of human rights as general normative standards, we should wonder with some curiosity how it is that a system such as the apartheid regime in South Africa came about. Indeed, Cassese makes the useful point that the formalisation of apartheid as a system of legalised exclusion took place in 1948, the year of the Universal Declaration of Human Rights. South Africa's refusal to be party to this, and, furthermore, its establishment of a system which went against everything the Declaration stood for, represented a severe blow to the ideals of the world political community. With apartheid, 'not only were immense, impenetrable walls erected between the various human groups in South Africa; an extremely high wall was also erected between South Africa and the rest of the world'.[26]

It is possible, Cassese suggests, to explain the development of apartheid according to three dimensions – historical, religious, and economic. Asheron also uses a threefold model, although his list includes political, cultural, and economic explanations.[27] In many respects, these lists are the same. The political and historical explanations relate to Afrikaner nationalism – so, the *politics of nationalism*. The cultural and religious explanations relate to values and beliefs inherited from the Calvinist faith – so, a *culture of separation*. The economic explanations relate to competition for resources and differentiation in industrial roles – so, the *economics of differentiation*. It is likely that a combination of these factors resulted in the decision to establish apartheid as a formal institution within South African society. In any event, the system was remarkable in the extent to which it showed how laws could be used as instruments of social control. Cassese suggests that in no other situation, not even Nazi Germany, were laws so tightly introduced to institutionalise an exclusivist ideology; in no other situation was the legal system itself so corrupted beyond its function as an arbiter of justice and equality into a mechanism of oppression.[28] Let us now turn to each of these possible explanations.

The first is a *political* explanation, which relates to the historical factors specific to the South African situation. While Dutch settlement in

South Africa in 1652 was in many ways typical of the racist ideologies of the European colonial powers, unlike other European settlers, the Afrikaners (or Boers) always felt separated from the Dutch homeland.[29] Thus, when the British invaded in 1795, these Boers treated it as an assault on them from the European colonisers, rather than on any of the native populations. The British assault was treated as an affront to an emerging Afrikaner nationalism. Even as they marched inland to steal land from the Zulu tribes, they fought for over a century against the British in the name of *their* native land. As Asheron states:

> Afrikaner nationalism developed out of the Boers' need both to re-establish their identity, and to create a group homogeneity through which they could ultimately rectify and overcome the humiliations and defeats which they had suffered since the events leading up to the Great Trek of 1836.[30]

The power struggle between the Afrikaners and the British culminated, of course, in the Boer War 1899–1902, which was won by the British. What followed was a period of 'peaceful struggle' between the two groups 'to obtain power through the white-dominated electorate'.[31] However, the resurgent Afrikaner nationalism, still wounded from its defeats at the hands of the British, never swayed from its primary objective: 'the total domination of South Africa in order to protect and promote the interests of Afrikanerdom'.[32] Fearing the possibility of the British stabilising their power base by extending the vote to non-whites, the Afrikaner nationalists worked to deliberately eliminate all non-whites from having any input at all into the political system.[33]

The second explanation is linked to the cultural traditions from which the Afrikaners originated. The Calvinist faith to which the Dutch settlers belonged took literally a passage from the Bible, Genesis 9: 25, in which Noah curses his son Ham and Ham's descendants (Hamites, or Africans) to always be servants to their brethren.[34] With the master–slave mentality already in place in the minds of many Europeans, it was only a short step to dehumanise the native populations, render them beyond salvation, and label them as nothing but cattle.[35] Alongside this existed a belief in the inherent divide between the good and the wicked, described in the Bible, to which the Calvinists offered an interpretation based on the colour of skin. Indeed, the Nationalist Party leaders happily justified apartheid as being based on Christian principles of fairness and justice.[36] Thus, it seemed natural, not only for the Dutch settlers but also for the British who arrived later, to accept the situation of inequality without question. That such a situation was already in place not only strengthened the political project of the Afrikaners, but also created tensions with the individualistic capitalist ideology favoured by the British.[37]

Of course, it is one thing to show how cultural traditions and beliefs influence the emergence of a racial ideology, and another to show how they perpetuate it. Leo Kuper has pointed out that various strategies were implemented in South Africa which allowed for the reproduction of the system.[38] For example, following legal requirements, an individual was forced to apply racial characteristics and definitions to a range of situations. This served to embed racial consciousness in the individual's perception of the world. This of course was further reinforced by the imposition of laws pertaining to all sorts of social activities: marriage, territorial interaction, education, employment, politics, leisure, healthcare, and so on. A further means of upholding this system was the distribution of punishments and rewards, which made it profitable, both socially and economically, for whites to support the dominant system.

Inevitably, then, the third explanation is to do with economics; that is, that someone was needed to do the difficult, dirty jobs, particularly in the mining of gold, upon which so much of South Africa's wealth depended.[39] Clearly, the British favoured the implementation of a *laissez-faire* capitalist economy, based on individualist principles. However, the architects of this economic policy readily accepted the existence of the racially segregated system, and their successors made effective use of these inequalities, and of the unskilled African labour force, to maximise their profits.[40] It would have made little sense, from an economic point of view, for the British to voice any opposition to Afrikaner nationalism and racist ideology.

Multicausal accounts such as these provide plausible sets of explanations as to how racist ideology becomes institutionalised, and it is senseless to deny that these factors were all present in the establishment of apartheid in South Africa. However, as other commentators note, they are very specific conditions which apply only to this extreme case of racial discrimination. Since institutionalised racism occurs in most countries in some form or another, there must be, say these critics, a general explanation for its role in the social structure. So although Marxist commentators would not deny the presence of particular cultural and historical conditions which steer racism in a particular direction, they would point out that these are not the underlying *causes* of institutionalised discrimination. Thus, according to such writers as Robert Miles and Oliver Cromwell Cox, the best way to understand racism in any form is to see it as a particular ideology which serves the interests of capitalist society.[41] These writers have sought to understand not only how capitalism initially *produces* racist ideologies – Cox, for example, understands racism as a consequence of colonialism, which is itself capitalist expansionism – but also how capitalism *reproduces* racism through hegemonic processes. One of the most influential figures associated with the radical critique of liberal histories of South Africa which emerged in the 1970s was Martin Legassick. Legassick actually published nothing on the subject but his doctoral dissertation and various unpublished papers cemented his status as the leading figure in the debate, tracing the origins of apartheid firmly back to British imperial strategies.[42] Legassick's thinking was complemented by Harold Wolpe's account of how the policy of segregation was maintained in order to uphold the convenient and efficient system of cheap labour.[43] In short, Wolpe pointed out that industrialists had been able to pay African workers cheap rates because of the complex family structure and division of labour in the rural communities. The possibility of mass urbanisation was threatening to this profitable arrangement; thus the need to embed spatial segregation through a policy of apartheid. Wolpe's account benefits from the subsequent analysis of gender divisions, family structures and patriarchy provided by Belinda Bozzoli, who has shown how the stable gender relations inherent in southern African societies – men migrating to work, women remaining on the land – have inadvertently contributed towards the system of segregation.[44]

Marxist and feminist theories have, then, been important in so far as they divert attention away from explanations of apartheid based solely on the perpetuation of racist ideologies. However, Marxists in particular have attracted considerable criticism from Weberian and anti-racist authors for their continued insistence upon reducing racial conflict to class struggles, and thus dismissing the significance of race and ethnicity as ends in themselves. Debates of this kind – which focus on race relations within a stratified system – thus connect the literature on apartheid as an abuse of human rights with that on forms of social stratification, a particular example of which we turn to now.

Apartheid, caste and social stratification

In his dissenting opinion on the case of *Plessy v. Ferguson*, Associate Justice Harlan, pointing to the absence of any legally recognised system of social stratification in the United States, illustrated his point with the statement: 'There is no caste here.' Was his use of caste in this respect appropriate? A lively debate took place during much of the 1960s and

1970s on the relationship between apartheid – including segregation in the USA – and the caste system in India, and the extent to which both could be included as forms of social stratification. Neo-Weberian, neo-Marxist, and structuralist sociologists and cultural anthropologists took sides on whether caste is unique to the Indian experience, or can be understood within wider debates and frameworks of stratification, class and power. The major contributors to the debate included W. Lloyd Warner, Oliver Cromwell Cox, and Louis Dumont.

Max Weber had himself declared that the caste system in India is an extreme form of status distinction.[45] Although Weber's distinctions between class, status and party are rather vague at times, we can at least use them as ideal types signifying one's position within the economic sphere (the market), social sphere (society) and political sphere (state) respectively. Thus, from a Weberian point of view, the Indian caste system, in so far as it is a form of *social* hierarchy, can interpreted as a kind of status distinction.[46]

There are those who, as we shall see, would accuse Weber of misunderstanding the nature of caste. Nevertheless, an obvious research project ensues from his observations; namely, if caste is not unique to Hindu society but is a particular representation of a kind of social divide not reducible to money, to what extent can parallels be drawn between it and such racially segregated systems as the colour bar in the American South, or apartheid in South Africa? The starting point for this debate is Lloyd Warner's claim that two forms of social stratification existed concurrently in the American South: a caste system, and a class structure.[47] Warner is careful in his description of caste:

> Caste as used here describes a theoretical arrangement of the people in a given group in an order in which the privileges, duties, obligations, opportunities, etc., are unequally distributed between the groups which are considered to be higher and lower. There are social sanctions which tend to maintain this unequal distribution.... (Also) marriage between two or more groups is not sanctioned and ... there is no opportunity for members of the lower groups to rise into the upper groups or (*vice versa*).[48]

This last point is that which separates caste from class: by its nature, a class system, which certainly imposes sanctions and is based on an uneven distribution of resources, must involve some degree of social mobility and interclass relationships. Caste is a wholly closed system. Warner makes the point that the racially segregated system of the

American South was in every respect a caste system, in so far as it relied upon this closed form of stratification; however successful a black person might have become, however 'high up' he or she might have reached within their group, that black person would still be considered inferior because he or she belonged to a lower caste, *regardless of whether he or she belonged to a higher 'class' than a white person.*[49] The inequalities which existed in the American South, inequalities in education, housing, status and so on, could therefore be best understood in terms of the strategies for the perpetuation of a caste system and not in terms of other divisions.

Warner's thesis has been heavily criticised for its misunderstanding of the nature of the Indian caste system. Gerald Berreman seeks to overcome this problem by understanding caste in terms of three distinct characteristics: stratification, pluralism, and interaction.[50] In other words, castes are defined:

1   as hierarchical and closed social systems, the ideal-typical model of which is India;

2   as culturally pluralist societies in which a particular group achieves a monopoly of power;

3   as societies in which interaction is restricted according to these power relations.

By adopting such a model, Berreman, like Warner, concludes that it is possible to understand segregation in America as a caste structure.

Oliver Cromwell Cox entered this debate by pointing out a major distinction between the two systems: segregation in America was based on racial characteristics, while caste in India was not:

> To use [caste] at all in describing race relationships in the South, we must mean racial identity, for a person of Negro blood born in England or France or the West Indies, who happens to be in the South, must expect to assume the racial status of all other Negroes. It should be gross, indeed, to hold that all Negroes in the world belong to the same caste by descent.[51]

Power relations, according to Cox, are defined in racially segregated societies along the lines of skin colour, which serves to divide, not unite. Furthermore, the *internal* power structures of these two systems stem from quite distinct origins: membership of a caste is dependent upon the caste itself, but membership of a 'race' is a biological fact. So, while it is possible to be cast out of one's caste (even though the caste system *presumes* life membership), one cannot be cast out in equivalent terms from one's 'race'.[52] In caste societies, distinctions are culturally inherited. Thus, 'the Hindu's racial heritage identifies him with all other Hindus, while his caste heritage differentiates him from all other-caste Hindus'.[53] In any case, racial segregation is a reflection of the power structure in the USA, which is necessarily a capitalist one. Racial ideologies, Cox claims, are created by and structured through the economic base, which manipulates them in order to reinforce the dominant capitalist ideology. Thus, 'race' struggles are wholly political class struggles. To discuss racial segregation as a caste structure, Cox warns, is to throw a 'comfort blanket' over the debate, thus obscuring the real problem of economic relations within a capitalist society.

The structuralist anthropologist Louis Dumont provides a critique of both the neo-Weberian and neo-Marxist approaches to caste and segregation.[54] Dumont is even more adamant than Cox in refuting the neo-Weberian claim that both can be understood as forms of stratification based on status. Instead, Dumont understands them in their localised contexts, and as reflections of quite distinct ideological systems. The major difference, Dumont argues, is that segregation in America and apartheid in South Africa are distortions of the dominant ideology of those regions, which, being Western, individualistic, and monotheistic, is the ideology of egalitarianism. The caste system, by contrast, is a true reflection of the dominant ideology in Hindu societies, which is hierarchical. The term 'caste' is specific to this setting, suggests Dumont, because caste is necessarily a manifestation of a particular configuration, a particular set of values and beliefs, about the 'pure' and 'impure'.[55] In a caste society, power and status must be dissociated, and it is not enough to identify the presence of a specific social group which might appear to be a caste; one must be able to identify an all-inclusive caste *system*.

Gender and apartheid

So far we have discussed apartheid only in terms of 'race' and ethnicity. However, in so far as apartheid is separation, and the legal justification for the relegation of whole groups of people to the level of second-class citizen or even non-citizen, it clearly need not be just a problem of race. In this volume, I have chosen not to include a separate section on 'women's rights'. I do not think it is helpful to section off women's concerns as if they are peripheral to wider debates. Women suffer as men suffer from such violations as those which constitute the chapters in this book. There are, of course, examples of human rights violations specifically directed at women, and I have sought to highlight them under the appropriate chapter heading. Thus, in so far as rape is primarily used as a torture technique against women, I have discussed it in the chapter dedicated to torture. It seems wholly appropriate, then, to make reference to the numerous instances in which women are socially and politically marginalised or excluded in this chapter. I refer, of course, to the denial of a woman's right to full and equal citizenship, to political and social participation, which is prevalent in many parts of the world. If such exclusion is legitimised by the state then it *must* be a concern for human rights scholars, regardless of cultural context or justification. I can see no logical way it could be possible to oppose apartheid in South Africa but stay silent on the social and political exclusion of women.

The civil and political rights of women – upheld in principle by all the United Nations human rights conventions – were laid down specifically in the Convention on the Political Rights of Women 1953, and passed into law with the Convention on the Elimination of All Forms of Discrimination Against Women 1979. The 1953 Convention clarifies women's entitlements to vote, to stand for election, and to hold public office, on equal terms with men and without discrimination. The 1979 Convention, which evolved from the 1967 Declaration on Elimination of Discrimination Against Women, and which came into force in 1981, took a broader perspective, seeking to ensure women's rights in all spheres. Article 1 reads:

> For the purposes of the present Convention, the term 'discrimination against women' shall mean any distinction, exclusion or restriction made on the basis of sex which has the effect or purpose of impairing or nullifying the recognition, enjoyment or exercise by women, irrespective of their marital status, on a basis of equality of men and women, of human rights and fundamental freedoms in the political, economic, social, cultural, civil or any other field.

This is followed by Article 2, which calls upon states to condemn and eliminate discrimination against women, to, among other things, 'embody the principle of the equality of men and women in their national constitutions or other appropriate legislation if not yet incorporated . . .'. States are subsequently required 'to establish legal protection of the rights of women on an equal basis with men' and 'to take all

Table 7.1   Selected years of full suffrage for women[56]

Country	Year
New Zealand	1893
Finland	1916
Canada	1918
Germany	1918
Sweden	1918
United States	1920
United Kingdom	1928
France	1944
Japan	1945
China	1949
India	1950
Mexico	1953

appropriate measures, including legislation, to modify or abolish existing laws, regulations, customs and practices which constitute discrimination against women'. Clearly, these ideals have not translated into
practice. Fingers are often pointed in the direction of the Islamic world
for its refusal to grant women social and political freedoms and equality
before the law. This is usually justified through appeal to the writings of
the *Quran*, although various scholars have suggested that such accounts
are often selective and open to alternative interpretation.[57] In truth,
women have fought for and won their right to vote over long periods of
struggle. Table 7.1 below shows how this was achieved at different times
in different countries.

   Of course, a number of countries – Kuwait, Saudi Arabia, Qatar,
Oman, the United Arab Emirates, Equatorial Guinea, Surinam, Taiwan
– still deny women the right to vote. However, this is not an issue of relevance only to non-Western societies. While it is true that the struggles
of the women's movement have indeed resulted in political enfranch-
isement, and in formal equality before the law, the reality is that
women's civil and political rights are denied through the patriarchal
structure of the political and legal systems. The state – a masculine construct – sustains this gender hierarchy through various practices and
forms of regulation.[58] Freedom to participate is not the same as freedom
from interference; equality before the law is not the same as equality of
access. These are without doubt human rights concerns because they
rest ultimately with the state and its responsibility for upholding civil
and political rights for all.

The state, apartheid and human rights

Are we all 'equal'? Clearly not. Some are born with greater intelligence than others; some are stronger; some wiser. Some members of society have the power to give birth to offspring; some are remembered best for their skills as footballers. But if we are not equal, what is the obsession within human rights circles with equality? And is equality so important that we must cherish it above all else?

Karl Popper clearly thought not. For Popper, any attempt to impose equality in society was necessarily an authoritarian assault on individual freedom. It is possible that freedom brings us greater happiness than equality. But if equality is restricted by law, then surely so is freedom. An individual is not free, in the *caste* system or under apartheid, to change his or her status, to attain full citizenship.

Does this matter? In his brilliant dystopia, *Brave New World*, Aldous Huxley introduced us to a future society in which everyone is born into a certain classification – Alphas, Betas, Gammas, Deltas, and Epsilons. The Alphas were the brains of the society, occupying the most important jobs, making the tough decisions. The Epsilons were the unskilled manual workers, who had no voice in politics at all. But they never cared, because from their conception they were reared to be Epsilons, and they would justify their position by saying how happy they were to be Epsilons, without any cares in the world. And the Gammas were so happy to be Gammas, because they were free from the pressures of being an Alpha but were not as stupid as those dumb Epsilons!

Huxley's story finds an interesting parallel in the South African case. Very often, South African leaders would justify their system by drawing attention to the fact that, despite the conditions, blacks in South Africa actually experienced a better standard of living than in neighbouring African countries. Cassese, examining with due care the content of the apartheid legislation, rightly criticises this defence. Such an account, he claims, judges human existence solely in material terms, and while it may be true, it does not remove from the fact that in these other countries blacks were at least regarded as equal, as *human*.[59]

Of course, we have already answered our initial question – no, we are not all 'equal', but the human rights concern is that we are equal *before the law*. That is to say, we are all allowed the same entitlements provided for us by the state and its agents, regardless of our characteristics. When a woman is denied her right to vote *because she is a woman*, when a black man is told where he can and cannot live *because he is a black man*, then a violation of fundamental human rights has clearly taken place. This, after all, is the claim which lies at the heart of

Associate Justice Harlan's brave speech in defiance of the Supreme Court's 'separate but equal' decision in *Plessy v. Ferguson*. So, once again we return critically to Table I.3 in the Introduction to this volume. According to that table, apartheid is a violation of the civil right to equality. While that is certainly true, it is not the reason for its inclusion as a human rights concern. Instead, it must be seen as a violation of equality before the law, and thus of *citizenship*, locating it firmly within the realm of the state.

Essay questions

1. What structural conditions existed in South Africa that allowed apartheid to emerge?

2. Can we treat both apartheid and caste as forms of social stratification?

3. Apartheid can be used to describe any political system in which entire groups of people are excluded from the decision-making process, and segregated either spatially or socially. Discuss.

Notes

1 Antonio Cassese (1988) *Human Rights in a Changing World*, Cambridge: Polity Press, p. 106.

2 Associate Justice Harlan's speech was reproduced in Charles Thompson (1996) 'Harlan's Great Dissent' in *Kentucky Humanities*, 1.

3 Human Rights Watch/American Civil Liberties Union (1993) *Human Rights Violations in the United States: A Report on U.S. Compliance with the International Covenant on Civil and Political Rights*, New York and Washington, D.C.: Human Rights Watch/American Civil Liberties Union.

4 Cassese, *Human Rights*, p. 106.

5 Cassese, *Human Rights*, p. 106.

6 Cassese, *Human Rights*, p. 107.

7 Cassese, *Human Rights*, p. 114.

8 Cassese, *Human Rights*, p. 107.

9 Cassese, *Human Rights*, p. 108.

10 Cassese, *Human Rights*, p. 108.

11   A. J. Christopher (1994) *The Atlas of Apartheid*, London: Routledge, p. 147.

12   This paragraph is a summary of Chapter 6 in Christopher, *Atlas of Apartheid*.

13   Following questions raised at the UN by India on South Africa's treatment of citizens of Indian origin; Donna Del Gaudio (1988) 'The Fight Against Apartheid' in Peter Davies (ed.) *Human Rights*, London: Routledge, p. 62; also Cassese, *Human Rights*, p. 114.

14   Del Gaudio, 'Fight Against Apartheid', p. 63.

15   Cassese, *Human Rights*, p. 114.

16   Cassese, *Human Rights*, p. 115.

17   Cassese, *Human Rights*, p. 116.

18   Geoffrey Robertson (1999) *Crimes Against Humanity: The Struggle for Global Justice*, Harmondsworth: Penguin, pp. 235–7.

19   Cassese, *Human Rights*, p. 117.

20   Christopher, *Atlas of Apartheid*, p. 6.

21   Del Gaudio mentions, in the US, General Motors, IBM and Coca-Cola as examples, and in the UK, Barclays Bank, which had been the target of vehement anti-apartheid demonstrations; 'Fight Against Apartheid', p. 73.

22   Robertson, *Crimes Against Humanity*, p. 237.

23   C.W. de Kiewiet (1941) *A History of South Africa, Social and Economic*, Oxford: Oxford University Press.

24   Saul Dubow (1989) *Racial Segregation and the Origins of Apartheid in South Africa*, Basingstoke: Macmillan; Heribert Adam and Hermann Giliomee (1979) *Ethnic Power Mobilized: Can South Africa Change?*, New Haven: Yale University Press; extracts from both reproduced in William Beinart and Saul Dubow (eds) (1995) *Segregation and Apartheid in Twentieth-Century South Africa*, London: Routledge.

25   John Rex (1970) *Race Relations in Sociological Theory*, London: Weidenfeld & Nicholson.

26   Cassese, *Human Rights*, p. 110.

27   Andre Asheron (1969) 'Race and Politics in South Africa' in *New Left Review*, 53, Spring.

28   Cassese, *Human Rights*, p. 109.

29   Cassese, *Human Rights*, p. 111.

30   Asheron, 'Race and Politics', p. 53.

31   Asheron, 'Race and Politics', p. 53.

32   Asheron, 'Race and Politics', p. 53.

33   Asheron, 'Race and Politics', p. 54.

34   Cassese, *Human Rights*, p. 111.

35   Asheron, 'Race and Politics', p. 54.

36   Cassese, *Human Rights*, pp. 112–13.

37   Asheron, 'Race and Politics', pp. 55–6.

38   Leo Kuper (1960) 'The Heightening of Racial Tension' in *Race* 2, 1, November; cited in Asheron, 'Race and Politics', p. 57.

39   Cassese, *Human Rights*, p. 113.

40   Asheron, 'Race and Politics', p. 56.

41   Oliver Cromwell Cox (1948) *Caste, Class and Race*, New York: Doubleday; Robert Miles (1982) *Racism and Migrant Labour*, London: Routledge & Kegan Paul.

42   Martin Legassick (1995; original 1972–3) 'British Hegemony and the Origins of Segregation in South Africa' in Beinart and Dubow, *Segregation and Apartheid*.

43   Harold Wolpe (1972) 'Capitalism and Cheap-Labour Power in South Africa: From Segregation to Apartheid' in *Economy and Society* 1; reproduced in Beinart and Dubow, *Segregation and Apartheid*.

44   Belinda Bozzoli (1983) 'Marxism, Feminism and Southern African Studies' in *Journal of Southern African Studies* 9; reproduced in Beinart and Dubow, *Segregation and Apartheid*.

45   Max Weber (1947) *The Theory of Social and Economic Organization*, Glencoe, Ill: Free Press.

46   Of course, complications arise from the rather vague definition Weber himself provides for status groups, which appear, as Immanuel Wallerstein says, to form a 'residual category which can be based on heredity, family, lifestyle, rank, honour, or privilege, and which may, at a stretch, even include "the nation"'. See Immanuel Wallerstein (1991) 'Social Conflict in Post-Independence Black Africa: The Concepts of Race and Status-Group Reconsidered' in Etienne Balibar and Immanuel Wallerstein, *Race, Nation, Class: Ambiguous Identities*, London: Verso, p. 188.

47   W. Lloyd Warner (1936) 'American Caste and Class' in *American Journal of Sociology*, 42.

48   Warner, 'American Caste', p. 234.

49   Warner, 'American Caste', pp. 235–6.

50   Gerald D. Berreman (1967) 'Stratification, Pluralism and Interaction' in A.V.S. de Reuck and J. Knight (eds) *Caste and Race: Comparative Approaches*, London: Churchill.

51   Cox, *Class, Race and Caste*, p. 455.

52   Cox, *Class, Race and Caste*, p. 457.

53   Cox, *Class, Race and Caste*, p. 456.

54   Louis Dumont (1972; original 1966) *Homo Hierarchicus: The Caste System and Its Implications*, London: Paladin.

55   Dumont, *Homo Hierarchicus*, p. 247.

56   Based on information from *Encyclopedia Americana* website, accessible on http://gi.grolier.com/presidents/ea/side/wsffrg.html.

57   See Taj I. Hashmi (2000) *Women and Islam in Bangladesh: Beyond Subjection and Tyranny*, Basingstoke: Macmillan.

58   See V. Spike Peterson and Laura Parisi (1998) 'Are Women Human?: It's Not an Academic Question' in Tony Evans (ed.) *Human Rights Fifty Years On: A Reappraisal*, Manchester: Manchester University Press.

59   Cassese, *Human Rights*, p. 109.

Further information

Books

Many of the definitive contributions to the debate over how apartheid in South Africa could be explained have been usefully brought together in one volume, *Segregation and Apartheid in Twentieth-Century South Africa*, edited by William Beinart and Saul Dubow (London: Routledge, 1995). Geography students might find A.J. Christopher's analysis of the spatial dimensions of apartheid, *The Atlas of Apartheid* (London: Routledge, 1994), useful. In addition, numerous personal accounts of life under apartheid add a human dimension to these academic analyses.

Documentaries

A comprehensive documentary in four parts covering the history and ethnology of apartheid has been produced and directed by John Blake. *Apartheid* begins with a discussion of *Origins*, proceeds to analyse the idea of *A New Order*, before discussing its *Divisions*. The fourth part is called, tellingly, *Adapt or Die*.

CHAPTER EIGHT

Slavery

> No one shall be held in slavery or servitude; slavery and the slave trade shall be prohibited in all their forms.
>
> *Universal Declaration of Human Rights, Article 4*

What is slavery?

Slavery, which throughout history has taken many forms, might be described as the formal (but not always legal) denial to individuals or groups of a particular freedom, to have control over their own lives. Yet even this simple attempt at a definition is unsatisfactory. It raises moral questions as well as intellectual ones. What, exactly, would such a freedom entail? Why should we treat it as a *right*? And if we are to approach slavery from the perspective of a social scientist, what exactly should we focus our attention on? We might, for example, concern ourselves with any number of the following: slavery as an institution and its various forms; the relationship between slavery and 'race'; the experience of slavery; the conditions which make slavery possible and/or profitable; slavery as a social relationship between master and slave; the relationship between slavery and capitalism, and the position of slaves within the class structure. Each of these raises sociological questions.[1] We would, then, agree with Orlando Patterson, who has described slavery as 'a remarkable case study of the nature of social values and of social change ... [and] ... the fundamental sociological problem of social order and control'.[2]

Geoffrey de Ste. Croix,[3] who usually talks about 'unfree labour' as a general category, makes the distinction within this between *chattel slavery*, *debt bondage*, and *serfdom*. We shall not be discussing serfdom in this chapter, and although debt bondage will be mentioned, most attention will be paid to chattel slavery. The League of Nations, in its 1926 Slavery

Convention, defined slavery as 'the status or condition of a person over whom any or all of the powers attaching to the right of ownership are exercised'.

Slavery has taken many forms and existed in many historical and geographical societies. One of the most wide-ranging comparative studies of slavery as a social institution was carried out by Orlando Patterson.[4] Patterson suggests that there are only three noticeable universal features common to all known slavery systems:

1   that the master has the right to threaten or punish the slave with violence

2   that all slaves experience what Patterson calls 'natal alienation', meaning, they are denied rights of birth

3   that all slaves are deprived of honour.

Various features commonly associated with slavery are excluded from Patterson's list. First, he says, we cannot say that all slaves are exploited for the purpose of economic gain, since in many African societies they were used to increase the number of dependants of the master, which would, in turn, increase his status but not result in direct economic benefit. Indeed, in *The German Ideology*, Marx and Engels had suggested that early slavery was a product of the kinship structure.[5] Secondly, we cannot say that slavery is always associated with ownership, in part because until Roman law there was no real concept of 'absolute property'. Thirdly, we cannot assume that all slaves are ethnic, cultural or territorial 'Others', since there have been rare examples of enslavement *within* ethnic groups.

In a more recent contribution, Bales and Robbins consider slavery to be comprised of three key features:[6]

1   that the slave is controlled by another person

2   that the owner appropriates the labour power of the slave

3   that the slave's activities are controlled by the threat or use of violence.

They then proceed to apply these criteria to some of the institutions which are commonly considered to be forms of slavery. Some of these institutions – 'white slavery', forced labour, debt bondage, child prostitution, forced prostitution, and sexual slavery – satisfy all the criteria Bales and Robbins employ. Two other institutions – prostitution and the use of migrant workers – sometimes but not always satisfy all three. Forced marriages involve the threat of violence but not always the other two. Apartheid, incest and (sometimes) organ harvesting all involve the threat of violence, but none of them involve the appropriation of labour power, and only sometimes do they involve loss of free will. The caste system may involve violence but does not satisfy the other criteria. Prison labour certainly involves the threat of violence but only sometimes involves the appropriation of labour power but never the loss of free will.[7]

Suffice it to say that a vast library of work has been carried out, primarily by historians, on chattel slavery as it existed in the United States prior to the Civil War. It is important to touch on some of this here. However, in so far as much of this was polemical in nature, we should treat it with care when addressing, as we shall below, some of the key sociological questions, such as those which relate to the role played by slavery *as an institution* within wider social, cultural, economic, and political conditions. Historians such as Ulrich Bonnell Phillips and those who followed him tended to discuss slavery not in terms of *rights* but in terms of its positive contribution to society, both as a means of social control, and also as an educational and civilising experience for the 'inferior' black slave.[8] If such pro-slavery pieces tended to be somewhat sympathetic towards the plight of the slaves, there were also those which adopted a far more aggressive, racist view on the issue. In the early part of the twentieth century, social Darwinism was beginning to take form as an intellectual perspective. Of course, as the century progressed, so did the academic debate, with various reports and studies setting out to counter either (or both) the paternalistic pro-slavery literature or the biological-reductionist rants. In this respect, studies by Gunnar Myrdal and Kenneth Stampp are significant.[9] However, as Stanley Elkins points out, even as thorough and ground-breaking a research project as that undertaken by Stampp could not escape from the agenda which had been set by the earlier writers – an agenda driven by moral polemic which betrayed 'all the characteristics one might expect of white men who knew nothing of what it meant to be reared in slavery'.[10]

In his important study of slavery in America, Elkins discusses the 'four major legal categories which defined the status of the American slave'.[11] This, at least, suggests an attempt to locate the institutional practice of slavery at the time in terms of a systemic denial of rights, and indeed of a process of dehumanisation. The first, he argued, was *terms of servitude*, and these had been established, from around the 1660s, to mean servitude for life, passed on to all descendants. The second, regarding *marriage and the family*, was agreed in the mid-nineteenth century to mean that, for the purpose of upholding ownership rights, slaves were denied the traditional securities and assurances of family life, and no marriage between slaves was recognised in law. The third, Elkins says, was on the matter of *police and disciplinary powers over the slave*. In the Southern states, Elkins suggests, it was customarily considered to be good practice for masters to adopt a paternalistic attitude towards their slaves, and to avoid unnecessary ill-treatment. But this was never defined in law, and where slaveholders were responsible for the gross torture, and in some cases murder, of their slaves, it was virtually impossible for courts to intervene. Finally, in the matter of *property and other civil rights*, it was accepted that slaves had no such rights at all under the law: whatever they did they did solely at their master's allowance, whatever they might have owned became the property of their master.

According to any definition, slaves constitute a social group (whether we take that to be a social class in the Marxist sense or choose to adopt some other form of classification), located firmly within a social hierarchy. To treat slavery solely as an economic institution would be short-sighted – even in its most economic aspect, its relationship with capitalism, we will see that slavery constitutes more of a social than an economic system. In what follows, we will take a journey not through the economics or the statistics of slavery, but through its sociology – that is, through some of the key sociological themes developed in the works of such writers as Stanley Elkins, Eugene Genovese, Orlando Patterson and Kevin Bales.

A brief history of slavery

We should not spend too long on a historical overview of slavery as an institution. Needless to say, any attempt to understand slavery without some knowledge of its role in various societies throughout history would be foolhardy. However, so common a practice was slavery that a full geo-historical overview would take up far more space than is available here. For the purpose of brevity, and to provide a brief introduction to the three slave-holding societies which have received the most academic attention, I shall concentrate solely on slavery as it existed: first, in ancient Rome and Greece; second in early colonial Latin America and the Caribbean; and third, in the Southern states of the USA. I will conclude with a discussion of its abolition.

Slavery in the ancient world

Slavery was already an ancient institution by the time history reached the period which we refer to as the 'ancient world'. We have already mentioned, albeit briefly, different aspects of the slavery systems of ancient Greece and ancient Rome. Historical studies inform us that ancient Greek society relied upon various forms of unfree labour, types of which included the *andrapodon* (war slave), the *oiketes* (household slave), and the *doulos* (common or chattel slave).[12] Debt bondage had been a common practice in Athens and other *poleis* until around 600 BC, when the statesman Solon abolished it in Athens.[13] Subsequent laws protected citizens from slavery. Wealthy Athenians needed a new source of cheap labour, and many Greek *poleis* turned to the enslavement of the various 'barbarians' (non-Greeks) who lived in the outside world, although some, including the Athenians, happily enslaved other Greeks. It would appear that by the early sixth century BC some form of slave economy existed between neighbouring cities, with the practice becoming increasingly popular throughout various outposts of the known world.[14] The Persian invasion of 480 BC appears to have been a crucial point in the expansion of the slave system. In the fifth and fourth centuries BC, there were some 80–100,000 chattel slaves in Athens alone.[15]

Debt bondage also appears to have been commonplace in earliest Rome (c. 450 BC).[16] This may have involved the 'leasing' of a child into servitude by a father, although it is possible that those sent into such bondage were not considered 'slaves', who were always foreigners, usually captured in war.[17] Aside from this difference in definition, there was a significant difference in terms of service which reflected the contrast between 'insiders' and 'outsiders'. Those under debt bondage were 'insiders', citizens, serving bondage for an agreed period of time, while slaves were 'outsiders', foreigners, prisoners of war, whose enslavement was permanent. Similarly, most references to debt bondage in the Old Testament (and there are many) regarding the ancient Near and Middle East suggest that the debt-bondsman or bondswoman had certain 'rights' which are protected under law.[18] By contrast, ancient Hebrews had happily kept Canaanites as slaves for centuries, content in the knowledge that not only were Canaanites 'Others', but their enslavement was enshrined in God's law, recounted in Genesis.[19] However, in Rome at least by the third century AD, the two groupings – *servi* (slaves) and *mancipia* (debt bondsmen) – were similar in status, and both were comprised of foreigners, enslaved by the army.[20]

Slavery in Latin America and the Caribbean

In around the fifteenth century, the practice of slavery reached a new level with the establishment of the transatlantic slave links connecting

Western Europe with West Africa and the New World of the Americas. This, of course, is inextricably linked to European expansionism and colonialism. The Europeans had come across slave economies during their earlier exploits in Africa, where relatively small numbers of prisoners of war were sold as goods. This was a system which the Europeans were eager to turn to their advantage.[21] Experiments with native American populations used as slaves had failed, primarily due to the native sensitivities to new diseases imported from Europe with the colonisers. The abundance of Africans made this mortality rate a less significant factor. Slaves were brought from West Africa to work on the sugar and coffee plantations of Latin America and the Caribbean, as well as the British colonies of North America. Portuguese conquest had brought the international slave trade to Brazil in the late 1500s. The Dutch replaced the Portuguese in various important outposts, including Brazil, in the mid-1600s. When the Dutch lost their tenuous grip on Brazil shortly afterwards, they turned their attentions north to the Caribbean islands, notably Barbados. British colonialism opened up Jamaica and Cuba to the slave trade in the seventeenth and eighteenth centuries.

In the lucrative sugar plantations of Brazil, the Portuguese had initially used native populations but, as was generally the case, soon came to realise that African slaves were more economical. Indeed, the Portuguese had experience of using African slave labour in their other colonies. As James Walvin points out, in the mid-1500s there were virtually no slaves in the sugar mills, but by the end of the sixteenth century they formed a 'striking minority', and by the early-1600s Africans dominated the labour force.[22]

In Jamaican society, slavery had been a feature since its colonisation by the British in 1655, and was not abolished until 1834. Although much work on slavery has focused on the distinctive character of the slave society of the American South, the practice as it was applied in Jamaica has also received its share of attention from academics, notably Patterson, who has shown that the system was wholly inefficient and ultimately disastrous, due largely to the absenteeism of the British landlords.[23] However, the 'triangular trade' which began in the European ports, made its way to the West African coast, and moved on to the Americas before finishing back in Europe, was extremely profitable for the English merchants. They would fill the ships with goods which were usually of a minimal value at home, and which could be readily exchanged for slaves in West Africa. These slaves were then exchanged in the Americas for goods of a higher value. Each exchange resulted in a huge profit, and the wealth contributed greatly to the development of commercial and then industrial capitalism in Britain.[24]

Slavery in the United States

The case of African enslavement in what is now the United States remains a particular, and peculiar,[25] case in the history of slavery. As Elkins points out, there was nothing natural about it, which could be understood in terms of any suitability on the part of the African slaves to work in the plantations. It could not be explained along purely *racial* lines as there is no necessary history connecting slavery to 'race'. And the English who controlled the colonial lands had no tradition of their own, in history or in law, of anything equivalent with slavery.[26] As with elsewhere in the Americas, the English first used native slave labour, but this proved unsatisfactory. There was a major demand for labour which was satisfied at first by the importing of indentured labour from England, Scotland and Ireland. Although the first 20 Africans arrived in Virginia in 1619, the question of servitude was not defined in law until 1660.[27] It was only around this time that, in part to encourage more white settlers to come to the colonies to work without fear of being forced into harsh servitude, certain rights were established which were not extended to include black workers, since it was felt that their arrival was not subject to such deterrence.[28] That, within only a couple of generations, what had started as an informal, and largely unenforceable, practice had suddenly become a unique and totalising form of institutionalised racial discrimination had much, Elkins argues, to do with the sweeping tide of capitalism.

The experience of the enslaved Africans was, undoubtedly, a harsh one. Despite the popular image of the kind Southern gentleman adopting a paternalistic attitude towards his slave, reports from the time reveal the relationship between master and slave to be one based primarily on sheer power, forged by the dominant social institutions, sustained by fear and violence. Very little was done if a master mistreated, tortured, or even killed his slaves. Women slaves were subject to sexual abuse. Punishments for indiscretions and offences, and even poor performance, were severe. Most severe were the punishments for rebellion. And yet, slave revolts did occur, and we should take care to recognise the history of slavery in America as being a history not only of domination but also of resistance.[29]

The abolition of slavery

It is perhaps fair, if rather curious, to say that the driving force behind the abolition of the slave trade, and slavery in general, came from Britain.[30] Inspired by the growing influence among intellectual circles of Enlightenment ideals of freedom and driven initially by concern amongst Oxford University students, the abolitionist movement grew steadily, and attracted increasing levels of support, from the eighteenth century onwards. One of the main protagonists involved in the struggle was the MP and missionary William Wilberforce. Under pressure from key quarters, the British parliament finally banned the slave trade in 1807 (although the British slave system was not formally ended until 1838). After this, the British took upon themselves the role of global champions of freedom, a posture which earned them scorn in other parts of the world. Nevertheless, thanks to the efforts of the abolitionists, the 1815 Declaration Relative to the Universal Abolition of the Slave Trade condemned the practice and called upon states to declare it illegal, as well as encouraging the establishment of duties aimed at deterring participation in the trade.[31]

British opposition to slavery was built upon a growing humanism associated with Enlightenment sensibilities. It was also closely associated with certain religious movements, notably the Quakers.[32] But the British had the luxury of not living with slavery on their doorsteps. With regard to the abolition of slavery in the United States, the growing anti-slavery movement in the Northern states was probably more significant. Elkins suggests that the abolitionist movement in America was unique among its kind, in so far as it was *wholly moral* in its outlook.[33] There appeared, he claims, to be something about the American perspective at the time which was quite fearful and dismissive of those sociological accounts which concerned themselves with institutions. By the 1830s, America was dominated by a wholly *individualistic* mentality. And yet, amidst this radical celebration of individualism as a virtue, the problem of slavery – that is, of slavery as a manifestation of sin – was becoming increasingly apparent. The result of this outrage was the American Civil War of 1861–1865, which resulted in the adoption of the Thirteenth Amendment to the American Constitution outlawing slavery in 1866.[34]

Forms of slavery continued, nonetheless, to thrive in various parts of the world: Cuba, Brazil, West Africa, India, South-east Asia, and the Middle East included. At the global level, the practice of slavery was finally declared illegal by the passing of the League of Nations Slavery Convention on 25 September 1926, which entered into force on 9 March 1927.[35] When the League of Nations gave way to the United Nations, the Convention was altered by protocol on 7 December 1953, and came into force on 7 July 1955. The Supplementary Convention on the Abolition of Slavery, the Slave Trade, and Institutions and Practices Similar to Slavery was adopted by the United Nations on 7 September 1956 and came into effect on 30 April 1957. Drawing heavily on the 1926 Convention, and on the 1948 Universal Declaration of Human Rights, the

Supplementary Convention made it clear that the practice or endorsement of, and any participation in, slavery, the slave trade, or similar institutions (including debt bondage and serfdom), was a criminal offence liable to severe punishment. In a related development, the International Covenant on Economic, Social and Cultural Rights of 1966 emphasised the right to work and to receive a fair wage from that work. The International Covenant on Civil and Political Rights of the same year added a provision prohibiting most forms of unfree labour. In an important case heard in 1970, the International Court of Justice made it clear that slavery is understood by the international community to be a criminal offence, regardless of whether a particular government has ratified the various treaties, by listing the protection from slavery as one of two obligations *erga omnes* (that is, obligations owed by a state to the international community itself).[36] Finally, at the Rome Final Act of 1998, slavery was defined as a crime against humanity and placed under the jurisdiction of the International Criminal Court. These major acts may be summarised, following Bales and Robbins, as shown in Table 8.1.

Slavery in the contemporary world

It would, sadly, be a mistake to believe that, thanks to the various international covenants and conventions discussed above, slavery has been fully abolished. Like so many other human rights violations, it is as common today as it has been at any point in the past, perhaps more common. Nor should we in the West seek comfort in a belief that, even if slavery does still exist, at least *we* have abolished it. In his groundbreaking investigation, published as *Disposable People*, Kevin Bales suggests that there are perhaps 3,000 household slaves in the city of Paris alone, and many more in other Western metropolises, from London to Los Angeles, Zurich to New York.[37] Add to these the 20 million or so 'bonded labourers' (primarily in South Asia) who are working to pay off a debt which can never be repaid, and other kinds of modern slave, and Bales suggests that, at a conservative estimate, there are some 27 million slaves in the world today.[38]

This 'new slavery', says Bales, is quite different from the 'old' slavery associated with the transatlantic slave trade. For one thing, slavery is officially *illegal* everywhere, so there is no such thing as a legal entitlement to ownership. But this, in a way, benefits the modern slaveholders, who are not bound by legal procedures. They can get away with whatever they want.[39] Also, in the 'old' slavery, buying a slave represented a considerable investment. Due to the relative shortage of slaves, and to the high purchase cost, slave-owners tended to treat their 'property' in

Table 8.1 Major slavery Conventions[40]

Slavery convention	Definition/Declaration regarding slavery
Slavery Convention (1926)	**Slavery defined:** The 'status or condition of a person over whom all of the powers attaching to the right of ownership are exercised' **Forced labour added:** States should 'prevent compulsory or forced labour from developing into conditions analogous to slavery'
Universal Declaration (1948)	**Servitude added:** 'No one shall be held in slavery or servitude; slavery and the slave trade shall be abolished in all their forms'
Supplementary Convention (1956)	**Servile status added:** Practices referred to as 'servile status' should be abolished: debt bondage serfdom unfree marriages the exploitation of young people for their labour
Economic, Social and Cultural Covenant (1966)	**Freedom to choose work added:** Recognises 'the right of everyone to the opportunity to gain his living by work which he freely chooses or accepts'
Rome Final Act (1998)	**Trafficking added:** Slavery defined as 'the exercise of any or all of the powers attaching to the right of ownership over a person and includes the exercise of such power in the course of trafficking in persons, in particular women and children'

Table 8.2 'Old' and 'new' forms of slavery[41]

'Old' slavery	'New' slavery
Legal ownership asserted	Legal ownership avoided
High purchase cost	Very low purchase cost
Low profits	Very high profits
Shortage of potential slaves	Surplus of potential slaves
Long-term relationship	Short-term relationship
Slaves maintained	Slaves disposable
Ethnic differences important	Ethnic differences not important

such a way as to ensure maximum longevity. In the 'new' slavery, the emphasis is on a quick and profitable turnover – low cost, minimal investment, high profit. Slavery is no longer defined (and justified) according to racial or ethnic characteristics, ensuring that there is a surplus of possible slaves, who become, in Bales's terms, wholly *disposable*.[42] Comparisons between the 'old' and 'new' slaveries are conveniently summarised in Table 8.2.

Bales lists various forms of modern slavery.[43] This is not an exclusive list, nor are the categories wholly independent. There are two key factors which unite them. First, they are defined by the threat of violence. Second, the slaves are used for the purpose of economic exploitation. These forms of slavery include:

1   *Chattel slavery*. As in 'old' slavery, a person is born or sold into servitude and the ownership of another. Bales claims this takes place most commonly in Northern and Western Africa and the Middle East, but represents a relatively small percentage of the total slave population.

2   *Debt bondage*. A person is not owned, but controlled and made to work as repayment of some kind of debt, which can never be repaid. The length and nature of the bondage is undefined, and the debt can be passed down to children. The most common form of slavery in the world, this is found most often in South Asia.

3   *Contract slavery*. A person is enticed into a place of work through promise of a contract and proper employment, but the reality is that she or he is kept as a slave, threatened with violence, paid nothing, and yet a contract makes this all appear legitimate. It is common throughout the world and Bales indicates that this is the fastest-growing form of modern slavery.

4   *War slavery.* In times of war, civilians are sometimes enslaved and used as labourers or made to work on projects which sustain the war effort. This (relatively uncommon) form of slavery is, unlike the others, usually sanctioned by the government, and can be found today in Burma and Sudan.

5   *Children as domestic servants.* Children are not owned but are controlled through violence to perform domestic chores in return for lodgings. This form of slavery usually lasts until adulthood, and occurs mainly in the Caribbean and western Africa.

6   *Ritual or religious slavery.* In some African or Asian countries, girls or young women are presented as slaves to local priests, usually as some kind of atonement for sins committed by their families. To appease the gods, the virgin girl becomes the domestic servant and sexual slave of the priest until he frees her.

'Race', citizenship and slavery

One of the key points to Elkins's argument is that the system of slavery that existed in ante-bellum America was in many respects unique. This is justified in part through Elkins's attempt to develop a social psychology of the slave mentality, which will be discussed in greater depth below. Another aspect of this system of slavery which, while not unique to the American case, is nevertheless most pronounced in it, is the relationship between slavery and 'race'. We should take care to remember that the various forms of slavery which took place before, and, as Bales's[44] recent research shows, those forms which exist in the world today, have not necessarily depended on racial characteristics. While in the American case, as Elkins himself says, the Southern slave-owners came to justify their practice along highly racial grounds, adopting social Darwinist theories of 'racial hierarchy',[45] studies of other slavery systems show different attitudes. The Brazilian sociologist Gilberto Freyre has claimed that in Brazil, friendly and informal relations existed between master and slave, and he puts this down to the absence of any history of colour prejudice in Portugal (which, he claims, can be explained according to Portugal's history and its geography between Europe and Africa).[46] Anglo-Saxons, Freyre suggested, were more racist in their views. Also, Frank Tannenbaum has pointed out that, in Brazil during the time of slavery, there were as many or more people of colour who were free as there were those who were enslaved.[47] This can be explained mainly through the emphasis paid to manumission, that is, the potential for a slave to achieve freedom. Tannenbaum's thesis is that in contrast to the Anglo-Saxon tradition, Catholic slave-owning societies saw the system as one aimed at 'educating' and 'preparing' the slave for future citizenship. A similar contrast existed in ancient times, between the Greek and the Roman models. The orthodox Greek view, held by Plato and Aristotle (and Herodotus) was that of 'natural slavery': that, for some people, enslavement is a natural state. The view adopted much later by the Stoics, which influenced later Roman perspectives, was that slavery was an accident, a matter not of nature but of fortune. It is no surprise, then, to learn that in ancient Greece, manumission did not lead to citizenship, whereas in ancient Rome, it often did.[48]

The views of Freyre and Tannenbaum have been heavily criticised by, among others, Marvin Harris, who suggests that even if the Portuguese resident in Portugal were not racist in their outlook, they certainly developed racist views when settling in overseas colonies such as Brazil.[49] Harris is harshly critical of one of Tannenbaum's key points, that, in contrast to the situation in the Southern states of America, in Latin America black slaves were not dehumanised. The difference between slavery and freedom was treated as an accident of history, and slaves were accorded a fair number of rights.[50] Harris concedes that this may have been true in law, but he argues that it was not the case in practice. But it does suggest another conundrum in the analysis of slavery: to what extent can a slave also be a citizen? Citizens are, by their very nature, accorded rights which allow them to participate in the political, social, cultural and economic practices of the community. The history of citizenship runs parallel to the history of slavery. In ancient Greece, a clear distinction was made between citizens and slaves. Where slaves have not been overtly defined as 'non-humans', they have at least been considered 'non-citizens', and this has tended to involve the enslavement, if not of people considered to be of different *colour*, then at least of people defined as being from a different *culture* or *nationality*: foreigners. One cannot understand the history of slavery without first confronting the history of *difference* and *Otherness*. How, we might ask, could we possibly justify owning slaves if we did not somehow separate *them* from *us*? In so far as *we* are free citizens, and, accordingly, 'complete' humans, *they* must somehow be subhuman, or not human at all.[51] After all, if we were to adopt a social contract perspective which is commonly used in moral philosophy, we would see that, so long as it is considered acceptable for us to own those who are otherwise no different from ourselves, what, then, stops others from similarly owning us? If the basis of any social or political system can be understood in these terms, there would necessarily have to be a clear demarcation, between citizens and slaves, humans or non-humans, in order to justify such a system.

Understanding slavery

Slavery is probably more closely connected to the structures of capitalism and colonialism than any other substantive issue discussed in this volume. Whereas our attempts to understand the conditions within which the other violations included here occur will almost certainly, thanks primarily to contributions from Marxist scholars, lead us in the direction of capitalism, in the case of slavery, we must *begin* with capitalism. In order to get some overview of the relationship between capitalism and slavery, we should look at how various major writers, notably Eugene Genovese, Geoffrey de Ste. Croix, Barrington Moore and Orlando Patterson, have studied it throughout history. Genovese and Ste. Croix both adopt an overtly Marxist perspective, which views history in terms of a series of epochs defined by their economic systems. Slavery is thus an early 'mode of production' – that is, it is a means of extracting surplus through exploitation. Ste. Croix in particular argues that in the ancient world slaves did indeed constitute what we refer to today as a 'social class'. Moore's contribution to this debate offers a different assessment of the relationship between slavery and capitalism. In one respect, he takes his theoretical lead from Max Weber, in so far as he seeks to develop a multi-causal historical sociology. But Weber had famously pointed out that, in order to reach maximum efficiency, capitalism requires a system of free labour.[52] Moore's thesis is that there are different forms of capitalism, and not all of them are incompatible with slavery. Patterson also seeks to produce a non-reductionist account of slavery, but one which develops close links to capitalism. Indeed, Patterson suggests that the idea of property as it developed in Roman law may have originated from the concept of slavery, and that we might reasonably argue that slavery was important in the initial development of trade. We should then consider how the 'new' slavery discussed by Bales relates to more recent developments in how the world capitalist economy functions. It would appear that, implicitly, Bales is taking a stance *contra* Weber and *pro* Marx, in so far as his interpretation of the global economy makes clear the crucial role played by slavery and its inherent power relations.

According to Marxists such as Geoffrey Ste. Croix, Tom Brass, and Eugene Genovese, slavery constitutes a mode of production in much the same way as feudalism and capitalism, which replaced it, do. Slavery is a system intended to exploit one group for the express purpose of producing a surplus which is beneficial to the lifestyle of the exploiting group. This is true of slave-holding societies in antiquity, such as the ancient Greek and Roman civilisations, and also of the colonialist slave systems which operated during early modernity in the Americas.[53] Such systems can be distinguished from other slave societies, such as those which existed in parts of Africa and in the Far East, precisely because of their relationship to capitalist production. As Brass has recently argued, the prevalence of slavery in the developing world is closely connected to the various struggles to develop a capitalist mode of production, which would liberate the exploited worker.[54] As Bales and Robbins, summarising Brass, state, slave labour 'stalls the political transformations that generally accompany the proletarianization of the workforce, as well as reimposing authority over a workforce where a proletariat already exists'.[55] Thus, a Marxian analysis of slavery need not reduce the practice to being simply a primitive mode of production. It can be located within a complex relationship with the more advanced capitalist mode. Capitalism can exploit slavery in a similar way to technology, to cheapen free wage labour or to quash the development of class consciousness.[56] Indeed, some Marxists regard the system of slavery employed by the plantation owners in the American South not, actually, as a slave mode of production but as an agrarian capitalism which utilises slave labour as an economic resource.

Genovese locates his attempt to devise a Marxian, *materialist* understanding of slavery within a (broadly) sympathetic critique of previous specialists, notably Tannenbaum and Elkins.[57] Following an earlier, harsher critique by Marvin Harris,[58] Genovese points out that Tannenbaum (and Elkins) operate within an *idealist* framework which 'ignores the material foundations of each particular slave society, especially the class relations, for an almost exclusive concern with tradition and cultural continuity'.[59] While slavery might be conceived of as a mode of production, the slaves themselves can be understood as a quasi-proletarian class. However, class analysis as applied to capitalist societies sits relatively uneasily with regard to what might be called 'pre-bourgeois' societies. Genovese rejects the thesis that slave-holding societies (such as the American South) are wholly agrarian societies 'fighting against the encroachment of industrial capitalism', but he is also critical of the opposing view which holds that plantation slavery was actually another manifestation of capitalism.[60] The mere presence of commercial activities within the slave-holding South does not alone qualify it to be a capitalist system. There have, Genovese rightly points out, been many pre-capitalist systems which operate some form of commercial operation. We can, however, work between these positions by locating the slave South within a wider world economy. There is no doubt that slavery, within this context, was entirely compatible with world capitalism, since it allowed for a relatively cheap and constant workforce. It therefore produced a 'small commercial bourgeoisie', the

profits of which went into slave-holding.[61] This, in turn, provided the
ruling classes with the luxury of a lifestyle suitable to their position,
which duly served to reinforce class relations.[62] The conflict, as
Genovese rightly says, was not so much between economic practices but
between the cultural ones which emerge from them – that is, between
the 'liberal individualism' of capitalism and the 'aristocratic elitism' of
pre-bourgeois slave society.[63] But for the most part in the ante-bellum
South, this conflict was kept in check through the hegemonic practices
adopted by capitalism as a *social* (as opposed to economic) system. Such
a social system is inherently based upon the uneven distribution of
wealth and power, and the strategies adopted by one, dominant social
group to maintain control over the other, subordinate one. It is in this
respect that Genovese, drawing heavily on Gramsci, offers a Marxian
interpretation of the Southern system of plantation slavery, a system in
which:

> economics, politics, social life, ideology, and psychology converged to
> thrust the system outward and ... beneath each factor lay the exigencies
> of the slaveholding class.[64]

Most leading industrialists, Genovese points out, supported slavery
and had considerable interest in the plantation system:

> The commercial bourgeoisie, such as it was, remained tied to the
> slaveholding interest, had little desire or opportunity to invest capital in
> industrial expansion, and adopted the prevailing aristocratic attitudes.[65]

However, as Genovese points out, the Southern system of plantation
slavery was wholly restrictive upon the economic development of the
South, limiting its purchasing power so that it could not sustain much in
the way of industrial development at a time when economic demand
favoured industrial over agrarian production.[66] For Genovese, the end
of slavery in the South was in no small way the result of a political-
economic crisis, not reducible to simple economics. The actual *profitability* of the system (contrasted with, say, the industrial capitalism of the
North), is not a major factor in understanding its role as a social institution. But in the long term, the expansive requirements of the system,
coupled with the threat to the slave-holders' hegemony, brought it into
crisis.

In contrast to the Marxist approach, which locates slavery within wider systems of economic exploitation, some social scientists and historians have sought to adopt a more multi-causal perspective on the relationship between slavery and capitalism. Writers such as Orlando Patterson and Barrington Moore, who come from otherwise distinct traditions, are both indebted to the works of Max Weber. Various key themes link Weber's ideas, even if, unlike Marx, they do not form a cohesive theory of society. Supporters of Weber might suggest that his writings take Marx's ideas to a different level. While Marx focused on conflict between social classes, based on relations of production, Weber concerned himself with conflict between various social groups, not just relationships between social classes but also power relationships and lifestyle or status group relationships. For Weberians, then, slaves do not necessarily constitute a social class, bound primarily by economic interests. Also, while Marx viewed economic development as the driving force of history, Weber suggested that social and cultural practices often produced 'ways of life' which influenced economic change.[67] Thus, for Weberians, the practice of slavery may have played an instrumental part in the development of modern capitalism. It is this point especially which unites Patterson and Moore – their belief that Western modernity (and, for Patterson, Western concepts of freedom) emerged out of a history of slavery.

In an important study, Eric Williams has argued that the accumulation of wealth produced by the slave trade played a significant role in the development of at first commercial, and subsequently industrial, capitalism, in Britain.[68] Orlando Patterson has adopted a similar view, arguing that early systems of slavery may have been hugely influential in the development of modern systems of industry, finance and trade. In keeping with the Weberian tradition (although quite critical of Weber), Patterson focuses on slavery less as ownership of property and more as assertion of power. Patterson does not restrict his claim to the emergence of capitalist societies. He suggests also that slavery was instrumental in the development of various cultures in Africa, east Asia, and the Islamic world.[69]

In his hugely influential study of the *Social Origins of Dictatorship and Democracy*, Barrington Moore also pays attention to how slavery makes possible a particular form of modern capitalist system, but his project, as we shall see, is quite different from that of Patterson. Moore focuses on what we might describe as a 'clash of cultural and economic systems'. He draws attention to what he calls the 'routes' to modernisation'.[70] The focus of Moore's project is to understand the relationship between various types of political system which have resulted from these 'routes', and the different power relationships within these societies. His schema is summarised in Table 8.3.

Table 8.3   Barrington Moore's 'routes to modernisation'

Route	Political system	Examples
Bourgeois revolution	Capitalist democracy	United Kingdom, United States, France
Revolution from above	Fascism	Germany, Japan
Peasant revolution	Communism	Russia, China

In studying America's transition to capitalist democracy, Moore concentrates on the role played by the system of plantation slavery, and thus on the political and economic tensions which resulted in the Civil War. This was, he claims, the key period in America's shift towards the capitalist democratic model. By the mid-1800s, he suggests, three distinct forms of economic system were already in place in the USA – the industrialising North-east, the free-farming West, and the South, which depended upon plantation slavery. He answers the question he sets himself – Is the presence of a plantation economy driven by unfree labour incompatible with the requirements for capitalist democratisation? – with a qualified 'no'.[71] Certain conditions needed to be present to bring about this conflict, this clash of ideologies.

Following Kenneth Stampp,[72] Moore suggests that slavery was a highly profitable institution, but that Southerners, ashamed to justify the practice solely on economic grounds, claimed it to be the natural, and mutually beneficial, form of human society.[73] However, for economic and environmental reasons, plantation slavery *per se* was becoming an increasingly non-profitable system. In the industrialising North, there was concern that the practice might spread to the largely unsettled West, and that this would upset the balance between the two main economic systems which were competing within the country at the time.[74] The key difference between them remained that between a largely urban structure celebrating achieved status, and a rural one defending the principles of social hierarchy and ascribed structure. While the North embraced modernity, the South appealed to tradition.[75] Furthermore, the North became less economically reliant upon Southern cotton, more advanced in its manufacturing techniques, and more open to export and import. As the influence of the North spread to the rapidly developing free-farming West, the South felt increasingly threatened. This combination of, on the one hand, economic differences, and, on the other, moral, social and cultural ones, resulted in tensions within the political administration. Amidst these political uncertainties and economic and social conflicts were found the seeds of a war which, it is often falsely taught, was fought solely over the issue of slavery. If it was fought in order to 'preserve the Union', there were those who saw it as a 'revolutionary struggle between a progressive capitalism and a reactionary agrarian society based on slavery'.[76] In a sense, the war was fought between competing economic ideologies to determine the future of the nation-state. If the latter had won, America might very well have developed into an authoritarian, fascist society. The qualified 'no' – as an answer to the question about the incompatibility of the two systems – thus becomes a contextualised 'yes'.

Moore's model does not reduce the practice of slavery solely to the level of economic factors, preferring instead to consider the complex relationship between economic, moral, social, and political causes. But, in the last instance, his is an economistic explanation. Slavery developed because it was economically profitable. Its continuation required the presence of a moral system which justified a social hierarchy. Indeed, in the South, slavery *necessarily* legitimised, and was legitimised by, a whole way of life. Thus, even as geographical and economic transformations rendered the practice less viable, Southerners felt it necessary to defend it.

Moore's model concentrates mainly on internal changes and adopts a comparative, as opposed to a transnational, approach. There is little recognition of external influences upon development. This is a criticism which could be levelled at Weberian historical sociology in general – that for Weberians, as for Weber, the nation-state has been the central unit of analysis.

So far we have restricted our discussion of the conditions within which slavery flourishes to historical dimensions. We should recall, though, how the 'new slavery' identified by Kevin Bales differs from these earlier forms. According to Bales, there are three main reasons for the rise of this 'new' slavery, none of which should be treated in isolation from the others. First, Bales draws attention to the huge population explosion in the post-1945 era. The expansion of the world population from two billion after the Second World War to six billion today means that there is a surplus of people. The bulk of this growth has been in the developing world. Secondly, the globalisation of capital has redirected economic practices away from the nation-state. The implications of these economic transformations brought about first by modernisation and then by globalisation have forced many people, especially once again in the developing world, into the major cities, and into increased poverty. The third ingredient required to produce the 'new slavery', Bales suggests, is the presence of high levels of corruption among government, police and military. In other words, Bales explains the 'new slavery' by pointing to a conspiracy between slave-holders and corrupt officials who often serve as slave-catchers.

Although Bales's research on the 'new slavery' is less concerned with locating the practice within the wider political economy than with identifying instances of it, there are links which can be drawn between it and what Leslie Sklair has called the 'global system' of economic exchange.[77] Bales points out that, while the *direct* value of contemporary slavery to the global economy is quite small, the *indirect* value is considerable.[78] Bales offers as an example the slave-assisted production of steel in Brazil:

> Much of this steel is then made into the cars, car parts, and other metal goods that make up a quarter of all Brazil's exports. Britain alone imports $1.6 billion in goods from Brazil each year, the United States significantly more. Slavery lowers a factory's production costs; these savings can be passed up the economic stream, ultimately reaching shops of Europe and North America as lower prices or higher profits for retailers.[79]

There is a subtext to Bales's research. The 'new' slavery thrives in 'new' economic conditions. These are conditions of disorganised capitalism, of disembedded economic practices, and of a borderless market economy. Bales is right to compare modern transnational corporations to the empires of a past age, in so far as they 'exploit natural resources and take advantage of low-cost labor', but adds that they no longer have to bear the added cost of governing the country.[80] The 'new' slavery is, in a similar fashion, 'control without ownership'.[81] Just as the global economy is fragmented, decentred, and relatively unstructured (both spatially and temporally), so too, in response to such economic needs, is the 'new' slavery driven by the demands of consumerism, rather than any sense of long-term ownership. The new slave, says Bales, 'is a consumable item, added to the production process when needed, but no longer carrying a high capital cost'.[82]

The experience of enslavement

Historical narratives recount the experience of slaves in the Southern American states. However, it is not always easy to distinguish truth from fiction. Southern writers, schooled in romanticism, often provided accounts of slave-owning families as noble, heroic and paternalistic. Whatever these accounts tell us, we should bear in mind that the experience of enslavement is the experience of a lack of freedom. In this section, we will discuss some of the work carried out on two aspects of the slave experience: the master–slave relationship (and with it the experience of violence), and the heavily criticised suggestion that the experience of slavery in America resulted in the development of a particular, docile personality.

The master–slave relationship

Many historical and literary sources present the relationship between the slave-owner and the slave in the Southern states as one of strict but sympathetic paternalism. In the case of some pro-slavery intellectuals, black slavery might have made possible the transition from 'savagery' to 'civilisation', which was in itself a noble thing even if it did require the slave to be 'disciplined' from time to time, in much the same was as one might discipline a dog.[83] Both views have, of course, enraged many academics, who have tried to counter them by diverting attention to the nature of the relationship between master and slave. From a sociological standpoint, this is a type of *social relationship*, akin to, say, the relationship between an employer and employee, a husband and wife, a teacher and student. Each different type of social relationship operates according to its own set of rules, which are usually determined by the expected outcome of the particular relationship. In this section, we look at two such approaches. One is drawn from a Hegelian-Marxian tradition which emphasises the unequal power relationship between the two social actors. A well-known example of this approach is Eugene Genovese's application of the Gramscian thesis on hegemony to the master–slave relationship. The other, associated with the work of Robert Fogel and Stanley Engerman, concentrates instead on the economic relationship between masters and slaves, and how, the authors argue controversially, this may have yielded benefits for both parties. Fogel and Engerman locate their argument within a wider perspective often referred to as 'rational choice' theory, or 'exchange' theory, which seeks to understand social behaviour using methods borrowed from economics.

The classical treatment of the relationship between master and slave comes from the Hegelian-Marxian tradition. It was Georg Hegel who first talked about the 'master–slave dialectic'.[84] For Hegel, the slave existed in a position between his master, and the master's 'object of desire', the slave's product. Viewing the master–slave relationship as a *dialectic of control* accords each party some degree of power. Clearly, in unequal conditions and with unequal access to resources, the vast majority of the power resides with the master. Nevertheless, the slave holds the capacity for rebellion. Hegel's dialectical approach was developed by Marx, who defined the master–slave relationship primarily as a relation of domination.[85] Marx's ideas developed from his historical materialism, in which slavery was considered to be a pre-capitalist mode of production. Neo-Marxists might wish to apply other aspects of Marx's thought to the question of slavery, notably, the question of ideology, and the respective roles played by the master (as bourgeoisie) and the slave (as proletariat). This would necessarily lead to the question of resistance and revolution. While in the classical Marxist sense, this would involve a kind of 'class consciousness' and a subsequent material and ideological revolution, micro-sociological analyses of resistance suggest alternative strategies.

In many respects, Elkins is an heir to this tradition. He sees the relationship between master and slave in the Southern plantations as being an extreme form of 'power relationship'.[86] Although Elkins, in keeping with Hegelian-Marxism in general, does not focus specifically on any empirical interactions, preferring instead to locate the relationship within wider structural conditions, he makes clear the extent to which it is a relationship based on 'dehumanisation'. Elkins shows, rightly or wrongly, that however particular instances may suggest otherwise, the interaction between master and slave can never be anything but a power relationship, so imbued as it is with inequality and 'Otherness'. Elkins thus presents the slave as a relatively docile recipient of power, and has been criticised for downplaying the extent to which slaves acting out roles can be interpreted as a form of resistance. Elkins's reading of the master–slave relationship forms part of his social psychology of the 'slave mentality', and it, and the criticisms made of it, will be discussed at greater length below.

Elkins, though, is no Marxist. Probably the most important analysis of master–slave relations to come from within the Marxian tradition is that offered by Eugene Genovese.[87] Genovese takes his lead from the Gramscian theory of hegemony, which relates to the strategies adopted to maintain power. This power, manifested in the pre-capitalist slave economy as control over the slave, involved a strategic process of negotiation, often involving compromises over the slave's privileges. The slaves were thus made to feel that, by receiving guidance and protection from their masters, and at the same time being rewarded for good service by various allowances, they were experiencing the extent of rights available to them. For Genovese, these conflicts over rights and privileges were class conflicts, but they took place within the system, slaves often competing with each other for privileges, rather than coming together to resist it. This divided sense of class consciousness duly allowed the masters to maintain the oppressive system.

Most of the historical literature concerning plantation slavery in the Southern states seems to agree upon a few basic points. It is widely believed, for example, that slavery was not, in fact, an economically efficient or (for the individual slave-holder) a profitable system, that it was detrimental to the Southern economy, and that, even before the Civil War, it was a dying institution. These four assumptions, plus that which holds slavery to have been a harsh and cruel experience for the slaves themselves, are attacked by the revisionist economic historians Fogel and Engerman, in their controversial book *Time on the Cross*. Fogel and Engerman counter these beliefs with the charge that slavery was profitable, rational, efficient, flourishing prior to the war, and seemingly on the ascendant, adaptable, and wholly beneficial to the Southern economy. Furthermore, they suggest that hard-working slaves not only experienced a better standard of living than many paid industrial workers, but also that they actually benefited from their production efforts.[88]

Justification for the controversial position adopted by Fogel and Engerman comes from their adoption of a position akin to behaviourism in psychology, or exchange theory and rational choice theory in the social sciences. Slave-holders, it is argued, behaved largely benevolently towards their slaves not because of some culturally embedded sense of paternalism, but because it was more profitable to do so. In return for benevolence and various incentives, slaves responded through hard work and loyalty. Just as the slave-holders were capitalists, imbued with the Protestant work ethic, driven by the desire to make money, so, claim Fogel and Engerman, were the slaves themselves committed to the bourgeois Protestant ethic of work as a value in itself.

Of course, it is in no small part because of their decision to adopt such a reductionist perspective that their conclusions can be criticised. David and Temin suggest that Fogel and Engerman's position is skewed by their overly economistic and instrumentalist understanding of human action.[89] Take, for example, Fogel and Engerman's claim that masters would use benevolence and gift-giving as individual incentives. In the same volume as the above critique, Gutman and Sutch[90] return to an earlier source to show how, in the state of Georgia, it was customary to allow slaves to grow, in small amounts, their own crops, for which they would receive either goods or money.[91] 'There is a great difference', the critics warn, 'between a "universal custom" and a selective labor incentive'.[92]

Once again, our discussion of the master–slave relationship has so far been restricted to historical accounts. The 'disposable people' who are the victims of contemporary slavery are, as we have seen, short-term investments. So, even if there was, in 'old' slavery, some aspect of paternal welfare, perhaps even some reciprocity, in the master and slave relationship, in contemporary slavery this relationship is based solely on power and cruelty. Bales begins his disturbing investigation with an account of a young woman named Seba, who had been taken to Paris from her home in Mali as a young girl to serve as a nanny, in return for which she would be sent to school to learn French. Seba never went to school. She was forced to work from daybreak until night-time. She was fed leftovers from the children's plates. She was beaten repeatedly. She tells of one occasion when she was stripped naked, whipped with wire, and had chilli pepper rubbed into her wounds and into her vagina until she passed out.

I was raised by my grandmother in Mali, and when I was still a little girl a woman my family knew came and asked if she could take me to Paris to care for her children. She told my grandmother that she would put me in school and that I would learn French. But when I came to Paris I was not sent to school. I had to work every day. In their house I did all the work; I cleaned the house, cooked the meals, cared for the children, and washed and fed the baby. Every day I started work before 7 a.m. and finished about 11 p.m.; I never had a day off. My mistress did nothing; she slept late and then watched television or went out.

One day I told her that I wanted to go to school. She replied that she had not brought me to France to go to school but to take care of her children. I was so tired and run-down. I had problems with my teeth; sometimes my cheek would swell and the pain would be terrible. Sometimes I had stomachaches, but when I was ill I still had to work. Sometimes when I was in pain I would cry, but my mistress would shout at me.

I slept on the floor in one of the children's bedrooms; my food was their leftovers. I was not allowed to take food from the refrigerator like the children. If I took food she would beat me. She often beat me. She would slap me all the time. She beat me with the broom, with kitchen tools, or whipped me with electric cable. Sometimes I would bleed; I still have marks on my body.

Once in 1992 I was late going to get the children from school; my mistress and her husband were furious with me and beat and then threw me out on the street. I had nowhere to go; I didn't understand anything, and I wandered the streets. After some time her husband found me and took me back to their house. There they stripped me naked, tied my hands behind my back, and began to whip me with a wire attached to a broomstick. Both of them were beating me at the same time. I was bleeding a lot and screaming, but they continued to beat me. Then she rubbed chili pepper into my wounds and stuck it in my vagina. I lost consciousness.

Sometime later one of the children came and untied me. I lay on the floor where they had left me for several days. The pain was terrible but no one treated my wounds. When I was able to stand I had to start work again, but after this I was always locked in the apartment. They continued to beat me.[93]

Seba endured this because she had no choice. She did not understand the language, and knew nothing of her rights as a person. Indeed, she did not understand the concept of choice, nor of time. Days and weeks meant nothing to her. Age meant nothing to her. Her understanding of the world, Bales says, was akin to that of a five-year old.[94]

The slave personality

One of the most important, and controversial, aspects of Elkins's work has been his attempt to apply social psychological perspectives on character and personality to the experience of American slavery. Elkins points out that in much (especially Southern) literature on slavery in the American South, the slave was portrayed as docile, humble, lazy, and childlike. This stereotype, of the slave as the infantile 'Sambo', was justified by many Southerners at the time as resulting from racial characteristics, while most Northerners sidestepped the issue of personality by claiming that no such essential characteristics could be defended so long as personalities were distorted by the experience of slavery as an institution.[95] While, Elkins argues, the Southern argument is scientifically untenable, the Northern one fails to account for the historical and geographical range of slave-owning societies which did not produce such a character type as the one found in the American experience. He opts to take a middle ground, accepting that the 'Sambo' personality was indeed a dominant one among Southern slaves, but explaining this in terms of social and cultural factors. Indeed, Elkins adds credibility to his endeavours by locating them within what was then a growing and influential body of literature on personality and character types, including studies operating within such diverse frameworks as structural-functionalism (Merton), critical theory (Fromm, Adorno *et al*.), and American radical and democratic sociology (Riesman, Mills).[96]

Elkins's theory is based on the premise that the American experience was unique, due to a combination of *shock* (the brutal experience of the process of enslavement) and *detachment* (the severity of adjustment required to fit into new roles in an alien world). There is little doubt that the experience of enslavement was one of brutality and mortality, and that the subsequent process of dehumanisation associated with institutional slavery did indeed result in a considerable sense of shock. Slavery in West Africa had taken the form of a cultural deference to tradition and hierarchy, and slaves were granted certain rights. The social structure of the plantation system was one of extreme closure and authoritarianism. This resulted in a real sense of detachment, of alienation, experienced by the slaves upon arrival in such a wholly unfamiliar environment, which would not have been the same for slaves in other parts of the world. The process of redefining the identity of the slaves included, for example, the replacing of traditional African names with pet names which were often ludicrous.[97] It is in these conditions that the 'Sambo' personality developed.[98] Indeed, Elkins adds that the new social role ascribed to the slaves, that of the child, had a lasting effect on the character and personality of blacks in the American South long after the eventual abolition of slavery.[99]

It is through his theory of the slave mentality and its relation to social structure that Elkins has perhaps courted the most controversy. It is certainly a hypothesis which is open to critique. From one viewpoint, one might question the validity of his historical account, and in particular the unique nature of the American experience. Perhaps Elkins is wrong to assume that the 'Sambo' personality only appeared in the American South. Perhaps he can be found elsewhere, in other slave-holding societies. Patterson, for example, has offered a sympathetic critique of Elkins's views in his own analysis of slave society in Jamaica.[100] According to Patterson, a similar stereotype to that of the 'Sambo' existed in Jamaica, and was known as the 'Quashee'. Traits associated with the Quashee included evasiveness and pathological lying. Or, as at least one leading critic has suggested, perhaps he represents a universal slave-type.[101]

From another perspective, one might criticise his rather generalised depiction of the black slaves as cultural dupes, merely reacting (negatively) to the conditions within which they found themselves, offering little or no resistance in the form of positive or creative action.[102] Elkins's analysis seems to ignore or downplay slave revolt. Perhaps, in similar vein, we can criticise Elkins for assuming that Sambo existed at all as anything other than an image presented by the slave to the slave-owner.[103] Such a criticism would, sociologically speaking, adopt a perspective which is less concerned with structure and culture (the influence Elkins takes from Merton and Mills) and more with the social construction of roles, akin perhaps to Erving Goffman's dramaturgical analysis of the 'presentation of self'.[104] It would, accordingly, treat slavery as some kind of 'total institution' in the Goffmanian sense, and pay attention to the strategies employed by slaves to resist the totalising system.[105] Patterson, although in some respects sympathetic to Elkins's findings, has suggested that the slave in Jamaica might have had much to gain from playing up to the 'Quashee' stereotype: he would confirm his master's prejudices, hide his own inner feelings and, if necessary, force the blame for his inefficiency to be passed to his overseer, should he dislike him.[106]

Patterson has also criticised Elkins's research for being perhaps too generalised. He makes the useful distinction between the 'sudden and traumatic' adjustment of the African slave to Jamaica, and the 'gradual and less painful' adjustment of the Creole slave. He also 'deglorifies' Elkins's general theory of the African experience, pointing out that many of those enslaved were prisoners of war, or criminals who would otherwise be facing execution, and for whom slavery may well have been the 'better option'.[107]

The state, slavery and human rights

Slavery is a violation of that right which many consider to be the definitive human right: the right to freedom. This, of course, is a contested issue in so far as freedom means many things to many people. The question of boundaries to freedom is one that is constantly being posed by politicians, journalists, academics, and activists. 'We are free, personally,' writes Orlando Patterson, 'to the degree that we are released from the power of another, or not prevented by the power of another, to do what we want'.[108] This may be a definition of *freedom*, or more specifically, of *personal* freedom, but to what extent does this constitute a human *right*? Are we free to violate the rights of another? Can our right to freedom be used to justify our refusal to obey certain laws, or be neglectful of certain duties? To avoid these philosophical conundrums, we need to talk perhaps of freedom not as an absolute right in itself, but as a qualified set of conditions within which we are able to exercise our rights. Accordingly, in the positive sense, we need to be free to control our own lives. Or, restated in the negative sense, we need to be free from external control over our lives. This relates to what Patterson has called *sovereignal* freedom, freedom as the ability to exercise power over ourselves and others.[109] But even here, we are on tricky ground. How many of us are truly free in such a way? We all depend in some way on external forces which serve to shape, influence, and in many ways control the direction our lives take. A social scientist should be able to critique such a pluralist notion of power (which is associated with a liberal notion of freedom) from any number of Marxian, Foucauldian, or feminist perspectives. We might want to go so far as to say that, to employ a cliché, we are all 'slaves to the machine', with no real control over our bodies or our lives. And yet slavery, which is a specific form of this, is considered abhorrent and has been made illegal. Why is slavery a special case? The only difference is that the forms of slavery outlined in this chapter are overt restrictions of freedom.

Perhaps to answer this we need, with some modification, to turn to a third kind of freedom Patterson outlines. This is the freedom to 'share in the collective power of the state that governs us',[110] which he calls *civic* freedom. Using this definition, subjects of a dictatorship are, like slaves, not free. We might even wish to expand this definition and talk about freedom 'to participate in the cultural life of the community', as the Universal Declaration of Human Rights, Article 27 (1) suggests. Such participation can be read as a form of *active* citizenship and thus of *empowerment*, through resources which were never available to tragic Seba or those like her. But such a freedom requires access to resources, and is thus inseparable from questions of equality.

In any respect, each of these forms of freedom, which locate in freedom some *value*, betrays a bias towards Western culture and values. It is difficult to translate this Western discourse on freedom into many non-Western tongues. But, as Patterson points out, this is in part because freedom is the socially constructed product of certain historical and sociological conditions, and only in the West did these conditions exist. In this sense, the *idea* of freedom is only possible because of the *reality* of slavery.[111] This dialectic is illustrated with reference to the rise of slavery and the subsequent construction of democracy in seventh century BC Athens,[112] as well as to the conditions which existed in colonial and post-colonial America.[113]

Hannah Arendt makes another (typically chilling) observation with regard to the relationship between slavery, freedom, and human rights. For Arendt, slavery (her references are primarily to slavery in the ancient world) constitutes such an offence against human rights not so much because it denies certain people *liberty* (because quite clearly, other institutions, which we find perfectly acceptable, do the same), but because it denies them the *possibility* of fighting for their freedom. Its greatest horror, she claims, is not in the enslavement of a people (which may have followed a military conquest), but in the establishment of an institution wherein some people are *born* as slaves, 'when it was forgotten that it was man who had deprived his fellow men of freedom, and when the sanction of the crime was attributed to nature'.[114] Slavery is vile because it serves to exclude certain people from the family of humanity, beyond even the boundaries to which the rights of man are supposed to apply.

But, to return to Patterson's debate, does freedom matter? We may take issue with Patterson's suggestion that freedom as we understand it only entered our language because of slavery. This is certainly a non-essentialist (and sociological) claim, in so far as Patterson refuses to grant pre-social or natural law status to the quality of freedom. Freedom, however, is not *in itself* a particularly useful sociological concept. Usually, when sociologists have talked about freedom, they have been referring to the more general, abstract question of *determinism*: whether our actions and our choices are determined by our biological or psychological make-up, or whether we exercise the capacity of making free choices. Social scientists would tend to deny that we are all slaves to our genes, but they might equally be sceptical about pure constructionist claims that human agency is the dominant factor. They might concede a little to the constructionists, but insist that all agencies exist within conditions which are often restrictive. What is at stake is power, or, more precisely, empowerment. Empowerment, of course, takes place within the political sphere – the state. Thus, an interesting sociological observation comes from Rousseau, who said, famously, in *Du Contrat Social*, 'L'homme est né libre, et partout il est dans les fers'.[115]

Essay questions

1. How does the social-psychological perspective of 'role theory' help us understand the personality of a slave?

2. What are the differences between the 'old' slavery and the 'new' slavery?

3. How is slavery related to capitalism and colonialism?

4. What do we mean when we refer to the 'master–slave relationship'?

5. How has the practice of slavery become embedded in the structure of different societies throughout history? What conditions have influenced its development and legitimation?

Notes

1 Orlando Patterson, in *Slavery and Social Death: A Comparative Study*, Cambridge, MA: Harvard University Press (1982), discusses various other

aspects of slavery and the slave system which we will not deal with in any depth here, including the processes and practices of enslavement, and the various forms of manumission.

2 Orlando Patterson (1967) *The Sociology of Slavery: An Analysis of the Origins, Development and Structure of Negro Slave Society in Jamaica*, London: MacGibbon & Kee, p. 10.

3 G.E.M. de Ste. Croix (1981) *The Class Struggle in the Ancient Greek World, From the Archaic Age to the Arab Conquest*, London: Duckworth. Also Ste. Croix (1988) 'Slavery and Other Forms of Unfree Labour' in Leonie Archer (ed.) *Slavery and Other Forms of Unfree Labour*, London: Routledge.

4 Patterson, *Slavery and Social Death*.

5 Karl Marx and Friedrich Engels (1970; original 1845–46) *The German Ideology*, New York: International Publishers, p. 33. For an interesting commentary on the theory developed by Marx and Engels on slavery, see Robin Blackburn (1988) 'Slavery: Its Special Features and Social Role' in Archer, *Slavery and Other Forms*.

6 Kevin Bales and Peter T. Robbins (2000) 'No One Shall Be Held in Slavery or Servitude: A Critical Analysis of International Slavery Agreements' unpublished paper, p. 16.

7 Bales and Robbins, 'No One', p. 17. The authors do go on to discuss these institutions in greater depth, but they can nevertheless be criticised for offering rash generalisations about them and for failing to contextualise these types of slavery.

8 Ulrich B. Phillips (1918) *American Negro Slavery: A Survey of the Supply, Employment and Control of Negro Labor as Determined by the Plantation Regime*, New York: D. Appleton; Ralph B. Flanders (1933) *Plantation Slavery in Georgia*, Chapel Hill: University of North Carolina Press. For a discussion, see Stanley M. Elkins (1959) *Slavery: A Problem in American Institutional and Intellectual Life*, Chicago: University of Chicago Press, Chapter One.

9 Gunnar Myrdal (1944) *An American Dilemma: The Negro Problem and Modern Democracy*, New York: Harper; Kenneth Stampp (1956) *The Peculiar Institution: Slavery in the Ante-Bellum South*, New York: Knopf.

10 Elkins, *Slavery*, p. 23.

11 Elkins, *Slavery*, pp. 52–63.

12 Paul A. Cartledge (1988) 'Serfdom in Classical Greece', p. 34, and F.D. Harvey (1988) 'Herodotus and the Man-Footed Creature', p. 42, both in Archer, *Slavery and Other Forms*. Herodotus is usually credited as the primary source for our understanding of slavery in ancient Greece.

13 Cartledge, 'Serfdom', p. 34.

14 Harvey, 'Herodotus', p. 43.

15 Cartledge, 'Serfdom', p. 34.

16 Bernard S. Jackson (1988) 'Biblical Laws of Slavery: A Comparative Approach' in Archer, *Slavery and Other Forms*.

17 Henri Levy-Bruhl (1934) *Quelques Problèmes du Très Ancient Droit Romain*, Paris.

18 Jackson, 'Biblical Laws'.

19 Blackburn, *Slavery*, p. 270. The holy justification comes from the 'curse' placed by Noah upon his grandson Canaan to forever be a 'servant among servants' in Genesis 9: 20–26.

20 Blackburn, *Slavery*, pp. 88–9, following Florentinus.

21 James Walvin (1996) *Questioning Slavery*, London: Routledge, pp. 3–4.

22 Walvin, *Questioning Slavery*, p. 5.

23 Patterson, *The Sociology of Slavery*, pp. 33–9.

24 See Eric Williams (1964) *Capitalism and Slavery*, London: André Deutsch, pp. 176–7; also Patterson, *The Sociology of Slavery*.

25 From the title of Stampp's book, *The Peculiar Institution*.

26 Elkins, *Slavery*, pp. 37–8.

27 Attributed by Elkins to Oscar Handlin and Mary F. Handlin (1950) 'Origins of the Southern Labor System' in *William and Mary Quarterly*, 3rd series, VII.

28 Also attributed by Elkins (*Slavery*, p. 40) to Handlin and Handlin, 'Origins of the Southern Labor System'. Elkins and the Handlins also add that slavery had been practised in Virginia and Maryland prior to this point. For Elkins, this practice was largely inherited from the West Indies: although no official slave code existed until 1663, in Barbados the enslavement of the black population received gubernatorial sanction in 1636 (Elkins, *Slavery*, p. 41ff).

29 For example, Walvin (*Questioning Slavery*, p. 122) lists the following slave revolts: South Carolina in 1739; French Louisiana in 1763; Virginia in 1800; Charleston in 1822; and the famous Virginia uprising of 1831 led by Nat Turner.

30 Walvin, *Questioning Slavery*, pp. 158–66.

31 On this, see Bales and Robbins, 'No One', p. 2.

32 For more on the abolitionists and their relationship to intellectual movements, see the concluding chapters in David Brion Davis (1966) *The Problem of Slavery in Western Culture*, New York: Oxford University Press.

33 Elkins, *Slavery*, p. 28.

34 Elkins, *Slavery*, pp. 34–6.

35 For an analysis of this Convention, see Bales and Robbins, 'No One', pp. 4–7.

36 Barcelona Traction, Light and Power Co. (*Belgium v Spain*) 1970 ICJ 3.32 (5 February). This information is drawn from Bales and Robbins, 'No One', p. 3.

37 Kevin Bales (1999) *Disposable People: New Slavery in the Global Economy*, Berkeley: University of California Press, p. 3

38 Bales, *Disposable People*, p. 9.

39 Bales, *Disposable People*, p. 5.

40 Adapted from Bales and Robins, 'No One', p. 11.

41 Bales, *Disposable People*, p. 15.

42 Bales, *Disposable People*, p. 12.

43 Bales, *Disposable People*, pp. 20–2.

44 Bales, *Disposable People*.

45 Elkins, *Slavery*, p. 82.

46 Gilberto Freyre (1956) *The Masters and the Slaves*, New York: Alfred Knopf.

47 Frank Tannenbaum (1947) *Slave and Citizen*, New York: Alfred Knopf.

48 Ste. Croix, *The Class Struggle*; Ste. Croix, 'Slavery and Other Forms'.

49 See Marvin Harris (1971) 'The Myth of the Friendly Master' in Ann J. Lane (ed.) *The Debate over Slavery: Stanley Elkins and His Critics*, Chicago: University of Illinois Press.

50 Tannenbaum, *Slaves and Citizens*.

51 Elkins, in *Slavery*, makes this point forcibly. He suggests that the process of dehumanisation is key to the process of enslavement, and draws parallels with Bruno Bettelheim's (1943) ground-breaking study of identity in Nazi concentration camps, 'Individual and Mass Behavior in Extreme Situations', *Journal of Abnormal Psychology*, XXXVIII, October.

52 Max Weber (1968) *Economy and Society: An Outline of Interpretive Sociology*, New York: Bedminster Press (original 1922).

53 Ste. Croix, *Class Struggle*; Tom Brass (1999) *The Political Economy of Unfree Labour*, Cambridge: Cambridge University Press; Eugene Genovese (1965) *The Political Economy of Slavery: Studies in the Economy and Society of the Slave South*, New York: Vintage.

54 Brass, *Political Economy*, p. 10.

55 Bales and Robbins, 'No One', p. 13.

56 Brass, *Political Economy*, p. 10.

57 Eugene Genovese (1971) *In Red and Black: Marxian Explorations in Southern and Afro-American History*, London: Allen Lane The Penguin Press.

58 Marvin Harris (1964) *Patterns of Race in the Americas*, New York: Greenwood Publishing.

59 Genovese, *In Red and Black*, p. 27.

60 Genovese, *Political Economy*, p. 14.

61 Genovese, *Political Economy*, p. 20.

62 Genovese, *Political Economy*, p. 18.

63 Genovese, *In Red and Black*, p. 340.

64 Genovese, *Political Economy*, p. 243.

65 Genovese, *Political Economy*, p. 20.

66 Genovese, *Political Economy*, p. 173.

67 Most famously, how capitalism emerged in part due to the Protestant work-ethic; see Max Weber (1930; original 1904–1905) *The Protestant Ethic and the Spirit of Capitalism*, London: Allen & Unwin.

68 Williams, *Capitalism and Slavery*, pp. 176–7.

69 Patterson, *Slavery and Social Death*, p. viii.

70 Barrington Moore, Jr (1966) *Social Origins of Dictatorship and Democracy: Lord and Peasant in the Making of the Modern World*, Harmondsworth: Penguin.

71 Moore, *Social Origins*, p. 114.

72 Stampp, *The Peculiar Institution*.

73 Moore, *Social Origins*, p. 118.

74 Moore, *Social Origins*, p. 120.

75 Moore, *Social Origins*, pp. 121–2.

76 Moore, *Social Origins*, p. 142.

77 Leslie Sklair (1991) *Sociology of the Global System: Social Change in Global Perspective*, Hemel Hempstead: Harvester Wheatsheaf.

78 Bales, *Disposable People*, p. 23.

79 Bales, *Disposable People*, p. 23.

80 Bales, *Disposable People*, p. 25.

81 Bales, *Disposable People*, p. 24.

82 Bales, *Disposable People*, p. 25.

83 This was the view taken by Phillips, in *American Negro Slavery*.

84 Georg Hegel (1967; original 1807) *The Phenomenology of Mind*, New York: HarperCollins.

85 Karl Marx (1973; original 1857–1858) *The Grundrisse: Foundations of the Critique of Political Economy*, London: Penguin, pp. 325–6.

86 Elkins, *Slavery*.

87 Eugene Genovese (1975) *Roll, Jordan, Roll: The World the Slaves Made*, London: Andre Deutsch.

88 Robert Fogel and Stanley Engerman (1974) *Time on the Cross*, Vol. 1: *The Economics of American Negro Slavery*; Vol. 2: *Evidence and Methods – A Supplement*, Boston: Little, Brown. For a fierce critique of this, see Kenneth M. Stampp (1976) 'Introduction: A Humanistic Perspective' in Paul A. David, Herbert G. Gutman, Richard Sutch, Peter Temin, and Gavin Wright *Reckoning with Slavery: A Critical Study in the Quantitative History of American Negro Slavery*, New York: Oxford University Press.

89 Paul A. David and Peter Temin (1976) 'Capitalist Masters, Bourgeois Slaves', pp. 35–6, in David *et al.*, *Reckoning with Slavery*.

90 Herbert Gutman and Richard Sutch (1976) 'Sambo Makes Good, Or, Were Slaves Imbued with the Protestant Work Ethic?', in David *et al.*, *Reckoning with Slavery*.

91 Flanders, *Plantation Slavery in Georgia*.

92 Gutman and Sutch, 'Sambo Makes Good', p. 73.

93 Bales, *Disposable People*, pp. 1–2.

94 Bales, *Disposable People*, p. 3.

95 Elkins, *Slavery*, pp. 82–3.

96 Robert K. Merton (1940) 'Bureaucratic Structure and Personality', *Social Forces* XVIII; Erich Fromm (1947) *Man for Himself*, New York: Rinehart; Theodor Adorno *et al.* (1950) *The Authoritarian Personality*, New York: Harper; David Riesman (1950) *The Lonely Crowd*, New Haven: Yale University Press; Hans Gerth and C. Wright Mills (1953) *Character and Social Structure: The Psychology of Social Institutions*, New York: Harcourt, Brace.

97 Walvin, *Questioning Slavery*, p. 52.

98 Elkins, *Slavery*, pp. 98–103.

99 Elkins, *Slavery*, p. 133.

100 Patterson, *The Sociology of Slavery*, pp. 174–8, and Patterson (1971) 'Quashee' in Lane, *The Debate Over Slavery*.

101 Eugene D. Genovese (1971) 'Rebelliousness and Docility in the Negro Slave: A Critique of the Elkins Thesis' in Lane, *The Debate Over Slavery*.

102 For example, Fogel and Engerman, *Time on the Cross*.

103 See Earl E. Thorpe (1971) 'Chattel Slavery and Concentration Camps', and Mary Agnes Lewis (1971) 'Slavery and Personality', both in Lane, *The Debate Over Slavery*.

104 Erving Goffman (1969; original 1959) *The Presentation of Self in Everyday Life*, Harmondsworth: Penguin.

105 Erving Goffman (1968; original 1961) *Asylums: Essays on the Social Situation of Mental Patients and Other Inmates*, Harmondsworth: Penguin. Those who to varying degrees adopt a similar approach in criticising Elkins's thesis include George M. Fredrickson and Christopher Lasch (1971) 'Resistance to Slavery', and Roy Simon Bryce-Laporte (1971) 'Slaves as Inmates, Slaves as Men: A Sociological Discussion of Elkins' Thesis', both in Lane, *The Debate Over Slavery*.

106 Patterson, *The Sociology of Slavery*, p. 180.

107 Patterson, *The Sociology of Slavery*, pp. 145–8.

108 Orlando Patterson (1995) 'Freedom, Slavery, and the Modern Construction of Rights', p. 133, in Olwen Hufton (ed.) *Historical Change and Human Rights: The Oxford Amnesty Lectures 1994*, New York: Basic Books.

109 Patterson, 'Freedom, Slavery', p. 34.

110 Patterson, 'Freedom, Slavery', p. 34.

111 Orlando Patterson (1991) *Freedom*, Vol. 1: *Freedom in the Making of Western Culture*, London: I.B. Tauris; Patterson, 'Freedom, Slavery', pp. 135–6.

112 Patterson, 'Freedom, Slavery', p. 136.

113 Patterson, 'Freedom, Slavery', pp. 148–156.

114 Hannah Arendt (2000) *The Portable Hannah Arendt*, ed. Peter Baehr, Harmondsworth: Penguin, p. 38, reproduced from Arendt (1951) *The Origins of Totalitarianism*, New York: Harcourt Brace.

115 'Man was born free, and everywhere he is in chains', in Chapter One of *The Social Contract*.

Further information

Books

An excellent comparative and historical introduction to slavery, which puts it into wider sociological perspective, is Orlando Patterson, *Slavery and Social Death: A Comparative Study* (Cambridge, MA: Harvard University Press, 1982). Patterson's earlier work, *The Sociology of Slavery: An Analysis of the Origins,*

Developments and Structure of Negro Slave Society in Jamaica (London: MacGibbon & Kee, 1967) is also useful. In terms of its attempt to develop a systematic, social scientific understanding of slavery using a combination of historical and literary analysis, and role theory, Stanley Elkins's *Slavery: A Problem in American Institutional and Intellectual Life* (Chicago: University of Chicago Press, 1959) remains perhaps the seminal contribution to the field. Elkins's theories on the unique development of slavery in America, and on the 'Sambo' personality, are discussed at length in Ann J. Lane's edited volume *The Debate Over Slavery: Stanley Elkins and His Critics* (Chicago: University of Illinois Press, 1971). Another extremely controversial piece, in so far as it presents a more benign picture of American slavery and in that it adopts a rational-economic model, is Robert Fogel and Stanley Engerman's *Time on the Cross* (Boston: Little, Brown, 1974). The collected volume by Paul A. David, Herbert G. Gutman, Richard Sutch, Peter Temin, and Gavin Wright – *Reckoning with Slavery: A Critical Study in the Quantitative History of American Negro Slavery* (New York: Oxford University Press, 1976) – offers a trenchant critique of this study. A good historical overview of the slave trade and its impact upon the development of, and life in, the Americas is provided by James Walvin in his *Questioning Slavery* (London: Routledge, 1996). For a truly multi-disciplinary approach which includes commentaries on slavery across time and space, Leonie Archer's edited volume, *Slavery and Other Forms of Unfree Labour* (London: Routledge, 1988) is worth a look. For an even more contemporary study, Kevin Bales's recent *Disposable People: New Slavery in the Global Economy* (Berkeley: University of California Press, 1999) is unique in that it discusses, with the help of case studies from around the world, the continued existence of slavery in the world today. The analytical distinction Bales makes between 'old' and 'new' forms of slavery is sure to become an important such distinction for social scientists working in this field.

Videos

Slavery, produced and directed by Brian Woods and Kate Blewett, and available from True Vision in London, is a useful documentary revealing the extent and nature of slavery in the modern world. Students should also consult the various campaigning and promotional videos available from Anti-Slavery International.

Web pages

Information on slavery practices in the modern world can be found on the Anti-Slavery International website, at www.antislavery.org.

CHAPTER NINE

Genocide

> The Contracting Parties confirm that genocide, whether committed
> in time of peace or in time of war, is a crime under international law
> which they undertake to prevent and to punish.
>
> *United Nations Convention on the Prevention and*
> *Punishment of the Crime of Genocide, Article 1*

What is genocide?

Apartheid and slavery, the topics discussed in the previous two chapters, are forms of social exclusion, which is to say, they are strategies
designed to divide societies by denying one or another group access to
the distribution of the scarce resource of *status*. In both cases, a dominant
group within a given society is to some degree or another seeking to
make distinctions between itself and its target group which can become
institutionalised in the legal system. This forced separation is often articulated with reference to some myth of *purity*, such that the dominant
group can be said to be engaging in an act of *population cleansing*, and
while this distinction is often based on ethnicity, there is nothing to say
it cannot equally be drawn from gender, social class, or any other such
characteristic.[1] The most extreme form of population cleansing is *geno-*
cide; it would not, perhaps, be an exaggeration to describe genocide as
'the ultimate crime: the gravest of all violations of human rights'.[2]

It was the Polish jurist Raphael Lemkin who, in 1944, coined the
term 'genocide'.[3] If the crime itself can be traced back to antiquity, recognition of it in terms of international politics only really took place during the twentieth century. The term – which literally means the killing
(*cide*, from the Latin) of a race or tribe (*genos*, from the Greek) – was used
by Lemkin to describe any act or attempted act of destruction aimed primarily at a given racial, religious, or social grouping. Given that it is now

commonplace to use the term 'nation' to describe such cultural collectives, which very often transcend regional borders, we can treat genocide as the systematic attempt to wipe out a particular nation, or, as the United Nations General Assembly described it in 1946, 'a denial of the right of existence of entire human groups, as homicide is the denial of the right to live of individual human beings'.[4] In its 1948 Convention on Genocide,[5] the United Nations clarified its definition:

In the present Convention, genocide means any of the following acts committed with intent to destroy, in whole or in part, a national, ethnical, racial or religious group, as such:

(a) Killing members of the group;

(b) Causing serious bodily or mental harm to members of the group;

(c) Deliberately inflicting on the group conditions of life calculated to bring about its physical destruction in whole or in part;

(d) Imposing measures intended to prevent births within the group;

(e) Forcibly transferring children of the group to another group.

It is clearly significant that the United Nations saw fit to include the latter two acts, because they serve to shift the focus away from solely physical acts of violence, which one tends to associate with warfare. Genocide can also be a strategy for the eradication of a people using non-military means, such as by imposing restrictions on reproduction. However, the most common usage of the term relates to massacres committed during wartime. Antonio Cassese lists three main factors which can be attributed to genocides throughout history: their association with *wars of conquest*; the use of *religion* to justify the wholesale massacre of groups; and *colonial domination* as a reason for the destruction of indigenous peoples.[6] Cassese also points out that among those issues not covered in the Convention are *cultural* genocide (the annihilation of the culture of a group) and the extermination of *political* groups.[7]

That genocide is understood largely as an attempt to annihilate a *cultural group* (albeit, apparently, not the culture itself) is significant. Commentators have identified problems which arise from treating an atrocity such as the Nazi Holocaust in the same way as other examples of genocide, or mass killings, such as the 'disappearances' in Argentina.[8] However, these political killings were excluded from the Genocide Convention at the insistence of the Soviet Union and its allies.[9] The

United Nations definition had initially referred to the 'many instances of such crimes (that) have occurred, when racial, religious, political, and other groups have been destroyed entirely or in part'.[10] The Soviet Union and its allies objected to the inclusion of political killings because political groups are transient and difficult to define, while genocides are distinguishable in so far as 'the victims are defined primarily in terms of their communal characteristics'.[11] Writers such as Leo Kuper have stressed that political affiliations are as important and often as permanent as ethnic, cultural or religious ones.[12] Much earlier, in recognition of the possibility that governments would exploit this limitation of the Convention, the Dutch lawyer Pieter Drost suggested that the definition be amended to 'the deliberate destruction of physical life of any individual human beings by reason of their membership of any human collectivity as such'.[13]

Recognising the limitations of the Convention in much the same way as Drost, Cassese and Kuper, commentators such as Harff and Gurr have made the useful distinction between genocides and *politicides*.[14] Politicides, they claim, are those instances where 'governments respond ... with violent tactics in an attempt to quell politically organized groups that actively seek to alter power relations within a nation state'.[15] Within this broad definition, the authors distinguish further between *hegemonical* genocide, in which 'the primary motive of the ruling group is to subordinate a communal group by killing enough of its members that the survivors have no will or capacity to resist'; and *xenophobic* genocide, in which 'elite ideology calls for the elimination of the "offending" communal group'.[16]

Typologies of this kind are common. Vahakn Dadrian adopts a broader perspective, listing five types of genocide. The first is *cultural* (that is, pertaining to the culture of a given group). The second is *violent-latent* (genocide as a by-product of some other operation). The third he calls *retributive* (i.e. taking place in the context of a violent exchange between groups). The fourth is *utilitarian* (that is, genocide for some other purpose, such as population reduction). The fifth is *optimal* (i.e. the intentional and often indiscriminate attempt at total annihilation).[17]

Another definition has been offered by Israel W. Charny. Charny argues that 'genocide' should be adopted as a generic category which can include all forms of mass killing, and which can be subdivided where necessary.[18] According to Charny, the definition needs to be inclusive so as to accommodate *accomplices to genocide* (such as those governments and businesses which knowingly sell arms to offenders), genocide as a result of ecological change, and even, in the future, *planeticide*. Charny defines genocide *in the generic sense* as:

> ... the mass killing of substantial numbers of human beings when not in the course of military action against the military forces of an avowed enemy, under conditions of the essential defenselessness and helplessness of the victims.[19]

Charny identifies four categories within the generic one, within which other subdivisions can be identified.[20] The first category is *actual mass murder*. This includes: genocidal massacre; intentional genocide; genocide in the course of colonisation or the consolidation of power; genocide in the course of an aggressive (unjust) war; war crimes against humanity; genocide as a result of ecological destruction or abuse; genocide as a result of purposeful or negligent famine. The second category is *attempted genocide*. The third category deals with *accomplices to genocide*. The fourth category is *cultural genocide or ethnocide*, which includes: biological or physical ethnocide; economic ethnocide; linguicide; religious and spiritual ethnicide; and social ethnicide.

Yet another useful attempt to classify types of genocide comes from Helen Fein.[21] Fein suggests four main categories. The first is *developmental genocide*, which includes the colonial 'cleansing' of indigenous populations. The second is *despotic genocide*, which includes the 'clearing away' of political and other opponents, such as occurred in Latin America. The third is *retributive genocide*, which includes clashes between ethnic groups, each trying to wipe out the other. An example might be the conflict in Rwanda. The fourth is *ideological genocide*. Here, one group defines another as undeserving of life, as typified by the Nazis' attitude towards the Jews. In an earlier work, Fein recognised how two types of retributive genocide – massacres driven by religion, and massacres of enemy tribes who could not be assimilated – predate the rise of the modern state, but that these other types have been made possible in part because of the nation-state.[22]

Jonassohn and Chalk, finding these typologies wanting in different respects, have provided an alternative framework.[23] These authors classify four types of genocide. The first involves acts committed *to eliminate the threat of a rival*. This, they suggest, includes most of the earliest accounts of genocide. The second is genocide *for the acquisition of economic wealth*. Also rooted in antiquity, this category includes genocide through colonial expansion. The third is genocide *for the creation of terror*, a classic exponent of which was Genghis Khan. Each of these three types, claim the authors, has virtually disappeared. The fourth, thriving and far more of a recent development, is genocide *for the implementation of a belief, a theory, or an ideology*, which can be based on religion or political security, real or perceived. So, this category is broad enough to include massacres of heretics, religious witch-hunts, political massacres such as the Armenian genocide, and of course the Nazi Holocaust.

Yet another typology, offered by Roger W. Smith, marries aspects of the frameworks proposed by Dadrian and Fein, and lists five 'pure' types:[24] *retributive genocide* (which has already been discussed); *institutional genocide* (which relates to the political use of terror); *utilitarian genocide* (such as population control in the competition for scarce land resources); *monopolistic genocide* (for the monopolisation of power and culture within a given territory); and *ideological genocide* (already discussed at length).

There have been numerous other worthy attempts by social scientists at providing a working typology of genocide.[25] Indeed, it would not be an exaggeration to suggest that a great deal of academic work on genocide (excluding historical studies of specific genocidal projects such as the Holocaust) has been concerned with debating its meaning and providing alternative typologies and definitions. Whichever definition one uses, genocide clearly has intense implications for social scientists, in so far as these practitioners study how societies work, and any attempt by one social grouping to annihilate another is revealing, to say the least. Nevertheless, with a few notable exceptions – especially ground-breaking studies by Helen Fein and Zygmunt Bauman[26] – sociology and its sibling disciplines have ignored the topic of genocide. Indeed, Fein points out that the vast majority of sociology texts which were produced after 1945 made no mention of genocide, and only in the 1970s did it receive any serious attention.[27] A similar ignorance of the Holocaust or genocide in general has existed in major psychological anthropology texts.[28] Given that some five to six million Jews were murdered in the Holocaust as a result of racial-ideological genocide; some 800,000 Armenians were massacred by the Turks because of national-political prejudices; some one to two million Cambodians were sent to the 'killing fields' by Pol Pot during his political project of internal 'cleansing'; and – as we saw in Chapter Four – between 9,000 and 30,000 political opponents were 'disappeared' by the Argentine regime, social scientists should certainly take such mass killings more seriously.[29]

A brief history of genocide

The Convention on Genocide became law in 1951, noticeably without the signed consent of the United States, which, having initially supported the Convention in 1946, only finally agreed to it in 1989. Significantly, it defined genocide as a crime during peace as well as war. It was widely believed that the experiences of the Second World War – of the Nazi Holocaust – had shaken the world sufficiently for its various leaders to ensure that such atrocities would never occur again. Clearly, their best efforts have been unsuccessful.

Any attempt to write a comprehensive history of genocide in this short space would be foolhardy. Given the controversies over the definition of genocide, it would be unwise to apply the term too liberally to the many mass killings reported throughout classical and medieval history. We will list some of these very briefly, before turning our attention to two major genocidal projects of the twentieth century – the massacre of the Armenians by the Ottoman Turks, and the Nazi Holocaust. We will conclude by outlining some of the all-too-frequent instances of genocide in the contemporary world.

Genocide in the ancient and early modern worlds

Chalk and Jonassohn do us the favour of providing an introductory history of genocides and massacres through the ages.[30] As they point out, such practices were quite common in the ancient Middle East, and the Assyrians were particularly aggressive practitioners, destroying countless populations and using fear as a weapon of war. A famous massacre took place in the second century BC when the Romans destroyed the city of Carthage. Reports exist of entire Middle Eastern populations wiped out by Genghis Khan and his Mongol army, but, as Chalk and Jonassohn point out, it is often difficult to assess these reports because much of the 'evidence' is contradictory, ambiguous, or missing.[31] In their excellent anthology, the authors cite various examples – the Anasazi people in what is now New Mexico; the native New Zealanders who predated the Maori; the inhabitants of Easter Island – who seem to have disappeared without trace.[32] It is possible that these populations were subjected to partial genocide, with survivors assimilated into the conquering group.

More recent historical examples of genocide took place in the era of colonialism. As Chalk and Jonassohn point out, Europe's expansion into the Americas, Asia and Africa resulted in a number of genocides. Various native American tribes, such as the Pequots of New England in 1637 and various communities in Virginia throughout the seventeenth and eighteenth centuries, were exterminated, as were other native groups in Canada, Australia, Africa, and South America.

The massacre of the Armenians

Evidence suggests that during the First World War the German and Turkish armies were both responsible for various 'crimes against humanity'. The genocide committed by the Turks, loyal to the Ottoman rule and espousing a rabid ideology of Pan-Turkism, against the Armenians in 1915–16 has received considerable attention from scholars attempting to make links to the later Nazi genocide, though the international response at the time was muddled.[33] The Ottoman Empire – once a great power – had been losing territory and control for some 50 years. Lacking a strong economic base, culturally pluralistic, and riddled with internal political strife, the Turkish territories were open to the sudden rise of a strong ideology of Turkish nationalism. The outcome was the massacre of the Armenians in what was then part of the Empire during these two years. Ervin Staub provides a useful summary of events:

> In the midst of World War I, during the night of April 24, 1915, the religious and intellectual leaders of the Armenian community in Constantinople were taken from their beds, imprisoned, tortured, and killed. At about the same time, Armenians in the Turkish army, already segregated in 'labor battalions', were all killed. Over a short time period Armenian men over fifteen years of age were gathered in cities, towns, and villages, roped together, marched to nearby uninhabited locations, and killed.
>
> After a few days, the women and children and any remaining men were told to prepare themselves for deportation. They were marched from Anatolia through a region of ravines and mountains to the Syrian Desert, where they were left to die. On the way, they were attacked by Turkish villagers and peasants, Kurds, and *chettis* – brigands who were freed from prison and placed in their path. The attackers robbed the marchers of provisions and clothes, killed men, women, and children, even infants, and raped and carried off women. Through it all, Turkish gendarmes urged the marchers on with clubs and whips, refused them water as they passed by streams and wells, and bayoneted those who lagged behind.
>
> Telegrams to provincial capitals captured by the British army and reports by witnesses . . . provide evidence that the extermination of the Armenians was planned and organized by the central government. Estimates of the number killed range from four hundred thousand to over a million; the actual number is probably more than eight hundred thousand.[34]

Although various governments, including those of Great Britain, France and Russia condemned the Ottoman massacre, the subsequent formation of new political alliances allowed the Turks amnesty for this dreadful incident. Even though the peace treaty, the Treaty of Sèvres, which was signed in 1920, demanded the establishment of an independent Armenian state, the Treaty of Lausanne in 1923 modified and diluted this and required only that the Turks cease their discrimination against the Armenians. There is little doubt that this instance of historical revisionism influenced Hitler in his course of action.[35] Indeed, a characteristic of modern genocide is the utilisation of technology for the purpose of mass destruction, and such technological aides as concentration camps, gas chambers, and medical equipment, which we associate with the Nazis, had earlier been employed by the Ottomans in their systematic destruction of the Armenians.[36] Furthermore, commentators have re-evaluated the significance of the Armenian genocide, pointing out that it may also become a 'paradigm for a type of "political" genocide' that may become increasingly common.[37]

The Nazi Holocaust

The Nazi assault on human rights was without precedent. After Hitler came to power in 1933, the civil and human rights of individuals and groups targeted by the Nazi ideology were swept aside indiscriminately and on a staggering scale.[38] Also, it is widely accepted that the Nazi commitment to their project of 'racial purification' was absolute, and that it took precedence over all other factors, even munitions. It is understood that during the Holocaust, some six million Jews (more than 60 per cent of all Jews living in Nazi-occupied Germany)[39] were butchered by the Nazis, as well as millions of Protestants and Catholics, and countless gypsies, Ukrainians, Poles, Slovenes, and homosexuals.[40] The outrage which followed this was considerably more voluble than that which had followed the Ottoman massacres in 1915–16. After the close of the war, leading Nazi soldiers and officials were held accountable and charged with 'crimes against humanity' in the London Charter of 1945 and the International Tribunal at Nuremberg in 1946.

How the Holocaust came about has been the subject of considerable debate among scholars. It seems that the sudden rise of the Nazi Party could be clearly understood in terms of historical and social conditions. For example, Germans took defeat in the First World War very hard, the decadence of the Weimar Republic proved an easy scapegoat, traditional value systems and social structures were being challenged by new lifestyles, and economic hardship and unemployment had become commonplace. Hitler, with his promises of law and order, employment, and the rebuilding of Germany, provided an obvious answer to these problems, but how does this relate to the genocide that followed?

Scholars have provided countless explanations as to why the Holocaust took place, a number of which are listed by Staub.[41] One, as suggested by Raul Hilberg and others, the bureaucratisation process, which differentiated functions within the state structure. Two, associated with Hilberg and also Hannah Arendt, the use of veiled, euphemistic language, such as the 'final solution'. Three, the argument associated with Erich Fromm, and also Alice Miller, of the authoritarianism of culture – that is, because people have the propensity for violence, and because they are influenced by their social environments, they are more likely to release their violent and evil tendencies if their socialisation takes place in authoritarian families or punitive regimes. Four, the suggestion that the First World War had a major psychosocial impact on German youth, and that, given this spirit of rebellion, the iconoclastic appeal of Hitler was difficult to resist. Five, Germany has a long history of anti-semitism. Six, the importance of the family structure. Seven, Hitler's personality and psychopathology. Eight, the role of the victims, and in particular, as suggested by Arendt, Bettelheim and others, the suggestion that the Jewish Councils made it easier for the Nazis to devalue their victims. Additionally, Staub suggests, there have been complex explanations put forward by scholars, which pay attention to the role played by elites, by big business, by mass politics, and by industrialisation. The role of the state structure, and the presence of a severe rupture between past and present, are also listed as possible explanations. This is not a wholly convincing list, although it is likely that many of these factors did indeed play a part in shaping the Holocaust. Some of these arguments have been used as explanations of genocide in general, and we will return to them when we discuss the social foundations of genocide later in this chapter.

Within the field of Holocaust studies, the role of Hitler has been especially contested. Was the Holocaust *directly* authorised by Hitler, as is claimed by 'intentionalists' such as Hilberg, or was it the consequence of bureaucratic rationalisation, as suggested by 'functionalists' such as Mommsen?[42] There seems little doubt that Hitler was himself committed to the racial ideology, which he expressed in his tome *Mein Kampf* written in 1923. In it, Hitler took biological essentialism to its cultural extreme, suggesting that racial purity is fundamental to the establishment of 'higher' culture. He made it quite clear that Jews and other groups were 'evil' and were the 'enemy' of German progress. Some commentators, however, have dismissed these writings as more political rhetoric, designed solely to win the support of the anti-Semitic

German population, cementing the Nazi power base by uniting sections of society against a common 'enemy'.[43] Certainly, elements of anti-Semitism existed in German culture prior to the Nazi ascent, some taken from religious leaders such as Martin Luther, so it is believed by some that Hitler and his associates merely exploited this lingering prejudice.[44] This is an equally contentious point among scholars of the Holocaust – how important was the compliance of the people to the success of the Nazi project? While propaganda and the dissemination of ideology are important political tools, an appeal to a particular sensitivity held by the people at the time is often crucial.

Another field which has been heavily researched has been the process of *victimisation* of the Jews. Fein identifies five key stages: definition, stripping, segregation (and stigmatisation), isolation, and concentration and killing.[45] The Nazi genocide was not of course unique in its use of ghettos and concentration camps in which to isolate and imprison its victims, but it was distinct in its use of Jewish councils (*Judenrat*) to participate in this victimisation.[46]

As numerous commentators rightly point out, there is an ongoing scholarly debate on the extent to which the Holocaust can be described as a 'unique' event, not comparable to other historical genocides.[47] Advocates of the Holocaust as 'unique' in this respect fall, Helen Fein says, into two camps. One camp adopts a 'metahistorical or theological position which absolutizes the Holocaust as a unique phenomenon outside history', while the other offers more empirical distinctions between the Holocaust and other genocides. One of the chief arguments advocated by those in this second camp involves the *scale* of the Nazi genocide. According to commentators such as Bauer, a distinction can be made between genocide (partial annihilation) and Holocaust (total annihilation) – Lemkin was mistaken in conflating the two.[48] For Bauer, the systematic attempt by the Nazis to destroy Jewry in its entirety is unique as an example of the latter, comparable but not equitable to the Armenian genocide, and distinct even from other forms of Nazi persecution and slaughter, such as against gypsies and Poles. Horowitz adds to this by drawing attention to how the Nazi obsession with the massacre of Jews took precedence over other factors, such as economic security, and duly damaged the Nazi war effort; testament indeed to the ideological significance of anti-Semitism for the Nazis and to their commitment to the Holocaust.[49] Bauman also affords the Holocaust a unique place in the study of genocide by showing how it produced extraordinary activities from otherwise ordinary people.[50] However, Rosenberg raises doubts about this separation, and questions the oddity of the question of the 'uniqueness' of the Holocaust, pointing out that, despite the scale of its atrocities, it is not a historically unique event.[51]

Genocide and ethnic cleansing in the modern world

We will not have space to discuss in any depth many of the other genocides which have taken place since the signing of the Convention. Table 9.1 is adapted from two separate lists, provided by Cassese and Harf.[52]

In each of these cases, the reaction from the United Nations and the international political community has been unsatisfactory; it has either been a muted response, or a case of 'too little, too late'. We cannot discuss these in depth here but readers are urged to consult Cassese's saddening account of how ineffectual these responses have been.[53]

Global awareness of the prevalence of genocide and ethnic cleansing in the modern world was heightened by the terrible massacres in Rwanda and in the Balkan region during the 1990s. In both cases, the United Nations failed to intervene, provoking harsh but necessary questions about its competence and, more importantly, its potency as an international peacekeeping force. Concerned observers expressed their disgust that the lessons of the Holocaust and its aftermath had not been learned. For its part, the international political community did nothing to prevent the onslaught in Cambodia, and although it expressed its disapproval of the Serbian massacres in Bosnia, its efforts stopped short of mounting a 'credible challenge to the Serbian operations'.[54] Similarly, events in Rwanda and Burundi appeared to confirm this commitment to minimal intervention by the world political community either in the protection of the victims or the punishment of the perpetrators.[55]

The following account of the Rwandan genocide is taken from the *Observer* newspaper, under the sober heading, 'The death of a nation':

Up to one million Rwandans were killed when Hutus massacred Tutsi neighbours in 1994. Within three months one seventh of the population, mainly Tutsis, had been wiped out.

Hundred of thousands of refugees fled to camps in neighbouring countries. Hutu radio urged Hutus to take part in a 'Final Solution' to eradicate Tutsis – referred to as cockroaches. Machete-wielding members of the extremist Hutu militia Interahamwe – meaning 'we kill together' – swept into villages on killing sprees.

Thousands of women were gang-raped, or raped with gun-barrels or sharpened sticks. Others were held in sexual slavery. Children were particularly affected. 100,000 of those slaughtered were children. About 95 per cent of children witnessed violence and killing; 80 per cent lost family; 55 per cent saw other minors take part in killings; 16 per cent of

Table 9.1 Genocidal acts between 1960 and 1987

Year	Location	Description
1955–72	Sudan	Massacre of some 500,000 inhabitants of southern Sudan by Sudanese army
1960	Congo	Massacre of hundreds of Balubas by Congolese army in Southern Kasai
1965–67	Indonesia	Between 200,000 and 500,000 alleged communists killed by vigilantes
1965–72	Burundi	Massacre of Hutu community by dominant Tutsi, with between 100,000 and 300,000 Hutu killed in 1972 alone
1967–70	Nigeria	2–3 million Ibos massacred by other Nigerians
1968–74	Paraguay	Massacre of thousands of Guayaki Ache Indians by government troops
1971	East Pakistan (Bangladesh)	Massacre of over 1 million, possibly 3 million, Bengalis by Pakistani army
1971–78	Uganda	Indiscriminate massacre of civilians, and members of Acholi and Lango ethnic groups, by government troops under Idi Amin
1975	East Timor	Up to 100,000 Timorese massacred by Indonesian army
1975–78	Cambodia	Massacre of some 2 million people, including minority Muslims and Buddhists, by Khmer Rouge under Pol Pot
1975–78	Iran	Persecution and murder of members of the Bahai faith by government troops
1978	Equatorial Guinea	Acts of genocide committed against civilians
1982	Lebanon	Massacre of Palestinians in Sabra and Shatila by Christian Falangist troops with alleged complicity from Israel
1986–87	Sri Lanka	Genocidal acts committed against the Tamils by the Singhalese majority

the children had to hide under corpses to avoid killers and 95,000 were separated from their parents. Only 25,000 have been reunited with their families – many children were too young to remember their own names. More than 60,000 Rwandan households are headed by minors, mostly girls; 60% of Rwandan children say they feel 'unbearable sorrow' and 130,000 Rwandans were imprisoned for participating in the genocide, including former Rwandan Prime Minister, Jean Kambanda, who received a life sentence in 1998.[56]

Writer and activist Linda Melvern has brought attention to the complicity of Western nations, through the failure of the United Nations to intervene, in the Rwandan genocide.[57] Melvern points out that this was carried out openly, without secrecy, and after months of careful preparation, which was also open, and yet the international political community sat back. Indeed, during this time of preparation, other countries, plus the World Bank and the International Monetary Fund, invested money in the Rwandan economy, or engaged in trade negotiations with the Rwandan authorities, thus contributing directly, Melvern claims, to the conditions which made these atrocities possible. But if the United Nations did not formally intervene to prevent the atrocities, why did individual nation-states turn their faces away? Perhaps the United States was still haunted by memories of Somalia.[58] In the case of the British, it is perhaps not unreasonable to adopt a more historical perspective, and to locate the causes of the Rwandan genocide in British colonialism, or more specifically, the disruption it brought to pre-colonial ethnic settlements.[59]

Understanding genocide

This section offers an introduction to some of the anthropological, sociological and psychological perspectives on genocide. While many early studies were influenced by primordialist or essentialist accounts of human 'nature', which are not wholly dissimilar to some of the theories already discussed with regard to torture, these have been challenged from various more sophisticated perspectives. Social psychological accounts, which often focus on the individual, remain popular but are increasingly becoming interwoven with sociological accounts of the conditions required for genocide to take place. Among the sociological perspectives, the dominant one appears to have emerged from the Weberian tradition which emphasises the role of the centralised authoritarian state in modern societies, and the existence of conflicting groups within the plural society. Thus, issues such as racial discrimination, national culture, and state centralisation are crucial to these accounts. However, alternative perspectives can be found within the functionalist and Marxist traditions in social theory.

The individual capacity for genocide

It is perhaps too easy to explain genocide and other tendencies towards violence and destruction (see, especially, our discussion of the 'making of a torturer' in Chapter Five of this volume) in terms of humans' animalistic nature. It certainly seems to be rather simplistic to say, as Staub does, that under suitable conditions:

> ...some human beings become capable of killing others as naturally as if they were animals to be slaughtered, without questioning the act. Some killers may even enjoy it, as they would not enjoy killing animals, because they exercise power over other people or are aware of the victim's suffering, which fulfils their desire to hurt.[60]

There are various traditions which presume that human 'nature' is evil (although, as Staub rightly points out, it is unfair to make moral judgements on people committing such acts when it is the norm in their culture).[61] For example, Pierre van der Berghe has sought to explain ethnic discrimination using an anthropological model of kin selection (and altruism), which he bases on a sociobiological understanding of the innate aggressiveness of the human animal.[62] Thomas Hobbes, of course, believed that power and self-interest are basic human needs and that the state controls these desires. Other commentators have adopted a psychobiological perspective which draws uncritically on Freud's concept of *Thanatos*, the instinct for destruction which is often suppressed by the conscience, socialisation, and 'civilisation'. However, such uncritical accounts should be treated with some caution. While other life-forms may behaviourally kill to survive, no other living creature exhibits such an apparent urge for destruction as the human species. The capacity for genocide may well have emerged along with increasing technological developments and 'civilising' processes as a social construction. The critical theorist and social psychologist – and Frankfurt School member – Erich Fromm has observed that:

> [Man] differs from the animal in the sense that he is a killer; he is the only primate that kills and tortures members of his own species without any reason, either biological or economic, and who feels satisfaction in doing so. It is this biologically non-adaptive and non-phylogenetically programmed 'malignant' aggression, that constitutes the real problem, and the danger to man's existence as a species.[63]

In one advance upon simple essentialism, Lorenz discusses how humans are innately and instinctively aggressive and destructive animals, and that evolution has in fact exaggerated this biological drive. However, in so far as this biological evolution has been kept in check by repressive 'civilisation', the urge to release it remains strong and is manifested in sudden, often spontaneous eruptions of violence born of frustration. At first, then, Lorenz appears to be offering a crude sociobiological theory of genocide, but in fact it is one peppered with sociological observations pertaining to 'progress' and 'modernisation'. Indeed, if one aspect of human evolution has been the development of an innate sense of ethics which counters this biological drive for destruction by inhibiting the violence, the emergence of modern forms of warfare and weaponry actually makes it easier to overcome these inhibitions, and thus surrender to this urge, because of the increasingly impersonal nature of killing.[64]

Of course, not all essentialist theories begin with the assumption that the human agent is 'evil'. Jean-Jacques Rousseau famously critiqued Hobbes's theory by suggesting that in the 'state of nature' individuals are basically good, but society influences them in other directions. Similarly, Reinhold Niebuhr has argued that individuals are naturally decent but that groups and collectives are selfish.[65] Elites may very well exploit this, perhaps adopting models of social psychology akin to some of those we discussed under 'the making of a torturer'. According to one such theory, torturers distanced themselves from their victims through a process of elite social closure. Certainly, this strategy was used by the Nazis when recruiting for their elite security force, the *Schutzstaffel*, or SS, which was responsible for carrying out the Holocaust:

> Joining the SS was to become part of an elite, an aristocracy, a religious order, a secret society, a gang, an army and a family all at the same time ... At times the SS was something of a mentality, a way of life.[66]

Another perspective which blends an essentialist ontology with a recognition of the role played by cultures and environments is developed by Staub, who begins from the perspective that *both* 'good' and 'evil' are inherent characteristics of the pre-social human. According to Staub:

> By themselves, difficult life conditions will not lead to genocide. They carry the potential, the motive force; culture and social organisation determine whether the potential is realized by giving rise to devaluation and hostility towards a sub-group.[67]

Staub suggests that cultural and social factors nurture the genetic propensity for altruism and aggression to varying degrees, and the outcome has much to do with family environment. This is a view shared by Steiner, who stressed the importance of authoritarian upbringings on the moral development of SS officers, many of whom subsequently developed cravings for military life, and who were susceptible to a belief in Nazi ideology.[68]

The structural conditions of genocide

Individualistic accounts may help us understand the psychology of perpetrators of genocide, but they should not be divorced from structural accounts which seek to understand, sociologically, the conditions within which genocides take place. Weberian, functionalist and Marxist scholars have all contributed to this debate.

Perhaps the most convincing account of the capacity for genocide appears to come from the Weberian conflict theory camp, which emphasises pluralism and political violence. Three aspects of Max Weber's sociological library are relevant for the study of genocide. The first is Weber's understanding of the modern state as being the epitome of administrative, bureaucratic rationality, which controls the centralised means of violence. The second is Weber's claim that modern societies are defined according to conflict between groups who are competing for scarce resources. The third, drawing on the other two, is that a dominant group, or elite, emerges to take control over the centralised means of violence and therefore suppress rival social groups.

The contributions of Leo Kuper clearly fit into this tradition.[69] Kuper has sought to emphasise the structural conditions which make genocide possible, and chief among these is his concept of the 'plural society'.

This, he says, is a society in which various social or ethnic groups are competing for resources of power and money, and such societies, he claims, are by their very nature rife with inequalities. In this respect, Kuper is clearly a conflict theorist in the Weberian tradition. He pays another debt to Weber by suggesting that genocide is not a determined result of macro social change, but is instead the outcome of political decision making which has to be understood in historical context.

Kuper begins with the not-unreasonable claim that the structural basis for genocide in the modern world rests in the pluralistic characteristics of societies. Such societies are, by their very nature, diverse in terms of ethnic, religious or racial groups. A plural society is not the same as a pluralistic one; the former relates to the presence of cultural difference, the latter to the practice of multicultural tolerance. In his comparison of the conditions for genocide and mass killings in Nazi Germany, Ottoman Turkey, Cambodia and Argentina, Ervin Staub concludes that each regime was monolithic, often totalitarian, at the time of the genocide.[70] However, both the German and Turkish instances could be described as 'plural' in Kuper's terms. Argentina and Cambodia do not fit this model so easily, but in these cases the massacres were primarily political-ideological as opposed to ethnic. We will discuss the political and ideological genocide in Cambodia later in this chapter. We have already discussed the political killings in Argentina in Chapter Four.

Kuper does not say that genocide is inevitable in plural societies, nor that it only occurs in these conditions, but he does point out that in such societies the structural conditions for domestic genocide are more pronounced, a claim which appears to be legitimate in the light of genocidal conflicts in India, Rwanda, Burundi and elsewhere.[71] In the plural society, inequalities tend to exist in the political, economic, cultural and social spheres. Discrimination is often rife, not only in individual prejudices but also in institutional processes such as education and employment. Groups compete for scarce resources as well as for power relations in the political sphere. Cultural conflicts and contradictions become apparent. 'The plural society, in its *extreme* form,' writes Kuper, 'is characterized by a super-imposition of inequalities', and these 'structural conditions are likely to be conducive to genocidal conflict'.[72]

This struggle for economic, social and cultural resources clearly took place in Germany prior to the Second World War and influenced Hitler, although, as we have discussed above, there is some debate over the extent to which Hitler's project was ideologically driven. Nevertheless, social and economic unrest was exploited by the Nazis, who appealed to Germanic 'purity' and delivered a manifesto of nationalism and racism. Staub recites the following account of how Nazi 'justice' treated five war veterans who 'shot, stabbed, and bludgeoned' a young Polish communist while he slept. After initially receiving the death sentence, the five were not only reprieved, but later released by Hitler, whose propagandist Alfred Rosenberg wrote of the affair:

> Bourgeois justice weights a single communist, and a Pole at that, against five German war veterans. In this example is mirrored the ideology of the past 150 years, displaying the mistaken substructure of its being...The unacceptability of this attitude explains the world view of National Socialism. It does not believe that one soul is equal to another, one man equal to another. It does not believe in rights as such: it aims to create the German man of strength, its task is to protect the German people, and all justice, all social life, politics and economics must be subordinate to this goal.[73]

Racial ideology may well be a general stimulant for genocidal action, but we should take care to distinguish between a racial thuggery driven by irrational hatred, and the more subtle and clever dissemination of racist beliefs through appeals to the cultural idea of the 'nation'. Racism and anti-Semitism maybe existed in Germany prior to Hitler's ascent, but only when couched in nationalist terms can these beliefs become serious political ideologies. In this respect, 'nation' is conflated with 'race'. One has to first assume the 'purity' of a nation, and then to believe that it has been 'corrupted' by 'Others'. Kuper is right to point out that the plural nation is a precondition for genocide. Would the Holocaust have become such an accepted course of action among the German people if there were *no* Jews or other targeted groups living *in* Germany at the time? In the case of Germany, the idea of the nation had been central to its intellectual history. When the German army was condemned for marching through neutral Belgium in 1914, prominent intellectuals in the arts and sciences defended the action on the grounds of 'German culture' and 'civilisation'.[74]

'Race' and 'nation' are certainly important concepts, then, for understanding the capacity for genocide. However, for either to become influential in more than abstract terms, a third component is required: the *state*. This is the machinery used to drive forward the projects of racial purity and national supremacy. It must be strong, and exist above and beyond the people. Certainly, while France, America and elsewhere were establishing a constitutional role for the state as a servant of the citizenry, German intellectuals were taking Hobbes's idea of the strong state to its extreme.[75] Figures such as Martin Luther and Georg Hegel defended the autonomy of the state and the subordination of individuals to it.

Indeed, the role of the state is crucial to the Weberian tradition. Kuper emphasises the *political* nature of genocide. Harff and Gurr, whose distinctions between genocide and *politicide* have already been discussed, also belong to this conflict perspective and stress the extent to which genocide is a crime of the state. A similar view is developed by Chalk and Jonassohn, who draw much of their inspiration from Weber's theory of state violence and from his typologies of social action.[76] They emphasise that for genocide to be carried out effectively it is necessary to first have in place a 'high degree of centralized authority and quasi-bureaucratic organization',[77] because mass killing, often of defenceless victims, on such a scale is likely to be resisted by the foot soldiers ordered to carry it out unless this machinery is in place to ensure it. They also suggest that, rather than being an irrational expression of animal rage, genocide is a kind of purposive-rational action used to protect and uphold the power of the dominant elites who manage the state apparatus, often through empire-building or the accumulation of wealth. Many recent examples of genocide, they suggest, are carried out for the purpose of expanding a particular ideology or political belief.

Another writer whose work fits into this tradition is Porter.[78] Like most of the others mentioned in this section, Porter understands genocide to be a crime carried out by the state. Within the Weberian tradition the modern nation-state is given a position of some importance in determining social structure. Among the traits Porter attributes to the modern nation-state are a dependence upon militarism, the presence of powerful and exclusionary political parties, the presence of minority groups ('Others'), a tendency towards nationalistic and racialistic ideologies, and ambitions towards territorial expansion – attributes we have already covered. The modern nation-state provides the foundations for genocide to take place, via the reliance upon ideology, technology and bureaucracy, and it is important, says Porter, to remember that the state is highly influential in involving other social actors, be they artists, scientists or intellectuals, in the wider programme of genocide. Porter's belief that the capacity for genocide is stronger in the highly bureaucratic, technologically rational modern nation-state is one which is shared by Kuper, among others. Many of the conditions listed by Porter are supported by Staub. After analysing the social conditions from which genocidal conflicts in Nazi Germany, Turkey, Cambodia, and Argentina emerged, Staub reveals a number of similarities which, he claims, might assist us in predicting the potential for genocide in other countries. A general summary of Staub's claims is provided in Table 9.2.

Table 9.2   Cultural preconditions and progressions leading to genocide[79]

Cultural preconditions	Characteristics common to the four genocides
Cultural self-concept, goals, and values	Nationalism; Belief in national superiority; Feelings of insecurity and loss of status
Devaluation of subgroups	Usually long history of prejudice
Orientation to authority	Strong culture of obedience
Monolithic vs pluralistic culture	Usually monolithic-totalitarian
Ideology (emerging or adopted)	Strong ideology, whether racial, nationalist, or political
Steps along the continuum to destruction	Increasing level of violence prior to genocide

It is not unreasonable to suggest that genocidal conflicts are initiated in order to protect or uphold existing dominant political groups. Making the link between genocide and political elites, Irving Horowitz writes:

> When the ruling elites decide that their continuation in power transcends all other economic and social values, at that point does the possibility, if not the necessity, for genocide increase qualitatively. For this reason, genocide is a unique strategy for totalitarian regimes.[80]

Staub also makes the link between genocide and elites, and stresses the role of the state in the execution of mass killings:

> Genocide is usually organized or executed by those in power, by a government or ruling elite. Governments will commit genocide if the way of thinking and motivations out of which genocide evolves are already consistent with the culture or if they become so under the influence of the government.[81]

If we consider again the example of the Nazi Holocaust, then we can easily accept this claim. However, of course, it is one thing for political elites to plan massacres and genocides and another for their citizens and soldiers to participate in such acts. Clearly, various other factors need to be in place. For one, the ruling establishment needs to be seen as legitimate, and to have the support of the people. Secondly, the establishment needs to concoct a blend of populism and social psychology to offer some kind of ethical justification for its actions. It needs to appeal to the fears and prejudices of ordinary citizens, and to exaggerate them. It might, for example, begin by playing upon the fears of one section of the population for its jobs. This strategy is frequently employed in modern societies by hate-groups on the far right of the political spectrum, particularly against blacks or Hispanics. It might, as was the case in Nazi Germany, exaggerate this fear by espousing some kind of conspiracy theory, or, as has been the case elsewhere, by drawing attention to the differences in lifestyles between cultural groups, suggesting, in apocalyptic fashion, that a clash of civilisations is inevitable and that the outcome might be the destruction of some assumed 'authentic' culture. The end result is, of course, the dehumanisation, or demonisation, of the 'Other'.

Functionalist and Marxist theories of genocide may not be as visible as Weberian ones, but they have both influenced the direction of the debate. In functionalist theory, the emphasis is primarily upon external factors which in some way upset social cohesion or damage the bonds of social control which are seen as important for the maintenance of a peaceful and functioning society. Genocide is thus understood in terms of the collapse of social structure. According to Dadrian:

> [E]ven though in conception, design and execution, genocide may be regarded as a phenomenon *sui generis*, in terms of underlying structural contingencies and projective goals, it is functional; it subserves the ultimate end of equilibrium of a system beset by disarray through acute group conflict.[82]

Dadrian defends this structural-functional position with reference to the genocide of the Armenians by the Turks. He suggests that various factors – including the rise of the hitherto subordinate Armenians as a new bourgeois class, the consequences of the First World War, and nationalistic tensions between the two groups – created a systemic imbalance, the response to which by the (dominant) Turks was genocide as a means of sweeping structural and systemic change. In similar vein, Staub points out that the Khmer Rouge exploited the collapse of social structure, and in particular family structure, for its autogenocide in Cambodia in 1975.[83] National upheavals, such as revolutions, rebellions, conflicts, and major political transformations, are central to Barbara Harff's etiology of genocide.[84] Another framework which falls broadly within the functionalist tradition, but with elements of the neo-Weberian one, is that proposed by Mazian.[85] Mazian outlines various determinants of genocide, which include the breakdown of cohesion and consensus through the creation of 'Others', and the collapse of social control. She also recognises the importance of ambitious elites seeking total control, in keeping with the neo-Weberian tradition.

A Marxist contribution to the debate over the structural conditions required for genocide was provided by the philosopher Jean-Paul Sartre. Sartre claimed that genocide is linked to colonialism and is inherent in the nature of capitalism.[86] Conflicting national groups, struggling for control over market resources, engage in 'total war', in which civilians are involved in the production of war resources, and therefore part of the process of warmaking. In war between major military powers, there is some balance which renders genocide unlikely, but in colonisation, which involves a war being waged by a stronger power against a weaker nation, genocide is not only possible but likely, and, according to Sartre, there have been countless examples of it. Once the colonising power achieves its inevitable victory, it must somehow control the rebellious native population which conspires against it, and this is achieved by perpetual massacre. Although full physical genocide is rare, cultural genocide is common and, Sartre suggests, necessary for the perpetuation of the unequal economic system. Although Sartre's argument is flawed in so far as it is based on only specific and rather limited examples, the insinuation of a close relationship between colonialism (viewed from a Marxist perspective as an attempt to expand capitalism through political and cultural domination) and genocidal massacre seems plausible. The history of European expansionism (imperialism) is rife with references to the massacres of indigenous peoples, such that genocide may be considered a 'universal tendency' among such 'developed cultures'.[87] Tony Barta has expanded upon Sartre's agent-centred Marxist approach to genocide, based loosely on an understanding of social relations within the capitalist system.[88] Barta locates the problem of genocide firmly within the objective relations operating within the system of colonialism and capitalist competition. Thus, in contrast to many earlier writers, Barta is content to treat genocide in no small way as an unintended consequence of historical social relations.

Political genocide

We have already suggested that there is considerable debate over whether genocide – usually the targeted extermination of ethnic groups – should include politicide, the systematic mass killing of political groups. Both atrocities involve deliberate projects of the state aimed at erasing one or another category of people from existence. Politicides are not easily distinguished from the 'disappearances' we discussed in Chapter Four. Both are, ultimately, mass killings carried out on the orders of the state against the state's political enemies. The term 'disappearances' is *usually* applied to targeted killings, the extermination of political opponents as an extreme form of political imprisonment which, *en masse*, constitutes a massacre. Politicides, like genocides, are *usually* directed at groups. It is useful for our purposes, then, to include politicides in this chapter. We have already seen how the massacre of the Armenians could be read as a model for subsequent political genocides:

> ...where the elite's vision was predicated upon the political and sociological dimensions of the society they wanted to rule over. The return to a traditional order where hierarchies are in place and unchallenged may be one such vision. Recent genocides, especially the Indonesian, the Cambodian, and the Ibo, have been more brazenly political in nature, confirming the worst fears that knowledge of evil does not necessarily result in abhorrence of evil; that human reasoning can always find ways to characterize evil as being something else and to conclude that some societies must be destroyed or must destroy parts of themselves to be saved.[89]

In this section, we concentrate on only one of these evils – the political and ideological genocide which took place in Cambodia in the 1970s. While we trace the historical events which are relevant here, we will also bear in mind the question which is at the heart of our thinking about all genocides: How, in spite of rationalisation, can this have come about?

In 1975, the Khmer Rouge, a political movement made up mainly of peasants from the Cambodian rural areas, invaded the capital city, Phnom Penh, and began to evacuate the city by force. The Khmer Rouge espoused an extreme Maoist doctrine, dedicated to the establishment of a rural, communist peasant society, and were necessarily distrustful of cities, and of those who lived in them – intellectuals, professionals, politicians. Such people were executed, and the Khmer Rouge came to apply the same justice to others who were perceived as a threat to their political and ideological plans, such as Buddhist monks and members of ethnic minorities. Those who were allowed to live were made to work the land in small communities.

The atrocities which occurred during the Khmer Rouge's reign of terror do not, of course, fit the purely culturalist definition of genocide. The people massacred were not necessarily targeted because of their ethnicity (although some were); the intention was not as such to deny a clearly defined group of people the right of existence. The Khmer Rouge targeted enemies, or those they perceived as enemies. Their intentions were political:

> The aim was to kill all actual or potential enemies, everyone who could not adopt the world view and way of life required in the new state. Some of the killing was seemingly casual, perhaps intended to terrorize the population and stifle resistance. Later, executions for transgressing rules became the normal operating procedure in certain places.[90]

The intentions may have been political but not in the narrow sense – victims were not targeted simply because they were enemies of Pol Pot's regime. Unlike specifically political mass killings, the Khmer Rouge atrocities were directed at people who for the most part posed no overt threat to the dominant order. The driving force behind these atrocities was ideological – the Khmer Rouge believed fanatically in the need to establish a specific way of life, and those who became their victims played no part in this grand scheme. Much like Hitler and the extermination of the Jews, Pol Pot and his associates sought to justify their actions on the grounds of building the 'good society'. When news of the massacres reached the outside world, their lasting image – piles upon piles of human skulls buried in the 'killing fields' – became as powerful an image of evil as many people had seen. It seems impossible to understand how such evil can be committed in the name of an ideology based on building the good society within the context of rationality. That, however, is the point. The Khmer Rouge were obsessed with breaking all ties with Western rationality and modernity. They wanted to build an agrarian commune out of the ruins of their country. The ideological genocide in Cambodia did not take place *in spite of* rationality, but *because of* it. It was a response to the world outside, and how that world was seen to be corrupting the people of Cambodia. Hitler dared to play God by establishing his 'final solution', by deciding who lived and who died. Pol Pot wanted nothing less than to isolate Cambodia from the outside world, to erase history, to begin again at Year One. Those he killed he killed in the name of renewal. By announcing this epochal shift, by making such a clear and clean break with the past, Pol Pot and his followers were making an announcement: 'The past is dead, the present begins now.' Or, to put it another way, '*Humanity begins now,* and all that came before do not matter, because they were never truly human.'

The experience of the concentration camp

The concentration camp – a place of incarceration where victims of genocide could be conveniently assembled prior to their imminent execution – is a particular feature of modern, rationalised genocidal processes. As these camps are effectively equivalent, in their functions at least, to the maximum security prisons which store inmates awaiting the death penalty, similar perspectives on how individuals behave in such 'total institutions', how they maintain a sense of self, can be applied to those discussed in Chapter Six. Of the studies which focus directly upon the experience of the Nazi concentration camps, Fein conveniently summarises four major works – those of Bettelheim, Des Pres, Pawelczynska, and Luchterhand.[91]

As Fein states, Bruno Bettelheim's work is the best known, but also, in terms at least of its intellectual rigour, the least adequate.[92] Bettelheim claimed that Jewish prisoners in the camps exhibited regression, submission to their captors and their inevitable deaths without resistance, which contributed to their own victimisation.[93] He also suggested that long-term prisoners came to adopt the various styles, manners of speaking and behaving, of their jailors. However, Bettelheim's thesis was largely extrapolated from his own experience in a concentration camp between 1938 and 1940. In fact, Bettelheim – like others in his camp – managed to secure an exit visa and was released, so it is difficult to see how his generalisations could be appropriately applied to those experiencing the harsher conditions of the extermination camps. Indeed, contrary to Bettelheim's portrait of the concentration camp inmate as docile and submissive, other studies, such as that by Des Pres, show the extent to which these inmates were capable of considerable ingenuity and strategic planning, as well as camaraderie, in order to survive the ordeal.[94] Pawelczynska's study also avoids the simplistic generalisations of Bettelheim's work.[95] She concerns herself with the dynamics of the camp, its informal divisions, the networks and groups established

among the prisoners, and the impact of social and biological characteristics upon survival chances. Like Des Pres, she identifies the various
strategies of cunning and camaraderie employed by the inmates. She
also discusses the value system which existed amongst the prisoners,
which usually involved adapting existing moral codes to suit the extrem-
ities of the situation. Thus, the moral rule against theft was modified at
first to relate only to theft from living prisoners – dead ones and SS
officers were acceptable targets – and then, as hunger and desperation
grew worse, the definition of those from whom it was considered inappropriate to steal became more restrictive. Many of Pawelczynska's
claims about the maintenance of identity and the importance of value
codes and social bonds within the extreme environment are supported
by the longitudinal research carried out through interviews with survivors by Luchterhand.[96]

Of course, as sociologists such as Goffman have informed us, the
maintenance of a sense of self-identity in extreme situations and in 'total
institutions' is a careful and strategic process.[97] The point of these institutions is to destroy individualism, to dehumanise, and ultimately (in the
case of Death Row and the concentration camp) to prepare for death.
Maintaining a sense of self in such conditions is an almost impossible
task, and sometimes it is only possible in the very last moment before
death, when there is nothing else to lose. Staub recites the story of:

> . . . the dancer who was recognized as a dancer by a Nazi officer in the
> line leading up to the gas chamber and told to dance. As she danced,
> she grabbed the officer's gun and shot him. By becoming a dancer
> again she had regained her identity and capacity to resist.[98]

The state, genocide and human rights

Sociological research has concentrated largely on the not-unreasonable
claim that genocide becomes a reality only under conditions of late
modernity. Genocide may be a crime as old as humanity itself, but when
one considers the sheer scale of the atrocities which have been committed since the beginning of the twentieth century, we can identify it in
its current form as a uniquely *modern* crime.[99] The Holocaust remains a
terrifying reminder of the human potential for destruction. This potential is released with the aid of modern punitive and transportation technology, the bureaucratic and rationalised state as a centralised means of
violence, and the dominance of instrumental, means–end reasoning – all
conditions associated with modernity. As much of the theoretical and

empirical literature on the subject testifies, modern genocide results from the ultimate triumph of the dark side of modernity, what the pessimistic Max Weber termed modernity's 'iron cage'. It results from 'the modern state, with its enormous bureaucratic apparatus, centralization of power and monopoly of economic and military resources'.[100] This, together, as Kuper observes, with the inequalities maintained within a 'plural' society, provides the foundations for genocide.

The role of the state in executing genocides needs careful consideration. Tony Barta – whose account of the genocide of the Australian aboriginals is recommended reading – makes the persuasive point that not *all* genocidal activity can be reduced to the level of the state.[101] He distinguishes between a genocidal *state* – such as Nazi Germany, which pursued an intentional policy of destruction – and a genocidal *society*. Australia, he claims, is an example of a genocidal society – while there has always been an absence of intent, the genocide has been executed through the social relations inherent in the system. Thus, he suggests, while Australians are not blameworthy *per se*, they are involved in an inseparable, dialectical relationship with their aboriginal neighbours. Barta's insistence on moving the debate beyond the confines imposed by intentionality and the role of the state has been contested by a majority of commentators, including Richard Rubenstein, who follows in the tradition of Hannah Arendt by carving out a central role for the state.[102] Following Arendt, Rubenstein says, 'in reality, there are no human rights, only political rights', realised through active membership of a political community.

Helen Fein, recognising the existence of religious and tribal genocides prior to the emergence of the nation-state, nevertheless stresses that new forms of genocide have been made possible *because* of the rise of the nation-state.[103] It has ever been the task of the territorial nation-state somehow to unify the various *nations* (cultures) which exist within its borders under a singular (monocultural) banner, administered by a singular political system, the *state*. Horowitz points out that genocide 'is a fundamental mechanism for the unification of the national state'.[104] This territorial aspect – the expansion of political space – is undeniable. How this is achieved is often dependent upon the fanaticism of the provocative agents. Catherine MacKinnon has suggested that Serb soldiers in Bosnia used rape as a method of genocide: they systematically raped and impregnated Bosnian Muslim women who were then imprisoned until termination was not an option, in order to 'ensure' that Bosnia was a Serb state.[105] Thus, questions of territoriality and the nation-state are, for MacKinnon, inseparable from those of gender. Kuper goes so far as to make the claim that genocide not only serves to maintain, but is itself *upheld by*, the nation-state system, and that the United Nations is unable to prevent this. He argues that

[T]he sovereign territorial state claims, as an integral part of its sovereignty, the right to commit genocide, or engage in genocidal massacres, against peoples under its rule, and that the United Nations, for all practical purposes, defends this right.[106]

How can we understand genocide in the context of rationalisation? Everything about genocide and mass killings seems contradictory to the principles of modernisation, and yet not only has genocide persisted, it has adapted because of modern technologies, modern sensitivities. The Argentine leaders we discussed in Chapter Four sought to hide their dirty secrets, their disappearances, from the gaze of the outside world; the Khmer Rouge desired nothing less than the end of history, the beginning of a new world without modernist rationality. In the case of Nazi Germany, modernity and rationality were not dismissed as enemies of the genocidal project, but used as justifications for it. It is the sociologist Zygmunt Bauman who is primarily associated with this interpretation of the Holocaust as a reflection of the drive towards modernity and rationalisation. Auschwitz, for example, seems to represent an exemplary extension of the modern factory system; the end product of industrialisation and the terrible development of Weber's dark modernity.[107] Bauman makes the point that the mass destruction of the Jewish people took shape not in the shooting and gassing of these victims but in the symbolic extermination of Jewish identity which was achieved through the bureaucratic structures.[108] Rights and privileges were removed, as part of a process of dehumanisation, after which the physical extermination of the Jews became an easier task. Politicians and bureaucrats had already told citizens and soldiers that the Jews were not human. Official paperwork supported this. From this perspective, for many perpetrators, their murders were then perceived as not dissimilar to the killing of an animal. Indeed, this analogy continues in other ways. Modernity is often associated with human control over nature, domination through technology and engineering.[109] For the Nazis, the extermination of the Jews was not conditional on whether or not they 'repented' of sins as their 'crimes' were not sins but 'evils' carried out during the natural course of their existence (like a bacteria which commits no sin but needs to be destroyed; a destructive, but innocent, moral patient).[110]

This extermination of identity, of being, and this assumption that moral guilt can reside in mere existence, are both important points. In the introduction to this volume, I referred to genocide as a violation of the right to *existence*, located within the *social* sphere but mediated by the *political* one. I want now to explain what I mean by each of these labels.

First, why does genocide constitute a threat to the right to *existence* – and what is existence? Of all the commentators who have made rich contributions to the human rights debate, Hannah Arendt is perhaps the most valuable. Arendt makes the point that the popular (political) discourse on the 'rights of man' is relevant only in so far as one is *included* in the category 'human'.[111] To *be* 'human', Arendt suggests, it is presumed that one must belong to a recognised nation-state, for only that nation-state is able to protect one *as a human* in the name of these rights. Arendt is thus making the distinction between 'the right to . . .' and 'the right *to be recognised as having the right to* . . .', which is in effect the right to be recognised as human; to be included. Arendt applies this wonderful insight primarily to refugees (we shall say more about her work in this area in the next chapter). But it is equally applicable to the study of genocide, for it presupposes a distinction between *life* and *existence*. The death penalty is a violation of the right to life, but it does not challenge one's right to existence. For one to have, or have denied, the right to life, one must first *exist*. Life is negated by death, but existence, which appears to be a pre-social characteristic, is negated by nothingness. The opposite of existence is an empty void, an indefinable space. Genocide is an atrocity directed at nothing less than wiping out a people, denying a given existence.

When I suggest that genocide is a human rights atrocity that occurs within the social sphere but is mediated through the political, I run the risk of wandering into highly complex and contested territory, but I do not make this claim in order to be controversial. It is merely to suggest that the *rationale* behind the act of genocide is (primarily) social, in so far as it is an articulation of intense disregard between social groups. In other words, genocide is an act committed by one group of people against another. It is not necessarily political, it is rarely legal, it need have nothing to do with economics, and although its motives are often grounded in culture, it is not an act which is performed in the cultural sphere. Like apartheid or slavery, genocide is an act of social exclusion, an atrocity aimed at ensuring an imbalance in the distribution of *status*, which is a currency of social relationships. Of course, by its very nature, genocide goes further than denying the right to equality before the law, or individual freedom. Indeed, in terms of the schema I have adopted in this book, one of the factors that distinguishes genocide from these other forms of social exclusion is that *in most cases* it is not enforced legally. That is to say, unlike historical instances of slavery, or apartheid in South Africa, social exclusion need not become a formalised, 'legitimate' policy. In this respect, in so far as it is not upheld through the law, genocide as a form of social exclusion becomes a political strategy, in which the currency is not only status but power. Entire groups of people thus become victimised, not for the purpose of ensuring an unequal society, but for the purpose of legitimising a particular political ideology.

Let us conclude by summarising some of the main points discussed in this chapter. First, genocides and mass killings take many forms. Some are strategic and political, such as the 'disappearances' in Argentina, but most are ideological, including the Holocaust and the massacres in Cambodia. Second, the ideology that drives the genocide targets a particular group or groups for the ultimate censorship, total annihilation. The selection of the target group is usually made on racial, nationalistic, or ethnic grounds, but there are examples of political targeting. Third, although genocide appears to be the antithesis of modernist rationality and postwar sensitivity, the conditions which make genocide possible exist within the structures of modernity itself. Rationalisation does not only lead to 'progress' and 'Enlightenment'; a darker route leads – through the implementation of scientific, instrumental logic – to racial classification (in the name of science), and to dehumanisation. Along with rationalisation, two other fictions are essential to the development of genocide, and they are considered by some to be inseparable: the nation, a cultural group, and the state, a political machinery. Nationalism, in its extreme form as a belief in national purity or superiority, provides the cultural legitimation for genocide; the state provides the means to carry it out.

Essay questions

1. Is the official definition of genocide satisfactory? If not, what might be a suitable alternative?

2. To what extent might we view genocide as a natural consequence of the drive towards modernity and rationality?

3. Leo Kuper claims that a plural society is an important prerequisite for genocide to take place. What does he mean by this, and is he right?

4. Is it fair to describe the Holocaust as a unique event?

Notes

1 Andrew Bell-Fialkov (1996) *Ethnic Cleansing*, New York: St Martin's Press.

2 Ben Whitaker (1988) 'Genocide: The Ultimate Crime' in Peter Davies (ed.) *Human Rights*, London: Routledge, p. 51.

3 Raphael Lemkin (1944) *Axis Rule in Occupied Europe*, Washington: Carnegie Endowment for International Peace, Chapter Nine.

4 On genocide as a denial of the right to existence, see Ervin Staub (1989) *The Roots of Evil: The Origins of Genocide and Other Group Violence*, New York: New York University Press.

5 Signed by 43 states, with 104 ratifications and assessions. See Ian Brownlie (ed.) (1971) *Basic Documents on Human Rights*, Oxford: Oxford University Press, pp. 31–4.

6 Antonio Cassese (1990) *Human Rights in a Changing World*, Cambridge: Polity Press, Chapter Four, 'How Does the International Community React to Genocide?', p. 71.

7 Cassese, *Human Rights*, p. 75.

8 Staub, *Roots of Evil*, p. xiii.

9 The Soviet Union and its allies insisted upon its exclusion primarily because such political commitments were heterogeneous and transient, and because its inclusion would grant the United Nations licence to intervene in internal disputes. Of course, there was some recognition of the possibility that *any* massacre could then be justified on 'political' grounds. See Cassese, *Human Rights*, pp. 75–6.

10 Leo Kuper (1981) *Genocide: Its Political Use in the Twentieth Century*, New Haven: Yale University Press, p. 23.

11 Barbara Harff and Ted Robert Gurr (1989) 'Victims of the State: Genocides, Politicides and Group Repression since 1945' in *International Review of Victimology*, vol. 1, p. 28.

12 Leo Kuper (1985) *The Prevention of Genocide*, New Haven: Yale University Press, p. 100.

13 Pieter N. Drost (1959) *The Crime of State*, 2 volumes, Leyden: A.W. Sythoff, p. 125.

14 In, for example, Harff and Gurr, 'Victims', pp. 23–41. See also Harff and Gurr (1988) 'Towards an Empirical Theory of Genocides and Politicides: Identification and Measurement of Cases since 1945' in *International Studies Quarterly*, 32, pp. 359–71, and also Harff and Gurr (1987) 'Genocides and Politicides since 1945: Evidence and Anticipation' in *Internet on the Holocaust and Genocide*, no. 13 (December).

15 Harff and Gurr, 'Victims', p. 24.

16 Harff and Gurr, 'Victims', p. 28.

17 Vahakn Dadrian (1974–5) 'The Structural-Functional Components of Genocide' in Drapkin and Viano (eds) *Victimology*, Vol. IV; Dadrian (1975) 'A Typology of Genocide' in *International Review of Sociology*, 2.

18 Israel W. Charny (1994) 'Toward a Generic Definition of Genocide' in George Andreopolous (ed.) *Genocide: Conceptual and Historical Dimensions*, Philadelphia: University of Pennsylvania Press, pp. 64–94.

19 Israel W. Charny (1999) 'Classification of Genocide in Multiple Categories' in Israel W. Charny (ed.) *Encyclopedia of Genocide*, volume 1, Oxford: ABC Clio, p. 7.

20 Charny, 'Classification'.

21 Helen Fein (1984) 'Scenarios of Genocide: Models of Genocide and Critical Responses' in Israel W. Charny (ed.) *Toward the Understanding and Prevention of Genocide*, London: Bowler Publishing, pp. 3–31.

22 Helen Fein (ed.) (1979) *Accounting for Genocide: National Responses and Jewish Victimization During the Holocaust*, New York: Free Press.

23 Kurt Jonassohn and Frank Chalk (1987) 'A Typology of Genocide and Some Implications for the Human Rights Agenda' in Isidor Wallimann and Michael N. Dobkowski (eds) *Genocide and the Modern Age: Etiology and Case Studies of Mass Death*, New York: Greenwood Press, p. 12.

24 Roger W. Smith (1987) 'Human Destructiveness and Politics: The Twentieth Century as an Age of Genocide' in Wallimann and Dobkowski, *Genocide and the Modern Age*.

25 For a comprehensive list, see the literature review in Part 1 of Frank Chalk and Kurt Jonassohn (1990) *The History and Sociology of Genocide: Analyses and Case Studies*, New Haven: Yale University Press; see also Jonassohn and Chalk, 'A Typology'.

26 Helen Fein (1990) 'Genocide: A Sociological Perspective' in *Current Sociology*, 38, 1; Zygmunt Bauman (1989) *Modernity and the Holocaust*, Cambridge: Polity Press.

27 Helen Fein (1979) 'Is Sociology Aware of Genocide?: Recognition of Genocide in Introductory Sociology Texts in the US, 1947–1977' in *Humanity and Society*, August, pp. 177–93.

28 Ailon Shiloh (1975) 'Psychological Anthropology: A Case Study in Cultural Blindness' in *Cultural Anthropology*, 16, 4, pp. 618–20.

29 Figures taken from Staub, *Roots of Evil*, p. 7.

30 Not only do they provide an introductory history, on pages 32–40 of their anthology, but they dedicate the majority of the book to case studies and readings which discuss these examples and more in greater depth.

31 Chalk and Jonassohn, *History and Sociology*, p. 33.

32 Chalk and Jonassohn, *History and Sociology*, p. 34.

33 And remains so to this day. Turkey has yet to recognise these incidents as constituting genocide, and the United Kingdom is another country that

adopts this view. For an interesting discussion, see the article by Julia Pascal (2001) 'A People Killed Twice' in the *Guardian Weekend*, 27 January, pp. 32–9.

34 Staub, *Roots of Evil*, p. 10.

35 See Fein, 'Genocide', p. 2; Cassese, *Human Rights*, p. 73.

36 Whitaker, 'Genocide', p. 52.

37 Gerard J. Libaridian (1987) 'The Ultimate Repression: The Genocide of the Armenians, 1915–1917' in Wallimann and Dobkowski, *Genocide and the Modern Age*, p. 204.

38 Ian Kershaw (1995) 'The Extinction of Human Rights in Nazi Germany' in Olwen Hufton (ed.) *Historical Change and Human Rights: The Oxford Amnesty Lectures 1994*, New York: Basic Books, pp. 223–4.

39 S.P. Oliner and P.M. Oliner (1988) *The Altruistic Personality: Rescuers of Jews in Nazi Germany*, New York: Free Press.

40 Whitaker, 'Genocide', p. 52.

41 Staub, *Roots of Evil*, pp. 28–9.

42 Paul Hilberg (1967) *The Destruction of the European Jews*, Chicago: Quadrangle; Hans Mommsen (1986) 'The Realization of the Unthinkable: The "Final Solution of the Jewish Question" in the Third Reich' in G. Hirschfeld (ed.) The Policies of Genocide: Jews and Soviet Prisoners of War in Nazi Germany, London: Allen and Unwin, pp. 187–204, both cited in Fein, 'Genocide', pp. 57–8. The term 'functionalist' as used in this context may be misleading. It does not appear to be synonymous with the term as it has already been used in this chapter, and seems to have more in common with Weberian themes of rationalisation and bureaucratisation.

43 Gordon Allport (1954) *The Nature of Prejudice*, Reading, MA: Addison-Wesley, p. 40; cited in Staub, *Roots of Evil*, p. 95.

44 Staub, *Roots of Evil*, pp. 100–4.

45 Fein, 'Genocide', pp. 59–60, adapting Fein, *Accounting for Genocide*.

46 On this, see Hannah Arendt (1963) *Eichmann in Jerusalem: A Report on the Banality of Evil*, New York: Viking, and the critique of Eichmann by Fein and others in *Accounting for Genocide*, summarised in 'Genocide', p. 63.

47 Fein, 'Genocide', p. 52. See also Alan Rosenberg (1987) 'Was the Holocaust Unique?: A Peculiar Question' in Wallimann and Dobkowski, *Genocide and the Modern Age*.

48 Yehuda Bauer (1978) *The Holocaust in Historical Perspective*, Seattle: University of Washington Press.

49 Irving L. Horowitz (1976) *Genocide: State Power and Mass Murder*, New Brunswick, NJ: Transaction Books, p. 38; cited in Cassese, *Human Rights*, p. 74.

50 Bauman, *Modernity*, pp. 6–7.

51 Rosenberg, 'Was the Holocaust Unique?', p. 146.

52 Cassese, *Human Rights*, pp. 79–80; Barbara Harff (1987) 'The Etiology of Genocides' in Wallimann and Dobkowski, *Genocide and the Modern Age*, p. 46.

53 Cassese, *Human Rights*, pp. 80–5.

54 Richard Falk (1999) 'The Challenge of Genocide and Genocidal Politics in an Era of Globalization' in Tim Dunne and Nicholas J. Wheeler (eds) *Human Rights in Global Politics*, Cambridge: Cambridge University Press, p. 184.

55 Falk, 'The Challenge of Genocide', p. 185.

56 From 'The Rwandan blood on the UN's hands' in the *Observer* newspaper, 3 September 2000, p. 19.

57 Linda Melvern (2000) *A People Betrayed: The Role of the West in Rwanda's Genocide*, London: Zed Books.

58 A. Destexhe (1995) *The Crime of Genocide*, New York: New York University Press.

59 This argument is drawn from Mahmood Mamdani (1996) 'From Conquest to Consent as the Basis of State Formation: Reflections After a Visit to Rwanda', unpublished paper, referenced in Falk, 'The Challenge of Genocide', p. 193.

60 Staub, *Roots of Evil*, p. 128.

61 Staub, *Roots of Evil*, p. 24.

62 Pierre van der Berghe (1981) *The Ethnic Phenomenon*, New York: Elsevier.

63 Erich Fromm (1975) *The Anatomy of Human Destructiveness*, Greenwich, Conn.: Fawcett Publications, p. 26; cited in Kuper, *Genocide*, p. 52.

64 Konrad Lorenz (1977) *On Aggression*, New York: Harcourt, Brace and World, pp. 265, 228–90, and Lorenz (1970) *Studies in Animal and Human Behaviour*, London: Methuen, pp. 3–5, 51–6; cited in Kuper, *Genocide*, p. 51.

65 Reinhold Niebuhr (1960; original 1932) *Moral Man and Immoral Society: A Study in Ethics and Politics*, New York: Charles Scribner's Sons; cited in Staub, *Roots of Evil*, p. 24.

66 Tom Segev (1977) *The Commanders of the Nazi Concentration Camps*, PhD dissertation, Boston University; cited in Staub, *Roots of Evil*, p. 130.

67 Staub, *Roots of Evil*, p. 14.

68 John Steiner (1980) 'The SS Yesterday and Today: A Sociopathological View' in Joel E. Dimsdale (ed.) *Survivors, Victims, and Perpetrators: Essays on the Nazi Holocaust*, New York: Hemisphere Publishing Co.; cited in Staub, *Roots of Evil*, pp. 132–3.

69 Kuper, *Genocide*. See also Kuper, *The Prevention of Genocide*; Kuper (1977) *The Pity of It All*, Minneapolis: University of Minnesota Press.

70 Staub, *Roots of Evil*, p. 233, 235.

71 Kuper, *Genocide*, p. 57.

72 Kuper, *Genocide*, p. 58.

73 From the *Volkischer Beobachter* 26 August 1932, quoted in De Jonge, *Weimar Chronicle*, p. 212; cited in Staub, *Roots of Evil*, p. 97.

74 Staub, *Roots of Evil*, p. 107.

75 Staub, *Roots of Evil*, p. 108, following G.M. Kren and L. Rappoport (1980) *The Holocaust and the Crisis of Human Behaviour*, New York: Holmes & Meier, p. 23.

76 Chalk and Jonassohn, *History and Sociology*; see also Chalk and Jonassohn (1988a) *Definitions of Genocide and Their Implications for Prediction and Prevention*, Montreal: Montreal Institute for Genocide Studies; Chalk and Jonassohn (1988b) 'The History and Sociology of Genocidal Killings' in Israel W. Charny (ed.) *Genocide: A Critical Bibliographic Review*, New York: Facts on File Publications.

77 Chalk and Jonassohn, *History and Sociology*, p. 28.

78 Jack N. Porter (1982) 'Introduction' in Jack N. Porter (ed.) *Genocide and Human Rights: A Global Anthology*, Washington, D.C.: University Press of America.

79 Staub, *Roots of Evil*, p. 233.

80 Horowitz, *Genocide*, pp. 38–9; cited in Kuper, *Genocide*, p. 49.

81 Staub, *Roots of Evil*, p. 24.

82 Dadrian, 'Structural-Functional Components', p. 123; cited in Kuper, *Genocide*, pp. 50–1.

83 Staub, *Roots of Evil*, p. 206.

84 Harff, 'Etiology of Genocide'.

85 Florence Mazian (1990) *Why Genocide?: The Armenian and Jewish Experiences in Perspective*, Ames, Iowa: Iowa State University Press.

86 Jean-Paul Sartre (1968) 'On Genocide' in *Ramparts*, February, pp. 37–42; see also Sartre (1968) *On Genocide*, Boston: Beacon Press.

87 The reference is to Kurt Glaser and Stefan T. Possony (1979) *Victims of Politics: The State of Human Rights*, New York: Columbia University Press, although the authors arrived at this charge via a different route.

88 Tony Barta (1987) 'Relations of Genocide: Land and Lives in the Colonization of Australia' in Wallimann and Dobkowski, *Genocide in the Modern Age*, p. 239.

89 Libaridian, 'Ultimate Repression', p. 227.

90 Staub, *Roots of Evil*, p. 193.

91 Fein, 'Genocide', pp. 60–3.

92 Fein, 'Genocide', p. 60.

93 Bettelheim's thesis is located in various forms in various works. See Bettelheim (1943) 'Individual and Mass Behavior in Extreme Situations' in *Journal of Abnormal and Social Psychology* 38, pp. 417–52; Bettelheim (1960) *The Informed Heart: Autonomy in a Mass Age*, Glencoe, Ill.: Free Press; Bettelheim (1979) *Surviving and Other Essays*, New York: Knopf.

94 Terence Des Pres (1976) *The Survivor: An Anatomy of Life in the Death Camps*, Oxford and New York: Oxford University Press.

95 Anna Pawelczynska (1979) *Values and Violence in Auschwitz: A Sociological Analysis*, Berkeley: University of California Press.

96 Elmer Luchterhand (1964) 'Survival in the Concentration Camp: An Individual or a Group Phenomenon' in B. Rosenberg, I. Gerver and F.W. Howton (eds) *Mass Society in Crisis: Social Problems and Social Pathology*, New York: Macmillan; Luchterhand (1970) 'Early and Late Effects of Imprisonment in Nazi Concentration Camps: Conflicting Interpretations in Survivor Research' in *Sozialpsychiatre* 2, pp. 102–10; Luchterhand (1980) 'Social Behavior of Concentration Camp Prisoners: Continuities and Discontinuities with Pre- and Postcamp Life' in Joel E. Dimsdale, *Survivors, Victims and Perpetrators*, Washington: Hemisphere.

97 Erving Goffman (1991; original 1961) *Asylums: Essays on the Social Situation of Mental Patients and Other Inmates*, Harmondsworth: Penguin.

98 Staub, *Roots of Evil*, p. 165 ff.

99 See Smith, 'Human Destructiveness and Politics', p. 22.

100 Cassese, *Human Rights*, p. 71.

101 Barta, 'Relations of Genocide', p. 240.

102 Richard L. Rubenstein (1987) 'Afterword: Genocide and Civilization' in Isidor Wallimann and Michael N. Dobkowski, *Genocide and the Modern Age*, London: Greenwood, p. 297.

103 Fein, *Accounting for Genocide*.

104 Horowitz, *Genocide*, p. 73; cited in Cassese, *Human Rights*, p. 72.

105 Catharine A. MacKinnon (1993) 'Crimes of War, Crimes of Peace' in Stephen Shute and Susan Hurley (eds) *On Human Rights: The Oxford Amnesty Lectures 1993*, New York: Basic Books.

106 Kuper, *Genocide*, p. 161.

107 Bauman, *Modernity*, p. 8; Henry L. Feingold (1983) 'How Unique is the Holocaust?' in Alex Grobman and Daniel Landes (eds) *Genocide: Critical Issues in the Holocaust*, Los Angeles: The Simon Weisenthal Centre.

108 Bauman, *Modernity*, p. 24.

109 Bauman, *Modernity*, p. 70.

110 Bauman, *Modernity*, p. 72.

111 Hannah Arendt (1951) 'The Perplexities of the "Rights of Man"' in *The Origins of Totalitarianism*, New York: Harcourt Brace.

Further information

Books

Perhaps the most important overview is Leo Kuper's *Genocide: Its Political Use in the Twentieth Century* (New Haven: Yale University Press, 1981). Frank Chalk and Kurt Jonassohn's *The History and Sociology of Genocide: Analyses and Case Studies* (New Haven: Yale University Press, 1990) is another good survey, which brings together critical analysis and useful case studies and readings. Various edited collections are extremely useful, the best of which is Isidor Wallimann and Michael N. Dobkowski's *Genocide in the Modern Age: Etiology and Case Studies of Mass Death* (New York: Greenwood Press, 1987). Others are also recommended, such as Jack N. Porter's *Genocide and Human Rights: A Global Introduction* (Washington, DC: University Press of America, 1982) and Israel W. Charny's *Genocide: A Critical Bibliographic Review* (New York: Facts on File Publications, 1988). Charny has also edited *Toward the Understanding and Prevention of Genocide: Proceedings of the International Conference on the Holocaust and Genocide* (London: Westview Press, 1984), which includes contributions from Kuper and Helen Fein. Fein has done more than anyone to bring the study of genocide into the mainstream of the social sciences. Her comparative study *Accounting for Genocide: National Responses and Jewish Victimization During the Holocaust* (New York: Free Press, 1979) is required reading, as is her special edition of *Current Sociology: The Journal of the International Sociological Association*, 38, 1, Spring 1990, entitled 'Genocide: A Sociological Perspective'. The *Encyclopedia of Genocide* (Oxford: ABC Clio, 1999) is edited by Israel W. Charny, and spans two volumes. It is by no means an easy thing to get through. One seems to go through pages upon pages of introduction and contents before reaching the first entry, and many entries are included under larger subheadings rather than in alphabetical order, which is a bit odd. It also bears the clearly dominant imprint of its chief editor. Nevertheless, the very fact that it exists is deserving of praise!

Ervin Staub's *The Roots of Evil: The Origins of Genocide and Other Group Violence* is a surprisingly unhelpful treatment of the subject. It is segmented to such a degree and so firmly rooted in social psychology that it is almost unreadable for the non-specialist, although it may be more useful to students of psychology. Finally, any scholar concerned with the ethical and theoretical dimensions of genocide should consult Zygmunt Bauman's majestic *Modernity and the Holocaust* (Cambridge: Polity Press, 1989).

CHAPTER TEN

Refugees

1. Everyone has the right to freedom of movement and residence within the borders of each State;
2. Everyone has the right to leave any country, including his own, and to return to his country.

Universal Declaration of Human Rights, Article 13

Everyone has the right to seek and to enjoy in other countries asylum from persecution.

Universal Declaration of Human Rights, Article 14 (1)

1. Everyone has the right to a nationality.
2. No one shall be arbitrarily deprived of his nationality nor denied the right to change his nationality.

Universal Declaration of Human Rights, Article 15

What is a refugee?

One of the problems of a book such as this one is that it is always going to be out of date. By the time it reaches you, its statistics and case studies will have been replaced by new statistics, new testimonies, new crises. As I write this chapter, the eyes of the world are on Afghanistan, where the United States and its allies have carried out aerial attacks designed to topple the Taliban regime and force the leaders of the Al Qaida terrorist network out of hiding. Thousands upon thousands of Afghans are fleeing to the borders, hoping to find refuge in neighbouring countries such as Pakistan. Afghanistan already has the world's largest community of displaced persons.

We will see, throughout this chapter, that the experiences of refugees and displaced persons raise particular issues and concerns in matters pertaining to human rights, citizenship, and racism. As Hannah Arendt accurately observes, there had always been a presumption behind the development of the so-called 'rights of man' that it was the task of governments to incorporate these rights into their own domestic laws, and thus enforce them through citizenship:

> All human beings were citizens of some kind of political community; if the laws of their country did not live up to the demands of the Rights of Man, they were expected to change them, by legislation in democratic countries or through revolutionary action in despotisms.[1]

Arendt makes the chilling claim that refugees are not, in effect, denied the so-called incontrovertible 'rights of man', which exist so as to be upheld in national communities, but are instead denied the right to exist within a community at all. 'Their plight is not that they are not equal before the law,' she says, 'but that no law exists for them; not that they are oppressed but that nobody even wants to oppress them'.[2] With reference, for example, to how the Nazis first denied the Jews citizenship status and then herded them into ghettos and concentration camps, outside of humanity, Arendt states that a condition of total *rightlessness* had been created before there was any challenge to the right to live.[3]

> The fundamental deprivation of human rights is manifested first and above all in the deprivation of a place in the world which makes opinions significant and actions effective. Something much more fundamental than freedom and justice, which are the rights of citizens, is at stake when belonging to the community into which one is born is no longer a matter of course and not belonging no longer a matter of choice ... They are deprived, not of the right to freedom, but of the right of action; not of the right to think whatever they please, but of the right to opinion.[4]

The standard – but possibly outdated – definition of a refugee is taken from the 1951 United Nations Convention Relating to the Status of Refugees:

> any person who, owing to a well-founded fear of being persecuted
> for reasons of race, religion, nationality, membership of a particular
> social group or political opinion, is outside the country of his
> nationality and is unable or owing to such fear, is unwilling to avail
> himself of the protection of that country...or unable or...unwilling
> to return to it.[5]

There is little doubt that the refugee crisis is one of the most dramatic concerns of the contemporary world. The number of refugees has risen from under 3 million in 1986 to 11.7 million *legally* recognised refugees in the world today.[6] The *actual* figure probably exceeds 20 million. There are some 5 million officially recognised refugees living in Western Europe alone. Internally displaced persons around the world – those forced to flee their homes who remain within their own country – amount to an estimated further 25 to 30 million. In total, one person in every 115 alive today is a refugee or displaced person.[7] It is estimated that around 52 per cent of the world's refugees are children.

The rights of refugees are protected, theoretically, by the United Nations High Commissioner for Refugees (UNHCR). In its mission statement, the UNHCR claims that its primary purpose is to 'safeguard the rights and well-being of refugees', and to 'ensure that everyone can exercise the right to seek asylum and find safe refuge in another state, and to return home voluntarily'. These efforts, it claims, are guided by the 1951 UN Refugee Convention, and by its 1967 Protocol. The UNHCR was established by the UN – 36 votes for, 5 against, 11 abstentions – in 1949, to operate for a period of three years from 1951 to oversee the immediate refugee crisis. A previously established UN organ, the International Refugee Organization, had been largely unable to solve the crisis through resettlement, and was eventually closed down in 1952. The UNHCR was intended to take a more proactive stance. In terms of its work in this respect, the UNHCR seeks to discourage displacement by 'encouraging states and other institutions to create conditions which are conducive to the protection of human rights and the peaceful resolution of conflicts'. The UNHCR also acts in partnership with governments, super-governmental organisations, and NGOs to assist in the returning and reintegration of refugees into their countries of origin. As well as refugees and asylum-seekers recognised as such by the various statutes and covenants, the UNHCR deals with cases pertaining to 'returnees' (repatriated refugees who remain a cause for concern for a period of time after return), war victims, those of undetermined nationality, and the internally displaced.

In Europe, a series of acts and conventions have been established in a bid to forge a common policy on immigration and asylum, the assumption being that through standardisation conflicts between state sovereignty and international standards will be removed. The 1990 Dublin Convention created a common set of guidelines for establishing which nation-state is responsible for evaluating an asylum application. The 1990 Schengen Convention sought to establish freedom of movement within and between member states (although not all such states signed up for it). The 1992 Maastricht Treaty also sought to standardise asylum and immigration policies and introduced the concept of European citizenship. A common means of evaluating the urgency and legitimacy of asylum applications was proposed by the 1992 London Resolutions. Other recommendations and resolutions have included agreements on the definition of a refugee (1996) and procedures for ensuring the safe return of failed asylum applicants (1994 and 1995). The 1997 Amsterdam Treaty gave members five years to establish common asylum and immigration policies. In 1999, in Tampere, the European Council representatives agreed to work towards the full implementation of the 1951 UN Refugee Convention into European law.

Among the European states, Germany receives the most applications for asylum, according to UNHCR statistics. Between 1991 and 2000, 1,765,260 applications were made, compared with 42,397 made to the United Kingdom, which ranks tenth out of 25 in Europe for asylum applications per capita.[8] In 2000, the UK received 76,040 applications for asylum, an increase of less than 7 per cent on the 1999 figure.[9] The most significant statistical difference pertaining to asylum seekers in the UK between 1999 and 2000 was the decline in the number of refugees arriving from Yugoslavia – 5,695 in 2000 compared to 11,645 in 1999. Indeed, Yugoslavia was displaced from its position as the most popular country of origin in 2000 by both Iraq and Sri Lanka. There was a huge increase in applications from Iraqi citizens, from 1,800 in 1999 to 7,080 in 2000. Flows of refugees across borders are clearly variable from year to year and reflect wider, structural political circumstances.

By 1999, the leading country of origin for refugees was Afghanistan, from which some 3,580,400 people had fled – mainly to neighbouring Pakistan and Iran. In a later section, we will return to the crisis of flight from Afghanistan, which has of course worsened in 2001, prior to and following the US bombings of that country. Table 10.1 lists the ten largest refugee populations in 1999, according to the UNHCR.

Displaced persons have traditionally been treated to less protection than other refugees, but of course continue to live in fear for their lives from their oppressive governments. Their number has increased alarmingly in recent years. In 1999, there were four million internally displaced persons in Sudan alone. However, the UNHCR is not

Table 10.1 Largest populations of refugees, 1999[10]

Country of origin	Main countries of asylum	No. of refugees
Afghanistan	Pakistan / Iran	3,580,400
Burundi	Tanzania	568,000
Iraq	Iran	512,800
Sudan	Uganda / DR Congo / Ethiopia / Kenya / CAR / Chad	490,400
Bosnia-Herzegovina	Yugoslavia / Croatia / USA / Sweden / Netherlands / Denmark	478,300
Somalia	Kenya / Ethiopia / Yemen / Djibouti	447,800
Angola	Zambia / DR Congo / Namibia	432,700
Sierra Leone	Guinea / Liberia	400,800
Eritrea	Sudan	376,400
Vietnam	China / USA	370,300

empowered to intervene in the internal politics of any nation-state. Arendt's observations about the role played by nation-states in the recognition of human rights seem disturbingly apt.

Historically, most refugees were fleeing political persecution, a famous example being the Jewish exodus from Nazi Germany. This emphasis has now altered. The plight of most of these refugees and displaced persons has been caused by economic or ecological reasons, as opposed to the original concentration of political refugees in the post-war era. Not only has the refugee issue become a central concern for politicians in many nation-states, but there has been a need to rethink the original definition in the light of these changes.

Table 10.2   Largest populations of internally displaced persons, 2000[11]

Country	Millions
Sudan	4.0
Angola	1.1–3.8
Colombia	2.1
Congo-Kinshasa	1.8
Burma	0.6–1.0
Sierra Leone	0.5–1.0
Turkey	0.4–1.0
Indonesia	0.75–0.85
Iraq	0.7
Burundi	0.6

Much could be said about the refugee issue. I do not, however, want to spend unnecessary time in this volume discussing the rhetoric of politicians in response to the contemporary crisis. I want, instead, to focus on some issues in the debate which are of interest to us as academics. First, naturally, I provide a brief history of refugee crises. Second, I discuss the relationship between refugees and citizenship, with an additional emphasis on 'race'. Third, I look at the role of border controls and ask whether we can justifiably claim that these controls operate in violation of human rights standards. Fourth, I consider the current media discourse on asylum seekers and connect it to the work carried out by critical sociologists on moral panics. Fifth, I relate some of the experiences of displacement. Finally, I look at the role played by the state in seeking to resolve this crisis.

A brief history of refugees

As with almost all of the other human rights concerns discussed in this volume, the plight of refugees is an ancient one. There have been refugees and asylum-seekers for as long as there have been political territories with recognisable borders. In view of this, it would be impossible to provide a comprehensive historical overview. It is, however, the twentieth century which provides us with the most significant and chilling history of refugees, and I shall dedicate this section and this chapter primarily to this period. What little I say about the issue before then is by way of an introduction only.

Refugees in the ancient, medieval and early modern worlds

One of the earliest references to refugees can be found in an oath made around 3,500 years ago. A Hittite king agreed a treaty with the ruler of another country which included the declaration:

> Concerning a refugee, I affirm an oath to the following: when a refugee comes from your land into mine, he will not be returned to you. To return a refugee from the land of the Hittites is not right.

The concept of asylum and refuge resurfaces time and again through-out subsequent literary and historical texts of the ancient world, and then the biblical one. One of the more famous examples from the Bible is the Hebrew flight from Egypt to escape from the threat of slavery. The practice continued into and throughout the middle ages. Historically, most displacement has been caused by racial or religious conflict. For example, in the fifteenth century, large numbers of Jews were expelled from Spain. It is often argued that the beginning of the modern tradition of asylum in Europe came with the revocation of the Edict of Nantes in 1685, after which some 250,000 French protestants, the Huguenots, were forced to flee their country for fear of religious persecution. Many of these were authorised to settle in the (now German) states of Brand-enburg and Prussia. In 1708 the British Parliament passed an act which granted naturalised status to foreign Protestants. The French Revolution led to mass numbers escaping France for fear of political persecution. The first recorded reference to the 'right of asylum' came in 1725.

The examples cited in the aftermath of the Huguenot flight may have been exceptions, in so far as legislations were passed to help the refugees at a time when there was no general agreement on the right of asylum, but prior to the nineteenth century – possibly because passports and visas were not yet required to cross borders – this right was gener-ally honoured and there was no crisis of refugees. Only in the twentieth century, with the tightening of border controls and the increasing level of state persecution, did such a crisis emerge.

Refugees in the twentieth century

Hannah Arendt points out that for much of the nineteenth and twen-tieth centuries, certain countries did operate an unofficial practice of offering asylum to those who had been persecuted by their own governments. However, these numbers grew increasingly larger, more categories of persecution were introduced, and it became apparent that the unofficial system was inadequate to deal with the problem. Also, many of the new refugees were suffering from persecution not because of their actions or their beliefs but because of their physical characteristics or the ideological whims of their governments.[12] Shamefully, the offending countries no longer saw these refugees as enemies, or liabilities, or causes for shame; they were not political exiles who spoke out against the atrocities of their governments, but innocent victims rendered unworthy or subhuman.

The huge expansion in the numbers of refugees and displaced persons in the twentieth century is directly linked to the modern resurgence of genocidal practices. Thus, this chapter should be read with memories of Chapter Nine still fresh in mind. One survivor of the Holocaust is quoted as describing how historians in the future will look back on the twentieth century:

> ... not only [as] the century of great wars, but also [as] the century of the refugee. Almost nobody at the end of the century is where they were at the beginning of it. It has been an extraordinary period of movement and upheaval.[13]

Towards the end of the second decade of the century, as a result of the First World War, the Armenian genocide, and the Russian revolution, millions were forced into exile or statelessness:

> A total of 1.3 million Greeks were repatriated to Greece, mainly from Turkey; 400,000 Turks were decanted into the state which claimed them; some 200,000 Bulgarians moved into the diminished territory bearing their national name; while 1.5 or perhaps 2 million Russian nationals, escaping from the Russian revolution or on the losing side of the Russian civil war, found themselves homeless ... At a rough guess the years 1914–22 generated between four and five million refugees.[14]

However, as dire as this situation seemed, it was to get even worse in the years during and immediately following the Second World War:

It has been estimated that by May 1945 there were perhaps 40.5 million uprooted people in Europe, excluding non-German forced labourers, and Germans who had fled before the Soviet advance ... About thirteen million Germans were expelled from the parts of Germany annexed by Poland and the USSR, from Czechoslovakia and parts of south-eastern Europe ... They were taken in by the new German Federal Republic, which offered a home and citizenship to any German who returned there, as the new state of Israel offered a 'right of return' to any Jew. When, but in an epoch of mass flight, could such offers by states have been seriously made? Of the 11,332,700 'displaced persons' of various nationalities found in Germany by the victorious armies of 1945, ten million soon returned to their homelands – but half of these were compelled to do so against their will.[15]

Other crises followed, including those resulting from the Soviet expansion to the West. Some 200,000 Hungarians fled their country in 1956 following the Soviet invasion, the first full crisis to face the newly formed UNHCR.[16] And, as Hobsbawm points out, this was only the European situation. Millions of Chinese residents were displaced under Japanese occupation.[17] Some 15 million refugees fled India after decolonisation in 1947. Some 5 million Koreans were displaced as a result of the Korean War. About 1.3 million Palestinians left the new state of Israel. Indeed, the attention of the UNHCR was forcibly shifted during the 1960s away from Europe, towards Africa. Wars were breaking out following demands for independence from the colonised nations. From the crises which ensued from the Algerian war of independence of 1954 to 1962, in which over a million Europeans were forced to flee the country, to the numerous crises in sub-Saharan Africa during the 1960s, the problem of refugees had taken on new meaning for the UNHCR and the world political community it represented.[18] The crisis in Nigeria alone, concerning the claims to independence of the Ibo Biafra region beginning in 1967, resulted in the displacement of some 2 million people, either within or beyond the Nigerian borders.[19] By 1965, Africa was home to some 850,000 refugees, displaced from their homelands because of the decolonisation struggles.[20]

In the 1970s, attention shifted once again, this time to Asia. In 1971, military unrest in East Pakistan (now Bangladesh) resulted in some 10 million refugees fleeing across the border into India within the year.[21] Over the two decades following 1975, approximately 3 million people fled Vietnam, Cambodia and Laos after communist regimes came to power.[22] Indeed, during the late 1970s considerable attention was being paid to human rights events in South-east Asia – the Cambodian 'killing fields', the plight of the Vietnamese boat people. In 1979 a special conference was held, in Geneva, under the auspices of the United Nations, to discuss the crisis of refugees from this part of the world, made all the more urgent once neighbouring countries announced that they would not be taking any more refugees. Ten years later, a follow-up conference was held, also in Geneva, where a comprehensive plan of action was drafted to deal with the Vietnamese situation, and, for possibly the first time, the country of origin, Vietnam, played a large part in the proceedings.

The contemporary global refugee crisis

By 1980, the official statistic had risen to some 6 million refugees and 2 million internally displaced persons around the world; by 1995, the number of refugees had doubled to some 13.5 million, while the number of internally displaced persons had reached the staggering total of some 30 million – and this is only the official figure.[23] Throughout this period, the UNHCR and other concerned organisations were faced with crises in the Great Lakes region of central Africa, North-eastern Africa, Central America, and Afghanistan. These troubles continue today. As with the cases of Laos, Vietnam and Cambodia, the countries most directly affected by the exodus from Afghanistan (for instance) have been those which border it. Table 10.3, adapted from a UNHCR report, gives an indication of the numbers of Afghan refugees seeking asylum in Afghanistan's neighbours between 1979 and 1999.

Nevertheless, by the 1990s, a new agenda had reached the UNHCR and the international political community in general. The end of the Cold War, and the gradual resolution of conflicts around the world, allowed for the possibility of the repatriation of refugees following successful United Nations peace-building missions.[24] Regions hitherto plagued by war, such as Central America, Southern Africa, and South-east Asia, came together under the UN's stewardship to discuss the prospects for peace, the possible transition to democracy, and the re-settlement of refugees and displaced persons. In 1975, the UNHCR oversaw the return of only approximately 100,000 refugees, and even fewer in 1976 and 1977. Although this number rose to over half a million in both 1979 and 1980, it remained otherwise stable, hovering around 250,000, until 1991, when the total figure exceeded 2 million. It stayed in that vicinity for a few years, occasionally slipping back to around 1 million (e.g. 1997 and 1998). In 1999 just over 1.5 million refugees were returned to their homes.[25] However, amidst this optimism,

Table 10.3 Afghan refugees by country of asylum 1979–99[26]

Year	Pakistan	Iran	India	Russia	Other	Total
1979	402,000	100,000	–	–	–	502,000
1980	1,428,000	300,000	–	–	–	1,728,000
1981	2,375,000	1,500,000	2,700	–	–	3,877,700
1982	2,877,000	1,500,000	3,400	–	–	4,380,400
1983	2,873,000	1,700,000	5,300	–	–	4,578,300
1984	2,500,000	1,800,000	5,900	–	–	4,305,900
1985	2,730,000	1,880,000	5,700	–	–	4,615,700
1986	2,878,000	2,190,000	5,500	–	–	5,073,500
1987	3,156,000	2,350,000	5,200	–	–	5,511,200
1988	3,255,000	2,350,000	4,900	–	–	5,609,900
1989	3,272,000	2,350,000	8,500	–	–	5,630,500
1990	3,253,000	3,061,000	11,900	–	–	6,325,900
1991	3,098,000	3,187,000	9,800	–	–	6,294,800
1992	1,627,000	2,901,000	11,000	8,800	3,000	4,550,800
1993	1,477,000	1,850,000	24,400	24,900	11,900	3,388,200
1994	1,053,000	1,623,000	22,400	28,300	12,300	2,739,000
1995	1,200,000	1,429,000	19,900	18,300	9,700	2,676,900
1996	1,200,000	1,415,000	18,600	20,400	10,700	2,664,700
1997	1,200,000	1,412,000	17,500	21,700	12,500	2,663,000
1998	1,200,000	1,401,000	16,100	8,700	8,400	2,634,200
1999	1,200,000	1,325,700	14,500	12,600	10,000	2,562,800

the United Nations and the UNHCR were aware that the situations in most of the countries accepting returnees remained unstable, and continued to monitor them carefully.

By the end of the century, the refugee crisis had worsened, due in no small part to the terrible atrocities that took place in Rwanda and the former Yugoslavia. Indeed, between 1990 and 1999, over one million refugees from the former Yugoslavia took up asylum in Western Europe, making it easily the largest population.[27] Similarly, following the 1994 genocide and civil war in Rwanda, over two million refugees had fled to neighbouring countries by August, as Table 10.4 indicates.

Events in the Balkans and the African Great Lakes region continue to trouble human rights agencies. In its 1999 mid-year report, the UNHCR highlights four main areas of concern: South-eastern Europe (primarily Kosovo); the Great Lakes region (refugees from the Democratic Republic of Congo fleeing to Tanzania and the Central African Republic, refugees from Congo arriving in Gabon, and refugees

Table 10.4   Rwandan refugees in neighbouring countries, August 1994[28]

Location	Number
Northern Burundi	270,000
Western Tanzania	577,000
South-west Uganda	10,000
Zaire (Goma)	850,000
Zaire (Bukavo)	332,000
Zaire (Uvira)	62,000
Total	**2,101,000**

from Congo and Angola fleeing to the Democratic Republic of Congo); South America (mainly Colombia); and East Asia and the Pacific (primarily East Timor). Table 10.5 indicates the total population of concern to the UNHCR for 1998, broken down by region.

'Race', citizenship and refugees

Refugees and asylum-seekers tend to find themselves, in terms of *law* and *politics*, in an ambiguous position. Decisions as to whether or not to allow entry or grant asylum depend largely upon the applicant's origins, the perception of his or her motives, and the current demand for entry into a particular nation-state, but this seems to be a wholly arbitrary process. The 1951 Convention and Protocol Related to the Status of Refugees clearly states that those escaping danger should not be penalised for entering a country illegally, but this is rarely upheld.

No refugee is automatically *entitled* to become a citizen of another country, but all refugees are protected, *at least theoretically*, by the 1951 Convention Relating to the Status of Refugees and by the 1948 United Nations Declaration of Human Rights.[29] Of course, the task of the UNHCR is to implement the 1951 Convention, which protects refugees from the laws applicable to other international migrants. Refugees are entitled, according to the Convention, to the right of resettlement and to protection from deportation.

However, as refugees are not entitled to citizenship status in any given country, they are, of course, not necessarily accorded the entitlements and rights which accompany such a status. From this, it seems apparent that citizenship is still very much a selective process. While, at

Table 10.5 Total Indicative Population of Concern to UNHCR 1998[30]

Region	Refugees	Asylum seekers	Returnees	Internally displaced persons	Returnee internally displaced persons	Others	TOTAL
Africa	3,270,860	63,350	1,296,200	1,592,200	1,100	60,670	6,284,950
Asia	4,744,730	27,610	317,180	2,037,100	180,400	167,720	7,474,740
Europe	2,667,830	576,970	285,500	1,306,300	266,600	1,109,420	6,212,620
Latin America & Caribbean	74,180	360	7,860	–	–	–	102,400
North America	659,800	645,600	–	–	–	20,000	1,305,400
Oceania	74,310	5,200	–	–	–	–	79,510
TOTAL	11,491,710	1,319,090	1,907,310	4,935,600	448,100	1,357,810	21,459,620

least in terms of the general use of the word, a 'citizen' is usually seen as any member of a given community, there are in fact more non-citizens in most countries than a cursory glance might suggest. The 'contract' of citizenship – to abide by certain duties in return for certain rights – thus becomes a process of selection made by a political elite, often based on arbitrary individual characteristics, in particular the wealth which a refugee might be bringing with her/him, and thus contributing towards the economy of the host nation. Such arbitrariness and inequality result in conflict – as Jürgen Habermas rightly says, writing about the asylum debate in Germany, to avoid conflict, refugees, asylum seekers, and guest workers must be granted citizenship in the legal as well as the political-cultural sense.[31]

The reality of the status of refugees appears to extend far beyond the absence of recognised citizenship rights – refugees are treated, in some cases, as if they do not even qualify for *human* rights. Hannah Arendt's warning on the perplexities of human rights once again comes to mind. Richard Dunstan of Amnesty International writes:

'I'm in such a hopeless situation that I wish I was never born. This prison, without hope and faith to survive, is hell. Please help me!' – This letter was like many received every day of every week in Amnesty International's postbag from prisons in countries as diverse as Algeria, China, Iran, Nigeria, Turkey and Zaire. But this letter was written in Wormwood Scrubs prison, west London, where the writer, a 28-year-old Algerian asylum-seeker, had been incarcerated for the past four months while the Home Office considered his asylum claim. The writer was to spend a further six months in Wormwood Scrubs before being released and granted asylum.[32]

The tragedy of this is that the writer of this letter had not been convicted of or even charged with a crime. Indeed, no court had considered his position, and nor did any have to. The writer's only 'crime' was to seek asylum, and, as Dunstan says, detentions such as this fall within the discretionary powers of 'low-ranking immigration officials, acting without reference or effective accountability to any court or independent review body'. These powers were ratified by the United Kingdom's 1971 Immigration Act. The result is that asylum-seekers can be held indefinitely without being given due reason for their incarceration, and with no legal right to appeal or any legally prescribed right to bail. When all this is taken into consideration, it is evident that asylum-seekers, who have committed no crime, are allowed fewer rights than violent criminals.

The United Kingdom has constantly sought to champion human rights causes around the world, and yet, in reality, it is one of the most exclusive and bordered nation-states imaginable when faced with the possibility of a high refugee intake. It demands that all asylum-seekers within the EC carry valid passports and visas, a quite ludicrous expectation designed solely to keep people out. In the 1930s, when vast numbers of Germans were fleeing the Nazis, the UK demanded visas upon entry. Now, it has gone so far as to fine airlines up to £2,000 for each passenger carried into the UK without these travel documents. Of course, those most in need of asylum are those who cannot obtain these luxuries. A former political prisoner from Eritrea, seeking asylum in the UK, describes her experience on arrival at Heathrow Airport:

> The official considered our passports. She began shouting at us, saying 'How can you come in this way without proper documents – you will be sent back to Addis Ababa.' When she said this we were so distressed that we fell on our knees, weeping and pleading. The woman laughed at us – she thought it was funny that we were on our hands and knees. She said, 'We don't want Ethiopians; there are too many.' They took my brother by his legs and dragged him along the ground. Then the woman took me by the wrists and pushed me onto the plane.[33]

The question of access to 'externals' is just as complex in the UK as that relating to refugees. This applies even to requests for entry made by British 'subjects', even though it is understood that UK citizens are entitled to be allowed into their own country 'without let or hindrance'.[34] Until 1962 any Commonwealth citizen or British subject had the right to enter Britain, but the Commonwealth Immigration Acts of 1962 and 1968 and the Immigration Act of 1971 defined those who had such a right in more specific terms. These tended to be those from the 'old Commonwealth' (and thus largely the white population) and the debate used the language of 'belonging' and 'right of abode'. Debates over racism reflected the realities of the situation: those who suffered most were Asians from East Africa, and in response to criticism from the European Commission on Human Rights, the government at the time sought to extend entry to these peoples. In 1981 the Nationality Act changed the definition of Commonwealth citizens, who became British overseas citizens with no specific rights of abode. Apparently this was to bring nationality law more in line with immigration law, which Nicol[35] describes as a case of tail wagging dog. Since 1981, right of abode has been restricted to British citizens and citizens of the Commonwealth who established patriality before the act came into effect in 1983. EC nationals have right of entry under EC law, but in respect of opening its borders to those in gravest need, the United Kingdom has consistently failed to meet international standards.

Similar complications pertaining to inclusion and exclusion exist elsewhere. One of the fears often raised within the (often ill-informed) public debate on the asylum question concerns national identity – but what, precisely, constitutes an 'authentic' national identity? Indeed, the sources of such an identity vary from country to country. Habermas makes the point that, in France, it developed within an existing territorial space, while in Germany it was constructed through a specific, imaginary, bourgeois ideal of the nation. Indeed, in Germany, a distinction continues to be made between *Deutschen* (German citizens of German descent), *Reichdeutschen* (German citizens of non-German descent), and *Volkdeutschen* (non-German citizens of German descent).[36]

The relationship between refugees and citizenship is unclear because the very term *citizenship* is contested. The Western liberal tradition presupposes that citizenship is a form of contract between an individual and a state, in respect of certain corresponding and reciprocal *rights* and *duties*. The presumption, of course, is that these rights and duties are protected and carried out within the confines of a particular territory, a *nation-state*, over which the state in question has powers of administration. However, if we study the history of this term we will see that citizenship need not be such a contract at all, and that it certainly need not be limited territorially to a nation-state. Indeed, the idea of the nation-state, which dominates our maps of the world, is a modern one, and is easily predated by the discourse on citizenship which, understood in terms of membership and participation within a political community, can be traced back to the ancient Greeks.[37] The borders which divide nation-states are necessarily fictions, constructions, with no more right to claim authenticity than any other model for dividing up the continents. Very often, political discussions on the legitimacy of territorial boundaries are conflated with cultural discussions over 'race' and ethnicity. It is not difficult to see how citizenship is often used as a device for *exclusion*, and how that exclusion is often ethnic or racial.

That these boundaries are transient fictions – something that has become increasingly evident with the unstable events in Eastern Europe since the end of the Cold War – indicates that citizenship is also a transient fiction, dependent upon time and place, and often regulated by a dominant ideology. This instability results not only in problems of definition but of practice, as the UNHCR has observed:

After the dissolution of the Soviet Union and Czechoslovakia and the break-up of Yugoslavia, millions of people needed to confirm a new citizenship status. Was a former Czechoslovak citizen now Czech or Slovak? Was someone born in Belgrade, raised in Sarajevo, now married to someone from Zagreb, and living in Ljubliana a Yugoslav, Bosnian, Croat or Slovene citizen? New states emerging from these dissolutions established their own criteria for citizenship. In some cases, people who did not meet those criteria became 'stateless'; in other cases they failed to acquire citizenship where they lived.[38]

The world is conveniently divided into territories which are governed by political administrations, each of which claims the right to enforce laws within its boundaries and, by extension, holds the responsibility for protecting the rights of its citizens. For sure, not all stateless persons are refugees, but like refugees, they lack recourse to the protection provided by citizenship. Which state is responsible for protecting the rights of the stateless? Without such protection, they remain noncitizens and therefore, turning once more to Arendt's illuminating observations, outside the remit even of *human* rights regulation.

Refugees and border controls

To reiterate, borders which separate nation-states are convenient fictions. Yet the governments of those states go to great lengths to monitor who crosses them, and often insist on proof of identity, in the form of a passport or a visa. They presume, therefore, the fixity and legitimacy of these borders. Contemporary debates over globalisation, which highlight stark inequalities in who does and who does not have the power to travel freely between borders, allow us to reconsider these assumptions as academics as well as activists, not to mention travellers. But these debates are not solely academic. Indeed, the most significant challenge to the legitimacy of any nation-state's right to maintain such control over travel and the crossing of borders came with the signing of the UDHR in 1948; Article 13 (2) states – in rather ambiguous fashion – that 'everyone has the right to leave any country, including his own, and to return to his country'.

It may seem far-fetched of me to suggest that this Article challenges the legitimacy of travel documents or border controls, as if these travel documents and border controls are in themselves violations of human rights. Certainly, no state has ever interpreted the Article in this way and gone on to abolish passports or border checks on the basis of it, even though 80 national constitutions, international covenants and the UDHR all affirm the right to freedom of movement. We have already seen how the UK government insists on all asylum-seekers possessing valid entry documents. Similarly, the US Immigration and Nationality Act of 1952 states quite clearly that anyone who enters or leaves the United States must have a valid passport.[39] And yet, in my own work, I have attempted to say precisely this, that nation-state passports and border controls *are* indeed violations of human rights.[40]

This is not a new idea. It was with refugees and stateless persons in mind that the idea of a *world passport* first came about. Shortly after the First World War, Fridtjof Nansen, Norway's delegate to the League of Nations, suggested the idea of the first non-national passport for refugees and stateless persons (mainly White Russians); this 'Nansen Passport' became the first international travel document. Nansen himself became the League of Nations High Commissioner for Refugees, and established the precursor organ to the United Nations High Commissioner on Refugees. With so many other priorities for the UNHCR to concentrate on, the idea of the passport faded into history. However, it was revived shortly after the Second World War by a radically different organisation, the World Government of World Citizens (WGWC).

This organisation came into being on 4 September 1953 in Ellsworth, Maine. Its founder was Garry Davis. In 1948, in Paris, Garry Davis had surrendered his US national citizenship and declared himself a citizen of the world. Instantly, he posed a challenge to the French authorities whose soil he was on at the time. He had no passport, and no visa, and no recognised citizenship – so what were they to do with him? After attracting considerable media attention, Davis returned to the USA and began his adventures around the world, carrying only a passport proclaiming him to be a citizen of the world. Border control officials were by and large confused by this – a passport, it is commonly held, attaches the bearer to a nation-state, a recognised territory on the world map. Nevertheless, Davis used his passport to gain entry to a number of countries, each of which stamped its pages or presented him with a visa.

Davis was not merely playing a practical joke at the expense of bewildered border officials. He was making a very serious political point. He argued that *because* nation-state borders are fictions, and *because* we are all born citizens of the world, border controls are technically illegal, and he wanted to show up their hypocrisy. Freedom of movement, freedom to travel, Davis claimed, is the most basic of rights, because it represents freedom to escape from persecution. Indeed, this is stated clearly in the Universal Declaration of Human Rights, Article 13

(2). Under the current system, numerous needy travellers are denied passports and visas. Davis and his organisation therefore distribute among these needy travellers – refugees and asylum seekers – world passports. Between 300,000 and a half a million passports have been issued. These passports duly reaffirm that right to travel, to cross borders, and serve to neutralise the power of border officials.[41] They fulfil a simple human rights need.

The first 'world passport' issued by the WGWC was released on 10 May 1954, written in English and Esperanto. In 1972, the second edition was released, and in 1975, the third edition emerged in seven languages: English, French, Spanish, Arabic, Russian, Chinese, and Esperanto. The passport has been recognized *de juris* by six governments – Burkina Faso, Ecuador, Mauritania, Tanzania, Togo, and Zambia, but *de facto* by at least 152 nation-states at one time or another. As a human rights tool, it has assisted countless refugees to cross borders otherwise closed to them. Clearly, it is a pragmatic response to the global conditions in which we live.

Border controls violate human rights in other respects. In an impassioned plea for the abolition of immigration controls, Teresa Hayter demands that 'the idea of international migration (needs) to be rescued, and enshrined in international declarations as a normal and natural human right'.[42] She suggests that by the nature of the harsh suffering they impose upon others, border controls undermine a list of human rights, including:

> the right not to be subjected to inhuman and degrading treatment, the right not to be tortured, the right not to be arbitrarily arrested and imprisoned, the right to a fair trial by a properly constituted court, the right to family life, the right to work ... Immigration controls as they are currently practised violate the provisions of several international treaties to which the British government is a signatory.[43]

Refugees and the media

Hayter's book also draws attention to a disturbing consequence of the contemporary flow of refugees across borders. She lists a number of examples of the British press perpetuating racism and stereotypical, negative images of asylum seekers through the use of sensationalist headlines. Among those she lists is a headline from the *Daily Mail* newspaper of November 1998, 'Brutal crimes of the asylum seekers', which allegedly uncovers 'the devastating impact of serious crime by asylum seekers' in a story illustrated by photographs of black criminals.[44] The following month the same newspaper 'exposed' the asylum seekers as shrewd benefit fraudsters in an article dubbed 'The good life on Asylum Alley'. In the *Mail* and other newspapers, asylum seekers are regularly described using negative, often violent, imagery and terminology, featured in headlines connecting them to riots, crime waves, disasters, and threats to the system – and the editor of one less-than-reputable national newspaper described asylum seekers in an editorial as 'human sewage' and 'the scum of the Earth'.[45]

Such racist and offensive use of language in the popular press is by no means new. Following the Boer War in South Africa, a number of refugees were granted passage to England on the transport *Cheshire*, paid for through the generosity of the Lord Mayor's Fund. The *Daily Mail* ran a malicious piece, attacking the large number of Jewish refugees on board as if they were not genuine refugees:

> They fought and jostled for the foremost places at the gang-ways; they rushed and pushed and struggled into the troopshed, where the Mayor of Southampton ... had provided free refreshments ... They fought for places on the train ... the women and children were left to take their chances unaided ... Then, incredible as it may seem, the moment they were in the carriages they began to gamble ... [t]hese ... penniless refugees and when the Relief Committee passed by they hid their gold and fawned and whined, and, in broken English, asked for money for their train fare.[46]

This demonisation of the Jewish refugees was then juxtaposed with the respect paid towards the Englishmen who were also on board the *Cheshire*, and who had also been forced to flee South Africa:

> One man, with scarcely a rag of warm clothing on him, whose only asset was a tin of sandwiches, admitted he was dead broke, but refused to take a half-penny. These men stood by each other in a proud, shame-faced sort of way, and looked on in silence ...[47]

Although the *Mail* has been targeted in these extracts, it is by no means the only perpetrator, nor is the problem restricted only to the national press. Kushner and Knox draw attention to the different positions adopted by the various newspapers on the arrival of Polish refugees in the aftermath of the Second World War:

> Communist and left-wing papers such as the *Daily Worker* and *Tribune* tended to be hostile to the Poles, viewing them as pro-fascist, while Catholic papers were more sympathetic as were the *Manchester Guardian*, *The Scotsman* and *Yorkshire Post*. The popular press, especially the *Daily Mirror*, tended to stir up opposition, while *The Times* showed greater ambiguity.[48]

Local newspapers – particularly in middle-class, Conservative-voting heartlands – often feel obliged to reflect the views of their local readers and uphold the exclusivity of their areas against unwelcome newcomers. Media responses of this kind are not uncommon, and are not applied only to asylum seekers. Many studies have shown how matters of 'race' and ethnicity are usually only covered in the media when associated with negative issues such as violence, conflict and crime, and rarely in respect of structural inequalities.[49] One of the most widely discussed topics within which issues of 'race' are mentioned is, and has always been, immigration.[50] In this respect, both 'race' and immigration are treated as *problems*. The coverage of asylum seekers in the media is thus conflated with such coverage of 'race' and subsumed within a wider programme aimed at problematising difference and 'Otherness'. Needless to say, the media are highly effective in framing public opinion on and mobilising opposition to asylum seekers. They are instrumental in the creation of a moral panic which necessarily serves the ideological interests of the state, which by its own logic is resistant to homogeneity and pluralism. According to Stan Cohen:

> Societies appear to be subject, now and then, to periods of moral panic. A condition, episode, person or group of persons emerges to become defined as a threat to societal values or interests; its nature is presented in a stylised and stereotypical fashion by the mass media; the moral barricades are manned by editors, bishops, politicians and other right-thinking people; socially accredited experts pronounce their diagnoses and solutions; ways of coping are evolved or (more often) resorted to; the condition then disappears, submerges or deteriorates and becomes more visible. Sometimes the object of the panic is quite novel and at

other times it is something which has been in existence long enough, but suddenly appears in the limelight. Sometimes the panic is passed over and is forgotten, except in folklore and collective memory; at other times it has more serious and long-lasting repercussions and might produce such changes as those in legal or social policy or even in the way society conceives itself.[51]

The experience of displacement

So far, we have touched upon the lived *experience* of refugees in objective fashion. We have discussed it in respect of citizenship, pointing out the harsh truth that for many refugees arriving in the UK, the initial experience is one of detention. We have also intimated that for many refugees the experience is one of fear, thanks largely to media irresponsibility in producing moral panics and instigating the threat of violence. These experiences are not confined to the contemporary situation – throughout the twentieth century groups of refugees in Britain were segregated from the host population.[52] At the same time, other groups have been integrated, even naturalised.[53] The history of the experience of displacement is not a uniform one.

Take, as one example, the experiences of Basque children fleeing the Spanish Civil War, who arrived in Britain in 1937. Kushner and Knox tell how these children were well received by their concerned new guardians, and housed within a camp which contained its own cinema, showers, toilets, concert stage and telephones.[54] They were visited by celebrities and politicians. Nevertheless, there were problems. Communication was difficult as the children spoke no English and the translators spoke poor Spanish, never mind Basque. Also, regulations demanded that the camp be divided into two sections, one for those who had already been decontaminated and given new clothes, and one for those still to undergo that treatment; subsequent distinctions were made along the lines of religion and parents' political affiliation. These divisions caused resentment, according to the historians and their sources, and resulted in some distrust of the camp authorities.[55]

In general, the refugee camps – often made-over RAF or army bases – were 'self-contained communities, with their own canteens, clinics and nurseries in addition to schools on the premises. English classes were provided for all those who wished to attend . . .'[56] Nevertheless, regardless of the social and functional amenities provided for the refugees, it would be difficult to see the camps as anything more than ghettos, designed to keep the alien population firmly segregated from wider society. This image continues to this day, and is a source of considerable unease among those pointing out the possible hypocrisy in 'humanitarian' decisions to welcome refugees into the UK.

Additional problems faced later refugee communities, such as the Ugandan Asians who arrived in Britain, fleeing Idi Amin's dictatorship in the early 1970s. Being people of colour, they faced not only the barrier of language, the difficulties in acclimatising to a new way of life, and the difficulties in finding work. They faced the added torment of racist abuse. However, the Ugandan Asians did have kinship and community networks already resident in cities such as London and Leicester to rely upon. The Vietnamese refugees arriving a decade later faced the prospect of building such a community from scratch – not an easy task in the face of economic, social, and racist hardship. Kushner and Knox cite one Vietnamese teenager:

> My parents are lonely. They just stay at home and learn English from the TV programme. My family are not happy to live there. We like [to] live in a noisy crowded city. We sat and cried when we came here. There was nothing.[57]

For refugees, entitlements to work have always proved controversial. Despite generally sympathetic feelings towards, for example, refugees from the Soviet-occupied states of Eastern Europe, many British residents have expressed concern at government-sponsored projects to provide work for the displaced, particularly where work was scarce. This problem is not limited to the UK. But herein lies one of the most depressing traits of the experience of displacement. Many of the refugees are, of course, skilled and professional people in their homelands. They have been forced to leave behind not only their possessions, their homes and their money, but also their dignity and their standing in society. Where work is made available to them, it is usually only of the most menial kind. Thus, the experience of displacement is an experience of the stripping of identity. One is no longer a doctor, a teacher, or a father able to support his children. One is merely 'a refugee', as if such a category is homogeneous. By classifying people of such diverse backgrounds into such a misleading category, we simply reaffirm those stereotypes, perpetuated in the media, which present refugees as members of an underclass. In so far as class analysis is based primarily on financial resources, this is in part reality, but by reducing all human qualities to material possessions and *using that as the basis of categorising members of a society into a hierarchy*, we duly construct the refugee as someone wretched, an object of pity, someone less fortunate but also less important than us – someone *less than human*.

These problems intensified during the late 1980s and into the 1990s, as European nation-states began to close their borders. Kurdish refugees had a particularly difficult time adapting to life in Britain, once again experiencing the racism and the problems of language. These problems were only made worse by their experiences of torture in Iraq or Turkey. Similarly, escapees from the conflicts in the former Yugoslavia were met with considerable suspicion by their new hosts, based in part on a misguided essentialist belief in the violence inherent in the nature of those from the Balkans. Of course, another reason for these negative welcomes was the increasingly misunderstood distinction being made by politicians and media spokespersons between 'political' and 'economic' refugees. Complications arising from the blurring of national boundaries and identities created even more problems. And, of course, one of the worst problems faced by the displaced is *not knowing*, not being able to communicate with loved ones back home, a general feeling of *powerlessness* which is often misrepresented by the media as the *weakness* of victims. One Ugandan asylum seeker makes an interesting point in respect of how refugees are usually treated by their host populations:

> Contrary to what I believed in Uganda, a refugee is not just a person who has been displaced and has lost all or most of his possessions. A refugee is in fact more akin to a child: helpless, devoid of initiative, somebody on whom any kind of charity can be practised; in short, a totally malleable creature.[58]

This analogy between a refugee and a child is apposite, because like refugees, children are often excluded from the discourse of human rights. Both groups are seen as subject to frailty and dependence. Neither is given credit for creativity, for humanity. None of these problems is assisted by the UK government's inability to recognise that human rights are applicable to asylum seekers as well as its own citizens. Earlier in this chapter, we encountered moving testimonies of asylum seekers detained upon their arrival in the country. Another such experience – by no means uncommon – was had by one asylum seeker from Zaire, describing his time in Haslar, a refugee camp 80 miles from London:

During my stay in Haslar I found the situation like being jailed for life. Nobody informed me about the progress of my case; no court recommended me to be detained; I was only told I was not entitled to bail rights. All I could do was sit and wait. Some of us chose hunger strikes as a means to draw attention to our plight; others saw suicide as a way out of their predicament... The ordeal of my detention has not been easy to recover from. After being released I can say the compensation is not enough even to release me from nightmares about what I had undergone...[59]

These terrible stories contribute to our understanding of the experience of displacement from the point of view of those who manage to cross borders and find refuge in another country. Disturbing though they are, they at least provide some comfort for us, in the knowledge that the escapees had found asylum of sorts. The experience of displacement for many never reaches that stage. Too many perish during the escape. For many refugees the ordeal of escaping across a border is the most traumatic experience of displacement. As I come to finish this chapter, the ordeal is being experienced by thousands of Afghans seeking refuge across the Pakistan border. A report in the *Guardian* newspaper describes this experience with some feeling:

Thousands of Afghan refugees fleeing allied attacks yesterday swarmed across the Pakistani border amid chaotic scenes, which aid agencies warned were likely to get worse. Families without water and food tramped over mountains to safety in a new surge which is expected to become a flood if Pakistan officially opens its border. More than 3,500 people, most of them women and children from the heavily bombed city of Kandahar, arrived in the southern Pakistani town of Chaman after the host authorities appeared to open the frontier temporarily for humanitarian reasons...

Those who failed to make it into Pakistan have swollen overcrowded villages in the countryside, with some mud houses now containing four families. Such conditions could breed variations of polio...

An even grimmer picture emerged from the former Soviet republic of Tajikistan, north of Afghanistan, where children in drought-hit areas have dug out rat holes to steal back the grain hoarded by rats.[60]

The state, refugees and human rights

From the initial crisis in post-war Europe, through the Cold War and the decolonisation struggles, to the contemporary 'identity-based conflicts built around religion, ethnicity, nationality, race, clan, language or region', the nature of the refugee problem has altered dramatically during the second half of the twentieth century.[61] The current wars are more often than not being fought out not between but within nation-states, and processes of genocide, ethnic cleansing, and territorial division are intimately connected to the destabilisation of national identities associated with globalisation. Ethnic groups spanning vast regions and crossing nation-state borders challenge the presumed authenticity of those borders, and the cultures they purport to sustain. If processes of globalisation threaten these borders in all walks of life, they are particularly challenging for those concerned with the plight of refugees, as the UNHCR recognises:

> The current structure of refugee protection was designed in and for a state-centric system. Under the terms of the 1951 UN Refugee Convention, a refugee is a person who cannot avail himself or herself of the protection of his or her own state, and who has crossed an international boundary marking the limits of the sovereign territory of that state. One is forced to question the relevance of notions such as sovereignty and national frontiers as states lose much of their ability to control what crosses their borders as well as what goes on within them.[62]

According to Jürgen Habermas, the contemporary refugee crisis is the result of the global economic imbalance, between the richer nations of the West and the poorer ones of the South and East.[63] Certainly, there has been a significant transformation in the conditions which result in the mobilisation of refugees, from political causes such as flight from repression to economic and environmental ones which reflect the structural imbalance in the world economic system. Habermas suggests that the only way to 'cure' this crisis is through the establishment of competitive economic systems in these parts of the world, the prospects for which are not good.[64] In other words, it is time for the international political community to adopt a more structural approach, to deal not with the refugee crisis in isolation, but with its intrinsic relationship to other human rights concerns, including political oppression, civil war, and poverty, and to environmental concerns as well.

As with the other human rights concerns discussed in this volume, refugee crises are global crises but, although there are United Nations organs like the UNHCR and transnational social movements ready and willing to assist with their plight, in many respects ultimate responsibility falls upon the state. As I have discussed elsewhere, border controls exist to uphold the division and exclusion which are the chief political project of modernity.[65] This undermines the alternative project which celebrates the emancipatory potential of freedom of movement and identification. Passports, flags and other symbols of national identity and identification are weapons of symbolic violence, designed to perpetuate this divisive project of the state through the appropriation of the cultural sphere.[66] At the same time, refugees, by the very act of fleeing one state and seeking protection from another, alien one, deny the Hobbesian principles upon which nation-states are built. As fellow humans, citizens of the world, we should not, morally, object to granting them safe haven, and yet to do so causes numerous problems. Without citizenship status, they are effectively – as Arendt pointed out – denied even the status of humans, because they are denied a voice in the political community. Yet the granting of such a status carries with it additional implications, not least for the economy of the nation-state in question. While human life can never be reduced to the level of economics, it is important to recognise this, because we know from experience or observations that a large influx of refugees can easily be met with violence by members of the host population. While some of this violence may be racist in nature, much of it and other types of negative reception are driven by fear over the possible redistribution of scarce resources. They are also driven, sadly, by the negative portrayal of refugees in the media, including the reproduction of stereotypical images. These issues should concern us all, as social scientists, as activists, and as people.

Essay questions

1. What are the main obstacles facing refugees and asylum seekers as they attempt to flee persecution in their home countries? Discuss with reference to the academic and legal literature on refugees.

2. What does Hannah Arendt mean when she says that human rights are only meaningful if you are recognised as human? What might this mean for the plight of refugees?

3. Why is the problem of refugees a peculiarly modern crisis?

4. Discuss the charge that passports and border controls are violations of the basic human right to travel.

Notes

1   Hannah Arendt (2000) *The Portable Hannah Arendt*, ed. Peter Baehr, London: Penguin, p. 34, reproduced from Arendt (1951) *The Origins of Totalitarianism*.

2   *Portable Hannah Arendt*, p. 36, reproduced from *Origins*.

3   *Portable Hannah Arendt*, p. 37.

4   *Portable Hannah Arendt*, p. 37.

5   United Nations Treaty, 28 July 1958: 'The 1951 United Nations Convention Relating to the Status of Refugees', 189, 2545, p. 137.

6   Refugee Council statistics, taken from www.refugeecouncil.org.uk.

7   Refugee Council, www.refugeecouncil.org.uk.

8   UNHCR statistics on www.unhcr.ch.

9   Refugee Council statistics on www.refugeecouncil.org.uk.

10   UNHCR statistics on www.unhcr.ch.

11   US Committee for Refugees (2001) *World Refugee Survey 2000*, Washington; reproduced in United Nations High Commissioner for Refugees (2000) *State of the World's Refugees: Fifty Years of Humanitarian Action*, Oxford: Oxford University Press, p. 215.

12   *Portable Hannah Arendt*, p. 35, reproduced from *Origins*.

13   Hugo Gryn, quoted in Tony Kushner and Katharine Knox (1999) *Refugees in an Age of Genocide*, London: Frank Cass, p. 1.

14   Eric Hobsbawm (1994) *The Age of Extremes: The Short Twentieth Century 1914–1991*, Harmondsworth: Penguin, p. 51.

15   Hobsbawm, *Age of Extremes*, p. 51; references and citations from Eugene M. Kulischer (1948) *Europe on the Move: War and Population Changes 1917–1947*, New York: Columbia University Press, pp. 253–73; Louis W. Holborn (1968) 'Refugees I: World Problems' in *International Encyclopedia of the Social Sciences* vol. XIII, p. 363; Wolfgang Jacobmeyer (1985) *Vom Zwangsarbiter zum heimatlosen Ausländer: Die Displaced Persons in Westdeutschland, 1945–1951*, Gottingen: Vandenhoeck & Ruprecht.

16   UNHCR, *State of the World's Refugees*.

17   UNHCR, *State of the World's Refugees*, p. 13.

18 UNHCR, *State of the World's Refugees*, p. 37.

19 UNHCR, *State of the World's Refugees*, p. 47.

20 UNHCR, *State of the World's Refugees*, p. 52.

21 UNHCR, *State of the World's Refugees*, p. 61.

22 UNHCR, *State of the World's Refugees*, p. 79.

23 Gil Loescher (1999) 'Refugees: A Global Human Rights and Security Crisis' in Tim Dunne and Nicholas J. Wheeler (eds) *Human Rights in Global Politics*, Cambridge: Cambridge University Press.

24 UNHCR, *State of the World's Refugees*, p. 133.

25 UNHCR, *State of the World's Refugees*, p. 151.

26 UNHCR, *State of the World's Refugees*, p. 119.

27 UNHCR, *State of the World's Refugees*, p. 160.

28 UNHCR, *State of the World's Refugees*, p. 251.

29 The UN Declaration ensures their rights to life, free of danger and hunger, and to seek asylum in any country, although it is worth pointing out that no country is *obliged* to give asylum.

30 Statistics taken from UNHCR Refugee Statistics, 1998 Overview at http://www.unhcr.ch/statist/980view/ch1.htm.

31 Jürgen Habermas (1994) *The Past as Future*, translated by Max Pensky, Cambridge: Polity Press, p. 123.

32 Richard Dunstan, 'Cell Culture' in *Amnesty*, Jan. / Feb. 1997, p. 13.

33 Jan Shaw, 'Beyond these castle walls' in *New Internationalist*, June 1993, p. 12.

34 Andrew Nicol (1993) 'Nationality and Migration' in Robert Blackburn (ed.) *Rights of Citizenship*, London: Mansell Publishing, p. 266.

35 Nicol, 'Nationality and Migration', p. 266.

36 Habermas, *The Past as Future*, p. 132.

37 On which, see Darren J. O'Byrne (2002, forthcoming) *The Dimensions of Global Citizenship*, London: Frank Cass; Derek Heater (1996) *World Citizenship and Government: Cosmopolitan Ideas in the History of Western Political Thought*, London: Macmillan; Gerard Delanty (2000) *Citizenship in a Global Age: Society, Culture, Politics*, Buckingham: Open University Press.

38 UNHCR, *State of the World's Refugees*, p. 189.

39 Garry Davis with Greg Guma (1992) *Passport to Freedom: A Guide for World Citizens*, Cabin John, MD: Seven Locks Press, p. 61.

40   See O'Byrne, *Dimensions of Global Citizenship*; Darren J. O'Byrne (2001) 'On Passports and Border Controls' in *Annals of Tourism Research* 28, 2, pp. 399–416.

41   David Gallup, representing WGWC, in a personal interview, 24 July 1996.

42   Teresa Hayter (2000) *Open Borders: The Case Against Immigration Controls*, London: Pluto Press, p. 151.

43   Hayter, *Open Borders*, p. 149.

44   Hayter, *Open Borders*, p. 30.

45   Hayter, *Open Borders*, p. 30.

46   'So-Called Refugees' in the *Daily Mail*, 3 February 1900; quoted in Kushner and Knox, *Refugees*, p. 23.

47   'So-Called Refugees', in Kushner and Knox, *Refugees*, p. 23.

48   Kushner and Knox, *Refugees*, p. 235.

49   For example, P. Hartmann (1974) 'Race as News' in J.D. Halloran (ed.) *Race as News*, Paris: UNESCO.

50   B. Troyna (1981) *Public Awareness and the Media: A Study of Reporting Race*, London: Commission for Racial Equality.

51   Stan Cohen (1972) *Folk Devils and Moral Panics: The Creation of the Mods and Rockers*, London: MacGibbon & Kee, p. 28; cited in Stuart Hall, Chas Critcher, Tony Jefferson, John Clarke, and Brian Roberts (1978) *Policing the Crisis: Mugging, the State, and Law and Order*, Basingstoke: Macmillan, pp. 16–17.

52   Kushner and Knox, *Refugees*, p. 5.

53   Kushner and Knox, *Refugees*, p. 5, drawing on John Hope Simpson (1939) *The Refugee Problem: Report of a Survey*, London: Oxford University Press, p. 339.

54   Kushner and Knox, *Refugees*, pp. 112–13.

55   Kushner and Knox, *Refugees*, pp. 113, 117–18.

56   Kushner and Knox, *Refugees*, p. 232, referring to the camps established for Polish refugees fleeing the Soviet occupation.

57   Felicity Edholm, Helen Roberts and Judith Sayer (1983) *Vietnamese Refugees in Britain*, London: Commission for Racial Equality, p. 16; cited in Kushner and Knox, *Refugees*, p. 320.

58   From Mahmood Mamdani (1973) *From Citizen to Refugee: Ugandan Asians Come to Britain*, London: Francis Pinter; cited in Kushner and Knox, *Refugees*, p. 406.

59 From Mark Ashford (1993) *Detained Without Trial: A Survey of Immigration Act Detention*, London: Joint Council for the Welfare of Immigrants, pp. 58–61; cited in Kushner and Knox, *Refugees*, p. 382.

60 Rory Carroll (2001) 'Border Chaos After Refugee Surge' in the *Guardian*, Saturday, 20 October, p. 5.

61 UNHCR, *State of the World's Refugees*, p. 275.

62 UNHCR, *State of the World's Refugees*, p. 276.

63 Habermas, *The Past as Future*, p. 122.

64 Habermas, *The Past as Future*, p. 122.

65 O'Byrne, *Dimensions of Global Citizenship*.

66 O'Byrne, 'On Passports'.

Further information

Books

Most of the topics, and the various crises, mentioned here are discussed in far greater depth in the United Nations High Commissioner for Refugees publication *The State of the World's Refugees: Fifty Years of Humanitarian Action* (Oxford: Oxford University Press, 2000). Students are also directed towards the fascinating historical account of refugees – the continuity of whose stories and experiences is cleverly maintained through an emphasis on a particular county in the south of England, Hampshire – provided by Tony Kushner and Katharine Knox, *Refugees in an Age of Genocide* (London: Frank Cass, 1999).

Websites

The United Nations High Commissioner for Refugees website is at www.unhcr.ch. The website of the Refugee Council is at www.refugeecouncil.org.uk. Both contain a rich combination of statistics, geographical and historical detail, and personal case studies.

Conclusion

New directions in human rights research

In this volume we have concentrated on some of the most prominent violations of civil and political rights in the world today. We have discussed them both as violations in themselves, perpetrated by the state or its agents, and as objects of social science research. Of course, we have left many areas untouched. We have not, for example, dealt with the rights of specific groups – children, women, and so on. Where it has been appropriate, we have incorporated relevant discussion of these groups into the suitable substantive chapter. Sometimes we have excluded key issues in human rights research because the violations themselves lie somewhere outside the state sector. This has been done to maintain continuity and focus, and not to suggest that such issues are not human rights concerns.

In this conclusion, we will look at some violations which are specific to certain groups in society. We will also look at some of those violations which are not, as yet, in the mainstream of human rights research, primarily because they are not carried out directly by the state, and which have not, for this reason, been given their own space in this book. These constitute new directions in human rights research, drawing us away from a state-centric perspective. Whether this is helpful, or whether it leads us into more confused terrain, remains to be seen. One thing is certain. The atrocities discussed in this concluding chapter – female genital mutilation, child labour, poverty, and so on – are most certainly human rights violations, whether one approaches the subject from a philosophical or an institutional-legal perspective. Also, in so far as they redirect our focus away from states and towards cultural and economic systems, they require us to make reference to the role played by such non-state actors as transnational corporations in promoting human rights worldwide.

Women and human rights

The inclusion of women's rights as a category of human rights is not, of course, a recent development in the field. The United Nations Convention on the Elimination of All Forms of Discrimination Against Women was adopted in December 1979 (it secured 130 votes in favour, none against, and ten abstentions) and became law in September 1981. However, earlier campaigners and commentators may have felt that the category of 'woman' was implicit in that of 'human'. With hindsight, it is easy for us to criticise the naivety of this assumption. Although feminists have criticised the gender-blindness of much universalistic theory,[1] human rights research has in practice always been aware of the specific abuses directed at women. In Chapter Five we discussed rape as a form of torture, while the political and social exclusion of women was analysed in Chapter Seven. Both examples constitute violations of traditional civil and political rights. In addition, women often suffer guilt by association, imprisoned, tortured and even killed simply because their (male) associates or relatives are believed by governments to be involved in political opposition groups.[2]

The 1979 Convention is primarily concerned with establishing equality and condemning discrimination on the basis of sex. It covers such general human rights concerns such as the right to vote and participate in political procedures (Articles 7 and 8); the right to acquire, change or retain a nationality (Article 9); the right to equality in education (Article 10); employment (Article 11); healthcare (Article 12); and economic and social life (Article 13). Article 15 states succinctly that 'States Parties shall accord to women equality with men before the law'. Very little that is included in the Convention, and is applied therein to the particular case of women, stands outside the more general framework of rights already in existence in the Universal Declaration and the 1966 Covenants. However, one important demand is made in Article 5 (a), which requires states to take all appropriate measures:

> To modify the social and cultural patterns of conduct of men and women, with a view to achieving the elimination of prejudices and customary and all other practices which are based on the idea of the inferiority or the superiority of either of the sexes or on stereotypical roles for men and women.

This rather innocuous passage seems at first to be saying much of the same, but contained therein is an important additional recognition

– that the rights of women are very often violated not in the civil and political sphere but in the realm of culture, of customs and practices. In so far as the discourse on human rights has struggled for some time with the inclusion of abuses which take place within the non-state (specifically, the cultural) sector, various areas of concern which are specific to women have served to highlight the need to intellectually incorporate these abuses within the wider framework. Indeed, among the many important issues raised by the feminist critique of human rights is that the traditional discourse maintains the distinction between state and non-state, between public and private.[3] This volume, one could argue, is no different. However, I have so far presented an overview of the traditional field, and this conclusion provides a space for a number of significant criticisms which could be made of that field, including the feminist one. In this section, I will outline some of the main developments and arguments pertinent to two such concerns: female genital mutilation and *sati*. Both atrocities highlight the extent to which human rights violations specific to women are often targeted at the body of the woman. The same is true of a third violation discussed below, which is more of a political practice than a cultural one, and that is the practice of forced sterilisation.

Female genital mutilation

Female genital mutilation[4] (FGM) is the term used to describe the removal of part, or all, of the female genitalia. It is a practice common to many parts of the world. It takes place extensively in many African countries by different ethnic groups; among Muslim populations in Oman, North and South Yemen, Bahrain, Qatar, Saudi Arabia, the United Arab Emirates, Indonesia, Sri Lanka, Malaysia, India, and Pakistan; among various indigenous groups in parts of Peru, Colombia, Brazil, and Mexico; and among Ethiopian Jewish Falashasas in Israel.[5] Although the extent of the practice is difficult to measure, it is believed by the World Health Organization that over 135 million girls and women are genitally mutilated in Africa alone, with some 2 million girls each year at risk from having to endure the procedure.[6] Global migration has resulted in the spread of the practice to parts of Europe, Australia, and North America, where it is sometimes performed illegally by doctors from within the ethnic community.

There are three main categories of FGM: clitoridectomy, excision, and infibulation.[7] Clitoridectomy involves the removal of the prepuce, or hood, which protects the clitoris. It is the least severe, and least common, form of FGM, and the only one which can truly be called 'circumcision'.

Excision is the removal of the prepuce, the clitoris itself, and all or parts of the labia minora. Some 80 per cent of FGMs practised in Africa involve some form of excision.[8] Infibulation is the most severe form of mutilation, and involves the removal of the prepuce, the whole of the labia minora and majora. The two sides of the vulva are then stitched together using thorns, leaving a very small opening preserved by a tiny piece of wood or reed to permit the flow of urine and menstrual blood. This form of mutilation is practised on up to 15 per cent of the girls and women of Africa.[9]

The age at which the FGM is carried out differs across cultures, from a few days old through to adolescence. The most common age is between four and eight, at which girls are less likely to resist the procedure or be aware of it and try to run away, and at which it is believed the pain is easier to forget.[10] In most cases, no anaesthetic is available to numb the pain, and the girl is held down by up to three adults while the surgeon carries out the operation.[11] An infibulated woman is expected to remain sewn up until her wedding night when the husband either opens her up with a dagger or is expected to force his way in with his penis. According to Jacques Lantier:

> ...the husband should have prolonged and repeated intercourse with her during eight days. This 'work' is in order to 'make' an opening by preventing the scar from closing again. During these eight days, the woman remains lying down and moves as little as possible in order to keep the wound open. The morning after the wedding night, the husband puts his bloody dagger on his shoulder and makes the rounds in order to obtain general admiration.[12]

Anthropological studies have traditionally, misleadingly, treated FGM as the female equivalent of male circumcision, and compared to the large-scale collective ceremonies associated with male circumcision, the more individualistic and less elaborate practice of FGM might have appeared somewhat tame.[13] As individuals and campaigning organisations began to take an interest in the practice (the United Nations paid some attention to it during its Decade for Women 1975–1985, and non-governmental organisations discussed it at the Copenhagen Forum in 1980), so did academics, although initial studies found the secrecy and taboo surrounding the event difficult to penetrate. Certainly, gender-based violence was only just beginning to receive attention as a human rights issue.[14] They did, however, reveal its complexity and its relationship to wider issues of repression and control over female sexuality.

FGM is justified according to cultural and belief systems, religion, myth, and superstition. Muslim justifications for the practice are usually based on a Koranic reading which suggests that the non-excised woman is 'impure'. However, there is considerable disagreement within the Muslim community over this interpretation, and many leading Muslim countries no longer observe the practice. In many African countries the practice is justified according to superstitious fears about the terrible consequences of not conforming to tradition. Other societies believe that the clitoris is a dangerous organ with the power to kill a man on penetration, or that the female sexual organs are ugly, or that a non-infibulated woman cannot conceive, or that the practice cures women of 'illnesses' such as hysteria or 'excessive' masturbation.[15] Anthropological readings of the practice have understood it as a rite of passage into adulthood, surrounded by elaborate celebrations,[16] but as the age of mutilation has lowered, so has any pretence towards this meaning.

In reality, other factors influence the practice, notably class position, education level, individual consciousness about rights, and economic independence.[17] Above all, the vast majority of ethnic groups which practise FGM are male-dominated: women are born into a subservient position, and are socialised to accept a role of domestic and sexual submissiveness.[18] Only through marriage do women gain access to land and resources. The position of women is one of complete dependency on a husband for economic survival, and so a woman must go to whatever lengths are necessary to make her a suitable bride, including enduring FGM. This would guarantee her virginity, which is considered an absolute prerequisite for marriage. Sexual activity is for the purpose of procreation only, and sexual desires, particularly among girls and women, must be controlled. FGM thus serves as an instrument for systemic or structural control, maintaining power over the bodies and identities of women. In this respect, it clearly violates Article 5 of the 1979 Convention, and is a serious concern for human rights scholars and activists.

Sati

Another such concern is the persistence of the practice of *suttee* or *sati*, the ritual suicide (self-immolation) of widows – *sati* actually means 'good woman' – on the funeral pyres of their husbands. Although illegal – it was prohibited by law in Bengal in 1829 by the British governor, William Bentinck – this has been defended as traditional practice by many upper-caste Hindus, particularly in Rajasthan. Feminists have raised concerns about how this brutal practice rationalised deep-rooted misogyny and violence, and how it benefits economic interests (the widow cannot become an economic burden, money can be saved on property, and even made on the shrine). The publication of an important book by Radha Kumar,[19] and the controversy surrounding the death of Roop Kanwar in 1987, have resulted in the mobilisation of anti-*sati* sentiment.

> Roop Kanwar had brought a large amount of gold in her dowry and had only been married for six months before her husband, who was suffering from mental disorder, died. Roop Kanwar's in-laws decided she would become *sati* – and did not inform her parents.
>
> The evidence that feminist organizations gathered pointed to murder: some of her neighbours said she had run away and tried to hide before the ceremony, but was dragged out, pumped full of drugs, dressed in bridal finery and put on her husband's funeral pyre. The feminists held counter-demonstrations along the route of the procession and were confronted by groups of hostile women, who had appropriated the language of rights, stating that they should have the right, as Hindus and as women, to commit, worship and practice *sati*.[20]

Cases like this remind us of a number of things. First, like the burning of witches at the stake (although as a means of celebrating virtue rather than punishing vice), this is a horrible, gruesome, painful practice. Second, while it appears to be (like female genital mutilation) a human rights concern which occurs within the cultural sphere, it clearly crosses over into the political sphere (when the state either sanctions it or turns a blind eye to its practice) and the economic sphere (in so far as there is dowry to be gained). Third, the language of rights can be appropriated by any sides to an argument. Fourth, there are certain instances of human rights violations which are unique to women, and which reflect nothing more or less than a system which is structurally misogynistic. What is at stake in the case of *sati* is *in the first instance* an individual's right to life, but *in the second instance* the rights of the entire female population to equality, to be treated with dignity, and to existence. These violations cannot be easily divorced from one another.

Forced sterilisation

China has long faced criticism from the international community for its 'one child' policy. Forced sterilisation is often used as a means of enforcing this policy, which is a violation of personal autonomy as well as a form of bodily mutilation. The 1979 United Nations Convention on the Elimination of Discrimination Against Women states that all women are entitled to adequate healthcare facilities, including family planning, and the freedom and responsibility to decide the number and age difference of children to be had. China clearly violates this. Also, in 1985, the Chinese government agreed to ensure that fertility control methods and drugs conform to adequate standards of quality, efficiency and safety, yet the forced birth control policy contradicts these promises. In Tibet, which has suffered numerous human rights violations at the hands of the Chinese, enforced abortion contradicts the Buddhist faith of many of the victims. Women are required to obtain permits from the government before conception to allow the child to be born legally. No women under the age of 22 may have children. Women up to seven months pregnant have been injected in the stomach so that they give birth to a dead foetus. Alternatively, the doctor may squeeze the foetus manually until the woman bleeds and ultimately miscarries. Electrical devices may be inserted into the womb which mince the foetus, which is then removed. Statistics suggest that in some Tibetan villages, roughly 70 per cent of the women are sterilised as a result of this procedure.

Children and human rights

Within academic circles, children's rights are often discussed separately from human rights. This is because, perhaps paradoxically, teaching and research on children's rights often adopt a broader approach; the rights discussed within this framework are rights of citizenship, of political exclusion, the subject matter of social policy analysis. Good textbooks on the subject, such as Bob Franklin's *The Handbook of Children's Rights*, include chapters on children's rights in education and criminal justice, as well as arguments for the establishment of a Minister for Children, and the implications of important matters of policy such as the UK government's Children Act 1989.[21]

As with the case of women, and consistent with the approach adopted in this book, it is not our task here to discuss in any detail any rights which are specific to children, for such rights would necessarily fall outside of the rubric of human rights. Indeed, a key problem with the idea of children's rights lies in the definition of childhood, which of course differs across time and space. In so far as children are human and therefore subject to human rights standards, specifics of age are irrelevant. However, in some areas, including those already discussed in this book, children are *legally* prevented from exercising what would be their basic civil and political rights (problematic, if we were to accept that such rights are universal, as discussed in Chapter One). Obvious examples which spring to mind include the right to vote, work, or own property.[22] In so far as these 'liberty rights' have not been enshrined in law, more attention, in the field of children's rights, has been paid towards 'welfare rights', such as education, health, and family protection.[23]

We should, however, pay some attention to those *violations* of *human* rights which are targeted specifically at children – even if by doing so we lead ourselves once again into the quicksand of defining childhood. In addition, though, it is not always easy to make a clear distinction between the specific and the general sets of rights. Indeed, the various Conventions which make specific reference to children and childhood do not always do so, from the Geneva Declaration on the Rights of the Child 1924, through the United Nations' Declaration of the Rights of the Child 1959, to the Convention on the Rights of the Child 1989.

The 1989 Convention is the most important, because it is legally binding and implements the standards outlined in the earlier Declarations in international law. The Convention is in three parts and contains 54 Articles.[24] Many of these Articles merely uphold the general rights and freedoms applicable to all humans according to the Universal Declaration of Human Rights, such as the right to life (Article 6); the right to freedom of expression (Article 13); the right to freedom of thought and religion (Article 14); the right to association (Article 15); and the right to protection from arbitrary arrest and interference from the state (Article 16). While in some cases (such as the case of freedom of thought and religion) an additional clause empowers responsible parents or guardians to 'direct' the child in a suitable manner, for the most part these Articles are designed to clarify the obvious but often contested point that *children are human*.

Other Articles uphold more child-specific rights but have wider implications and interpretations. For example, Article 7 (which includes reference to the broader human right to a nationality) talks of the child's right to be registered after birth, to be given a name, and to know and be cared for by her or his parents. Article 8 develops this, demanding that states recognise the right of the child to *preserve* that identity, name, nationality, and family structure 'as recognised by law without unlawful interference'. Article 9 stipulates that, except in situations of abuse or neglect or where parents are separated, the child 'shall not be separated from his or her parents against their will', and Article 11 bars the 'illicit transfer and non-return of children abroad'. In so far as these Articles relate to the rights to identity and autonomy of the body, they are reflections of broader human rights concerns. Article 19, which specifies the role of the state in preventing 'physical or mental violence, injury or abuse, neglect or negligent treatment, maltreatment or exploitation' towards the child, is clearly a focused application of human rights conventions outlawing torture or cruel and degrading treatment. Article 37 (a) makes this link directly, and – unlike the more general human rights Conventions – makes it clear that the death penalty shall not be imposed upon persons under the age of 18.

Social and economic rights are also covered in ways specific to the child. Not surprisingly, the right to a family is stressed, directly or indirectly, in many of the Articles, with additional clauses and Articles designed to ensure the welfare of the child in respect of parents who are separated, abusive parents, adoption or foster care. Other social and economic rights – such as those to health, social security, and, of course, education – are included.

The 1989 Convention has been ratified by almost all the UN member states at an incredibly speedy rate. Only Somalia and the United States are not at present signatories. However, like all Conventions, it is frequently ignored by governments. In a critical interpretation of the Convention, Michael Freeman shows how one country – the United Kingdom – fails to uphold the rights and freedoms contained therein.[25] His argument rests on the way Article 3 – in which it is claimed that in all actions concerning children, public or private, *'the best interests of the child shall be a primary consideration'* – is interpreted. In various institutional settings, he argues, basic rights, laid down in the Convention, are legally denied. Freedom of expression and information – Article 13 – is restricted, for example, by 'government intrusions on school curricula' such as the limitation of sexual education to heterosexual relations, and the banning of partisan political activities or education, as well as by the requirement to wear school uniforms. Similarly, freedom of assembly – Article 15 – is ignored whenever schools deny children their right to form associations. The right to privacy – Article 16 – is meaningless in practice, as privacy is controlled either by parents or by state institutions. English law, Freeman claims, falls short of other standards set out in the Convention pertaining to adoption, neglect and abuse, health care, and religion.

The targeting of children as victims of human rights abuses has received considerable attention from groups such as Amnesty International. Over the years, Amnesty has collected evidence from numerous countries showing how children are often kidnapped, imprisoned, tortured, even killed by government forces in an attempt to intimidate or punish their parents.[26] In global terms, three areas pertaining to childhood and human rights have attracted considerable attention from activists and academics – child labour, child soldiers, and street children.

Child labour

Article 32 of the Convention reads:

> 1. States Parties recognize the right of the child to be protected from economic exploitation and from performing any work that is likely to be hazardous or to interfere with the child's education, or to be harmful to the child's health or physical, mental, spiritual, moral or social development.
> 2. States Parties shall take legislative, administrative, social and educational measures to ensure the implementation of the present article. To this end, and having regard to the relevant provisions of other international instruments, States Parties shall in particular:
> (a) Provide for a minimum age or minimum ages for admission to employment;
> (b) Provide for appropriate regulation of the hours and conditions of employment;
> (c) Provide for appropriate penalties or other sanctions to ensure the effective enforcement of the present article.

Nevertheless, according to the International Labour Organisation, there are at present in the world some 250 million children between the ages of 5 and 14 working, '120 million full-time, and some 50–60 million in hazardous conditions'.[27] These figures do not include many children doing manual work in rural agricultural areas, nor the many girls employed as domestic servants in wealthy households, nor the multitude of children carrying out unpaid work for their families for the benefit of the family business. In 1997, UNESCO estimated that the actual figure is closer to 400 million, while a *New Internationalist* survey has suggested it is 500 million. International Labour Organisation figures from 1995 suggest that the vast majority of these children are employed in agricultural work, as Table 11.1 suggests.

South Asian countries such as India are among the world's leading exporters of hand-knotted or hand-woven carpets. Child labour is frequently employed because children are cheap, and many are brought in as bonded labourers. Bonded labour is a system in which children are either born or sold into slavery in order to pay off a family debt. In India the carpet industry grows some 10 per cent every year and, according to UNICEF estimates, the number of child labourers grows by 5 per cent every year. Often, these child labourers eat and work in the same shed, under unhealthy conditions, and may work up to 18 hours a day, seven

Table 11.1 Percentage of economically active children 5–14 years old by industry[28]

Industry	%
Agriculture, hunting, forestry and fishing	70.4
Wholesale, retail, restaurants and hotels	8.3
Manufacturing	8.3
Community, social and personal services	6.5
Transport, storage and communication	3.8
Construction	1.9
Mining and quarrying	0.9

© The Guardian/Observer

days a week, often in crouched positions which leave them physically deformed.

Everyone has the right to decent conditions in which to work, to fair payment for that work, to rest and leisure. Child labour is a violation of the most basic standards of human rights, not only because moral standards dictate that children should be free from work, but because when they are forced to work, it is because they are the cheapest source of labour, and the most easily exploited and manipulated. They therefore suffer conditions at work – in violation of the standards mentioned above – far worse than might be experienced by adults.

Child soldiers

Article 38 of the Convention requires states to 'take all feasible measures to ensure that persons who have not attained the age of fifteen years do not take a direct part in hostilities', and that states shall 'refrain from recruiting any person who has not yet attained the age of fifteen years into their armed forces'. Children's rights campaigners have argued that the age of 15 is inappropriate, and that the minimum age for active service in conflict situations should be raised to 18. However, according to Amnesty International statistics, there are an estimated 300,000 children under the age of 18 – some as young as 7 – participating in armed conflicts around the world today, across some 30 countries.[29]

One such country is Sri Lanka, where the anti-government Tamil Tigers frequently recruit children – either with consent or by force – into their ranks. This is despite their promise to the United Nations Special Representative for Children and Armed Conflict that they would not use children under 18 in combat situations and would not recruit for any purposes children under 17.[30] Others include Pakistan and Afghanistan, where children are commonly recruited into the armed forces through religious schools, without parental consent.[31] Many military leaders believe that children make good soldiers because they rarely question the orders of their commanders. Jean-Pierre, 14, fights for the rebel movement in the Democratic Republic of Congo:

> The rebels came to our village in Kivu and said that we would get both food and money if we became soldiers and helped them defeat Kabila's army. They said that it would be easy to defeat Kabila and that we didn't need to be afraid because the enemy escaped as soon as it saw the rebels. Several of the rebels were boys my age and they had nice uniforms and new guns. I and three other boys from my village went with them and fought in both Katanga and Kindu. Many died during the fighting, I was scared but my commander said that I was a good soldier. When we took Kindu we first had to cross the Congo river by boat. The enemy shot at us the whole time but I was more afraid of drowning because I cannot swim. It has been over two years since I was home and saw my mother and brothers and sisters. If there is peace I will go home and try to get a job.[32]

In 2000, the United Nations Security Council announced its plans to establish a war crimes tribunal in Sierra Leone in the aftermath of the civil war in that country. This was met with some opposition from Save the Children UK and other groups, because it specified that children from the age of 15 would be liable to prosecution, if not imprisonment. According to the children's rights campaigners, 'former child combatants are already undergoing an extremely delicate process of rehabilitation and reintegration into society and that most of them were abused, drugged, tortured or brainwashed to unimaginable extents, then made to commit atrocities against their families or neighbours in order to survive'.[33] Amnesty International reports that some 5,000 children have been involved in armed conflict in Sierra Leone.[34]

Street children

In Chapter Four, we saw how government-sponsored death squads were responsible for the 'disappearances' of thousands of political opponents in many countries. These secret paramilitary units perform other tasks for repressive regimes as well – not least the task of 'cleaning up' neighbourhoods. In Colombia, this operation costs little more than £3,000. But this 'community service' provided by the vigilantes is not one to be applauded. The 'rubbish' that is removed from the streets is not litter but the many destitute children who sleep there. There are thousands of street children in the cities of Colombia, and every month, as many as 40 of them simply 'disappear',[35] murdered by the death squads and buried in unmarked graves. In 1991, official statistics revealed that 2,800 children in Colombia – and 1,500 in Brazil – were killed in this way. Usually, the murderers are hired by local businesses which see the street children as a nuisance, and damaging to trade. Often, they are advertised in advance, in the form of posters displayed in the city, with such messages as the following:

> The industrialists, businessmen, civic groups, and community at large in the Zone of Martyrs invite you to the funerals of the delinquents of this sector, events that will commence immediately and will continue until they are exterminated.[36]

These atrocities take place in other parts of Latin America. Amnesty International recounts the following incident in Guatemala:

> On the morning of 6th June 1990 in Guatemala City, a group of street children were sitting chatting in a park when a black van pulled up. Three armed men got out, dragged four boys and a girl into the back of the van and drove off.
>
> The men sprayed a chemical in their faces and placed a bag over each of their heads, causing the children to inhale and pass out. They were taken to a cemetery where the others came round to see one boy hung by his hands from a tree and being beaten. The girl was the only one not handcuffed ... [so] [s]he ran through the graveyard, chased by one man in the truck, and escaped. She passed out inside a rubbish bin and was later found and taken to hospital.
>
> The four boys were found 11 days later. Two of them were without ears; their eyes had been gouged out and their tongues cut off. They had been shot in the head.[37]

While governments deny involvement in these atrocities, it is widely believed that they often turn a blind eye to the killings in order to maintain the support of businesses. Investigations into the killings are often initiated, and arrests made, but more often than not they are stalled. According to activists like Bruce Harris – who founded the organisation Casa Alianza to raise awareness of the plight of the street children in Central America – the description of the death squads' activities as 'social cleansing' is made without irony. The children are not, 'in the eyes of society . . . seen as children, and so they are killed, in much the same way as stepping on a cockroach'.[38] Children – like the refugees we discussed in Chapter Ten – are easily and frequently targeted for human rights violations simply because it is easy for 'society' to deny them the most basic of labels, *humanity*.

Business and human rights

The dangers faced by the street children of Colombia, Guatemala and elsewhere draw attention to the role played by businesses in human rights violations. Traditionally, organisations such as Amnesty International have focused their campaigning attentions on governments, who are both principal violators and, allegedly, principal defenders of human rights. However, the increasing power wielded by businesses – particularly transnational corporations – in the world system requires us to ask questions about the relationship such corporations have with respect to human rights. When, in 1995, the activist Ken Saro-Wiwa and eight others were executed in Nigeria for their role in supporting the Movement for the Survival of the Ogoni People, questions were raised not only with the Nigerian officials but also with the multinational oil corporation Shell, which has had considerable influence in Nigeria through its sizeable economic activities in and around the River Niger delta. These activities were met with some opposition from tribal groups concerned about their environmental impact. Shell and other corporations with investments in Nigeria have at times needed to rely upon the protection of the police during protests. In November 1990 Shell called in the paramilitary Mobile Police Force to protect its sites and investments, and 80 members of the Etche ethnic group were massacred. Shell distanced itself publicly from these events, and in 1994 established a policy of not accepting police or military help. This act of conscience was negated, though, by revelations in 1996 that for a decade and a half Shell had been paying for and arranging for the import of various arms – from handguns to heavy weaponry – for the use of the Nigerian forces. Shell suffered further criticism for its alleged inadequacy in using its influence to speak out against the executions of the Ogoni activists.

Would it have made any difference if Shell had made more of an effort to voice its concerns? Sir Geoffrey Chandler has suggested that the influence of corporations such as Shell could constitute a very powerful weapon in the struggle for human rights worldwide.[39] Chandler suggests that, despite the fact that many corporations deny they have any responsibility in such matters, human rights necessarily transcend all boundaries and cannot be seen as solely the responsibility of the state to protect. 'In the public mind,' writes Chandler, 'profiting *under* an oppressive regime finds an easy, if unjust, transition to profiting *from* it. Corporate silence in the context of world condemnation risks being taken by the offending government to be acquiescence in what it does.'

Like Shell, the sportswear manufacturer Nike has been subjected to criticism for contracting the manufacture of its training shoes to companies in Asia which operated sweatshops, in violation of even the most minimum labour standards and in clear violation of human rights regulation. Nike and companies like it have, like Shell, sought to distance themselves from these revelations. In some cases, of course, campaigns against human rights violations are directed at the corporations themselves, for their active involvement rather than their tacit consent. In Chapter Five we discussed the trade in arms and torture equipment worldwide – a lucrative trade, certainly. Despite attempts by nation-states to regulate such transactions, these corporations have been able to manipulate the loopholes in the global marketplace to continue their trade. Similarly, those concerned with the deaths of numerous babies in economically poor countries due to an over-reliance upon artificial baby milk powder laid the blame firmly at the feet of multinational corporations such as Nestlé.[40]

Transnational corporations are key players in world politics, just as they are dominant players in world economics. Only six nation-states have revenues larger than the nine largest transnational corporations, excluding transnational banks.[41] However, the largest 200 transnational corporations are based in only ten nation-states, primarily the United States and Japan. Thus, there are clear inequalities in the distribution of power and resources.

Global corporations may wield this economic power, but they are not accountable to international law in the same way that nation-states are. In this respect, it is difficult to utilise campaigning techniques with a view to forcing these corporations to respect human rights standards. Nevertheless, in so far as this economic power translates into political power (the power to influence decisions made by governments), transnational corporations must be a legitimate target for human rights

Table 11.2 Comparison of nation-states and TNCs by revenue[42]

Rank	State or TNC	Revenues ($ billion)	Year
1.	UNITED STATES	1,248	1994
2.	GERMANY	690	1994
3.	JAPAN	595	1995
4.	UNITED KINGDOM	389	1994/5
5.	ITALY	339	1994
6.	FRANCE	221	1993
7.	Mitsubishi	184	1995
8.	Mitsui	182	1995
9.	Itochu	169	1995
10.	General Motors	169	1995
11.	Sumitomo	168	1995
12.	Marubeni	161	1995
13.	Ford Motor	137	1995
14.	Toyota Motor	111	1995
15.	Exxon	110	1995
16.	NETHERLANDS	110	1992
17.	Royal Dutch / Shell Group	110	1995
18.	SWEDEN	109	1995/6
19.	Nissho Iwai	98	1995
20.	SPAIN	97	1994

campaigns. At the same time, one of the defining traits of the new *global* marketplace is the decreasing power of nation-states to regulate the activities of such corporations, which can easily relocate their operations across borders in search of maximum profit. So, there is much power and little or no accountability, except to shareholders. This paints a depressing picture. Nevertheless, there is room for optimism. No corporation – or nation-state – wants to be 'named and shamed' as having played a part in some human rights violation somewhere in the world. Corporations rely on good publicity and, like Shell, would want to be seen by the watching world to be implementing and enforcing an ethical business policy. It is now widely accepted that corporations, like nation-states, must play a part in protecting the environment, and the same ethics can be applied to the protection of human rights in an increasingly globalised world.[43]

Poverty and human rights

As we begin to draw this volume to a close, let us turn briefly to two areas of concern which have always – like human rights – attracted the attention of campaigning organisations, but which have rarely been discussed *in the context* of human rights. The first of these is poverty. We can, broadly, treat poverty as a violation of Article 25 of the Universal Declaration of Human Rights, which stipulates the right to a 'standard of living adequate for the health and well-being' of persons 'including food, clothing, housing and medical care and necessary social services, and the right to security in the event of unemployment, sickness, disability, widowhood, old age or other lack of livelihood'. Needless to say, this Article attempts to pack a considerable range of social and economic rights into a relatively small space. The International Covenant on Economic, Social and Cultural Rights 1966 elaborates on this right to an 'adequate standard of living' in its Article 11 (2), in which it calls on states to recognise 'the fundamental rights of everyone to be free from hunger'. The Social Policy (Basic Aims and Standards) Convention of the International Labour Organisation 1962 also required states to recognise that 'the improvement of standards of living shall be regarded as the principal objective in the planning of economic development' (Article 2), and that 'all practicable measures shall be taken in the planning of economic development to harmonize such development with the healthy evolution of the communities concerned' (Article 3 (1)).

Social scientists have been concerned with the causes and extent of poverty (primarily within their own Western nation-states) since the social sciences themselves came of age in the late nineteenth century. Seebohm Rowntree's classic 1901 study of poverty in York, for example, began by describing the minimal requirements for an acceptable standard of living, based on a minimum amount of money required to have access to the necessities of life.[44] Subsequent writers, such as Peter Townsend, have sought to improve upon Rowntree's methodology.[45] Meanwhile, numerous sociologists of all schools and traditions, from Marxist to functionalist, have sought to explain or understand poverty by locating it within the wider social structure (for example, within a wider system of social stratification, or according to its functions for the social system as a whole).

The work of researchers such as Townsend is significant in the development of social policy as an academic discipline in the United Kingdom, just as equivalent research projects have helped it develop elsewhere. However, social policy has traditionally been concerned with welfare provision within nation-states. While poverty could be understood in terms of *citizenship* and according to those rights allegedly guaranteed by a functioning welfare state system, it was rarely discussed in terms of human rights. Similarly, Marxist accounts have seen poverty as an inevitable consequence of the wider project of capitalism, which necessarily creates inequality in the name of the maximisation of profit.[46]

The emergence of neo-Marxist perspectives which focused on the structural inequalities of the *world* capitalist system should have made it easier for researchers to make the relevant links between global poverty and issues of human rights. Sadly, this challenge was largely ignored. The major contributors to world-systems theory, such as André Gunder Frank and Immanuel Wallerstein, have tended to prefer long-term historical analyses to specific studies.[47] Indeed, the model they have adopted and adapted over the years was set up as an alternative to Walt Rostow's conservative, evolutionist one, in which it was presupposed that all nation-states undergo a five-stage process of development before they attain a particular level of modernisation.[48] Frank's – and Wallerstein's – point is that not every nation-state can attain this level, because the world's economic resources are finite, and that some nation-states are poor *because* others are rich, and *vice versa*. This is explained according to long-term studies of the world economy, and although these writers have been keen to link capitalist growth to processes of colonialism and slavery, little attention is paid to them *per se*. While we might find these neo-Marxist approaches useful for understanding certain motives behind the practices of oppressive regimes in poorer countries (that is, that these regimes are part of the wider system, and dictatorships can be profitable if they are organised well enough), we would not find in them a framework for locating global poverty within the context of human rights.

One very important volume which has attempted – with a considerable degree of success – to bring together the issues of poverty and human rights is Willem van Genugten and Camilo Perez-Bustillo's *The Poverty of Rights*.[49] Clearly, the inspiration for such an analysis that links poverty with human rights comes from Marx. However, it can be recast using the language of the Universal Declaration of Human Rights, Article 28, which declares that 'everyone is entitled to a social and international order in which the rights and freedoms set forth in this Declaration can be fully realized'. This seems to be what Patricia Helena Massa Arzabe has in mind when she states:

> Human rights norms are intended to ensure every person the means for the full development of his / her personality and citizenship in the social system, and are necessary for productive interaction in a democratic society. These are the rights without which the person will not be able to exist completely nor have her / his dignity fully respected, because of unsatisfied needs or unavailable possibilities of self-development.[50]

The author recognises, like Marx, that human rights are not changeless – they are 'historically and spatially conditioned'. Therefore they must be understood in the context of social structure, as resulting from 'social struggles between interests and between groups'. Central to the idea of human rights is the idea of human dignity, and this dignity must be concrete, grounded in material conditions and realities. She concludes that this paradigm of human dignity effectively marries the principles of human rights with the problem of global poverty. Other contributors to this volume share this concern with emphasising the human dimension of poverty, pointing out that poverty results from a lack of compassion by others.[51] As one commentator clearly states, poverty 'denigrates, excludes, mutilates and kills (and) has become the single greatest violator of human rights in the world today'.[52]

The reality of human rights is that they are based on an equality of access to the ways and means of civil society. The reality of poverty is that it is based on the uneven distribution of life chances and necessarily produces inequalities in access to principles of justice and self-development.[53] Poverty is the negation of rights.[53] Poverty violates the fundamental right to security of the person (Article 1 of the Universal Declaration). None of this, of course, is in doubt. What is contested is the extent to which the blame can be laid at the feet of the state. Indeed, if one adapts Wallerstein's perspective, the nation-state can only be accorded minimal responsibility for conditions of poverty. Even so, while the state may not be directly involved in the validation and execution of poverty, in the way that it is with torture or the death penalty, it is responsible for its perpetuation within the social structure, in much the same way that slavery becomes embedded in the social structure. Poverty, like slavery, apartheid, or the problem of refugees, is a form of social exclusion, which can be and often is targeted at certain groups in society. It is achieved through the (political) state's manipulation of the economic sphere, via the uneven distribution of life chances, and in this respect the state's relationship with poverty is akin to that with refugees. Poverty is clearly a human rights concern, and the boundaries between human rights research and poverty research are rightly being eroded with the recognition that the state has as active a role in upholding social and economic rights as it does civil and political ones.

The environment and human rights

The second concern related to human rights but rarely discussed in that context is the environment. As with the case of poverty, the relationship between human rights and the environment can be interpreted in respect of Article 28. However, poverty has at least been recognised by United Nations acts and conventions as a human rights concern since the signing of the UDHR in 1948, because it is easily located within the broad category of economic, social and cultural rights passed into international law with the 1966 Covenant. Environmental concerns have entered the discourse on human rights far more recently, via the largely undefined category of *third-generational rights*. If *first-generational* rights – civil and political – are freedoms of the individual, and *second-generational* rights – economic, social and cultural – locate that individual within the social structure by recognising that she or he has certain needs within a world of others, then *third-generational* rights are those collective rights which locate both the individual and the community within a physical structure. Land rights, for example, grant communities self-determination and autonomy over their immediate physical environment. Environmental rights, controversially, grant each individual the right to exist in a clean and healthy environment, and duly charge the state (among other political actors) with the task of ensuring that environmental conditions are kept in a way suitable for human existence. Thus:

> The environmental crisis which surrounds us is indissolubly linked to patterns of social exclusion, to such a degree that the environmentalist cause and that in defence of human rights are but two faces of the same coin. One battle cannot be won if the other is lost... [A] holistic vision of environmental problems is necessary which connects them to the current challenges confronting us in terms of human rights across all their civil, political, economic, social and cultural dimensions.[54]

These claims, which echo Norberto Bobbio's belief that human rights, democracy and peace are intrinsically linked through the need to establish the appropriate conditions within which human rights can be exercised, are undeniable. Human rights are meaningless unless such conditions exist. With this in mind, the United Nations Stockholm Declaration made at the 1972 Conference on the Human Environment makes the links between human rights and the environment explicit. Its opening proclamation states that:

> Man (*sic*) is both creature and moulder of his environment, which gives him physical sustenance and affords him the opportunity for intellectual, moral, social and spiritual growth. In the long and tortuous evolution of the human race on this planet a stage has been reached when, through the rapid acceleration of science and technology, man has acquired the power to transform his environment in countless ways and on an unprecedented scale. Both aspects of man's environment, the natural and the man-made, are essential to his well-being and to the enjoyment of basic human rights – even the right to life itself.

The Declaration makes even clearer the links between humanity's responsibilities towards its environment and the practices of human rights abuses in its Principle 1:

> Man has the fundamental right to freedom, equality and adequate conditions of life, in an environment of a quality that permits a life of dignity and well-being, and he bears a solemn responsibility to protect and improve the environment for present and future generations. In this respect, policies promoting or perpetuating apartheid, racial segregation, discrimination, colonial and other forms of oppression and foreign domination stand condemned and must be eliminated.

The wording of the 1972 Declaration carefully passes the responsibility upon individuals to serve as caretakers of their environment, while assigning to states the burden of planning and policy-making in environmental matters. Like poverty, environmental concerns are not solely the result of states' actions. Individuals and businesses are also at fault. Like poverty, environmental damage is produced through the capitalist logic of maximising profits.[55] In respect of both global poverty and the global environmental crisis, global action is surely required by an authority to which both nation-states and transnational corporations are accountable.

Commentators have already succeeded in bringing environmental issues into the discourse on citizenship.[56] Indeed, this seems inevitable as global citizenship becomes a more realistic understanding of our political identities than the more restrictive, exclusive nation-state citizenship. After all, citizenship is about rights *and duties*, and as global citizens, we can appreciate our duties *towards the environment* in much the same way that nation-state citizens could respect their duties towards the state (such as through the paying of tax or the performance of military service). To talk of the environment within the discourse on human rights, though, is not the same thing. Here, we must focus not on our role as 'stewards' of Planet Earth (the role given to us by the Stockholm Declaration) but as humans who deserve, require, *and demand* a healthy environment for us to live our lives with dignity, and within which all other rights can be exercised. Just as *genocide* is interpreted as the planned denial of the right to existence to entire groups of people, and is accordingly condemned in international law, so must human rights research recognise that *ecocide* is the indiscriminate denial of the right to existence to future generations, and must be equally condemned.

Human rights in a globalised world

Commentators wishing to expand the scope of human rights research beyond the simplistic individualism of the traditional paradigm call for a more holistic perspective to be adopted. In this respect they echo the calls made by feminists to break down the distinctions between the public and private realms, which have seen the discourse on human rights restricted to the former. In the twenty-first century, such developments seem inevitable. The rapid expansion of capitalism across borders and the increasing power wielded by transnational corporations within the global system without political accountability require us to broaden our horizons as academics and activists. By couching the language of human rights in terms of human dignity, we are able to both intellectualise and campaign as easily on poverty, ecocide, and female genital mutilation and other oppressive cultural traditions, as we are on direct forms of state oppression, such as torture, censorship or the death penalty. The traditional paradigm of human rights campaigning has, rightly, focused its attention on the state, because the state has been the principal political agent. If anything, globalisation weakens the power of the state, and disrupts the world map by challenging the presumed legitimacy of borders. Human rights research must respond to the challenges posed by globalisation.

Of course, globalisation is a multi-layered thing, and can be both enabling and disabling to the advancement of human rights. While the spread of global capitalism in a manner detached from any equivalent spread of global political accountability may be disabling, the spread of human rights ideology is enabling. Globalisation – as it is understood in the media and in political circles – undoubtedly produces huge inequalities in economic and political power, most evidently between the North and South or what Wallerstein calls the 'core' and 'periphery'. But this is only half the story. Globalisation is a process noun, and as such can be used to refer to almost anything. One does not need to endorse a macro-theory of historical social change in order to talk about 'the globalisation' of something or another. Certainly, the term is stripped of any potential value or meaning if it is solely used to describe the processes of capitalist expansion across borders. One can also talk about the 'globalisation of human rights'. This may sound odd at first – how can an idea based on universalism become globalised? Various commentators have sought to determine the relationship, using different intellectual influences, between these competing processes. One group has countered the dominant form of globalisation – the 'globalisation from above' associated with the 'new world order' – with an alternative model, 'globalisation from below' aimed at the establishment of a 'one-world community'.[57] In my own work, I have made use of Jürgen Habermas's theory of modernity as *competing projects*.[58] Habermas understands modernity to be a tension between competing forms of rationalisation, one of which is located in instrumental reason and articulated through the economic and political spheres (the 'system'), the other of which is located in communicative reason and articulated through the social, cultural and personal dimensions (the 'lifeworld'). While the former has been dominant, the latter has been ever-present as its antithesis. Human rights are best understood as articulations of this latter modernity, given greater force after 1945 during an era of globalisation, and can provide a powerful alternative to the dominant systemic globalisation, the global marketplace.

A similar view has been presented by Leslie Sklair.[59] Sklair begins by distinguishing between 'capitalist globalisation' (exemplified by the spread of the global market) and 'socialist globalisation'. Locating these two projects in a dialectical relationship, Sklair follows Gramsci by distinguishing between economic, political, and cultural-ideological practices, represented in capitalist globalisation by transnational corporations, the transnational capitalist class, and the culture-ideology of consumerism. Sklair suggests that there are specific crises inherent in capitalist globalisation – class polarisation and ecological unsustainability – and that socialist globalization emerges as an alternative through the globalisation of human rights. Human rights, Sklair argues, provide the socialist globalisation alternative to the culture-ideology of consumerism, but (as we have seen in this volume) much of the discourse on human rights is restricted to the civil and political spheres (where, as Sklair indicates, globalisation has had a fairly positive influence), and he points out that this discourse needs to reach out to the economic and social spheres. Sklair's contribution is interesting because it does adopt a holistic approach to human rights (connecting them *necessarily* to human development and human dignity), and in doing so interprets human rights as *socialist* (rather than individualist) qualities. This, of course, inverts the criticism so often levelled at human rights. Sklair makes use of a United Nations Development Programme report which comes close to redefining human rights by erasing the distinction between individual freedoms and social needs, and which bears a strong resemblance to the calls made by the contributors to *The Poverty of Rights* for a more holistic approach:

Human rights and human development share a common vision and common purpose – to secure the freedom, well-being and dignity of all people everywhere. To secure:

- Freedom from discrimination – by gender, race, ethnicity, national origin or religion.

- Freedom from want – to enjoy a decent standard of living.

- Freedom to develop and realize one's human potential.

- Freedom from fear – of threats to personal security, from torture, arbitrary arrest and other violent acts.

- Freedom from injustice and violations of the rule of law.

- Freedom of thought and speech and to participate in decision-making and form associations.

- Freedom for decent work – without exploitation.[60]

Globalisation challenges intellectual as well as national boundaries. No sooner have I sought, in this volume, to shape the foundations of human rights studies than I am opening the door for its evolution. Peace studies, environmental studies, and development studies must all play important roles in the development of human rights research, so that it maintains its focus on the structural conditions within which human rights violations take place. Human rights research is meaningless unless it is located within economic, social, political and cultural contexts. But these structural conditions change across time and space. If human rights are to be timeless and universal, then they must be applicable in all such conditions. While it may be true, as Norberto Bobbio has suggested, that the *discourse* of human rights came into existence with the inversion of the state–citizen relationship,[61] human rights *per se* do not begin and end with the nation-state. The nation-state is only one kind of political formation, and a relatively recent one as well. The state – the means through which we order and administer our political actions – takes many forms. The nation-state may torture and execute its citizens, but torture and the death penalty are violations of human rights whether they are committed by state or opposition forces, or by other agents claiming to wield 'legitimate' authority. These structural conditions are also intrinsically interlinked. According to some commentators, globalisation has allowed us to reinvigorate the idea of society by delinking it from the state.[62] If this is true, and if it is true that our role as citizens is acted out not within the political state but within society, then surely the same can be said of human rights. Society is comprised of people and institutions. We interact with and acknowledge the presence of other people, and we construct institutions, such as the state and the market, so as to order our lives. If human rights violations, such as those which subordinate or degrade women, are perpetuated in the name of culture and tradition (and in many cases conveniently overlooked by the state, which may have added its support to international treaties opposing such practices), then the principles of society are violated. If slavery or poverty persist because of the unregulated expansion of the global economy, then the principles of society are broken. The state is not alone in violating human rights, but it alone can protect them, because the state, in whatever form it takes, is the manifestation of the political will of its citizens, and the machinery of law and social control. So the 'end' of the nation-state, if such a thing is at present imaginable, does not mean the end of human rights – far from it. 1948, when representatives of different states, different nations, different traditions, first came together to turn a set of abstract ideals about the 'good society' into a workable and (eventually) binding set of legal principles, may seem like ancient history, but on the contrary it is only a recent memory. Despite the apparent failures of the UN and its organs to effectively regulate human rights around the world, we find ourselves only at the *beginning* of the 'age of rights'. There is still much for academics and activists to do in the infant field of human rights research.

Essay questions

1. How might we explain the persistence of female genital mutilation in many cultures?

2. In what ways are children often targeted as victims of human rights abuses?

3. Does globalisation mean the end of the nation-state, and if so, what are the implications of this for the regulation of human rights?

4. What role must corporations and businesses play in safeguarding human rights? What obstacles exist which make their compliance difficult to guarantee, and how might we overcome those obstacles?

5. Human rights mean little unless we live in a clean, healthy world free from poverty and war. Discuss.

Notes

1 See V. Spike Peterson and Laura Parisi (1998) 'Are Women Human? It's Not an Academic Question' in Tony Evans (ed.) *Human Rights Fifty Years On: A Reappraisal*, Manchester: Manchester University Press. For another excellent entry into the debate on women's human rights, see Georgina Ashworth (1999) 'The Silencing of Women' in Tim Dunne and Nicholas J. Wheeler (eds) *Human Rights in Global Politics*, Cambridge: Cambridge University Press.

2 'Women's Rights, Human Rights' in *Amnesty*, 73, May–June 1995, p. 6.

3 Petersen and Parisi, 'Are Women Human?', p. 134.

4 I am grateful to Debra Wetherston for carrying out the research on FGM.

5 E. Dorkenoo (1995) *Cutting the Rose: Female Genital Mutilation, Its Practice and Its Prevention*, London: Minority Rights Publications.

6 Amnesty International (2000) 'Female Genital Mutilation: A Human Rights Information Pack' at www.amnesty.org/ailib/incam/femgen.fgm1.htm.

7 O. Koso-Thomas (1987) *The Circumcision of Women: A Strategy for Eradication*, Avon: The Bath Press.

8 Dorkenoo, *Cutting the Rose*.

9 Dorkenoo, *Cutting the Rose*.

10 Minority Rights Group (1982) *Female Circumcision, Excision and Infibulation: The Facts and Proposals for Change*, Report no. 47.

11 Amnesty International, 'Female Genital Mutilation'.

12   Jacques Lantier (1972) 'La Cité Magique', cited in Minority Rights Group, *Female Circumcision*, Paris: Fayord, p. 3.

13   Nancy Lutkenhaus and P.B. Roscoe (eds) (1995) *Gender Rituals: Female Initiation in Melanesia*, New York: Routledge.

14   Dorkenoo (1995) *Cutting the Rose*.

15   Koso-Thomas, *Circumcision*.

16   Lutkenhaus and Roscoe, *Gender Rituals*.

17   Dorkenoo, *Cutting the Rose*.

18   Koso-Thomas, *Circumcision*.

19   Radha Kumar (1993) *The History of Doing: An Illustrated Account of Movements for Women's Rights and Feminism in India, 1800–1990*, London: Verso.

20   Global Frontlines: India – 'Religion and Family Violence' www.fvpf.org/global/gf_india.html.

21   Bob Franklin (ed.) (1995) *The Handbook of Children's Rights: Comparative Policy and Practice*, London: Routledge.

22   Bob Franklin (1995) 'The Case for Children's Rights: A Progress Report' in Franklin, *Handbook*, p. 9.

23   Franklin, 'Case', p. 9; following a distinction made by C.M. Rogers and L.S. Wrightsman (1978) in 'Attitudes Towards Children's Rights: Nurturance or Self-Determination' in *Journal of Social Issues*, 34, 2.

24   See Ian Brownlie (ed.) (1992) *Basic Documents on Human Rights*, 3rd edition, Oxford: Clarendon Press, pp. 182–202.

25   Michael Freeman (1995) 'Children's Rights in a Land of Rites' in Franklin, *Handbook*.

26   Jonathan Power (1981) *Amnesty International: The Human Rights Story*, Oxford: Pergamon Press, pp. 39–41.

27   See www.crin.org.

28   International Labour Organisation figures reproduced in *Guardian Education*, Tuesday, 16 November 1999, p. 10.

29   See www.amnesty-usa.org/children/soldiers/about.html.

30   See www.amnesty-usa.org/news/2001/srilanka10112001.html.

31   Amnesty International (1998) *Securing Their Rights: Children in South Asia*, London: Amnesty International Publications.

32   Text by Peter Strandberg, taken from www.rb.se/chilwar/ett_01/news.htm, *Children of War* 2001, 2.

33 www.rb.se/chilwar/tre_fyra_00/news2.htm, *Children of War* 2000, 3 / 4.

34 Amnesty International (2000) *Childhood: A Casualty of Conflict*, London: Amnesty International Publications.

35 Minna Lacey (1994) 'Invited to Their Own Funerals' in *Amnesty* January / February, pp. 14–15.

36 Reported in Lacey, 'Invited', p. 15.

37 Susan Kobrin (1996) 'Killed Like Cockroaches' in *Amnesty* January / February, p. 16.

38 Kobrin, 'Killed', p. 16.

39 Geoffrey Chandler (1996) 'People and Profits' in the *Guardian*, Thursday, 14 November, p. 17.

40 See Antonio Cassese (1990) *Human Rights in a Changing World*, Cambridge: Polity Press, Chapter 8.

41 David P. Forsythe (2000) *Human Rights in International Relations*, Cambridge: Cambridge University Press, p. 191.

42 Forsythe, *Human Rights*, p. 192, using data drawn from sources including *'Fortune*'s Global 500: The World's Largest Corporations' in *Fortune* 5 August 1996, and the CIA-accumulated *The World Factbook*.

43 Forsythe, *Human Rights*, p. 210.

44 Seebohm Rowntree (2000) *Poverty: A Study of Town Life*, Bristol: Policy Press.

45 See, for example, Peter Townsend (ed.) (1970) *The Concept of Poverty*, London: Heinemann; Brian Abel-Smith and Peter Townsend (1965) *The Poor and the Poorest*, London: G. Bell & Sons.

46 Classic Marxist accounts of poverty include J.C. Kincaid (1973) *Poverty and Equality in Britain: A Study of Social Security and Taxation*, Harmondsworth: Penguin; Ralph Miliband (1974) 'Politics and Poverty' in Dorothy Wedderburn (ed.) *Poverty, Inequality, and Class Structure*, Cambridge: Cambridge University Press; John Westergaard and Henrietta Resler (1976) *Class in a Capitalist Society*, Harmondsworth: Penguin.

47 See André Gunder Frank (1969) *Capitalism and Underdevelopment in Latin America: Historical Studies of Chile and Brazil*, New York: Monthly Review; Immanuel Wallerstein (1979) *The Capitalist World Economy*, Cambridge: Cambridge University Press; and numerous other volumes written by these two prolific writers.

48 Walt Rostow (1971; original 1960) *The Stages of Economic Growth: A Non-Communist Manifesto*, 2nd edition, Cambridge: Cambridge University Press.

49 Willem van Genugten and Camilo Perez-Bustillo (eds) (2001) *The Poverty of Rights: Human Rights and the Eradication of Poverty*, London: Zed Books.

50   Patricia Helena Massa Arzabe (2001) 'Human Rights: A New Paradigm' in van Genugsten and Perez-Bustillo, *Poverty of Rights*, p. 31.

51   Marco Aurelio Ugarte Ochoa (2001) 'Poverty and Human Rights in the Light of the Philosophy and Contributions of Father Joseph Wresinski' in van Genugten and Perez-Bustillo, *Poverty of Rights*, p. 55.

52   Ugarte Ochoa, 'Poverty and Human Rights', p. 60.

53   Ugarte Ochoa, 'Poverty and Human Rights', p. 61.

54   Juan Antonio Blanco (2001) 'Natural History and Social History: Limits and Urgent Priorities which Condition the Exercise of Human Rights' in van Genugten and Perez-Bustillo, *Poverty of Rights*, p. 40.

55   Blanco, 'Natural History', p. 45.

56   See, for example, Bart van Steenbergen (1994) 'Towards a Global Ecological Citizen' in Bart van Steenbergen (ed.) *The Condition of Citizenship*, London: Sage; Fred Steward (1991) 'Citizens of Planet Earth' in Geoff Andrews (ed.) *Citizenship*, London: Lawrence & Wishart.

57   Jeremy Brecher, John Brown Childs and Jill Cutler (eds) (1993) *Global Visions: Beyond the New World Order*, Boston: South End Press.

58   Darren J. O'Byrne (2002, forthcoming) *The Dimensions of Global Citizenship*, London: Frank Cass.

59   Leslie Sklair (2002) *Globalization: Capitalism and Its Alternatives*, Oxford: Oxford University Press.

60   United Nations Development Programme (2000) *Human Development Report 2000*, New York: United Nations Publications, p. 1; cited in Sklair, *Globalization*.

61   Norberto Bobbio (1996) *The Age of Rights*, Cambridge: Polity Press, pp. ix–x.

62   Martin Albrow (1996) *The Global Age: State and Society Beyond Modernity*, Cambridge: Polity Press.

Further information

Books

A good and fairly critical survey of the 1989 Convention on the Rights of the Child is found in Bob Franklin (ed.) *Children's Rights: Comparative Policy and Practice* (London: Routledge, 1995). For a good overview of the relationship between business and human rights, see Lance A. Compa and Stephen F. Diamond (eds) *Human Rights, Labor Rights, and International Trade* (Philadelphia: University of Pennsylvania Press, 1996). For an excellent overview of the relationship between human rights and poverty, see Willem van Genugten and Camilo Perez-Bustilo (eds) *The Poverty of Rights: Human Rights and the Eradication of Poverty* (London: Zed Books, 2001). Among the numerous books on globalisation, see Barrie Axford's *The Global System: Economics, Politics and Culture* (Cambridge: Polity Press, 1995), Malcolm Waters's *Globalization* (London: Routledge, 1995) and Leslie Sklair's *Sociology of the Global System* (Hemel Hempstead: Harvester Wheatsheaf, 1991), each of which contains a summary of the key debates in global development.

Websites

For more information on children's rights, go to the Child Rights Information Network on www.crin.org. Also check out the Amnesty International USA section's Children's Rights Network on www.amnesty-usa.org/groups/crn. The United Nations Children's Fund is accessible on www.unicef.org. Sites with useful information on children and armed conflict include http://oneworld.org/child_rights/ch_war.html and www.rb.se/chilwar. Casa Alianza, which works on behalf of street children, is accessible on www.casa-alianza.org.

Appendix

The Universal Declaration of Human Rights was adopted and proclaimed by General Assembly resolution 217A (III) on 10 December 1948. Forty-eight countries voted in favour, none against, with eight abstentions.[1] The Declaration is not in itself a legally binding document, but it did provide the foundations for subsequent documents, particularly the International Covenant on Civil and Political Rights and the International Covenant on Economic, Social and Cultural Rights, both of which have force under international law. Taken together, these form the International Bill of Rights. The International Covenant on Civil and Political Rights was adopted on 16 December 1966, and came into force on 23 March 1976. The International Covenant on Economic, Social and Cultural Rights is not reproduced here because it does not relate directly to the issues discussed in this book. For the full text of that, plus other conventions and declarations passed by the United Nations and its organs, and the human rights charters of Europe, Africa and the Americas, see Ian Brownlie (ed.) (1992) *Basic Documents on Human Rights* (Oxford: Oxford University Press).

Universal Declaration of Human Rights

Preamble

Whereas recognition of the inherent dignity and of the equal and inalienable rights of all members of the human family is the foundation of freedom, justice and peace in the world,

Whereas disregard and contempt for human rights have resulted in barbarous acts which have outraged the conscience of mankind, and the advent of a world in which human beings shall enjoy freedom of speech and belief and freedom from fear and want has been proclaimed as the highest aspiration of the common people,

Whereas it is essential, if man is not to be compelled to have recourse, as a last resort, to rebellion against tyranny and oppression, that human rights should be protected by the rule of law,

Whereas it is essential to promote the development of friendly relations between nations,

Whereas the peoples of the United Nations have in the Charter re-affirmed their faith in fundamental human rights, in the dignity and worth of the human person and in the equal rights of men and women and have determined to promote social progress and better standards of life in larger freedom,

Whereas Member States have pledged themselves to achieve, in co-operation with the United Nations, the promotion of universal respect for and observance of human rights and fundamental freedoms,

Whereas a common understanding of these rights and freedoms is of the greatest importance for the full realization of this pledge,

Now, Therefore THE GENERAL ASSEMBLY proclaims THIS UNIVER-SAL DECLARATION OF HUMAN RIGHTS as a common standard of achievement for all peoples and all nations, to the end that every individual and every organ of society, keeping this Declaration constantly in mind, shall strive by teaching and education to promote respect for these rights and freedoms and by progressive measures, national and international, to secure their universal and effective recognition and observance, both among the peoples of Member States themselves and among the peoples of territories under their jurisdiction.

Article 1

All human beings are born free and equal in dignity and rights. They are endowed with reason and conscience and should act towards one another in a spirit of brotherhood.

Article 2

Everyone is entitled to all the rights and freedoms set forth in this Declaration, without distinction of any kind, such as race, colour, sex, language, religion, political or other opinion, national or social origin, property, birth or other status.
Furthermore, no distinction shall be made on the basis of the political, jurisdictional or international status of the country or territory to which a person belongs, whether it be independent, trust, non-self-governing or under any other limitation of sovereignty.

Article 3

Everyone has the right to life, liberty and security of person.

Article 4

No one shall be held in slavery or servitude; slavery and the slave trade shall be prohibited in all their forms.

Article 5

No one shall be subjected to torture or to cruel, inhuman or degrading treatment or punishment.

Article 6

Everyone has the right to recognition everywhere as a person before the law.

Article 7

All are equal before the law and are entitled without any discrimination to equal protection of the law. All are entitled to equal protection against any discrimination in violation of this Declaration and against any incitement to such discrimination.

Article 8

Everyone has the right to an effective remedy by the competent national tribunals for acts violating the fundamental rights granted him by the constitution or by law.

Article 9

No one shall be subjected to arbitrary arrest, detention or exile.

Article 10

Everyone is entitled in full equality to a fair and public hearing by an independent and impartial tribunal, in the determination of his rights and obligations and of any criminal charge against him.

Article 11

(1) Everyone charged with a penal offence has the right to be presumed innocent until proved guilty according to law in a public trial at which he has had all the guarantees necessary for his defence.

(2) No one shall be held guilty of any penal offence on account of any act or omission which did not constitute a penal offence, under national or international law, at the time when it was committed. Nor shall a heavier penalty be imposed than the one that was applicable at the time the penal offence was committed.

Article 12

No one shall be subjected to arbitrary interference with his privacy, family, home or correspondence, nor to attacks upon his honour and reputation. Everyone has the right to the protection of the law against such interference or attacks.

Article 13

(1) Everyone has the right to freedom of movement and residence within the borders of each state.

(2) Everyone has the right to leave any country, including his own, and to return to his country.

Article 14

(1) Everyone has the right to seek and to enjoy in other countries asylum from persecution.

(2) This right may not be invoked in the case of prosecutions genuinely arising from non-political crimes or from acts contrary to the purposes and principles of the United Nations.

Article 15

(1) Everyone has the right to a nationality.

(2) No one shall be arbitrarily deprived of his nationality nor denied the right to change his nationality.

Article 16

(1) Men and women of full age, without any limitation due to race, nationality or religion, have the right to marry and to found a family.

They are entitled to equal rights as to marriage, during marriage and at its dissolution.

(2) Marriage shall be entered into only with the free and full consent of the intending spouses.

(3) The family is the natural and fundamental group unit of society and is entitled to protection by society and the State.

Article 17

(1) Everyone has the right to own property alone as well as in association with others.

(2) No one shall be arbitrarily deprived of his property.

Article 18

Everyone has the right to freedom of thought, conscience and religion; this right includes freedom to change his religion or belief, and freedom, either alone or in community with others and in public or private, to manifest his religion or belief in teaching, practice, worship and observance.

Article 19

Everyone has the right to freedom of opinion and expression; this right includes freedom to hold opinions without interference and to seek, receive and impart information and ideas through any media and regardless of frontiers.

Article 20

(1) Everyone has the right to freedom of peaceful assembly and association.

(2) No one may be compelled to belong to an association.

Article 21

(1) Everyone has the right to take part in the government of his country, directly or through freely chosen representatives.

(2) Everyone has the right of equal access to public service in his country.

(3) The will of the people shall be the basis of the authority of government; this will shall be expressed in periodic and genuine elections

which shall be by universal and equal suffrage and shall be held by secret vote or by equivalent free voting procedures.

Article 22

Everyone, as a member of society, has the right to social security and is entitled to realization, through national effort and international co-operation and in accordance with the organization and resources of each State, of the economic, social and cultural rights indispensable for his dignity and the free development of his personality.

Article 23

(1) Everyone has the right to work, to free choice of employment, to just and favourable conditions of work and to protection against unemployment.

(2) Everyone, without any discrimination, has the right to equal pay for equal work.

(3) Everyone who works has the right to just and favourable remuneration ensuring for himself and his family an existence worthy of human dignity, and supplemented, if necessary, by other means of social protection.

(4) Everyone has the right to form and to join trade unions for the protection of his interests.

Article 24

Everyone has the right to rest and leisure, including reasonable limitation of working hours and periodic holidays with pay.

Article 25

(1) Everyone has the right to a standard of living adequate for the health and well-being of himself and of his family, including food, clothing, housing and medical care and necessary social services, and the right to security in the event of unemployment, sickness, disability, widowhood, old age or other lack of livelihood in circumstances beyond his control.

(2) Motherhood and childhood are entitled to special care and assistance. All children, whether born in or out of wedlock, shall enjoy the same social protection.

Article 26

(1) Everyone has the right to education. Education shall be free, at least in the elementary and fundamental stages. Elementary education shall be compulsory, Technical and professional education shall be made generally available and higher education shall be equally accessible to all on the basis of merit.

(2) Education shall be directed to the full development of the human personality and to the strengthening of respect for human rights and fundamental freedoms. It shall promote understanding, tolerance and friendship among all nations, racial or religious groups, and shall further the activities of the United Nations for the maintenance of peace.

(3) Parents have a prior right to choose the kind of education that shall be given to their children.

Article 27

(1) Everyone has the right freely to participate in the cultural life of the community, to enjoy the arts and to share in scientific advancement and its benefits.

(2) Everyone has the right to the protection of the moral and material interests resulting from any scientific, literary or artistic production of which he is the author.

Article 28

Everyone is entitled to a social and international order in which the rights and freedoms set forth in this Declaration can be fully realized.

Article 29

(1) Everyone has duties to the community in which alone the free and full development of his personality is possible.

(2) In the exercise of his rights and freedoms, everyone shall be subject only to such limitations as are determined by law solely for the purpose of securing due recognition and respect for the rights and freedoms of others and of meeting the just requirements of morality, public order and the general welfare in a democratic society.

(3) These rights and freedoms may in no case be exercised contrary to the purposes and principles of the United Nations.

Article 30

Nothing in this Declaration may be interpreted as implying for any State, group or person any right to engage in any activity or to perform any act aimed at the destruction of any of the rights and freedoms set forth herein.

International Covenant on Civil and Political Rights
Preamble

The States Parties to the present Covenant,

Considering that, in accordance with the principles proclaimed in the Charter of the United Nations, recognition of the inherent dignity and of the equal and inalienable rights of all members of the human family is the foundation of freedom, justice and peace in the world,

Recognizing that these rights derive from the inherent dignity of the human person,

Recognizing that, in accordance with the Universal Declaration of Human Rights, the ideal of free human beings enjoying civil and political freedom and freedom from fear and want can only be achieved if conditions are created whereby everyone may enjoy his civil and political rights, as well as his economic, social and cultural rights,

Considering the obligation of States under the Charter of the United Nations to promote universal respect for, and observance of, human rights and freedoms,

Realizing that the individual, having duties to other individuals and to the community to which he belongs, is under a responsibility to strive for the promotion and observance of the rights recognized in the present Covenant,

Agree upon the following articles:

Part 1

Article 1

(1) All peoples have the right of self-determination. By virtue of that right they freely determine their political status and freely pursue their economic, social and cultural development.

(2) All peoples may, for their own ends, freely dispose of their natural wealth and resources without prejudice to any obligations arising out of international economic co-operation, based upon the principle of mutual benefit, and international law. In no case may a people be deprived of its own means of subsistence.

(3) The States Parties to the present Covenant, including those having responsibility for the administration of Non-Self-Governing and Trust Territories, shall promote the realization of the right of self-determination, and shall respect that right, in conformity with the provisions of the Charter of the United Nations.

Part II

Article 2

(1) Each State Party to the present Covenant undertakes to respect and to ensure to all individuals within its territory and subject to its jurisdiction the rights recognized in the present Covenant, without distinction of any kind, such as race, colour, sex, language, religion, political or other opinion, national or social origin, property, birth or other status.

(2) Where not already provided for by existing legislative or other measures, each State Party to the present Covenant undertakes to take the necessary steps, in accordance with its constitutional processes and with the provisions of the present Covenant, to adopt such legislative or other measures as may be necessary to give effect to the rights recognized in the present Covenant.

(3) Each State Party to the present Covenant undertakes:
    (a) To ensure that any person whose rights or freedoms as herein recognized are violated shall have an effective remedy, notwithstanding that the violation has been committed by persons acting in an official capacity;
    (b) to ensure that any person claiming such a remedy shall have his rights thereto determined by competent judicial, administrative or legislative authorities, or by any other competent authority provided for by the legal system of the State, and to develop the possibilities of judicial remedy;
    (c) To ensure that the competent authorities shall enforce such remedies when granted.

Article 3

The States Parties to the present Covenant undertake to ensure the equal right of men and women to the enjoyment of all civil and political rights set forth in the present Covenant.

Article 4

(1) In time of public emergency which threatens the life of the nation and the existence of which is officially proclaimed, the States Parties to the present Covenant may take measures derogating from their obligations under the present Covenant to the extent strictly required by the exigencies of the situation, provided that such measures are not inconsistent with their other obligations under international law and do not involve discrimination solely on the ground of race, colour, sex, language, religion or social origin.

(2) No derogation from articles 6, 7, 8 (paragraphs 1 and 2), 11, 15, 16 and 18 may be made under this provision.

(3) Any State Party to the present Covenant availing itself of the right of derogation shall immediately inform the other States Parties to the present Covenant, through the intermediary of the Secretary-General of the United Nations, of the provisions from which it has derogated and of the reasons by which it was actuated. A further communication shall be made, through the same intermediary, on the date on which it terminates such derogation.

Article 5

(1) Nothing in the present Covenant may be interpreted as implying for any State, group or person any right to engage in any activity or perform any act aimed at the destruction of any of the rights and freedoms recognized herein or at their limitation to a greater extent than is provided for in the present Covenant.

(2) There shall be no restriction upon or derogation from any of the fundamental human rights recognized or existing in any State Party to the present Covenant pursuant to law, conventions, regulations or custom on the pretext that the present Covenant does not recognize such rights or that it recognizes them to a lesser extent.

Part III

Article 6

(1) Every human being has the inherent right to life. This right shall be protected by law. No one shall be arbitrarily deprived of his life.

(2) In countries which have not abolished the death penalty, sentence of death may be imposed only for the most serious crimes in accordance with the law in force at the time of the commission of the crime and not

contrary to the provisions of the present Covenant and to the Convention on the Prevention and Punishment of the Crime of Genocide. This penalty can only be carried out pursuant to a final judgment rendered by a competent court.

(3) When deprivation of life constitutes the crime of genocide, it is understood that nothing in this article shall authorize any State Party to the present Covenant to derogate in any way from any obligation assumed under the provisions of the Convention on the Prevention and Punishment of the Crime of Genocide.

(4) Anyone sentenced to death shall have the right to seek pardon or commutation of the sentence. Amnesty, pardon or commutation of the sentence of death may be granted in all cases.

(5) Sentence of death shall not be imposed for crimes committed by persons below eighteen years of age and shall not be carried out on pregnant women.

(6) Nothing in this article shall be invoked to delay or to prevent the abolition of capital punishment by any State Party to the present Covenant.

Article 7

No one shall be subjected to torture or to cruel, inhuman or degrading treatment or punishment. In particular, no one shall be subjected without his free consent to medical or scientific experimentation.

Article 8

(1) No one shall be held in slavery; slavery and the slave-trade in all their forms shall be prohibited.

(2) No one shall be held in servitude.

(3)(a) No one shall be required to perform forced or compulsory labour;
   (b) Paragraph 3(a) shall not be held to preclude, in countries where imprisonment with hard labour may be imposed as a punishment for a crime, the performance of hard labour in pursuance of a sentence to such punishment by a competent court;
   (c) For the purpose of this paragraph the term 'forced or compulsory labour' shall not include:
      i. Any work or service, not referred to in subparagraph (b), normally required of a person who is under detention in consequence of

a lawful order of a court, or of a person during conditional release from such detention;

 ii. Any service of a military character and, in countries where conscientious objection is recognized, any national service required by law of conscientious objectors;

 iii. Any service exacted in cases of emergency or calamity threatening the life or well-being of the community;

 iv. Any work or service which forms part of normal civil obligations.

Article 9

(1) Everyone has the right to liberty and security of person. No one shall be subjected to arbitrary arrest or detention. No one shall be deprived of his liberty except on such grounds and in accordance with such procedure as are established by law.

(2) Anyone who is arrested shall be informed, at the time of arrest, of the reasons for his arrest and shall be promptly informed of any charges against him.

(3) Anyone arrested or detained on a criminal charge shall be brought promptly before a judge or other officer authorized by law to exercise judicial power and shall be entitled to trial within a reasonable time or to release. It shall not be the general rule that persons awaiting trial shall be detained in custody, but release may be subject to guarantees to appear for trial, at any other stage of the judicial proceedings, and, should occasion arise, for execution of the judgment.

(4) Anyone who is deprived of his liberty by arrest or detention shall be entitled to take proceedings before a court, in order that that court may decide without delay on the lawfulness of his detention and order his release if the detention is not lawful.

(5) Anyone who has been the victim of unlawful arrest or detention shall have an enforceable right to compensation.

Article 10

(1) All persons deprived of their liberty shall be treated with humanity and with respect for the inherent dignity of the human person.

(2)(a) Accused persons shall, save in exceptional circumstances, be segregated from convicted persons and shall be subject to separate treatment appropriate to their status as unconvicted persons;

 (b) Accused juvenile persons shall be separated from adults and brought as speedily as possible for adjudication.

3. The penitentiary system shall comprise treatment of prisoners the essential aim of which shall be their reformation and social rehabilitation. Juvenile offenders shall be segregated from adults and be accorded treatment appropriate to their age and legal status.

Article 11

No one shall be imprisoned merely on the ground of inability to fulfil a contractual obligation.

Article 12

(1) Everyone lawfully within the territory of a State shall, within that territory, have the right to liberty of movement and freedom to choose his residence.

(2) Everyone shall be free to leave any country, including his own.

(3) The above-mentioned rights shall not be subject to any restrictions except those which are provided by law, are necessary to protect national security, public order (*ordre public*), public health or morals or the rights and freedoms of others, and are consistent with the other rights recognized in the present Covenant.

(4) No one shall be arbitrarily deprived of the right to enter his own country.

Article 13

An alien lawfully in the territory of a State Party to the present Covenant may expelled therefrom only in pursuance of a decision reached in accordance with law and shall, except where compelling reasons of national security otherwise require, be allowed to submit the reasons against his expulsion and to have his case reviewed by, and be represented for the purpose before, the competent authority or a person or persons especially designated by the competent authority.

Article 14

(1) All persons shall be equal before the courts and tribunals. In the determination of any criminal charge against him, or of his rights and obligations in a suit at law, everyone shall be entitled to a fair and public hearing by a competent, independent and impartial tribunal established by law. The Press and the public may be excluded from all or part

of a trial for reasons of morals, public order (*ordre public*) or national security in a democratic society, or when the interest of the private lives of the parties so requires, or to the extent strictly necessary in the opinion of the court in special circumstances where publicity would prejudice the interests of justice; but any judgment rendered in a criminal case or in a suit at law shall be made public except where the interest of juvenile persons otherwise requires or the proceedings concern matrimonial disputes or the guardianship of children.

(2) Everyone charged with a criminal offence shall have the right to be presumed innocent until proved guilty according to law.

(3) In the determination of any criminal charge against him, everyone shall be entitled to the following minimum guarantees, in full equality:

    (a) To be informed promptly and in detail in a language which he understands of the nature and cause of the charge against him;

    (b) To have adequate time and facilities for the preparation of his defence and to communicate with counsel of his own choosing;

    (c) To be tried without undue delay;

    (d) To be tried in his presence, and to defend himself in person or through legal assistance of his own choosing; to be informed, if he does not have legal assistance, of this right; and to have legal assistance assigned to him, in any case where the interests of justice so require, and without payment by him in any such case if he does not have sufficient means to pay for it;

    (e) To examine, or have examined, the witnesses against him and to obtain the attendance and examination of witnesses on his behalf under the same conditions as witnesses against him;

    (f) To have the free assistance of an interpreter if he cannot understand or speak the language used in court;

    (g) Not to be compelled to testify against himself or to confess guilt.

(4) In the case of juvenile persons, the procedure shall be such as will take account of their age and the desirability of promoting their rehabilitation.

(5) Everyone convicted of a crime shall have the right to his conviction and sentence being reviewed by a higher tribunal according to law.

(6) When a person has by a final decision been convicted of a criminal offence and when subsequently his conviction has been reversed or he has been pardoned on the ground that a new or newly discovered fact shows conclusively that there has been a miscarriage of justice, the person who has suffered punishment as a result of such conviction shall be compensated according to law, unless it is proved that the non-disclosure of the unknown fact in time is wholly or partly attributable to him.

(7) No one shall be liable to be tried or punished again for an offence for which he has already been finally convicted or acquitted in accordance with the law and penal procedure of each country.

Article 15

No one shall be held guilty of any criminal offence on account of any act or omission which did not constitute a criminal offence, under national or international law, at the time when it was committed. Nor shall a heavier penalty be imposed than the one that was applicable at the time when the criminal offence was committed. If, subsequent to the commission of the offence, provision is made by law for the imposition of a lighter penalty, the offender shall benefit thereby. Nothing in this article shall prejudice the trial and punishment of any person for any act or omission which, at the time when it was committed, was criminal according to the general principles of law recognized by the community of nations.

Article 16

Everyone shall have the right to recognition everywhere as a person before the law.

Article 17

(1) No one shall be subjected to arbitrary or unlawful interference with his privacy, family, home or correspondence, nor to unlawful attacks on his honour and reputation.

(2) Everyone has the right to the protection of the law against such interference or attacks.

Article 18

(1) Everyone shall have the right to freedom of thought, conscience and religion. This right shall include freedom to have or to adopt a religion or belief of his choice, and freedom, either individually or in community with others and in public or private, to manifest his religion or belief in worship, observance, practice and teaching.

(2) No one shall be subject to coercion which would impair his freedom to have or to adopt a religion or belief of his choice.

(3) Freedom to manifest one's religion or beliefs may be subject only to such limitations as are prescribed by law and are necessary to protect

public safety, order, health, or morals or the fundamental rights and freedoms of others.

(4) The States Parties to the present Covenant undertake to have respect for the liberty of parents and, when applicable, legal guardians to ensure the religious and moral education of their children in conformity with their own convictions.

Article 19

(1) Everyone shall have the right to hold opinions without interference.

(2) Everyone shall have the right to freedom of expression; this right shall include freedom to seek, receive and impart information and ideas of all kinds, regardless of frontiers, either orally, in writing or in print, in the form of art, or through any other media of his choice.

(3) The exercise of the rights provided for in paragraph 2 of this article carries with it special duties and responsibilities. It may therefore be subject to certain restrictions, but these shall only be such as are provided by law and are necessary:

(a) For respect of the rights or reputations of others;

(b) For the protection of national security or of public order (*ordre public*), or of public health or morals.

Article 20

(1) Any propaganda for war shall be prohibited by law.

(2) Any advocacy of national, racial or religious hatred that constitutes incitement to discrimination, hostility or violence shall be prohibited by law.

Article 21

The right of peaceful assembly shall be recognized. No restrictions may be placed on the exercise of this right other than those imposed in conformity with the law and which are necessary in a democratic society in the interests of national security or public safety, public order (*ordre public*), the protection of public health or morals or the protection of the rights and freedoms of others.

Article 22

(1) Everyone shall have the right to freedom of association with others, including the right to form and join trade unions for the protection of his interests.

(2) No restrictions may be placed on the exercise of this right other than those which are prescribed by law and which are necessary in a democratic society in the interests of national security or public safety, public order (*ordre public*), the protection of public health or morals or the protection of the rights and freedoms of others. This article shall not prevent the imposition of lawful restrictions on members of the armed forces and of the police in their exercise of this right.

(3) Nothing in this article shall authorize States Parties to the International Labour Organization Convention of 1948 concerning Freedom of Association and Protection of the Right to Organize to take legislative measures which would prejudice, or to apply the law in such a manner as to prejudice, the guarantees provided for in that Convention.

Article 23

(1) The family is the natural and fundamental group unit of society and is entitled to protection by society and the State.

(2) The right of men and women of marriageable age to marry and to found a family shall be recognized.

(3) No marriage shall be entered into without the free and full consent of the intending spouses.

(4) States Parties to the present Covenant shall take appropriate steps to ensure equality of rights and responsibilities of spouses as to marriage, during marriage and at its dissolution. In the case of dissolution, provision shall be made for the necessary protection of any children.

Article 24

(1) Every child shall have, without any discrimination as to race, colour, sex, language, religion, national or social origin, property or birth, the right to such measures of protection as are required by his status as a minor, on the part of his family, society and the State.

(2) Every child shall be registered immediately after birth and shall have a name.

(3) Every child has the right to acquire a nationality.

Article 25

Every citizen shall have the right and the opportunity, without any of the distinctions mentioned in article 2 and without unreasonable restrictions:

(a) To take part in the conduct of public affairs, directly or through freely chosen representatives;

(b) To vote and to be elected at genuine periodic elections which shall be by universal and equal suffrage and shall be held by secret ballot, guaranteeing the free expression of the will of the electors;

(c) To have access, on general terms of equality, to public service in his country.

Article 26

All persons are equal before the law and are entitled without any discrimination to the equal protection of the law. In this respect, the law shall prohibit any discrimination and guarantee to all persons equal and effective protection against discrimination on any ground such as race, colour, sex, language, religion, political or other opinion, national or social origin, property, birth or other status.

Article 27

In those States in which ethnic, religious or linguistic minorities exist, persons belonging to such minorities shall not be denied the right, in community with the other members of their group, to enjoy their own culture, to profess and practice their own religion, or to use their own language.

Part IV

Article 28

(1) There shall be established a Human Rights Committee (hereafter referred to in the present Covenant as the Committee). It shall consist of eighteen members and shall carry out the functions hereinafter provided.

(2) The Committee shall be composed of nationals of the States Parties to the present Covenant who shall be persons of high moral character and recognized competence in the field of human rights, consideration being given to the usefulness of the participation of some persons having legal experience.

(3) The members of the Committee shall be elected and shall serve in their personal capacity.

Article 29

(1) The members of the Committee shall be elected by secret ballot from a list of persons possessing the qualifications prescribed in article 28 and nominated for the purpose by the States Parties to the present Covenant.

(2) Each State Party to the present Covenant may nominate not more than two persons. These persons shall be nationals of the nominating State.

(3) A person shall be eligible for renomination.

Article 30

(1) The initial election shall be held no later than six months after the date of the entry into force of the present Covenant.

(2) At least four months before the date of each election to the Committee, other than an election to fill a vacancy declared in accordance with article 34, the Secretary-General of the United Nations shall address a written invitation to the States Parties to the present Covenant to submit their nominations for membership of the Committee within three months.

(3) The Secretary-General of the United Nations shall prepare a list in alphabetical order of all the persons thus nominated, with an indication of the States Parties which have nominated them, and shall submit it to the States Parties to the present Covenant no later than one month before the date of each election.

(4) Elections of the members of the Committee shall be held at a meeting of the States Parties to the present Covenant convened by the Secretary-General of the United Nations at the Headquarters of the United Nations. At that meeting, for which two thirds of the States Parties to the present Covenant shall constitute a quorum, the persons elected to the Committee shall be those nominees who obtain the largest number of votes and an absolute majority of the votes of the representatives of States Parties present and voting.

Article 31

(1) The Committee may not include more than one national of the same State.

(2) In the election of the Committee, consideration shall be given to equitable geographical distribution of membership and to the representation of the different forms of civilization and of the principal legal systems.

Article 32

(1) The members of the Committee shall be elected for a term of four years. They shall be eligible for re-election if renominated. However, the terms of nine of the members elected at the first election shall expire at the end of two years; immediately after the first election, the names of these nine members shall be chosen by lot by the chairman of the meeting referred to in article 30, paragraph 4.

(2) Elections at the expiry of office shall be held in accordance with the preceding articles of this part of the present Covenant.

Article 33

(1) If, in the unanimous opinion of the other members, a member of the Committee has ceased to carry out his functions for any cause other than absence of a temporary character, the Chairman of the Committee shall notify the Secretary-General of the United Nations, who shall then declare the seat of that member to be vacant.

(2) In the event of the death or the resignation of a member of the Committee, the Chairman shall immediately notify the Secretary-General of the United Nations, who shall declare the seat vacant from the date of death or the date on which the resignation takes effect.

Article 34

(1) When a vacancy is declared in accordance with article 33 and if the term of office of the member to be replaced does not expire within six months of the declaration of the vacancy, the Secretary-General of the United Nations shall notify each of the States Parties to the present Covenant, which may within two months submit nominations in accordance with article 29 for the purpose of filling the vacancy.

(2) The Secretary-General of the United Nations shall prepare a list in alphabetical order of the persons thus nominated and shall submit it to the States Parties to the present Covenant. The election to fill the vacancy shall then take place in accordance with the relevant provisions of this part of the present Covenant.

(3) A member of the Committee elected to fill a vacancy declared in accordance with article 33 shall hold office for the remainder of the term of the member who vacated the seat on the Committee under the provisions of that article.

Article 35

The members of the Committee shall, with the approval of the General Assembly of the United Nations, receive emoluments from United Nations resources on such terms and conditions as the General Assembly may decide, having regard to the importance of the Committee's responsibilities.

Article 36

The Secretary-General of the United Nations shall provide the necessary staff and facilities for the effective performance of the functions of the Committee under the present Covenant.

Article 37

(1) The Secretary-General of the United Nations shall convene the initial meeting of the Committee at the Headquarters of the United Nations.

(2) After its initial meeting, the Committee shall meet at such time as shall be provided in its rules of procedure.

(3) The Committee shall normally meet at the Headquarters of the United Nations or at the United Nations Office at Geneva.

Article 38

Every member of the Committee shall, before taking up his duties, make a solemn declaration in open committee that he will perform his functions impartially and conscientiously.

Article 39

(1) The Committee shall elect its officers for a term of two years. They may be re-elected.

(2) The Committee shall establish its own rules of procedure, but these rules shall provide, *inter alia*, that:
    (a) Twelve members shall constitute a quorum;
    (b) Decisions of the committee shall be made by a majority vote of the members present.

Article 40

(1) The States Parties to the present Covenant undertake to submit reports on the measures they have adopted which give effect to the rights recognized herein and on the progress made in the enjoyment of those rights:

(a) Within one year of the entry into force of the present Covenant for the States Parties concerned;

(b) Thereafter whenever the Committee so requests.

(2) All reports shall be submitted to the Secretary-General of the United Nations, who shall transmit them to the Committee for consideration. Reports shall indicate the factors and difficulties, if any, affecting the implementation of the present Covenant.

(3) The Secretary-General of the United Nations may, after consultation with the Committee, transmit to the specialized agencies concerned copies of such parts of the reports as may fall within their field of competence.

(4) The Committee shall study the reports submitted by the States Parties to the present Covenant. It shall transmit its reports, and such general comments as it may consider appropriate, to the States Parties. The Committee may also transmit to the Economic and Social Council these comments along with the copies of the reports it has received from States Parties to the present Covenant.

(5) The States Parties to the present Covenant may submit to the Committee observations on any comments that may be made in accordance with paragraph 4 of this article.

Article 41

(1) A State Party to the present Covenant may at any time declare under this article that it recognizes the competence of the Committee to receive and consider communications to the effect that a State Party claims that another State Party is not fulfilling its obligations under the present Covenant. Communications under this article may be received and considered only if submitted by a State Party which has made a declaration recognizing in regard to itself the competence of the Committee. No communication shall be received by the Committee if it concerns a State Party which has not made such a declaration. Communications received under this article shall be dealt with in accordance with the following procedure:

(a) If a State Party to the present Covenant considers that another State Party is not giving effect to the provisions of the present Covenant, it may, by written communication, bring the matter to the attention of that State Party. Within three months after the receipt of the communication, the receiving State shall afford the State which sent the communication an explanation or any other statement in writing clarifying the matter, which should include, to the extent possible and pertinent, reference to domestic procedures and remedies taken, pending, or available in the matter.

(b) If the matter is not adjusted to the satisfaction of both States Parties concerned within six months after the receipt by the receiving State of the initial communication, either State shall have the right to refer the matter to the Committee, by notice given to the Committee and to the other State.

(c) The Committee shall deal with a matter referred to it only after it has ascertained that all available domestic remedies have been invoked and exhausted in the matter, in conformity with the generally recognized principles of international law. This shall not be the rule where the application of the remedies is unreasonably prolonged.

(d) The Committee shall hold closed meetings when examining communications under this article.

(e) Subject to the provisions of subparagraph (c), the Committee shall make available its good offices to the States Parties concerned with a view to a friendly solution of the matter on the basis of respect for human rights and fundamental freedoms as recognized in the present Covenant.

(f) In any matter referred to it, the Committee may call upon the States Parties concerned, referred to in subparagraph (b), to supply any relevant information.

(g) The States Parties concerned, referred to in subparagraph (b), shall have the right to be represented when the matter is being considered in the Committee and to make submissions orally and/or in writing.

(h) The Committee shall, within twelve months after the date of receipt of notice under subparagraph (b), submit a report:

i. If a solution within the terms of subparagraph (e) is reached, the Committee shall confine its report to a brief statement of the facts and of the solution reached;

ii. If a solution within the terms of subparagraph (e) is not reached, the Committee shall confine its report to a brief statement of the facts. The written submissions and record of the oral submissions made by the States Parties concerned shall be attached to the report.

In every matter, the report shall be communicated to the States Parties concerned.

(2) The provisions of this article shall come into force when ten States Parties to the present Covenant have made declarations under

paragraph 1 of this article. Such declarations shall be deposited by the States Parties with the Secretary-General of the United Nations, who shall transmit copies thereof to the other States Parties. A declaration may be withdrawn at any time by notification to the Secretary-General. Such a withdrawal shall not prejudice the consideration of any matter which is the subject of a communication already transmitted under this article; no further communication by any State Party shall be received after the notification of withdrawal of the declaration has been received by the Secretary-General, unless the State Party concerned has made a new declaration.

Article 42

(1)(a) If a matter referred to the Committee in accordance with article 41 is not resolved to the satisfaction of the States Parties concerned, the Committee may, with the prior consent of the States Parties concerned, appoint an ad hoc Conciliation Commission (hereinafter referred to as the Commission). The good offices of the Commission shall be made available to the States Parties concerned with a view to an amicable solution of the matter on the basis of respect for the present Covenant;

(b) The Commission shall consist of five persons acceptable to the States Parties concerned. If the States Parties concerned fail to reach agreement within three months on all or part of the composition of the Commission, the members of the Commission concerning whom no agreement has been reached shall be elected by secret ballot by a two-thirds majority vote of the Committee from among its members.

(2) The members of the Commission shall serve in their personal capacity. They shall not be nationals of the States Parties concerned, or of a State not party to the present Covenant, or of a State Party which has not made a declaration under Article 41.

(3) The Commission shall elect its own Chairman and adopt its own rules of procedure.

(4) The meetings of the Commission shall normally be held at the Headquarters of the United Nations or at the United Nations Office at Geneva. However, they may be held at such other convenient places as the Commission may determine in consultation with the Secretary-General of the United Nations and the States Parties concerned.

(5) The secretariat provided in accordance with article 36 shall also service the commissions appointed under this article.

(6) The information received and collated by the Committee shall be made available to the Commission and the Commission may call upon the States Parties concerned to supply any other relevant information.

(7) When the Commission has fully considered the matter, but in any event not later than twelve months after having been seized of the matter, it shall submit to the Chairman of the Committee a report for communication to the States Parties concerned:

(a) If the Commission is unable to complete its consideration of the matter within twelve months, it shall confine its report to a brief statement of the status of its consideration of the matter.

(b) If an amicable solution to the matter on the basis of respect for human rights as recognized in the present Covenant is reached, the Commission shall confine its report to a brief statement of the facts and of the solution reached;

(c) If a solution within the terms of subparagraph (b) is not reached, the Commission's report shall embody its findings on all questions of fact relevant to the issues between the States Parties concerned, and its views on the possibilities of an amicable solution of the matter. This report shall also contain the written submissions and a record of the oral submissions made by the States Parties concerned;

(d) If the Commission's report is submitted under subparagraph (c), the States Parties concerned shall, within three months of the receipt of the report, notify the Chairman of the Committee whether or not they accept the contents of the report of the Commission.

(8) The provisions of this article are without prejudice to the responsibilities of the Committee under article 41.

(9) The States Parties concerned shall share equally all the expenses of the members of the Commission in accordance with estimates to be provided by the Secretary-General of the United Nations.

(10) The Secretary-General of the United Nations shall be empowered to pay the expenses of the members of the Commission, if necessary, before reimbursement by the States Parties concerned, in accordance with paragraph 9 of this article.

Article 43

The members of the Committee, and of the ad hoc conciliation commissions which may be appointed under article 42, shall be entitled to the facilities, privileges and immunities of experts on mission for the United Nations as laid down in the relevant sections of the Convention on the Privileges and Immunities of the United Nations.

Article 44

The provisions for the implementation of the present Covenant shall apply without prejudice to the procedures prescribed in the field of human rights by or under the constituent instruments and the conventions of the United Nations and of the specialized agencies and shall not prevent the States Parties to the present Covenant from having recourse to other procedures for settling a dispute in accordance with general or special international agreements in force between them.

Article 45

The Committee shall submit to the General Assembly of the United Nations, through the Economic and Social council, an annual report on its activities.

Part V

Article 46

Nothing in the present Covenant shall be interpreted as impairing the provisions of the Charter of the United Nations and of the constitutions of the specialized agencies which define the respective responsibilities of the various organs of the United Nations and of specialized agencies in regard to the matters dealt with in the present Covenant.

Article 47

Nothing in the present Covenant shall be interpreted as impairing the inherent right of all peoples to enjoy and utilize fully and freely their natural wealth and resources.

Part VI

Article 48

(1) The present Covenant is open for signature by any State Member of the United Nations or member of any of its specialized agencies, by any State Party to the Statute of the International Court of Justice, and by any other State which has been invited by the General Assembly of the United Nations to become a party to the present Covenant.

(2) The present Covenant is subject to ratification. Instruments of ratification shall be deposited with the Secretary-General of the United Nations.

(3) The present Covenant shall be open to accession by any State referred to in paragraph 1 of this article.

(4) Accession shall be effected by the deposit of an instrument of accession with the Secretary-General of the United Nations.

(5) The Secretary-General of the United Nations shall inform all States which have signed this Covenant or acceded to it of the deposit of each instrument of ratification or accession.

Article 49

(1) The present Covenant shall enter into force three months after the date of the deposit with the Secretary-General of the United Nations of the thirty-fifth instrument of ratification or instrument of accession.

(2) For each State ratifying the present Covenant or acceding to it after the deposit of the thirty-fifth instrument of ratification or instrument of accession, the present Covenant shall enter into force three months after the date of the deposit of its own instrument of ratification or instrument of accession.

Article 50

The provisions of the present Covenant shall extend to all parts of federal States without any limitations or exceptions.

Article 51

(1) Any State Party to the present Covenant may propose an amendment and file it with the Secretary-General of the United Nations. The Secretary-General of the United Nations shall thereupon communicate any proposed amendments to the States Parties to the present Covenant with a request that they notify him whether they favour a conference of States Parties for the purpose of considering and voting upon the proposals. In the event that at least on third of the States Parties favours such a conference, the Secretary-General shall convene the conference under the auspices of the United Nations. Any amendment adopted by a majority of the States Parties present and voting at the conference shall be submitted to the General Assembly of the United Nations for approval.

(2) Amendments shall come into force when they have been approved by the General Assembly of the United Nations and accepted by a two-thirds majority of the States Parties to the present Covenant in accordance with their respective constitutional processes.

(3) When amendments come into force, they shall be binding on those States Parties which have accepted them, other States Parties still being bound by the provisions of the present Covenant and any earlier amendment which they have accepted.

Article 52

Irrespective of the notifications made under article 48, paragraph 5, the Secretary-General of the United Nations shall inform all States referred to in paragraph 1 of the same article of the following particulars:

(a) Signatures, ratifications and accessions under article 48;

(b) The date of the entry into force of the present Covenant under article 49 and the date of the entry into force of any amendments under article 51.

Article 53

(1) The present Covenant, of which the Chinese, English, French, Russian and Spanish texts are equally authentic, shall be deposited in the archives of the United Nations.

(2) The Secretary-General of the United Nations shall transmit certified copies of the present Covenant to all States referred to in article 48.

Note

1   Those being: Byelorussian S.S.R.; Czechoslovakia; Poland; Saudi Arabia; Ukrainian S.S.R.; U.S.S.R.; South Africa, and Yugoslavia.

INDEX

Name index

A

Adorno, Theodor, 2, 109, 131, 181–2, 287
Althusser, Louis, 2, 109, 125, 128, 131, 141, 147, 232
Aquinas, St Thomas, 28–9
Arendt, Hannah, 2, 16, 35–6, 46–7, 59, 61, 72, 101, 109, 131, 150, 153, 154, 157, 290, 307, 325, 327, 338, 341, 343, 350, 353, 363
Aristotle, 28, 39, 53–4, 57, 274
Ascheron, Neal, 249–50
Augustine, St, 28

B

Bales, Kevin, 264, 266, 271, 273–4, 276–7, 281–2, 286–7
Bamber, Helen, 188
Barta, Tony, 320, 325
Bauer, Yehuda, 308
Bauman, Zygmunt, 2, 58–9, 150, 303, 308, 326
Beccaria, Cesare, 34, 165, 207, 219–20
Benenson, Peter, 95, 143–4, 149
Benn, Melissa, 128
Bentham, Jeremy, 33–4, 36, 56
Berreman, Gerald, 254
Bertrand, Maurice, 80–1
Bettelheim, Bruno, 307, 323
Bobbio, Norberto, 2, 16, 40–1, 46, 53–4, 59–61, 72, 387, 392
Bonnell Phillips, Ulrich, 265
Booth, Ken, 41, 44

Bozzoli, Belinda, 252
Brass, Tom, 276–7
Bull, Hedley, 79
Burke, Edmund, 33

C

Camus, Albert, 198
Carol, Avedon, 128
Cassese, Antonio, 75, 156–7, 249–50, 258, 300–1, 309
Chalk, Frank, 302, 304, 317
Chandler, Geoffrey, 382
Charny, Israel W., 301–2
Cicero, 28
Cohen, Stan, 357–8
Conrad, John, 222
Cromwell-Cox, Oliver, 20, 242, 251–2, 253–5
Curry Jansen, Sue, 131–2

D

Dadrian, Vahakn, 20, 301, 303, 319
Darnton, Robert, 111, 113
Davis, Garry, 354–5
Des Pres, Terence, 323–4
Descartes, Rene, 50, 52
Devlin, Patrick, 129
Dewey, John, 56–7
Donnelly, Jack, 41, 43–4
Drost, Pieter N., 301
Dumont, Louis, 20, 242, 253, 255
Dunne, Tim, 63

Durkheim, Emile, 59–60, 64–5, 142, 222
Dworkin, Andrea, 127

E

Elkins, Stanley, 265–6, 269–70, 274,
    277, 284, 287–9
Engerman, Stanley, 23, 283, 285

F

Fein, Helen, 2, 302–3, 308, 323
Festinger, Leon, 19, 181, 183
Fogel, Robert, 23, 283, 285
Forsythe, David P., 73, 76, 77
Foucault, Michel, 2, 24, 57–8, 109,
    124–5, 129, 131–3, 142, 143, 147,
    158–9, 208, 211, 231–3
Frank, Andre Gunder, 79, 385
Franklin, Bob, 374
Freeman, Michael, 376
Freyre, Gilberto, 274–5
Fromm, Erich, 287, 307, 312–13

G

Genefke, Inge, 171–2
Genovese, Eugene, 20, 266, 276–8,
    283, 284
Giddens, Anthony, 93
Glover, Jonathan, 219
Goffman, Erving, 288–9, 324
Gordon, Haim, 191
Greer, Germaine, 129
Gregory, Martyn, 189–90
Grotius, Hugo, 30
Gunther, Gerald, 119
Gurr, Ted Robert, 301, 317

H

Habermas, Jürgen, 2, 24, 39–41, 43,
    57, 61, 63, 102, 109, 117–18, 122,
    132–3, 153, 350, 352, 362, 390

Harff, Barbara, 301, 309, 317, 320
Haritos-Fatouros, Mika, 182
Harlan, John Marshall, 243, 252, 259
Harris, Marvin, 275, 277
Hart, Herbert, 129
Hayter, Tessa, 355
Hegel, Georg, 54–5, 93, 130, 221,
    283–4, 316
Helvetius, Claude-Adrien, 31
Hentoff, Nat, 119
Herodotus, 275
Hilberg, Raul, 307
Hobbes, Thomas, 16, 19, 22, 29–30, 31,
    38, 46, 77, 93, 110, 119, 127, 130,
    151, 153, 312–13, 316
Hobsbawm, Eric, 345
Hobson, John M., 78
Hood, Roger, 223
Horowitz, Irving, 308, 318, 325
Huggins, Martha, 145–6, 159, 175–6,
    183
Hugo, Victor, 169, 216, 232
Huxley, Aldous, 258

J

Johnson, Robert, 19, 226–7
Jonassohn, Kurt, 302, 304, 317

K

Kant, Immanuel, 2, 16, 21, 31–2, 35–6,
    38–9, 46–7, 50, 52–5, 55–9, 63–4,
    75, 93, 154, 217, 221
Kiewiet, C. W. de, 248
Knox, Katharine, 357–9
Kumar, Radha, 373
Kuper, Leo, 21, 251, 301, 314–16, 317,
    325
Kushner, Tony, 357–9

L

Lantier, Jacques, 371
Lawrence, Charles, 119, 127

Legassick, Martin, 252
Lemkin, Raphael, 299, 308
Levinas, Emmanuel, 59
Locke, John, 16, 22, 30, 31, 32–3, 36, 38, 46, 48, 52, 60, 63, 75, 78, 93, 108, 110, 116, 130
Lorenz, Konrad, 19, 313
Luchterhand, Elmer, 323–4
Luhmann, Niklas, 142, 150, 159

M

Marcuse, Herbert, 2, 3, 109, 124–5, 131–2, 153, 200
Marshall, Thomas H., 62
Marton, Ruchama, 165–6, 185–6
Marx, Karl, 20, 23, 33, 34–5, 53–5, 59–60, 64–5, 93, 112, 130, 153, 214, 264, 276, 279, 284, 385–6
Massa Arzabe, Patricia Helena, 385–6
Mazian, Florence, 320
Mazzini, Giuseppe, 33
McElroy, Wendy, 128
McIntyre, Alisdair, 40, 54–5, 63
McKinnon, Catherine, 127, 325
Melvern, Linda, 311
Milgram, Stanley, 19, 181–2
Mill, John Stuart, 22, 56, 93, 116, 118, 133, 217
Miller, Alice, 307
Mills, C. Wright, 215, 287–8
Milne, Seamus, 117–18, 126
Mommsen, Hans, 307
Montesquieu, Charles-Louise de, 31, 111
Moore, Barrington, Jr., 130, 276, 279–81
Myrdal, Gunnar, 265

N

Niebuhr, Reinhold, 313
Nietzsche, Friedreich, 53
Nino, Carlos Santiago, 37
Normand, Marcel, 220

O

O'Higgins, Paul, 107

P

Paine, Thomas, 32–3, 35–6, 46, 48, 110
Patterson, Orlando, 1, 21, 263–4, 266, 276, 279, 288–9, 289–91
Pawelczynska, Anna, 323–4
Plato, 28, 56, 221, 274
Popper, Karl, 2, 22, 109, 130–2, 258
Porter, Jack N., 317
Power. Jonathan, 164–5, 168

R

Radelet, Michael, 1, 210–11, 228
Rawls, John, 39, 41, 63
Regan, Tom, 40, 41, 46–7, 48–9, 51, 57
Reiman, Jeffrey, 217–18, 221
Rex, John, 248
Ricardo, David, 22, 78
Robertson, Geoffrey, 28
Robespierre, Maximilien-Francois de, 223
Rorty, Richard, 39, 43–4, 51–2, 63
Rosenberg, Alan, 308
Rostow, Walt, 385
Rousseau, Jean-Jacques, 30–1, 32, 34, 75, 93, 111, 291, 313
Rowntree, Seebohm, 384
Rubenstein, Richard, 325

S

Sartre, Jean-Paul, 20, 165, 320
Schilling, Paulo, 175
Seaton, Jean, 128
Sellin, Thorstein, 1, 218
Seneca, 28
Singh, Baljit, 153
Sjoberg, Gideon, 52, 65
Sklair, Leslie, 102, 282, 390–1
Smith, Adam, 22, 78

Smith, Roger W., 303
Smolla, Rodney A., 116
Sophocles, 28
Stampp, Kenneth, 265, 280
Staub, Ervin, 305, 307, 312, 314, 315,
    317, 320, 324
Ste. Croix, Geoffrey, 20, 263, 276

T

Tannenbaum, Frank, 274–5, 277
Townsend, Peter, 384
Toynbee, Polly, 117–18, 122, 126,
    128
Turner, Bryan S., 46–7, 51–2, 61, 64–5

V

Van den Haag, Ernst, 22, 217–19, 226
Van der Berghe, Pierre, 19, 312
Vaughan, Ted R., 52, 65
Vincent, R. J., 63

Voltaire, Francoise-Marie Arouet, 31,
    111, 117

W

Wallerstein, Immanuel, 79, 385–6
Walvin, James, 268
Warner, W. Lloyd, 21, 253–5
Waters, Malcolm, 40, 65
Weber, Max, 20, 22–4, 36, 59–61,
    64–5, 93, 125, 141, 146, 158,
    183–4, 200, 253, 276, 279, 281,
    314–15, 317, 325–6
Wheeler, Nicholas J., 63
Wilkes, Adrian, 122
Williams, Lindsay, 165, 174
Wollstonecraft, Mary, 33
Wolpe, Harold, 252

Z

Zimbardo, Phillip, 19, 181

Acts and Conventions index

A

American Declarations 1776–1789
    (United States), 75, 76, 100
Amsterdam Treaty 1997 (Europe), 340

B

Bill of Rights 1688–89 (England), 30,
    75

C

Children's Act 1989 (United
    Kingdom), 374

Civil Rights Act 1964 (United States),
    244
Commonwealth Immigration Acts
    1962 and 1968 (United Kingdom),
    351
Convention Against Torture, and
    Other Cruel, Inhuman or
    Degrading Treatment or
    Punishment 1984, 86, 167, 170
Convention on the Elimination of All
    Forms of Discrimination Against
    Women 1979, 86, 256, 369, 372, 374
Convention on the Political Rights of
    Women 1953, 86, 256
Convention on the Prevention and
    Punishment of the Crime of
    Genocide 1948, 85, 87, 93, 299,
    300–1, 303–4, 309

Convention Relating to the Status of
Refugees 1951, 86, 87, 338–9, 340,
348
Convention Relating to the Status of
Stateless Persons 1954, 86
Convention on the Rights of the Child
1989, 86, 375–8

D

Declaration on the Elimination of All
Forms of Intolerance and of
Discrimination Based on Religion
or Belief 1981, 86
Declaration on Protection of all
Persons from Being Subjected
to Torture and Other Cruel,
Inhuman or Degrading
Treatment of Punishment 1975,
86, 167, 170
Declaration Relative to the Universal
Abolition of the Slave Trade
1815, 270
Declaration of the Rights of the Child
1959, 375
Declaration of the Rights of Man and
the Citizen 1789 (France), 33,
34–5, 73, 75, 76, 100, 111
Dublin Convention 1990 (Europe), 340

E

European Communities Act 1972
(Europe), 89
European Convention on Human
Rights 1953 (Europe), 89, 111,
115, 140
European Convention on the
Prevention of Torture and
Inhuman or Degrading
Treatment or Punishment 1987
(Europe), 89
European Convention for the
Protection of Human Rights and
Fundamental Freedoms 1950
(Europe), 88–9

European Social Charter 1961
(Europe), 89

F

Fox's Libel Act 1792 (England), 110
Freedom of Information Act 1966
(United States), 113, 115, 123

G

Geneva Conventions 1864 and 1949,
88, 93, 169
Geneva Declaration on the Rights of
the Child 1924, 375
Group Areas Act 1950 (South Africa),
245

H

Hague Conventions 1899 and 1907,
88
Human Rights Act 2000 (United
Kingdom), 73, 76, 90

I

Immigration Act 1971 (United
Kingdom), 350
International Convention on the
Elimination of All Forms of
Racial Discrimination 1966, 86
International Convention on the
Protection of the Rights of All
Migrant Workers and Their
Families 1990, 86
International Convention on the
Suppression and Punishment of
the Crime of Apartheid 1973, 86,
246
International Covenant on Civil and
Political Rights 1966, 85, 86–7,
89–90, 99, 100, 109, 111–12, 140,
167, 170, 177, 244, 271, 369

International Covenant on Economic, Social and Cultural Rights 1966, 85, 86–7, 89–90, 99, 100, 271–2, 369, 384, 387

L

Land Act 1913 (South Africa), 244
London Resolutions 1992 (Europe), 340

M

Maastricht Treaty 1992 (Europe), 340
Magna Carta 1215 (England), 74, 75
Mines and Works Act 1911 (South Africa), 244
Murder (Abolition of the Death Penalty) Act 1965 (United Kingdom), 202

N

Nationality Act 1981 (United Kingdom), 351–2
Native (Abolition of Passes and Coordination of Documents) Act 1952 (South Africa), 245
Native Affairs Act 1920 (South Africa), 244

O

Obscene Publications Acts 1857, 1959, 1964 (United Kingdom), 111
Official Secrets Acts 1889, 1911, 1920, 1939 (United Kingdom), 111, 122

P

Peace of Westphalia 1648, 76
Population Registration Act 1950 (South Africa), 245
Prohibition of Mixed Marriages Act 1949 (South Africa), 245

R

Rome Final Act 1998, 92, 271–2

S

Schengen Convention 1990 (Europe), 340
Slavery Convention 1926, 85, 87, 270, 272
Social Policy (Basic Aims and Standards) Convention 1962, 384
Stockholm Declaration 1972, 388–9
Supplementary Convention on the Abolition of Slavery, the Slave Trade, and Institutions and Practices Similar to Slavery 1956, 270–2
Suppression of Communism Act 1950 (South Africa), 245

U

Universal Declaration of Human Rights, 1948, 5, 26, 36, 45, 53, 55, 60, 62, 72, 75–6, 85–7, 89–90, 99, 100–1, 106, 115, 139–40, 164, 169, 198, 241, 249, 263, 270, 272, 290, 337, 348, 353–5, 369, 375, 384–6, 387
Urban Area Act 1922 (South Africa), 244

Subject index

A

aboriginals, 64–5
Amnesty International, 8, 94–8, 99,
    100, 381
  mandate of, 15, 95–6
  opposition to censorship, 108, 123,
    125
  opposition to child soldiers, 378–9
  opposition to the death penalty,
    207, 209–10, 223, 226
  opposition to political imprisonment,
    140, 143–4, 147, 149
  opposition to torture, 170, 171, 176,
    190
  work on behalf of refugees, 350
  work on behalf of street children,
    380
apartheid, 12–13, 15–16, 241–59, 265,
    327, 386
  definition of, 241
  and discrimination against women,
    242, 255–7
  history of, 242–7
  relationship to caste, 15–16, 241–2,
    252–5
  and segregation in the American
    south, 241, 242–4, 252–4
  in South Africa, 8, 73, 81, 158, 241,
    242–7, 248–52, 253, 256, 258,
    327
  structural conditions of, 248–52
  theoretical perspectives on, 20–1,
    248, 251–2, 253–5

B

behaviourism, behavioural
    psychology, 19, 23, 182, 247, 285
British Medical Association, 185, 229
British National Party, 117, 122, 126
Buddhism, 54
  and the death penalty, 214
business and human rights, 14, 381–3

C

capitalism, 65, 389
  and apartheid, 251–2
  development of, 129–30
  and genocide, 320
  and Marxist theory, 20, 21, 23, 53,
    233
  and poverty, 385–6
  and slavery, 263, 269, 276–82
Casa Alianza, 381
caste, 15–16, 21, 241–2, 252–5, 265
categorical imperative (Kant), 31–2,
    47, 56
Catholic Church, opposition to
    pornography, 127
  opposition to the death penalty,
    207, 214
causalism, and censorship, 21, 125–6
  and the death penalty, 201, 219
  as a theory of ethics, 21, 109
  and torture, 179–80, 191
censorship, 5, 8, 11, 13, 31, 106–38,
    226, 389
  and democracy, 2, 115–25
  and discipline of media studies,
    1–3
  in Europe, history of, 110–14
  theoretical discourse on, 21, 22,
    125–6
  in the United States, history of, 113,
    115
  varieties of, 107, 165, 191
chattel slavery 263, 265, 267, 273
child labour, 368, 376, 377–8
child prostitution, 264
child soldiers, 376, 378–9
children's rights, 5, 7, 14, 368, 374–81
Church of England, and the death
    penalty, 213–14
citizenship, and children's rights,
    374
  development of rights of, 62
  and duties, 47–8
  and the environment, 389

citizenship, and children's rights
    (*continued*)
    political right to, 13, 34, 35–6, 46
    and poverty, 385–6
    and refugees, 338, 342, 348–53, 354,
        363
    rights of embedded in the state, 26,
        45, 60–1, 64–5, 72–3, 259, 392
    and slavery, 274–5
civil and political rights, 4, 8, 11–12,
    16, 62, 86–7, 89, 123, 257, 368, 369,
    375, 387
civil liberties, 26, 41, 45, 49, 112
collective rights, 11, 387
communitarianism, 38–9, 42, 54–5,
    62–3
concentration camps, experiences of,
    323–4
Confucianism, 54
constructivism, 18, 39
corporal punishment, 11, 167, 169
critical theory, 23–4, 132–3, 181, 200,
    287
cruel and inhuman treatment, 4, 164,
    167, 170, 199, 203, 207

D

death penalty, 1, 4, 11, 13, 15–17, 22,
    24, 34, 96, 198–233, 389, 392
    abolition of, 202–4, 207–8, 213,
        219
    as brutalisation, 201, 219
    as censorship, 165, 191
    cost of, 213, 216
    as deterrent, 199, 201, 204, 212, 215,
        217–21, 230, 232
    economic inequalities in, 199–200,
        224–5
    in Europe, 202–3
    history of, 201–8
    and incompetence of trial attorneys,
        224–5
    and the medical profession, 216,
        228–30
    and problem of innocence, 222–3
    and public opinion, 212, 215–16
    racial inequalities in, 199–200,
        223–4
    and religion, 213–14, 231
    as retribution, 200–1, 203, 212, 217,
        221–2, 230–1, 233
    for terrorists, 154
    in the United States, 8, 203–5,
        215–16, 218, 223–5, 226–7, 228,
        232
    worldwide statistics on, 5–6, 10,
        206
death row, experience of, 226–7, 324
debt bondage, 263, 264, 267, 271–2,
    274
democracy, and democratization,
    59–62, 109
    and the death penalty, 215–16
    censorship as incompatible with, 2,
        115–25
desert island scenario, 38
disappearances, 5–6, 8–9, 88, 96,
    141–2, 155–8, 300, 321, 328,
    379–80
Dreyfus affair, 111, 131, 143

E

ecocide, 14, 389
economic, social and cultural rights,
    11, 13, 16, 62, 86–7, 89, 376, 387
environment and human rights, 5, 14,
    45, 47, 55, 62, 387–9
equality, right to, 12–13, 34, 258–9,
    388
essentialism, 18–19, 39–41, 43, 78, 181,
    313–14
ethical subjectivation (Foucault),
    57–8
ethics, theories of, 18, 21, 55–9
ethnomethodology, 199
European Court of Human Rights,
    89
European law, 88–9, 90, 340, 351–2
European Union, 74, 78, 89, 170, 202
execution methods, 200, 208–12
exile, 141, 154–5
existence, right to, 12–14, 326–7, 389

F

fair trials, 7, 9, 95, 109, 139–40, 147
female genital mutilation, 1, 4, 14–15,
    43, 64, 368, 370–2, 373, 389
feminism, 21, 43, 61, 62, 64, 252, 389
    and apartheid, 248
    and pornography, 127–9
forced sterilisation, 14, 373–4
freedom, 24, 31, 32, 132–3, 233, 263,
    289–91
    right to, 12–13, 16–17, 31, 35–6,
        46–7, 154, 263, 289, 388
freedom of information, 13, 108, 110,
    115, 122–5, 133, 376
freedom of movement, 7, 99, 155, 337,
    354–5
freedom of speech, opinion,
    expression, 4, 6, 13, 31, 62, 95,
    106–8, 110–12, 113, 115–21, 122,
    375–6, 391
    and racist language, 117–19, 122,
        126, 127–8, 133
functionalism, 19–20, 23, 79, 217–18,
    287, 307, 314, 319, 384
Furman v Georgia (1972), 203–4

G

genocide, 1–2, 5, 12–13, 198, 299–328,
    389
    of Armenians, 304, 305–6, 308, 319,
        321, 344
    in Australia, 324
    in the Balkans, 309, 325
    in Cambodia, 303, 309–10, 315, 317,
        320, 321–3, 326, 328
    and capitalism, 320
    as a crime of the state, 191–2,
        316–18, 324–8
    history of, 303–11
    individual capacity for, 312–14
    and international law, 87–8, 92–3
    and modernity, 324–8
    in Rwanda, 309, 311, 315
    structural conditions for, 314–20

theoretical discourse on, 20, 21
typologies and definitions of,
    300–3
global economy, 191, 281–2, 382–3,
    385, 389, 390–2
globalisation of human rights, 35, 65,
    101, 389–92
Gregg v Georgia (1976), 203–4

H

Hinduism, 54
    and the caste system, 253–5
    and the death penalty, 214
    and sati, 372–3
Holocaust, the, 1, 52, 131, 181, 300,
    303, 304, 306–8, 309, 313, 316,
    319, 324, 326, 328, 344
house arrest, 141, 154–5
human nature, theories of, 18–19, 22,
    29–30

I

ideal moral judgement (Regan),
    40
ideal speech situation (Habermas),
    40
ideological state apparatuses
    (Althusser), 2, 125, 131
incontrovertibility of rights, 16–17, 27,
    31, 36, 44–9
    and problem of duties, 27, 45,
        47–9
    and problem of the hierarchy of
        rights, 27, 45–7
International Criminal Court, 81,
    91–3, 96, 247, 271
International Labor Organization, 76,
    84, 377, 384
international law, 30, 35, 65, 73–4,
    76–7, 79, 87–8, 89–91, 139, 247
International Monetary Fund, 80, 84,
    311
international relations, 21–2, 26, 72,
    74, 76–7

Islam, 54
  and the death penalty, 213, 232
  and female genital mutilation, 370, 372
  and women's rights, 257
Israeli Medical Association, 187

J

Jim Crow laws, 242–4
Judaism, and the death penalty, 214

L

land rights, 11, 14, 387
League of Nations, 76, 80, 85, 263, 270, 354
liberalism, and apartheid, 248
  and censorship, 116–19, 130, 132–3
  and pornography, 127–9
  as a theory of progress, 23
  as a theory of the state, 16, 22, 30, 42, 62, 65, 76, 78, 109, 115
  as a theory of world politics, 22, 44, 78–9
life, right to, 4, 11–15, 17, 30, 36, 45–6, 199, 375

M

Marxism, 20–1, 22, 23, 61, 65, 79, 200, 233
  and apartheid, 248, 251–2, 253, 255
  and genocide, 314, 320
  and poverty, 384–6
  and slavery, 266, 276–9, 283–4
master–slave relationship, 263–4, 266, 283–7
Medical Foundation for the Care of Torture Victims, 188
modernity, modernisation, 28, 59–62, 130–1, 142, 146, 232, 279–81, 313, 324–8, 363, 385
  theories of, 18, 22–4, 390

moral universalism, 28
moralism, and censorship, 21, 125–6
  and the death penalty, 200–1
  as a theory of ethics, 21, 109
  and torture, 179–80, 191

N

natural law, 27, 29, 32, 33, 37–41, 42, 43–4, 56, 60, 64, 150–1
  utilitarian critique of, 34, 62
natural rights, 30, 40
Nestlé affair, 382

O

Operation Condor, 156

P

patriarchy, 21, 128, 147–8
personal autonomy, right to, 14, 155
phenomenology, 19, 182–4, 199
Pinochet case, 90–1
Plessy v Ferguson (1896), 243, 252, 259
political policing, 145–6, 159
political prisoners, 3, 5–6, 11, 13, 95, 97, 139–60, 165, 226, 321
  definitions of, 147–9
  history of, 142–5
politicide, political genocide, 156, 301, 317, 321–3
politics, theories of, 18, 21–2
pornography, 21, 108–9, 126–9, 133
postmodernism, 38, 42–4, 58–9, 63–4
post-structuralism, 23–4, 200
poverty, 4, 5, 14, 368, 384–7, 388, 389, 392
prisoners of conscience, 9, 95, 97, 144, 147, 149–52
privacy, right to, 107, 155, 376
property, right to, 30, 34, 46
prostitution, 264
psychoanalysis, 23, 181, 200

R

racism, individual capacity for, 247–8
rape, as act of genocide, 305, 325
　as form of torture, 177–9, 256, 369
rational choice theory, 23, 283, 285
realism, and censorship, 130
　and the death penalty, 218
　and pornography, 127–8
　as a theory of the state, 22, 109, 151
　as a theory of world politics, 22,
　　77–9, 83
Red Cross, 76, 88
refugees, 5, 8, 12–13, 35, 64–5, 87, 99,
　327, 337–63, 381, 386
　from Afghanistan, 337, 340–1,
　　346–7, 361
　and border controls, 342, 353–5,
　　363
　and citizenship, 338, 342, 348–53,
　　354, 363
　and displaced persons, 339–41
　and experiences of displacement,
　　358–61
　and the media, 355–8, 359, 363
　in the modern world, 343–8, 362–3
　policies pertaining to, 340
　in the United Kingdom, 340, 350–2,
　　355–7, 358–61
　worldwide statistics on, 339, 340–2,
　　344–9
religious freedom, 7, 41, 375
religious universalism, 28–9
repressive state apparatuses
　　(Althusser), 3, 125, 131, 141–2,
　　147, 226, 232–3
reproduction, right to, 14
respectful treatment, right to, 11, 13,
　　46

S

'Sambo personality' (Elkins), 287–9
sati, 14, 64, 370, 372–3
security, right to, 14, 29–30, 34, 45–6,
　119, 127, 133, 155, 386

serfdom, 263, 272
Shell affair, 381–3
Sinn Fein, 117, 120
slave trade, 1, 263, 268, 269, 271, 279
slavery, 1, 2, 5, 12–13, 14–17, 198,
　263–98, 327, 386, 392
　abolition of, 242, 269–71
　in the ancient world, 266–7, 275,
　　276, 290
　and capitalism, 263, 269, 276–82
　history of, 266–74
　and international law, 87–8
　in Latin America and the
　　Caribbean, 266, 267–8, 274, 282,
　　288–9
　and manumission, 274–5
　modern or 'new', 15–16, 271–4,
　　281–2, 285–7
　and 'race', 263, 265, 273, 274–5
　and social class, 263, 266, 276, 278
　as a social institution, 263, 264–6,
　　280
　as a social relationship, 263, 283–7
　theoretical discourse on, 20–1, 23,
　　58
　types of, 263, 264–5, 267, 273–4
　in the United States of America,
　　265, 266, 268, 269, 270, 274–5,
　　277–8, 280–1, 285, 287–8, 290
society, theories of, 18, 19–21
sociobiology, 19, 181, 247, 312–13
state, the, 4, 11–17, 18, 21–2, 23, 26,
　29–30, 38, 61, 368
　and apartheid, 258–9
　and bureaucratic rationalization,
　　146, 157–8, 314, 326
　as censor, 107–9, 112–13, 128,
　　129–33
　and the death penalty, 199, 221–2,
　　230–3, 392
　and genocide, 191–2, 316–18, 324–8
　and human rights regulation, 72–4,
　　77–8, 100–1, 112, 389–92
　and human rights theory, 62–5
　and political prisoners, 141–2, 150,
　　157, 159
　and poverty, 384–7
　and refugees, 362–3

state, the (*continued*)
  and slavery, 289–91
  and torture, 167, 170, 183, 191–2, 392
Stoics, 28, 60, 275
street children, 376, 379–81
structuralism, 20, 24, 253, 255
subjectivity of rights, 27, 36, 49–55
  and problem of individuality, 52–4
  and problem of the rational agent,
    27, 49–52

T

terrorists and freedom fighters, 149,
    152–4
torture, 2, 3, 11, 13, 15–16, 34, 73, 89,
    164–92, 198, 207, 232, 389
  abolition of, 31, 96
  as censorship, 106, 165, 191
  as crime of the state, 191–2, 392
  as deterrent, 218
  equipment, trade in, 179, 189–91,
    382
  and European law, 89
  history of, 168–71
  medical involvement in, 184–9
  methods, 167, 168, 171–9
  of political prisoners, 145, 156, 160,
    171
  purpose of, 164–7
  theoretical discourse on, 21, 24, 43,
    58, 179–80, 191
  varieties of, 167
  victims of, 167, 187–9
  worldwide statistics on, 5–6, 9
torturers, the making of, 1, 19, 167,
    181–4

U

United Nations, 5, 26, 73–4, 76–8,
    79–87, 89, 91–3, 94, 96, 100–1,
    346, 363, 387, 392
  history of, 80–1
  and human rights, 85–7, 144, 167,
    170

and opposition to apartheid,
    245–7
and opposition to the death
    penalty, 207
and opposition to genocide, 300–1,
    309, 311
and opposition to slavery, 270
structure of, 81–4
and women's rights, 256, 371
United Nations Children's Fund, 84,
    377
United Nations Educational, Scientific
    and Cultural Organization, 84,
    377
United Nations High Commissioner
    on Human Rights, 84, 85
United Nations High Commissioner
    for Refugees, 84, 339–40, 345–9,
    354, 362–3
United Nations Security Council, 81,
    82–3, 92, 379
universality of rights, 27, 31–2, 36,
    37–44, 45, 56, 63
  and problem of cultural difference,
    27, 37, 41–5, 63
  and problem of natural law, 27,
    37–41, 42
utilitarianism, 21, 23, 33–4, 53, 56–7,
    65, 125, 179–80
  and critique of natural law, 34,
    62
  and the death penalty, 217, 219–20

V

validity claims (Habermas), 40, 118
violence, justifications of, 153–4

W

Weberian conflict theory, 20–1,
    314–17, 319
welfare, right to, 14, 32
Wolfenden Report, 129
women's rights, 5, 7, 33, 255–7, 258,
    368, 369–74

World Bank, 77, 80, 84, 311
World Health Organization, 84, 370
World Medical Association, 166,
      184–5
world passport, 99, 354–5

World Service Authority/World
      Government of World Citizens,
      98–100, 354–5
World Trade Organization, 77, 80, 84
world-systems theory, 385